BODY and *Soul*

D0468829

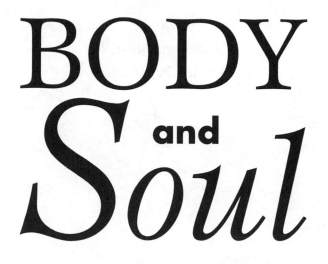

BODY and Soul

Rethinking Sexuality as Justice-Love

Marvin M. Ellison and
Sylvia Thorson-Smith, eds.

THE
PILGRIM
PRESS
Cleveland

To

Frank and Mike

Our Partners in Justice-Love

The Pilgrim Press
700 Prospect Avenue
Cleveland, Ohio 44115-1100
pilgrimpress.com

© 2003 by Marvin M. Ellison and Sylvia Thorson-Smith

All rights reserved. Published 2003

Printed in the United States of America on acid-free paper

08 07 06 05 04 03   5 4 3 2 1

Library of Congress Cataloging-in-Publication Data

   Body and soul : rethinking sexuality as justice-love / edited by Marvin M.
Ellison and Sylvia Thorson-Smith.
     p. cm.
   ISBN 0-8298-1561-9 (pbk. : alk. paper)
   1. Sexual ethics. 2. Sex–Religious aspects. 3. Body, Human–Religious aspects.
4. Homosexuality–Religious aspects. 5. Religion and justice. 6. Social ethics.
7. Spiritual life. I. Ellison, Marvin Mahan. II. Thorson-Smith, Sylvia.
HQ32.B634 2003
306.7–dc21
                                       2003051184

Contents

Part Three
PLEASURE AND HEALTH

Editors' note: The report of the Special Committee on Human Sexuality, titled "Keeping Body and Soul Together: Sexuality, Spirituality, and Social Justice," is referred to throughout this volume. The report is included in the publication *Presbyterians and Human Sexuality 1991,* published by the Office of the General Assembly, Presbyterian Church (U.S.A.). The publication also includes the 203rd General Assembly's response to the report of the Special Committee, as well as a minority report. The publication can be ordered from Distribution Management Services (DMS), 100 Witherspoon Street, Louisville, KY 40202-1396, or by calling 800-524-2612. Specify DMS order #OGA-91-001. All references to "Keeping Body and Soul Together" in this volume are taken from *Presbyterians and Human Sexuality 1991.*

Foreword

John J. Carey

With this book, editors Sylvia Thorson-Smith and Marvin M. Ellison have brought together a composite of voices that give English-speaking readers a broad perspective on contemporary issues related to human sexuality. All authors were asked to review the 1991 Presbyterian sexuality report entitled "Keeping Body and Soul Together: Sexuality, Spirituality, and Social Justice" and focus their thoughts on what has happened in North American discussions of sexuality since that time.

As the chair of the Presbyterian Special Committee on Human Sexuality that met from 1988 to 1991, I applaud this new publishing venture. All authors here are authorities in the areas of their essays, and the two editors of this volume are both well established and nationally recognized leaders in this field. This volume is surely the most comprehensive study of sexuality issues in America to be written since the publication of the 1991 Presbyterian report.

The General Assembly of the Presbyterian Church (U.S.A.) rejected the report at its meeting in Baltimore in June of 1991. That General Assembly marked, in my opinion, a sad day for the Presbyterian Church. The sexuality committee was given charge to investigate trends, issues, and problems in human sexuality in American culture and to report back to the General Assembly about what those trends, issues, and problems might imply for the church. The report includes an extensive theological introduction about the mood, climate, and assumptions of American culture and has ten chapters on sexuality related to particular groups and issues: women, men, adolescents, gays and lesbians, persons with disabilities, older adults, sexual violence, clergy sexual misconduct, AIDS, and reproductive technologies.

Almost all of the Presbyterian interest, however, focused on what the report says about gay and lesbian concerns. Semi-hysteria swept across the church for fear that any positive word from our committee concerning gay and lesbian persons might split the church. Conservatives in the church galvanized church opinion against the report even before it was published. The report went to the 1991 General Assembly with forty-seven recommendations, simply suggesting that the church should study the entire report for two years before it took any action. The fears and resentments of the conservatives prevailed, however, and the committee was thanked for its four years of work even as the report was rejected.

I analyzed the background issues of the Presbyterian debate (as well as what was going on in other Protestant denominations) in my book *The Sexuality Debate in North American Churches, 1988–1995.*[1] All of the controversy surrounding that report was not confined to sexuality. The keenest issues, in fact, were related to biblical interpretation and matters of power. In talking about the report around the country, I always maintained that none of the issues addressed in the report had any "Presbyterian" label. Rather, we spoke about deep problems of power and relationships in our whole culture. The report evidently had something to say to Christians of all denominations, as well as to others, and that's no doubt why it sold more than a hundred thousand copies.

Several factors, however, make this current book more germane and interesting to Americans of many different backgrounds. First of all, it is not commissioned by, nor does it have to answer to, any religious denomination. As I acknowledged in a 1992 article in *Christianity and Crisis,* we were aware as we worked on the Presbyterian report that there are many complex issues in human sexuality that we could not discuss in a report to the Presbyterian Church (U.S.A.).[2] Issues of bisexuality and the subtle dynamics and tensions within the gay and lesbian culture, for example, were not addressed. This book examines a much wider range of issues.

Second, although our culture still wrestles with sexuality problems on many fronts, the discussion reflected in this book has not taken place in a mood of semi-hysteria. Justice struggles are being won slowly in our society. In this book we read pieces from thinkers who stand in various relationships to their religious traditions, including those who stand at (or have been pushed to) the margins. Their voices are important and need to be heard.

Third, none of these essays has to conform to a particular theological tradition. Most religious traditions, in fact, want us to look backward in formulating contemporary sexual ethics. These essays attempt to speak to people who are not religiously affiliated, as well as to those who are struggling to renew and transform their religious traditions. The contributors to this book want to expand and refocus our religious thinking in all traditions, as well as remind us that sexuality problems are not confined to churches and synagogues.

Of course, the agenda of sexuality issues has changed in the past decade, too. Some issues remain constant, and others have emerged with considerable intensity. In recent times we have all become more aware of the problem of pedophilia, especially as evidenced in the Roman Catholic Church. This scandal, involving both the priesthood and actions of church bishops, has severely compromised the leadership and moral credibility of the church. The problem seems to widen day by day. This problem is not unique to the Roman Catholic Church, but it has heightened our concern for children, and other vulnerable people, in many different settings.

Another change has been the way that many denominations (and the broader society as well) have paid more attention to transgender persons. Some denominations, including the United Church of Christ, have established offices to address issues of gay, lesbian, bisexual, and transgender persons, thus linking together many people who have been traditionally marginalized by both churches and society. There has developed an implicit understanding that to support one of these constituencies is to support them all.

A third observation about change, although not a positive one, is the continuing conflict over gay and lesbian persons in the military. Despite President Clinton's effort to rectify the historic injustices directed against gay and lesbian personnel in our armed forces, rigid military attitudes have proven almost impossible to change. This non-ecclesiastical issue was not taken into account in various denominational studies, but it still exists as a problematic aspect of our culture. Recent studies show that dismissals from the armed forces as a result of sexual preference remain at the same percentage as a decade ago.[3] In the meantime, the military attitude reminds us that prejudice remains deeply embedded in our society.

Since 1991, has our society become more just? More sensitive to minorities and pluralism? Have churches become more open and compassionate? Initially it does not seem so. The authors in this book acknowledge that in some ways things are changing, but they also recognize that there's ample work left to do, including work that we scarcely imagined a decade ago.

Anyone committed to an ethic inclusive of sexual justice will be indebted to the editors and authors of this book for bringing us up to date on so many important issues. May its readership be wide and its light influential.

Notes

1. John J. Carey, *The Sexuality Debate in North American Churches, 1988–1995* (Lewiston, N.Y.: Edwin Mellen, 1995).

2. John J. Carey, "Sexuality: What We Couldn't Say," *Christianity and Crisis* 51, no. 12 (August 1991): 258–59.

3. I examine this issue in my edited book *Gays and Lesbians in the Military* (Lewiston, N.Y.: Edwin Mellen, 1996).

Acknowledgments

In the early 1990s we helped write and edit a major theological study on sexuality and social justice for the Presbyterian Church (U.S.A.). Because of ongoing conflict in church and society about these matters, we thought it a good idea, some dozen years later, to invite a number of United States womanist, feminist, and queer theologians to revisit these issues and share their considerable wisdom. We also wanted to experience, once again, the joy of collaborating on just this kind of project, and we have not been disappointed. Working with this amazing lineup of contributors, as well as with Timothy Staveteig, Pamela Johnson, and John Eagleson at The Pilgrim Press, has been pleasurable for us both.

We have also received support from a variety of other quarters. Marvin was granted a generous sabbatical leave by the Trustees of Bangor Theological Seminary and has received ongoing encouragement from President William Imes, Dean Glenn Miller, and his faculty colleagues. Leta Bilodeau at the seminary's Portland campus worked her magic at several junctures to keep both authors and editors on track. In addition, the Eleanor H. Haney Fund provided grant money that made timely completion of this book possible.

Sylvia received a faculty research grant from Grinnell College that allowed her to travel to Maine for an extended work session. She has been warmly encouraged throughout this project by colleagues and staff in the sociology and religious studies departments of the college and by Grinnell College students whose intellectual curiosity, creative imagination, and energy for social justice sustain the delights of teaching.

Finally, we wish to express our gratitude to John Carey and our colleagues on the 1991 Presbyterian Special Committee on Human

Sexuality. In bravely speaking a fresh and bold word to the church about sexuality and spiritual integrity, they managed to "trouble the waters" and, thank God, keep hope alive that body and soul really do belong together—intimately, justice-lovingly.

Acknowledgment is gratefully extended for permission to include the previously published articles:

Marvin M. Ellison, "Setting the Captives Free: Same-Sex Domestic Violence and the Justice-Loving Church," adapted from *The Spirituality of Men: Sixteen Christians Write about Their Faith*, edited by Philip Culbertson, copyright © 2002 Augsburg Fortress. Used by permission (*www.augsburgfortress.org*).

Judith Plaskow, "Authority, Resistance, and Transformation: Jewish Feminist Reflections on Good Sex," in *Good Sex: Feminist Perspectives from the World's Religions*, edited by Patricia Beattie Jung, Mary E. Hunt, and Radhika Balakrishnan, copyright © 2001 by Judith Plaskow. Reprinted by permission of Rutgers University Press.

Contributors

Rita Nakashima Brock is a visiting scholar at the Starr King School for the Ministry, Graduate Theological Union, in Berkeley, California. She is the author of the award-winning *Journeys by Heart: A Christology of Erotic Power* and co-author of *Proverbs of Ashes: Violence, Redemptive Suffering, and the Search for What Saves Us.*

Thelma B. Burgonio-Watson, the first Filipina ordained in the Presbyterian Church (U.S.A.), is the Director for Training and Education at the Center for the Prevention of Sexual and Domestic Violence in Seattle, where she also coordinates the Asian and Pacific Islander Program. She served as a member of the Presbyterian committee that produced the 1991 "Keeping Body and Soul Together: Sexuality, Spirituality, and Social Justice."

John J. Carey is Wallace M. Alston Professor of Religious Studies, Emeritus, at Agnes Scott College in Decatur, Georgia. He chaired the Presbyterian Special Committee on Human Sexuality that produced the 1991 document "Keeping Body and Soul Together: Sexuality, Spirituality, and Social Justice," and edited *The Sexuality Debate in North American Churches, 1988–1995: Controversies, Unresolved Issues, and Future Prospects* (Edward Mellen, 1995). He now lives in Tallahassee, Florida.

Susan Halcomb Craig is ordained in the Presbyterian Church (U.S.A.) and pastor of United University Church at the University of Southern California campus in Los Angeles. She serves More Light Presbyterians as their liaison for bisexuality and lives with her partner, the Rev. Bear Ride, in Pasadena, California.

Virginia (Ginny) West Davidson, at eighty-six, readily acknowledges with Nelle Morton that the whole journey is home! She graduated with a degree in church history and theology from Colgate

Rochester Divinity School at the age of seventy-two, has served the Presbyterian Church as Vice-Moderator and in many other positions of leadership, and has an irreverent longing to partner with others in ministries of welcome and extravagant caring for all of Sophia God's creation.

Kelly Brown Douglas is professor of religion at Goucher College in Baltimore, Maryland. A priest in the Episcopal Church, she is the author of *Sexuality and the Black Church* and *The Black Christ.*

Marvin M. Ellison teaches Christian social ethics at Bangor Theological Seminary. His publications include *Erotic Justice: A Liberating Ethic of Sexuality* and *Same-Sex Marriage and Other Queer Notions: A Progressive Christian Ethical Analysis* (Pilgrim, forthcoming). Along with the community educator from a local domestic violence project, he regularly co-teaches a course for seminarians on ministry in relation to sexual and domestic violence. He was a principal author of "Keeping Body and Soul Together: Sexuality, Spirituality, and Social Justice."

Chris Glaser is the author of nine books, including *Coming Out as Sacrament* and most recently *Henri's Mantle: One Hundred Meditations on Nouwen's Legacy.* Chris served on the Presbyterian Task Force to Study Homosexuality from 1976 to 1978.

Robert E. Goss teaches Religious Studies at Webster University. He is author of *Jesus ACTED UP: A Gay and Lesbian Manifesto* and *Queering Christ: Beyond Jesus ACTED UP.* He also co-edited *Take Back the Word: A Queer Reading of the Bible* and *Our Families, Our Values: Snapshots of Queer Kinship.*

Debra W. Haffner is an ordained Unitarian Universalist minister and director of the Religious Institute on Sexual Morality, Justice, and Healing. A sexuality educator for more than twenty-five years, she is former president and CEO of SIECUS, the Sexuality Information and Education Council of the United States.

Scott Haldeman is assistant professor of worship at Chicago Theological Seminary. While his research focuses on the history and practice of worship among Protestants in North America, what catches his interest is the interpretation of many types of practice, ritualized and everyday, traditional and transgressive.

Beverly W. Harrison is Carolyn Williams Beaird Professor Emerita of Christian Ethics at Union Theological Seminary (New York) and past president of the Society of Christian Ethics, the first woman elected to that position. She is author of *Making the Connections* and *Our Right to Choose* and now lives in western North Carolina.

Carter Heyward, an Episcopal priest, is the Howard Chandler Robbins Professor of Theology at Episcopal Divinity School in Cambridge. Author or editor of more than a dozen books, she continues to be involved in movements for justice and peace. Heyward has also founded a center for therapeutic horseback riding in the mountains of North Carolina, where she lives in a small intentional community.

Mary E. Hobgood is associate professor of religious studies at the College of the Holy Cross in Worcester, Massachusetts. She is the author of *Dismantling Privilege: An Ethics of Accountability* and co-editor of *Welfare Policy: Feminist Critiques,* both published by The Pilgrim Press.

Mary E. Hunt is a Catholic feminist theologian and co-director of WATER, the Women's Alliance for Theology, Ethics and Ritual, in Silver Spring, Maryland. She is the author of numerous publications and the co-editor (with Patricia Beattie Jung and Radhika Balakrishnan) of *Good Sex: Feminist Perspectives from the World's Religions.*

Daniel C. Maguire is a professor of ethics at Marquette University. The author or editor of thirteen books and some two hundred articles, he is also president of the Religious Consultation on Population, Reproductive Health and Ethics, an international collegium of eighty scholars from all the world religions. *Ms.* magazine in their tenth anniversary issue listed Maguire as "one of the forty male heroes of the past decade, men who took chances and made a difference."

Virginia Ramey Mollenkott is a feminist and queer theologian who is grandmother to three children and emeritus professor of English at William Paterson University. Her book *Omnigender: A Transreligious Approach* (Pilgrim, 2001) won the 2002 Lambda Literary Award in the bisexual/transgender category. Following a reading of *Stone Butch Blues* and her ensuing research, she came to identify herself not simply as lesbian, but as a "masculine woman," that is, as a transgender or Two-Spirited person.

Rebecca Todd Peters is assistant professor of religious studies at Elon University, where she also holds the Distinguished Emerging Scholar chair. Her research interests, in addition to gender and sexuality, include economic and environmental ethics and globalization.

Judith Plaskow is professor of religious studies at Manhattan College. Author of *Standing Again at Sinai: Judaism from a Feminist Perspective*, she is currently at work on a book entitled *Just Sex: Judaism and Sexuality in American Culture*.

Michael D. Smith has been pastor of First Presbyterian Church in Grinnell, Iowa, since 1986. He has served the Presbyterian Church (U.S.A.) as a presbytery stated clerk, has been a longtime member of women's advocacy committees, and is currently co-moderator of the strategy committee of More Light Presbyterians.

Jane (Janie) Adams Spahr is the twin sister of Joanie, daughter of Sue and Chet, mother of Jim and Chet, partner emerita of Jim, preacher, pastor, lesbian, feminist, minister/director/evangelist for "That All May Freely Serve," and lover of justice, people, and creation.

Daniel T. Spencer is ordained in the United Church of Christ and currently associate professor of religion and ethics at Drake University in Des Moines, Iowa. His book *Gay and Gaia: Ethics, Ecology and the Erotic* was published by The Pilgrim Press in 1996.

Sylvia Thorson-Smith is a lecturer in religious studies and sociology at Grinnell College in Grinnell, Iowa. She has been a consultant and writer of several studies for the Presbyterian Church (U.S.A.), as well as a sexuality educator for Planned Parenthood of Southern Kansas.

Anne Underwood, an attorney, has been a mediator for the State of Maine judicial system since 1982 and currently consults with Protestant and Jewish denominations and chaplain associations on professional ethics. Raised Presbyterian and now a Catholic by choice and "for choice," she co-chairs the Religious Coalition Against Discrimination in Maine and serves on the boards of the Maine Council of Churches and the Center for Post-Holocaust Studies.

Johanna W. H. van Wijk-Bos is Dora Pierce Professor of Bible and Professor of Old Testament at Louisville Presbyterian Theological Seminary, where she has taught for over twenty-five years. She and her husband, David, are both ordained ministers in the Presbyterian Church (USA), and they struggle in solidarity with others for a church where justice is an integral part of peace.

– Introduction –

Keeping Body and Soul Together, Again for the First Time

Marvin M. Ellison and Sylvia Thorson-Smith

Hope and fear

Although conflict about religion and sexuality is nothing new, in recent years the heat seems to have been turned up. As Christian ethicist James B. Nelson and his colleague Sandra P. Longfellow observe, "The past twenty-five years [have been] without parallel in the long history of the church in terms of the amount of critical focus on sexuality issues."[1] As evidence, merely consider the vast array of books, articles, and denominational reports that have been produced on a wide range of topics dealing with human sexuality. In addition, a tremendous amount of ferment and debate has been stirred up, both by those seeking to change attitudes and policies about sex and by those working just as diligently to block change. "So much hope and so much fear," Nelson and Longfellow write, are being expressed about religion and "things sexual."[2]

When and where we enter

For more than two decades the two of us have participated, in one way or another, in these religious "sex wars." At the start of a third millennium we can also testify how things have hardly slowed down. As educators, one located in a seminary and the other in an undergraduate college, and as people of faith, one ordained as clergy and the other as elder, both European Americans, both feminists, one gay, the other straight, both partnered and each a parent of an

1

adult child, we come to this book of essays with a bias that has (fortunately, we think) shaped the entire project. Frankly, to us it only makes sense to put scholarship and activism together.

Editing this book has been an opportunity to work on concerns we care deeply about and also to enjoy ourselves, taking delight in how this professional collaboration gives us more time and "excuse" for deepening our connection as friends. As Presbyterians, we are quite aware that the Calvinist tradition has long emphasized doing one's *duty,* but the fact of the matter is that soliciting and editing these essays has been for us a very great *pleasure.* For that we're grateful both to The Pilgrim Press and to the over two dozen contributors to this volume. We want to offer this word of gratitude up front because readers should appreciate, if they do not already, that, first of all, there are real joys in making justice and, second, when it comes to these matters, it's important not to go it alone. In fact, in these endeavors it's especially wise to take along all manner of friends and allies.

Here we want to underscore the importance to progressive Christians and others that a small denominational press such as The Pilgrim Press has wholeheartedly embraced a mission to educate and inform the church and wider society on issues of religion and justice. Among the pressing justice concerns that must be kept in front of congregations, many address the pain and the pleasure of human sexuality. Courage begins with gaining awareness, and education promotes action for change. To those who provide the precious printed page and support social transformation with the expression of new ideas, we say "bravo," "brava" for connecting faith to action and making the expansion of justice movements possible.

Where and how, then, do we enter this project? We are Christian advocates for a comprehensive justice that includes gender, race, economic, and sexual justice and also incorporates respect and care for the earth and for nonhuman as well as human life. Sylvia teaches courses on human sexuality, gender, and religion at Grinnell College and has worked in a variety of contexts to make church and society more hospitable, particularly for women and sexual minorities. Her previous writing projects include studies on pornography,[3] gay and lesbian concerns,[4] and the challenges and joys of being a heterosexual ally.[5] She is also a "founding mother" of "Voices of

Sophia," an organization of pro-feminist, anti-racist Presbyterians who seek a renewal of faith by advocating justice for women and all marginalized peoples. Such justice-seeking means, in part, challenging the church to be more open to the Spirit's "doing a new thing" in women's theologies and liturgies.

Marvin teaches Christian social ethics at Bangor Theological Seminary and describes himself vocationally as a theological educator for justice. In Maine he co-chairs an interfaith network of pro-choice religious leaders who advocate for public policy that promotes reproductive rights and responsibility and also promote comprehensive sexuality education in congregations and schools.[6] As an out gay man, he has been active in movements for civil rights for lesbian, gay, bisexual, and transgender people (LGBT) and others denied their full humanity and rights as citizens, including the right of same-sex couples to marry. His publications include a study that develops a progressive Christian sexual ethic, a co-authored guide on religious responses to sexual and domestic violence, and a forthcoming book on same-sex marriage.[7] Along with Sylvia, he was a primary author and editor of the 1991 Presbyterian sexuality study, "Keeping Body and Soul Together: Sexuality, Spirituality, and Social Justice," the touchstone for this collection of essays.

Justice-making and spiritual renewal

In working for social justice and the renewal of religious tradition, we have been far from alone. Countless numbers of women and men, older and younger, of various racial and sexual identities have raised persistent cries for justice and compassion in their churches, synagogues, mosques, and temples and throughout the social order. This diverse assortment of folks constitutes a grassroots progressive movement, in the United States and globally, seeking a new moral order or *bios,* way of life. Some of us recognize and speak of this also as the movement of the Sacred in our midst.

Within this engagement, we've been learning, again and again, that a passion for justice lies at the heart of any spirituality worth having. Moreover, justice-making begins not by looking on from a distance, but by making connections with others, especially those deemed Other, outcast, and enemy, and by listening deeply, heeding their (and our own) cries of protest and lament, and joining the effort to set wrongs right.[8] These days the spiritual crisis that is so pervasive in the United States and elsewhere has everything to do, we suggest, with the fact that so few self-identified religious people express a genuine commitment to do justice and hold themselves accountable to marginalized peoples. Ethicist Beverly Harrison puts the matter this way: "Why is it, I ask myself, that so many people like us—white and relatively affluent—do not hear the calls for solidarity (not just advocacy or concern, but solidarity) with the poor, as a call to community?...Is it not the case that the politics of liberation makes little sense to us, and frightens us so badly, precisely because the longing—our will and desire—for genuine community is so nearly dead among us?"[9]

It is from this vantage point, as advocates for justice and renewal of community, including communities of faith, that we have invited the contributors to this volume to share their considerable wisdom about religion, sexuality, and sexual ethics. They, along with us, are persuaded that it is necessary to break through what poet Adrienne Rich calls the "lies, secrets, and silence"[10] and discern anew how to offer a genuinely life-giving word, both spoken and embodied. Given the negative track record of most religious traditions about sex and sexuality, who can seriously doubt that individuals and communities alike are in great need of Spirit-filled good news about sexuality, spirituality, and social justice?

Our working assumption in preparing this volume has been that religion, including Christian tradition, may well contribute to the doing of justice, but only if it undergoes its own reformation. Such a reformation will happen most readily, we wager, by means of embracing the Other and receiving with gratitude the moral wisdom of feminist, womanist, mujerista, and queer theologians, as well as people everywhere who are struggling for bodily integrity, spiritual well-being, and life itself. At the same time, we recognize that personal and communal struggles around gender, sexuality, and sexual difference are often intense, deeply divisive, and not likely to be resolved any time soon. Indeed, this collective effort to "keep body and soul together" may, indeed, be the "longest revolution," one in which many others will need to follow and stand upon our shoulders, just as we now stand on the shoulders of so many people, known and un-known, who have gone ahead of us. This "great peace march"[11] is not for the faint-hearted, for as Carter Heyward rightly contends, "Sexual justice [has been] the most trivialized, feared, and postponed dimension of social justice in western society and, possibly, in the world."[12]

"Keeping Body and Soul Together," the first time

The decade of the 1980s was pivotal for many people of faith, including Presbyterians. A reunion in 1983 of the two largest Presbyterian denominations—the United Presbyterian Church in the U.S.A. and the Presbyterian Church (U.S.) —marked the culmination of more than a century of efforts to heal the painful division within Presbyterianism brought about by slavery and the Civil War. In the 1960s and 1970s, the roots of the nineteenth-century abolitionist and women's movements continued to bear fruit in the civil rights, women's, and gay liberation movements. Conflict in both denominations over these justice issues remained intense after reunion and gave rise to even larger debates within the newly formed Presbyterian Church (U.S.A.). It was the continuing impasse over gay ordination that led the 1987 General Assembly to call, once again, for "more study" and to direct Isabel Wood Rogers, a highly respected Christian educator and moderator of the Assembly, to appoint a committee whose assignment would be to conduct a comprehensive study of human sexuality in the context of Christian faith and practice.

Within months, Rogers had assembled a group of ethicists, health professionals, counselors, sexuality educators, theologians, biblical scholars, and parish ministers to undertake this study, and the committee met for the first time in early 1988. Almost immediately, however, we realized how high the stakes would be in undertaking this work. We had hardly begun to delineate our task when two conservative members, Diogenes Allen of Princeton Theological Seminary and Roberta Hestenes of Eastern College, challenged the central objective of the committee and resigned in protest over its composition. New members had to be appointed (for a total of seventeen), and because of the vast amount of work before us, we were given an extension (originally 1990) until the 1991 Assembly to produce our report.

For three years we met in various locations around the country, listening in open forums to the stories and perspectives of widely diverse people struggling with issues of sexuality in their lives. Some traveled many miles to meet with us and share their hopes and concerns. Many pleaded for recommendations that would open up the church to ordination and welcoming the full gifts of gay and lesbian members. Others pled with us to do nothing that would change church policies and positions. In the context of prayer, theological study, and social/scientific research, the committee wrestled with its assignment, ever mindful that we were under the watchful scrutiny of the whole church and well aware that our conclusions—whatever they would be—would likely not be welcome within some segments of the denomination.

Over a year before our report was written and released, denominational executives invited (summoned) our chair, John Carey, and Sylvia to a meeting in Louisville where they were questioned about the committee's progress, cautioned about rumors, and given a not-too-subtle signal that what we were doing had generated, at the very least, great cause for concern. Of interest, in retrospect, is how *much fear* and how *little hope* was expressed about our work. Fear, as a matter of fact, became the driving force in the institutional pressure that surrounded us. Whereas many people were eager for a fresh word on human sexuality, those responsible for denominational peace and unity (primarily white men) voiced increasing caution, restraint, and even threat that we dare not do what it seemed we were about to do. Looking through our notes on meetings during the final year, we find remarks by those who testified before us: "go slow," "use softer language," "no policy recommendations," "let others make policy later," "don't be divisive," "you'll split the church," "think of peace and unity," "don't go the limit just to shock."

Surrounded by intense outside pressures, once the committee studying human sexuality began to make decisions, our internal differences and divisions emerged. Majority opinion began to solidify around a passionate justice-seeking framework for our report, with additional chapters on particular issues ranging from women's issues to clergy sexual misconduct, AIDS, reproductive technologies, and a series of recommendations on a wide range of church policy. A minority group held out for various alternatives, none of which was persuasive to the majority. In early 1991, a majority (eleven out of seventeen) of the committee adopted its two-hundred-page report and released it to the Presbyterian Church, recommending that the entire volume be approved by the General Assembly for two years of study. Statements of the six dissenting members comprise a minority view that was released as well.

"Keeping Body and Soul Together: Sexuality, Spirituality, and Social Justice" represents yet another good faith effort within a long history of Presbyterians and people in many other religious traditions who have sought to discern the "good news about sex" and a liberating sexual ethic for these times. In a framework entitled "Putting Sex in Perspective," the 1991 report contends that now is the time to rethink sexuality and reclaim a passionate spirituality of justice. This involves affirming "a gracious God, delighting in our sexuality," a call to holiness as inclusive wholeness, and the need to decenter conversations by actively listening to marginalized voices (since Western culture has been shaped primarily by white male heterosexuals). Sexual "justice-love" of mutuality and respect means honoring the goodness of sexuality, having gratitude for diversity, granting special concern for the sexually abused and violated, and acknowledging accountability for sexual behavior. The report advocates a single moral standard of justice-love as a test for all sexual relationships and proposes a seven-point ethic of "common decency" as a test of our values and commitments. In addition to the framework, "Keeping Body and Soul Together" includes ten issue chapters and forty-seven recommendations. From the outset, press coverage reflected the firestorm set off by the report:

- The *News of the Presbyterian Church (U.S.A.)* began its announcement article with the following statement: "Controversial even before its release, the report...is now out, and the emotional topic of homosexuality is only one of its many facets."[13]

- An editorial in the same newspaper warned: "The disagreement over this report is almost certain to be of monumental proportions. Let us pray that the struggle will result in growth."[14]

- Moderator Price Gwynn remarked in an interview: "Enough information has come out, I think, to indicate that it's going to be what I consider potentially damaging, damaging to the community of the Presbyterian Church....I'm in hopes that the General Assembly will put that report to bed in whatever way it finds appropriate."[15]

- An April 1991 headline in the *Des Moines Register* read: "Church Shaken by Panel's Report Endorsing the Joy of Sex."[16]

- An editorial in the *New York Times* declared that the report would be "virtually dead on arrival" when the General Assembly met in June 1991, calling it "an undeniably revolutionary statement on sex" and noting that more than half of the presbyteries (regional governing bodies) had called for the report's rejection while not a single one endorsed it.[17]

The *New York Times* had it right. "Keeping Body and Soul Together" was dead on arrival. Efforts to sustain its life and study were ultimately defeated. Opting not even to debate the content and recommendations of the report, commissioners to the General Assembly issued a pastoral letter declaring that they did not adopt either the majority or minority report and dismissing the committee with "thanks for their work, and with regret for the cruelties its members have suffered."[18] Perhaps the only bright moment was the church's refusal to accept even more conservative recommendations to scuttle the entire report, erase it from the Assembly minutes, and keep it from ever circulating again in print. However, by the time of the voting, the "cat," so to speak, was already well "out of the bag," insofar as about a hundred thousand copies of the report had been distributed far and wide, inside and outside the United States and far beyond the confines of Presbyterianism. One national church executive was heard to lament, not the report's controversial content, but that the church hadn't managed to put a higher price tag on this study paper and thereby failed to collect all the revenues its runaway bestseller might have earned!

Our experience of watching the Assembly fail to seriously engage the substance of our work is best described by the T-shirt worn by a young gay man the day after the General Assembly concluded. On the front it said, "I had sex with the Presbyterian Church," and on the back, simply: "And it was awful."[19]

Significance of the report

Immediately following Presbyterian debate, "Keeping Body and Soul Together" continued to garner attention from a wide range of media, critics, and supporters. During the week of the Assembly in Baltimore and all summer, members of the committee who wrote the report were interviewed by television networks, National Public Radio, magazines, and newspapers. Scholars and cultural icons of varying credibility weighed in on the report, assessing its significance with both welcome and dismissal:

- Ethicist Karen Lebacqz wrote in *Christianity and Crisis:* "At last: A report on sexuality worth reading. At last a report that places sexuality squarely within the framework of concerns for *justice* in church and society."[20]

- Social commentator Camille Paglia, in an article entitled "The Joy of Presbyterian Sex," observed that the report "offers itself as a profound, compassionate, and expertly researched statement on contemporary sexuality, [b]ut it is a repressive, reactionary document.... It is the revival of the old Protestant ethic, masquerading in hip new clothes."[21]

- Describing Paglia as a "feminist fatale" who "romps...into the rockless pastures of intellectual deception," Naomi Wolf denounced Paglia's "distortion of the relationship between sex and feminism" in assessing the Presbyterian report and her "remarkable liberty to misrepresent feminism."[22]

- Theologian Tom F. Driver charged that Paglia's attacks on the report and its feminist framework are "as full of fury as they are empty of sense and substance." As for the thousands of copies sold, Driver notes that "the presses are still rolling," and a "lot of folk seem to want to know what the committee

said. Some may even find it helpful. God preserve them if they
do not hear Paglia's warning that this document presages the
collapse of civilization."[23]

- Geneva Overholser, editor of the *Des Moines Register* and later
  ombudswoman for the *Washington Post,* devoted a column
  to the report in which she decried the church's denial about
  changing sexual norms that led to the report's defeat and
  celebrated its language of justice-love, integrity, faithfulness,
  and responsibility. "I have a new hope. In my days as a
  Presbyterian preacher's kid, not even a task force could have
  said such loving, sensible things about sex."[24]

Why did "Keeping Body and Soul Together" elicit such a national
chorus of opinion, not only in religious circles but also in nearly
every media forum that debates social trends? First of all, the secular press is always drawn to religious sex controversies. The history
of the church's suspicion about, repression of, and antagonism toward human desire imprisons honest sexual discussion in a tightly
regulated zone of ecclesiastical control so that when, unexpectedly,
a genuine breath of fresh air threatens to challenge the institutional
status quo, an event of disproportional consequence appears to be
in the making. Perhaps the most interesting alignment of medium
and message was found in a substantive and effusively grateful review by Craig Vetter in *Playboy* magazine, entitled "The Serpent in
the Chapel," which begins as follows:

For a while last summer, it looked as if the Presbyterian church
was about to lose its virginity to the real-world notion that it
might be possible to enjoy a healthy, moral sex life outside
of traditional Christian marriage. It was the best chance any
mainstream denomination has ever had to modernize and hu-
manize Christian morality, and it arrived with the publication
of an official church report....When the committee members
sat down to write, they didn't pull any punches....As they
launched bravely into their tough-minded and enlightened proposals for a modern Christian sexual ethic, they suggested
perhaps the way to start was to imagine the Lord Himself as "a
gracious God, delighting in our sexuality." That phrase alone

was enough to keep me reading, because it blew away the dark spirit of everything I'd ever been taught about Christian sexual morality.[25]

Another reason for the report's high-profile attention was the thoroughgoing shake-up portended by its analysis. Since the framework of this report is unapologetically feminist, liberationist, and ethically provocative, its critique of patriarchal sexuality and its call for a complete dismantling of sexist and heterosexist practices in sexual relationship and church practice are unsettling at the very least to the comfortably privileged keepers of the status quo. Nothing less than the bedrock of normative sex, marriage, and ecclesiastical gender arrangements are at risk when a church document proclaims boldly that human sexual pleasure is godly, that same-sex couples deserve religious approval, and that the substance (justice-love) rather than the form (marriage) should govern ethical relationships. No wonder those within and outside the church recognized how high the stakes were. No wonder a Presbyterian newspaper ran a post–General Assembly headline story that was intended to calm fears: "Assembly Rejects Report, Strongly Affirms Marriage."[26]

On this score, a British theologian, Adrian Thatcher, has written recently of the 1991 Presbyterian report as "the now notorious document." It is his judgment that "perhaps there has never been a more positive church sexuality report for advancing a self-critical understanding of the gender inequalities, patriarchal influences, sexual violence and attempts at social control which can be found in Christian thought and practice, together with a deeply Christian affirmation of people who have suffered from these malign influences or who are found beyond the customary parameters of approved sexual behaviour." At the same time, he suggests that the church rejected this work because it marginalized marriage in favor of a "justice-love ethic." "If the sanctity and centrality of marriage had been upheld by the report writers," Thatcher surmises, "much of their reforming agenda might have been retained. The marginalization of marriage made the rejection of the report inevitable."[27] Without a doubt, a majority of Presbyterians did rally to "save marriage," but we question Thatcher's analysis and conclusion. Interestingly, the 1991 report does not disregard or "marginalize" marriage; rather, it refuses to *privilege* marriage or make it the exclusive location for responsible sexual expression. However, by not privileging marriage, the committee is misjudged as discounting it altogether, a response characteristic of patriarchal church politics. That dismissive maneuver is certainly familiar to feminist (and even nonfeminist) women who, by refusing to cater to men or place men's interests consistently above their own, are perceived to be "man-haters."

Since 1991, theological and ethical analysis of sexuality issues has become only more complex. Many other religious bodies have developed similar studies and offered their proposals for revising ethical standards. The Presbyterian conflict over ordination intensified into a decade-long contest of overtures, constitutional amendments, judicial procedures, and demonstrations of civil disobedience.[28] Women who attended a global ecumenical event called Re-Imagining were charged with bringing denominations to the brink of split by worshiping the Goddess and celebrating female sexuality. Academic institutions and activist organizations debate queer theory and "identity politics," and every issue of sexuality has become more complicated because of race, gender, and class analyses.

A host of sexuality issues has held center stage, both nationally and internationally, in reports about the global HIV/AIDS pandemic, the murders of Matthew Shepard and other victims of hate crimes, the Methodist trial of Rev. Jimmy Creech for performing same-sex marriages, children's access to pornographic Internet sites, free speech debates over library Internet restriction, increased evidence of widespread sexual abuse, murders of abortion providers and decreased availability of abortion services, contested laws on same-sex adoption, increased benefits for domestic partners, ecological dangers, transsexual and intersexed medical developments, international sex tourism, and the list goes on. These cultural markers date "Keeping Body and Soul Together" as a particular product of the late twentieth century, but also attest to its continuing viability as a critical theo-ethical lens for rethinking and reevaluating emerging issues of human sexuality.

Wherever people live as sexual persons, there will be the longing for a "good word about sex." A hopeful message is needed about how to realize justice as well as love in sexual relationship. We believe that the 1991 Presbyterian report deserves its place as one key touchstone for addressing issues of human sexuality from a progressive religious perspective, and we are grateful to all who have used it to delve into deeper waters than we were prepared and able to enter ourselves.

Risks then and now

During the time when the Presbyterian committee was producing "Keeping Body and Soul Together" and engaging in its own theological reflection about human sexuality, we received many letters. Some offered words of encouragement; others warned us against wasting the church's time and money on questions that Bible-believing people shouldn't even be asking. Many others expressed a range of concerns, as did one young woman who wrote the following:

> What the youth and young adults of today are crying out for is guidance for responsible sexual behavior. God created us as sexual beings and we should be able to rejoice and explore God's love with our chosen partner through our sexuality, but unfortunately the opposite often occurs and sex is viewed as sinful, dirty, and wrong. There are many who don't understand their sexuality, and they are the ones our church must help, and they are silently crying out for help. I was.[29]

For people trapped in pain, silence, or worse, a church that does not speak a truthful and healing word only adds to their suffering. This is not only inhumane; it is unfaithful. As the 1991 report affirms: "We cannot keep silent and remain faithful to the God who creates, redeems, and sustains human sexuality as a good gift. God intends well-being for all creation, including sexual well-being. Since God is far from indifferent about human welfare, the community seeking fidelity to God should reflect God's own abiding care and compassion."[30]

Speaking a healing and truthful word may well be the faithful thing to do, but it is also risky, especially in an ecclesiastical and sociocultural context in which organized, well-financed forces of fear and reaction strike to punish dissenters and keep them silent.

Perhaps if "Keeping Body and Soul Together" had been a study document only for the church's edification and rumination, it might have raised controversy, but surely not the hysteria that ended up

being generated in large part because of the forty-seven recommendations that accompanied the study material. These recommendations were offered as ways to change the church so that it would
more fully reflect a gospel-mandated commitment to sexual and
gender justice. No doubt the single recommendation that sparked
most anxiety and furor was the call for the ordination of qualified
gay, lesbian, and bisexual persons to the pastoral ministry, but other
recommendations also incited right-wing groups and fueled their
massive efforts to generate a denominational backlash against the
report. Take note: this backlash was mounted even *before* the report
had been distributed or read. (Recommendations included calling
for a national event on sexuality for college-aged young people,
advocacy of comprehensive sexuality education in public schools,
development of educational materials for men in congregations on
men's issues, preparation of a resource on date and acquaintance
rape, revision of church pension and health insurance policies to
include same-sex couples, and adding a requirement that all seminarians complete at least one course in human sexuality.) When all
was said and done, not a single recommendation was debated, much
less accepted by the church.

Those most closely associated with the report, including its courageous and politically astute chairperson, John Carey, experienced
more and more heat as the time approached for circulating the document throughout the denomination, in anticipation of a formal vote,
up or down, at the church's national meeting. As the media coverage increased with headlines such as "Roll Over, John Calvin,"[31]
one committee member, an African American woman, lost a job
offer within the denomination because of her refusal to disown the
committee and recant her stand with the majority. This was a sober-
ing lesson about the risks involved in advocating justice, especially
gender and sexual justice. It was also a vivid reminder that not
everyone is equally vulnerable. Those with various degrees of social power and privilege, especially those of us who are white, male,
heterosexual, married, gainfully employed in positions beyond denominational leverage, and combinations thereof, may have taken
personal risks, but we typically did not have to pay as high a price
as did more vulnerable members of our committee. A similar lesson

would be made clear when, later in 1994, a nationally orchestrated and horrendously vicious backlash was launched against the ecumenical Re-Imagining conference on global feminism and spirituality. Again, women employed by the church, women of color, and lesbians took the greatest hit, as right-wing groups shamelessly maligned womanist theologies and hurled homophobic insults as part of their efforts to discredit those who sought to dismantle gender and sexual injustice.[32]

Because advocacy for sexual justice is risky business, contributors to this volume have shown significant courage in sharing their wisdom with an audience that may well include not only sympathetic readers and (always welcome) constructive critics, but also those wishing to discredit critics of the status quo and seeking to cause them grief. Several contributors to this volume decided late in the game that they had to withdraw, some for health and other personal reasons, others because they reassessed their personal and professional lives and concluded that appearing in this collection would put them at too great a risk. No collection of essays is perfect, but because of these unintended gaps, we do not cover some topics we had hoped to address specifically, including reproductive rights, disabilities, and lesbian concerns.

Because all are diminished when anyone is excluded or not heard in full voice, this experience has given us even more incentive to work for the day when the price of doing sexual justice will not be paid disproportionately by people of color, women, sexual minorities, and those employed by the church and church-related institutions. Race—or, better said, white racial supremacy—does and will impact sexuality at every turn, and unless white-skinned people become responsible, even the well-intentioned among them may try to protect themselves by stepping aside and letting people of color "take the heat," especially women and those who are not heterosexual. Keeping the costs of risk-taking in mind, we would do well to remember John Dominic Crossan's wise observation:

> It is impossible (fortunately) to have justice without compassion, but it is possible (unfortunately) to have compassion without justice.... Compassion, no matter how immediately necessary or profoundly human, cannot substitute for justice, for the

right of all to equal dignity and integrity of life. Those who live by compassion are often canonized. Those who live by justice are often crucified.[33]

Outline and content

The contributors to this volume know full well that the religious and ethical project is to end crucifixions, not perpetuate them. They speak as justice-lovers fully committed to keeping body and soul together. Part One, "Authority, Sources, and Norms," begins with Beverly W. Harrison's analysis of sexuality as a justice issue. Recognized as the pioneer of Christian feminist liberation ethics, she looks at the obstacles that prevent the integration of sexuality and spirituality in the lives of many people and encourages progressive people of faith to retrieve the best from the liberal theological tradition of holding love and justice together. Judith Plaskow then addresses the thorny question of authority and what actually legitimates efforts to speak a fresh word about sexuality and sexual ethics from a Jewish perspective. A third essay, by Johanna W. H. van Wijk-Bos explores the yield of reading biblical traditions through a feminist lens. Carter Heyward finishes this section with her review of teaching sexuality in a seminary context and identifies some of the changes in content, process, and perspective that have most intrigued her and her students.

Part Two, "Sexualities," explores some of the diversity of human sexualities. The plural is used intentionally here to underscore that human sexuality is replete with variation and difference, as well as to challenge an older paradigm that naturalizes heterosexuality and evaluates other modes as deviant and inferior. Kelly Brown Douglas, along with other authors in this volume, is both appreciative and critical of the 1991 Presbyterian report. Her essay pushes for an analysis of sexuality that takes into account how white racism influences sexual paradigms in both black and white communities and church traditions. Susan Halcomb Craig then addresses one of the variations of sexual identity, bisexuality, and in doing so speaks from her vantage point as a bisexual woman in a committed relationship with another woman. Chris Glaser, well-known writer and gay Christian denied ordination, writes about aging, sexuality, and the subtle differences between a "young" and an "old" love. An essay follows on adolescents and sexuality by Debra W. Haffner, former executive director of SIECUS (the Sex Information and Education Council in the U.S.) and someone eager to enlist religious leaders in promoting comprehensive sexuality education for all ages.

Three essays complete this section by looking at various components of gender and sexuality. Rebecca Todd Peters writes about gendered theological images and why naming the divine as female matters to women and men seeking sexual and spiritual wholeness. Daniel C. Maguire looks at male myths and how men and male experiences of sexuality might benefit from a "gender revolution." Virginia Ramey Mollenkott completes this section with her proposal for a gender paradigm that shatters the familiar binary gender code and makes room for transgender people, their lives, and their spirituality.

Part Three, "Pleasure and Health," addresses the "good news about sex" and how engagement in sexual ethics promotes sexual health and well-being. Two gay men first take up this theme, starting with Robert E. Goss's analysis of gay erotic spirituality and his appeal for recovery of sexual pleasure at the heart of religious experience. Scott Haldeman follows with a discussion of revelation and receptive anal sex, an essay that will no doubt spark conversation and reflection. Two women then enter to press matters of health and well-being, beginning with Sylvia Thorson-Smith, whose essay suggests that honesty requires us to struggle with what among us is *unhealthy* and notes the difficulty of finding appropriate resources for sexual health. Mary Hunt then examines the global pandemic of HIV/AIDS and offers a religious "reality check" about understanding how this and every other sexuality issue is further complicated by race, gender, and poverty.

Part Four, "Pain and Violence," begins with Thelma Burgonio-Watson's passionate call for an end to domestic violence and a turn from private pain to public — and global — concern, especially for Asian American immigrant women. Marvin M. Ellison follows with an essay on the churches' response to same-sex domestic violence and contends that to do justice in these matters, the church must first be willing to recognize and honor same-sex relationships.

Anne Underwood concludes this section by sketching a justice frame-work for addressing clergy sexual misconduct and calls upon faith communities to learn from the legal system in doing what justice demands.

To introduce Part Five, "Struggle and Hope," we cite an insight at-tributed to Augustine: "Hope has two beautiful daughters, anger and courage: anger at the way things are, and courage to do something in response."[34] Authors in this section share their wisdom about a variety of justice struggles and insights gained from engaging those struggles rather than "standing apart." Daniel T. Spencer, in wisely noting the absence in the 1991 report of sustained attention to keep-ing body, soul, *and earth* together, outlines a theological ethic of sexuality that recasts justice-love as an *ecological* ethic of right re-lation. Mary E. Hobgood redresses another deficiency in that earlier study by focusing on global economic arrangements that are always at work shaping, and often misshaping, gender and sexuality. Rita Nakashima Brock then looks at marriage as a troubled institution and asks what changes must take place if the church is to promote marriage that is genuinely ethical. The concluding essay, produced collaboratively by Virginia West Davidson, Michael D. Smith, and Jane Adams Spahr, uses Presbyterian conflict over gay ordination as a case study to examine far-reaching issues of church leadership.

Again, for the first time

For many who attended the Presbyterian General Assembly in 1991, an unforgettable moment is etched indelibly in memory. Commis-sioners, after voting overwhelmingly not to adopt the sexuality re-port, issued a "pastoral" letter designed to "calm the waters" by reaffirming church policy on ordination for heterosexuals only and upholding marriage as the exclusive norm for sexual relating. The movement toward sexual justice, at least among Presbyterians, had been successfully squelched, or had it?

As soon as the General Assembly had taken its action, a protest followed, giving pause to some and hope to many more. Express-ing deep feelings of pain and anger, as well as love and support for lesbians and gay men and all those made to suffer by the church's negative sexual theology and ethic, the demonstration was described by Sylvia in an essay published soon after this momentous Baltimore General Assembly:

> From the back of the convention center, a huge wooden cross was borne high as a small group of gays, lesbians, and their friends moved silently forward. The procession became larger as hundreds of people got up from their seats and joined our ranks. Tears streaming down faces, arms linked, we stood and listened as 10–inch nails were driven into the cross, the silence pierced by those who felt crucified. Then we sang: "We are a gentle, angry people…a gay and lesbian people…a resurrection people." With a crucifixion and a song, the 203rd General Assembly of the Presbyterian Church (U.S.A.) concluded its deliberation on human sexuality.[35]

Again and again throughout history, in waves of movements for social justice, people have joined in solidarity to give voice to the voiceless, take self-jeopardizing risks, challenge powers and principalities, and muster deep reservoirs of courage to go against the comfort-seeking tide of the status quo. With the determination and conviction of Susan B. Anthony, who didn't live to see women get the vote but kept hope alive with her conviction that "failure is impossible," masses of change agents are standing together, across religious traditions, to apply a justice-loving ethic to all matters regarding human sexuality. What looks like folly to many is, to those committed, nothing short of life-giving participation in a movement that sustains body and soul.

The two of us have found blessings abundant as part of this justice-loving community. Not the least is the gift of our deep friendship, a connection that over the years continues to spark creative energy and endless good times as we seek to find ways to live in both church and world as a fearless gay man and an uppity heterosexual woman. Above and beyond this mutual richness, we are blessed daily by a broad network of justice-loving friends, family members, colleagues, and partners, a network that has grown over the years and often surprises us with its multiple new intersections and expanding connections. Who would have ever thought that life had this in store for the two of us—a Tennessee-born Presbyterian teaching at a UCC seminary in Maine and an Alaskan Lutheran-turned-Presbyterian teaching at a historically UCC college in Iowa? Kate Millett had it so right when she wrote: "The work of enlarging human freedom is such nice work we're lucky to get it."[36]

Christian ethicist Larry Rasmussen describes the Jesus movement as a radical experiment in "creative deviance on the frontline."[37] Being deviant means not accepting the given definitions, being creative means pursuing real alternatives, and being frontline means staying engaged for the long haul. Regardless of the religious tradition or social convictions in which one is anchored, this definition speaks powerfully of the call to radical, transformative work that justice-lovers believe is so central to their values and commitments. Such a call to deviance confirms the wisdom in Flannery O'Connor's quip: "You will know the truth, and the truth will make you *odd*."

As editors and contributors to this volume, we invite readers now to savor the wisdom of the essays that follow and, then, to be emboldened to become (ever more) odd themselves, showing forth a distinctive kind of oddity in their own lives and work: an odd, even quite brazen passion for justice and a never-ending delight in the goodness of being sexual persons. As two of the authors of the earlier Presbyterian study, we risk repeating ourselves here, but given how this *Body and Soul* collection has renewed in us our encouragement to "keep body and soul together, again for the first time," we offer once more the heartfelt words that close the framework section of the 1991 document:

> As Christians whose deep desire is for justice-love, we find ourselves grateful beyond words for the gift of sexuality and for God's gracious call to be in loving, caring, mutual relation with others. Above all, we are invited to new life in solidarity with the marginalized and oppressed. In responding to this calling, may God bless and keep us while empowering us, each and all, to make justice-love abound in a world where there is precious little of it.[38]

Notes

1. James B. Nelson and Sandra P. Longfellow, "Introduction," in *Sexuality and the Sacred: Sources for Theological Reflection,* ed. James B. Nelson and Sandra P. Longfellow (Louisville: Westminster John Knox, 1994), xvi.

2. Ibid., xvii.

3. Sylvia Thorson-Smith, et al., *Pornography: Far From the Song of Songs* (Louisville: Presbyterian Church [U.S.A.], 1988).

4. Sylvia Thorson-Smith, *Reconciling the Broken Silence* (Louisville: Presbyterian Church [U.S.A.], 1993).

5. Sylvia Thorson-Smith et al, eds., *Called Out With: Stories of Solidarity* (Louisville: Westminster John Knox, 1997).

6. The website for the Maine Interfaith Council for Reproductive Choices is at *www.MICRC.org.*

7. *Erotic Justice: A Liberating Ethic of Sexuality* (Louisville: Westminster John Knox, 1996); *Clergy and Domestic Abuse, Child Abuse, and Substance Abuse: A Cross-Disciplinary Training Curriculum,* with Francine Stark (Augusta: Maine Department of Human Services and the Edmund S. Muskie School of Public Service, 2000); *Same-Sex Marriage and Other Queer Notions: A Progressive Christian Ethical Analysis* (Cleveland: Pilgrim, forthcoming).

8. See Iris Marion Young, *Justice and the Politics of Difference* (Princeton: Princeton University Press, 1990), 4–5.

9. Beverly Wildung Harrison, "The Dream of a Common Language: Towards a Normative Theory of Justice in Christian Ethics," *Annual of the Society of Christian Ethics* (1983): 18.

10. Adrienne Rich, *Lies, Secrets, and Silence* (New York: Norton, 1979).

11. Holly Near, *The Great Peace March* (Boston: Horn Book, 1993).

12. Carter Heyward, *Touching Our Strength: The Erotic as Power and the Love of God* (San Francisco: Harper & Row, 1989), 4.

13. Michael E. Jones and Jerry Van Marter, "Sexuality Panel Report Includes Much More Than Same-Sex Issues," *News of the Presbyterian Church (U.S.A.)* 4, no. 1 (January–February 1991): 1–N.

14. Michael E. Jones, "Human Sexuality Report Doesn't Fool Around," *News of the Presbyterian Church (U.S.A.)* 4, no. 1 (January–February 1991): 2–N.

15. Robert H. Bullock, *The Presbyterian Outlook,* 173, no. 7 (February 25, 1991): 11.

16. Laura Sessions Stepp, "Church Shaken by Panel's Report Endorsing the Joy of Sex," *Des Moines Register,* April 22, 1991, 3A.

17. Peter Steinfels, "Beliefs," *New York Times,* May 25, 1991.

18. Office of the General Assembly, Presbyterian Church (U.S.A.), June 11, 1991.

19. Sylvia Thorson-Smith, "I 'Had Sex' with the Presbyterian Church," Synod of Lakes and Prairies *Presbyterian Life and Times* (summer 1991): 4–5.

20. Karen Lebacqz, "Sex: Justice in Church and Society," *Christianity and Crisis* (May 27, 1991): 174.

21. Camille Paglia, "The Joy of Presbyterian Sex," *New Republic,* December 2, 1991, 24.

22. Naomi Wolf, "Feminist Fatale," *New Republic,* March 16, 1992, 23.

23. Tom F. Driver, "Presbyterians, Pagans, and Paglia," *Christianity and Crisis* (February 3, 1992): 20.

24. Geneva Overholser, "The Last Bastion of Denial," *Des Moines Register,* June 30, 1991.

25. Craig Vetter, "Serpent in the Chapel," *Playboy* (fall 1991): 138.

26. Ann Anderson, "Assembly Rejects Report, Strongly Affirms Marriage," *News of the Presbyterian Church (U.S.A.)* 4, no. 5 (June 1991): 1.

27. Adrian Thatcher, *Living Together and Christian Ethics* (Cambridge: Cambridge University Press, 2002), 85–87.

28. See chapter 22 in this volume, "No More Second-Class Members: Rethinking the Church's Continuing Debate over the Ordination of Lesbian, Gay, Bisexual, and Transgender Persons."

29. *Presbyterians and Human Sexuality 1991* (Louisville: Presbyterian Church [U.S.A.], 1991), 6.

30. Ibid., 6–7.

31. Kenneth L. Woodward, "Roll Over, John Calvin," *Newsweek,* May 6, 1991, 59.

32. On the use of homophobia and sexism as strategies of division, see Suzanne Pharr, *In the Time of the Right: Reflections on Liberation* (Berkeley, Calif.: Chardon, 1996).

33. John Dominic Crossan, *The Birth of Christianity* (San Francisco: Harper-Collins, 1998), 586.

34. Augustine is paraphrased in Robert McAfee Brown, *Spirituality and Liberation: Overcoming the Great Fallacy* (Philadelphia: Westminster, 1988), 136.

35. Thorson-Smith, "I Had Sex with the Presbyterian Church," 5.

36. Kate Millett, *Sexual Politics* (New York: Simon & Schuster, 1990), xii.

37. Larry Rasmussen, "Shaping Communities," in *Practicing Our Faith: A Way of Life for a Searching People,* ed. Dorothy C. Bass (San Francisco: Jossey-Bass, 1997), 124–26. Rasmussen draws here on Ronald Heifetz's *Leadership without Easy Answers.*

38. *Presbyterians and Human Sexuality 1991,* 29.

Part One

Authority, Sources, and Norms

Christianity's Indecent Decency

Why a Holistic Vision of Justice Eludes Us

Beverly W. Harrison

The title I have chosen is intended to "conjure" the religious culture into which I was confirmed, now the Presbyterian Church (U.S.A.). This denomination was created in 1983 out of two other "denominational tribes," both of which claimed deep love for John Calvin and the traditions of his followers. Calvin, it should be recalled, was a lawyer, and his church's political order has always appealed to those with a deep desire to do things "decently and in order."

Unfortunately, starting in the early 1960s, a powerful group of corporate executives came together and agreed to pour their considerable largesse into getting Presbyterians out of the justice business.[1] Their initial agenda targeted the strong anti-racism commitments of the former "northern church," the UPCUSA. As a result, when issues of gay/lesbian ordination arose in the 1970s and feminism also gained stature and voice, these laymen were already organized to manipulate the sexuality issues that frightened Presbyterians and rendered most liberals speechless in the debate. Since that time, the most vulgar forms of indecency, masked as piety, have prevailed in most official gatherings of the denomination. Many pockets of resistance to the weird and un-Reformed "Kill the Queers" theology now endorsed by Presbyterians struggle to exist. However, what I will here refer to as Virtual Reality Theology remains the official teaching of this church tradition.

To keep these Virtuals mindful of the many better things in the history of their church, I dedicate this essay to three of the most powerful, though frequently maligned, Presbyterian practitioners of theological justice-love.[2] All three were/are my teachers and ongoing guides: Maggie Kuhn, who still empowers us to pray for the coming of the Gray Panther Revolution;[3] that incomparably beautiful theologian of lucidity and simple wonder, Robert McAfee Brown, who taught us to see the complexity and theological depth in all things, with an eye to finding humor in embracing the theological vocation of St. Hereticus;[4] and my friend and gentle spiritual teacher, Delores S. Williams, who is Paul Tillich Professor of Theology and Culture at the Union Theological Seminary in New York. She not only teaches the subtleties of white racism, but also has led the way in showing us how to suffer the battery of white patriarchal *libel* and get on with one's critically important work.[5]

The current situation of progressive Christians: a hypothesis from a proudly queering Gray Panther

Initially, our editors' invitation to me to address the question of why Christian people and communities have so much trouble connecting human sexuality, in all its variegated colors and dimensions, to matters of justice (not to say love!) sounded like a delicious request, even a luscious opportunity! It was, I imagined, an assignment I could do with at least one hand tied behind my back. After all, I had long been putting together theses about theological and political liberalism's entrapments in the Reagan/Bush/Shrub era. My list of the theoretical (i.e., theo-moral teaching) and the practical mistakes of present and former liberals in both church and academy is, to tell the truth, very long. That many who were originally educated in "modernist" Christian thinking are now headed into what I perceive as the new "virtual" theology of neoliberalism troubles me mightily. Many now fashionably "postmoderns" have, in fact, moved into reaction. So this assignment, I imagined, would be a fairly easy one. However, since all forms of insensitivity to justice blind us to hope, the question, once posed, turned out to be not so easy to answer.

Recent changes in the venue where I do my work contributed something to the unexpected difficulties this assignment posed. In my none-too-retiring mode as a replaced academic, I have left the city for the country. Among other things, my lack of familiarity with my new environment led me to imagine that my move to what was once

"Helmsland" (and what may now become "Doleville"), would bring me to a place where few would be interested in what I had long been teaching. Since I had no intention of hiding my light under a BUSHel, even here, I began by acknowledging that I need to learn how to do my theological teaching anew. I decided to talk about religion in any place where anyone would listen and engage, be it in grocery store conversations, coffee klatches, or in the vast and interesting array of religious- and/or community-based gatherings that the mountains of western North Carolina spawn.

My earlier life had taught me that the lecture platform and the graduate school classroom are incredibly rich sites for my own learning, but I feared it had not taught me much about translating across the chasms that have developed between what learned Christians have to say and what grassroots folks want to hear. I had imagined that the problem would chiefly be reluctance on the part of people to listen. What I have found is that, outside of the academic geopolitical regions where those who deem themselves "the best and the brightest" dwell, there is great openness. I have quickly learned enthusiasm for this stance of "perpetual teaching," seeking out and, when I can, empowering diverse and clear-sighted queering types of every hue and persuasion.

To be sure, here as elsewhere, we who long for a resurrection of progressive Christianity are undermanned (i.e., too few men who can hear) and decidedly underpaid and understaffed (i.e., not enough money or volunteers). My confidence grows, however, that we can still find ways to launch creative skirmishes against neoliberalism, which is being advanced by a new fundamentalism[6] that insists that any who deserve recognition must be of their Rightful persuasion. All other voices, we should note, invite erasure on the Virtuals' screen of the *truly* Great.

Happily, at the same time, learning to live in a culture where this new fundamentalism seeks to erase any alternative religious views has given me some hope. It has enabled me also to witness the resistance of many evangelical Christians to the Right's admonitions that they *must* be mean-spirited toward sexual deviance and terrified of doctrinal flexibility. Given the Christian Right's activities for over a decade, our appreciation for grassroots decency has to be chastened, however, by recognition of the economic power of the newly minted

Virtual Theology. Observing at first hand the active creation of the new fundamentalism has helped me to recognize that there have been devastating costs attached to liberal theology's three decades of passivity and willingness to surrender, without an engagement, to the new Christianity of the Righteous.[7]

The move from the now deindustrialized and newly technologized Northeast to the rapidly deindustrializing and still technologizing Southeast makes me aware of the extent to which the problem is not people at the grassroots but the national script of salvation forged in Washington. This region still awaits the full promise of the military-industrial complex, which took center here as a scheme by Democrats to address regional poverty. The South continues to embrace the dream of unlimited affluence that has long been re-iterated. However, deindustrializing is now a whiplash dynamic in the globalized economy, and it again brings to this region poverty rather than the greater largesse that monopoly capitalism promises to those who believe.

While many in the South still harbor hope in the prophets of the military-industrial national dream and trust neoliberalism to de-liver, the mood here, as elsewhere, is becoming surly. The historical contradiction of simultaneously destroying the agencies of govern-ment aimed at social well-being while accelerating the growth of a new "homeland security" apparatus strains the people's power of resistance. Turning social caring over to the "charity" of corpo-rations and megachurches is beginning to fray the populace since it requires more work, less money, and more charity than working poor people can afford. While the most ardent Republicans claim to be confident, they grow ever more enraged at any deviance. Further-more, all live under the stress of so-called productivity (more work, less money), as well as more rapid and more violent trajectories of change than anyone is naming. It is in this atmosphere that I have also been busy studying the nation's new religious demographics at close range.

The result of all this is that I have come to feel great urgency about a recovery of *some* of the tenets and more of the practices of an earlier liberal theological era. People here are actually quite hungry for a re-turn to the simpler conditions of human decency. While enthusiasm for any visible signs of success commends the social form of the mega-churches to many (read: churches designated by diverse labels that have become mini- or maxi-corporations), the longing for a recovery of caring community and the small decencies of human kindness is palpable. It should be a good time for that Old Time Religion of love of God and neighbor. Alas, however, the liberal denominations continue to be mostly silent and, for the most part, very gray and aged. What is most worrisome, however, is the timidity of the leadership of these denominations.

Formerly liberal churches mired in sexual fear

At least as far back as 1975, when what I now call the "old-line"[8] Protestants first began to break out in agony at the very mention of sexuality, I have puzzled over the question, "Whatever happened to all that talk about the relationship of justice and love that filled the pages of the massive tomes of Protestant Christian theology produced in the first half of the twentieth century?"[9] As I have listened over the last quarter century to the distressingly barren ecclesiastically generated discourses about sex, it has become appallingly clear that within most denominational parishes the fear has not dissipated, and little has been learned. The truth is that those reared in older liberal theologies are still all but speechless in the face of any expression of human sexuality that deviates from a simple, even simple-minded, nineteenth-century Victorian script. Sex, many of our most churchly voices proclaim, is a part of our "lower animal nature," a fearful force that must be controlled. The only "good sex" that the dominant Protestant churchly imagination can still conjure is captive to the idea that no one should, in any way, be sexual outside of the marital bed.[10] Christian conventionality must hold all other desires at bay. Furthermore, the once deemed "natural" missionary position — the physical and spiritual placement of men over women — must still prevail. Fathers, they insist, must be heads of households even if most younger men no longer have interest in the job.

Meanwhile, since the baby boomers took over in town and country, the rest of the world has moved on sexually. Victorian sexual theory has been replaced, and many are learning from the new biology, the new sexology, and myriads of anthropological and psychosocial perspectives, not to mention the new cultural studies that often refer to themselves as "queer theory." As a result most "oldline" Protestant churches have become a spiritual embarrassment to all but the elderly who have missed the new hip cultural changes. The "neoevangelicals,"[11] as I like to call some of my neighbors who buy in on political and economic neoliberalism, are as far from Victorian sexuality as the rest of us. Neo-fundamentalist Beverly LaHaye's work to encourage "women aglow" has made luscious sexiness a must.[12] "Concerned Women of America" is quite a glamorous group, since most of these neoevangelical women have husbands who can well afford to provide the cost of their newly pious glamour. All across the Southeast, as much as in the Northeast, whether neoliberal or not, women are assertive in demanding their "marital rights" in ways that would have shocked "Victorian Southern ladies" and that warm the hearts of Gray Panther feminists like me.

One of the results of all this is that even though the churches are busy and well attended, more and more people in city *and* in country say that they no longer are much interested in "religion." They seem to mean organizations that declare something to be definitive "theological truth." By contrast, everybody in and out of the churches is interested in "spirituality," and among most of those, sexuality is pretty much of a good thing and fun to boot. Is it any wonder that the children born to leaders of once liberal churches have wandered off, taking some of their parents' moral sensitivity with them, into what might be termed a respectful secularity?

Meanwhile, outside of "the secular cities,"[13] many remain in the churches, where the challenging work of learning to explain liberalism's problems goes on. What I find hopeful is that most of my new neighbors think of themselves as evangelicals and as genuine lovers of Scripture. As a result, they also tend to believe that professing Christian faith means that they must take a stab at the practice of neighbor love in their daily lives. What I find worrisome is the ease with which the new nationalist "Market God" theology shapes such uncomplicated spirituality in a privatizing direction and obscures the role of the struggle for justice in recovering genuine spiritual depth.[14]

Neoliberal public theology, so-called anti-terrorism, and its erasure of "liberality" from the spirit of the people

It should be clear, then, that it is not the sensibilities of grassroots Christians that are problematic. What we must address is the media-focused accounts of the self-evident truths of neoliberalism, which claim that politics (read: the struggle for a good community) is irrelevant and that "the market" will provide the wisdom to meet our needs. Because the current neoliberal assault is leading to ongoing erasure of much that was best in historically grounded theological and political liberalism, we must learn to name its violence. Neoliberal violence is subtle. It batters only ambitious and strong women, poor women, children, gays, and old men at home and abroad. These "outsiders" to neoliberal progress are the distinctive "collateral damage" of their "virtual wars." But the carnage hardly ends there. The New Punditry takes aim at truth-tellers of many sorts who must be defaced and discredited if the Right is to prevail. Disinformation and libelous "spins" abound. Though the rhetorical weapons of the New Righteousness are not as lethal as the high-tech toys they propose to visit on Muslim strangers and others who have reason to hate us, their verbal invectives leave many voices of wisdom and an earlier understanding of "decency" defaced or silenced. Currently, all genuine prophets (i.e., those who can see why our present cannot yield decent visions of the future) are doomed to contemptuous dismissal in the Market God's pantheon.

It is, I think, time to issue a warning to all presumed liberals who aspire to stardom and elite status: The path you are traversing leads, at best, to historical amnesia and triviality and, at worst, to high crimes and far more than misdemeanors. All who seek the ear of the new Patriarchal Warlords and play by their rules are doomed to fall under the spell of the Market God. This understood, we can get on with setting aside our fears and doing our work with vigor. Once freed from the captivity of the sound-bite mentality and worry about our status, it is easy to uncover "old fashioned" lovers of justice and compassion who share our suspicion of pundit-generated theology. To do that, we must gain a strongly renewed sense of the role that justice plays as a nonnegotiable condition for the embodiment of love.

Relearning some of the virtues of liberalism: justice as love's only handmaiden

More than once, in the pile of class notes I borrowed from folks who actually sat in his classroom, I found evidence that H. Richard Niebuhr admonished his students *not* to watch their enemies (i.e., those whom they especially feared) too closely. It was, he said, very easy to imitate those we fear and to become like them. (Long ago I discovered that theologians utter the wisest and most memorable adages in their classrooms, but frequently omit them from their writings.)

Though I have often been critical of many of the most celebrated U.S. theologians, we need to pause and consider what happened to the legacy of those like H. Richard Niebuhr, Reinhold Niebuhr, and Paul Tillich, who were recognized both as theologians and social critics. We need to recall Reinhold Niebuhr's uncompromising insistence that love cannot be love in the absence of justice. We need to recover Paul Tillich's conviction that cultural depth and creativity are signs of genuine cultural godliness. However, even with a recovery of these earlier aspirations to connect love to the concrete life of justice and injustice, the road ahead will be stony in our struggle to resurrect a tradition and voice of progressive Christianity.

Life on actual "ground zero" (i.e., where people in real towns and cities live and die through the way public events shape their daily lives) gives us reasons to resist being mesmerized by the *virtual* "ground zeros" created by those shaped by inane Virtual Religion. Such religions mimic the fanatical fears that fed earlier fascisms. What still strikes real terror in my heart, however, is the blindness liberal-spirited folk have to Virtual Theology's *apocalyptic visions* created by the "rich and famous" and those who identify with them. H. Richard Niebuhr was right. It is easy to mimic the enemy, and on the national level, many former liberals and current timid liberals are swayed by their appeals to fear. Frightened people are easy to lead astray.

We all need to disentangle liberal faith from the "Market God" and "Kill the Queers" theologies. "Queers," as I use the term, refers not only to anyone gay, lesbian, bisexual, or transgender, but to any woman who refuses to surrender self-affirming labels like feminist, womanist, and mujerista, and also to any pro-feminist man brave enough to challenge this new Virtual Theology. It most especially includes all strong, self-respecting women who resist compulsory pregnancy, which has become the *truly* Christian public policy in relation to abortion and female health.[15]

We also need to be clear that the dominant Public Theology of Death is now held in place by a fierce *nationalism*. The endless "war on terrorism" hype is aimed at getting people to confuse patriotism with nationalism, so that the newly constructed scenario of "Imperial-Savior America" can prevail. Connecting the work of justice-making to the endlessly trivialized matters of sexual justice has become all the more difficult because of the apocalyptic cleverness of the neo-war mentality.

Digging deeper to recover the historical accomplishments of liberalism

Working on an early draft of this essay, I was stunned to hear news of the death of Minnesota Senator Paul Wellstone, his extraordinary wife, Sheila, and their daughter Marcia, all firm advocates of justice for women, children, and all sorts of people of nonwhiteness. Their deaths and those of their five friends, eight wonderful people altogether, were tragic. All spoke for humane public practices toward children, working people, and grassroots communities. The grief that seized me at this awful news was far more than personal. It was, I recognized, grief at the assault on the "prairie populism" that had shaped my own earliest visions of what community ought to be. Ironically, the Wellstones were products of Southern agrarian populism of the region where I now live.

Paul, a child of Russian Jewish immigrants, was, more than any current member of the United States Senate, a clear outsider of that "millionaires club." Ardent in his advocacy of working families, he was a Southern populist who believed that politics should serve the grassroots. Sheila, also a modern girl-child of the South, was uncompromising in her vision of a world where women could grow up free of violence and where children matter. Marcia Wellstone, their daughter, carried the hopes of many for the Wellstone political legacy, due especially to her own growing concern for a community welcoming to multicultural and multiracial voices.

What the trauma of these deaths conjured for me was an awareness of how far we have wandered, as a nation, from the roots of
progressive Catholic and Protestant populism and from the social
teaching both these traditions have engendered in our national collective memory.[16] Pondering the passion for genuine democracy I
learned in my youth, a passion animated in both Protestant and
Catholic communities, made me realize anew how much has been
lost in the public memories of all our current political leaders who
espouse Christianity. The loss of genuine feeling for democracy as a
central religious longing is apparent in the souls of many of our elites,
whether they profess neoliberalism or claim to offer alternative politics. But at one time, liberal Protestants and Catholics shared with
immigrant Jews a resounding commitment to equality and justice.

To be sure, Protestants originally held a suspicion of the role of
the strong state (or, better, a suspicion of state-imposed religion)
and a preference for local political organization. Earlier Protestant
populism had a rather "old Republican" cast, a political sensibility now erased by the new Republican Warriors. By contrast, many
Catholics arrived on these shores with expectations that the state
could and should act "for the working people." Jews, whether secular or religious, also brought a more urban expectation that the state
could and should act for the public welfare, especially the welfare of
working people.

In spite of a clear commitment to democracy, almost all Europeans brought the myopia of whiteness, i.e., a "naïve preference"
for a Euro-centric culture. It is not surprising that white racism has
now become our nation's *deepest problematic.* Even so, the ardor for
progress in democracy, so central to a vision of good society, *was
not in question* for earlier liberals, whether Catholic, Protestant, or
Jewish. What troubles me most in our present situation is the weak
purchase that not only neoliberals but also nonrepentant liberals
have on the importance of genuine democracy in any religious or
spiritual "recovery."

The result is that many Christian traditionalists, drifting into neoliberalism, have joined the reigning neoliberal practices of berating
feminists, pounding the "queers," and blathering about saving their
denominations. In the face of this, we need to get clear that theological liberalism's failure is that we have been far too timid and

unimaginative in shaping alternatives to traditionalism, alternatives that could move us further toward being builders of bridges across lines of alienation and difference. While women within Judaism, Islam, and Christianity have struggled to address differences creatively, few others have joined us in that project. Without such aggressive efforts to forge common strategies across the lines of difference, especially across past and present structures of violence, concrete democracy is doomed in this nation.

Nearly twenty years ago, in print and in lecture, I frequently quoted Mariana Valverde's insightful point that the world historical task of feminism is to make equality (read democracy) sexy.[17] The full import of her observation only now dawns on me. Today I write with greater awareness of how *utterly unsexy* genuine equality has become in this culture. What we need to grasp is the fear of difference that is bred by the *actual pervasive inequality rampant among us.* When people feel deeply vulnerable and unsafe, we prefer to leave palpable untruths and propagandistic distortions unchallenged, if only to persuade ourselves that the powerful actually know what they are doing. It is more urgent than ever to understand that this nation's movement into subtle forms of "friendly fascism," which wear a smiling face and offer endless professions of our national decency and righteousness, threaten democracy as never before.[18] The scandal is that Christianity is colluding in and even providing a sanctified "American Christianity" every bit as idolatrous as the so-called "German Christianity" of the first part of the twentieth century. That collusion, I submit, is clearly related to the earlier lessons progressive Christians failed to learn.

Overcoming sources of liberal theology's myopia to injustice

We desperately need to recall and reread my own generation's "great" teachers as progressives. The Niebuhrs, Paul Tillich, Karl Barth, and Emil Brunner did their work in the face of their fear of "German Christian" idolatry. Fear of fascism led each of them to seek a road to the recovery of a "Christian depth" in their theologies. My generation might be said to have over-learned the "fear of idolatry" from our reading of their work. Instead, we need to learn the cost of departing from justice-love and fear the new temptations to baptize state-sponsored Christianity.

The similarity between "German Christian" theology and "Anti-Terrorism Market God" theology seems easy to miss in present Christian discourse. We have tended to turn our theological mentors into voices to be imitated rather than rereading their work to winnow wisdom from unwisdom. Each of these theologians needs revisiting, but with less reverence and deeper appreciation for what each intended. For example, H. Richard, along with his younger friend Daniel Day Williams, was perhaps the most poetically gifted imaginer of what it would mean for Christians to make love of God and neighbor the heart of Christian communal practice.[19] However, perhaps because of a fear learned in German-American culture of social disorder and "laboring people," he carried a deep suspicion of politics.[20] Although the most "churchly" of the U.S. born theologians, he never found a way to make clear the public vocation of Christianity, nor was he ever able to make peace fully with "secularity." Given his late-life fixation on "divine sovereignty," his "radical monotheism" spoke less and less to justice and the common life. His longing to locate a deep and subtle love in a "cosmic imagination" gave way to James Gustafson's "frozen vision" of God.[21]

Paul Tillich's fate as a lost voice of liberal theology should also be noted. Tillich pioneered in revisioning theology as cultural critique and called for theological analysis that "discerned the signs of the times." Though his family background was relatively privileged, he threw his lot with the Left and situated his voice firmly in the call for a socialist decision within a German Christian environment hostile to that stance.[22] He elected to stand with a number of the Frankfurt School scholars, most of them Jewish, who sought to clarify the destructive social and cultural consequences of growing economic inequity in Germany.[23] His need to leave Germany in the face of the impending Nazi threat and his move into exile in the United States were closely related to his political critique of Nazism and his endorsement of socialism.

Only a few of Tillich's friends and interpreters in this country ever mention this reality. Among his near contemporaries, only his distinguished younger friend James Luther Adams fully recognized the actual setting of his work. Most also fail altogether to situate his theological perspective in the traditions of German critical theory, with its commitment to demystify class relations that mask the concrete economic suffering of so many. Though Ronald Stone has recently edited and published some of Tillich's political writings, and even though a few of his interpreters, such as Tom Driver and Delores Williams, have carried on the tradition of cultural criticism that situates culture in its political and economic context, Tillich's work is usually read apolitically and abstractly. Many other so-called Tillichians who profess to follow his lead in discerning the spiritual depths of culture have, in fact, focused exclusively on the depth dimensions of persons, ignoring entirely the nonpersonalistic and thoroughly socialized reading of life that critical theory presumes and emphasizes. While Tillich himself demurred from analyzing political life in the country of his exile, he never looked to psychological perspectives for their own sake. His focus was always on the alienation that social repression produces. His was an effort to find ways to free people and their communities from brokenness. Ripped from this context, the real depth of his perspective is lost in captivity to individual narcissism.

The dissipation of Reinhold Niebuhr's legacy has also been all but complete with the passage of time. More than other theologians rooted in German traditions, he overcame the suspicion of politics that runs deep in the German Lutheran culture transplanted to the United States and emphasized the irreducible necessity of political responsibility. While his own theory of justice never reached the complexity of some earlier Christian theories, and while he worked largely within a rather "thin" liberal theory in which justice requires a continuous balancing between freedom and equality, he nevertheless made clear that there is no genuine love in the absence of proximations of justice. No perspective on Niebuhr can read him as compromising on this point.[24]

Niebuhr has, in fact, been read in a bewildering number of ways and has been invoked by many whose neoliberalism he would deplore. Perhaps because he was less than explicit methodologically and because he became something of a Cold Warrior himself, he was often embraced by Cold War partisans without deference to his religious convictions. His repudiation of Christian anti-violence traditions, a complex mixture of anti-perfectionism and historical pessimism, led to seriously unfair readings of much of value in Christian moral traditions.[25] Even so, Niebuhr's work can give no comfort to the antipolitical ardor of neoliberalism. His embrace of welfare liberalism was unqualified, and there is simply no justification for any neoliberal readings of him. Furthermore, his closest friend and collaborator, John Coleman Bennett, should be credited with continuing the liberal legacy without apology. In fact, no one better demonstrated that the liberal tradition could embrace new challenges from emerging liberationist voices and have no concern for any presumed loss of spiritual substance.[26]

There is a great deal more to be said about the Reagan/Bush era retreat of Protestant and Roman Catholic social teaching from far more communitarian and justice-oriented postures held in more liberal times. That fears about sexuality and a deeply imbedded misogyny have been factors in the move of many to the Right, including the Catholic hierarchy, is, I believe, indisputable. Nothing has made the appallingly inadequate response to sexual justice clearer than the current pedophilia crises within Roman Catholicism. In the eloquent words of Anna Quindlen,

> We understand that in the world of "Father knows best" in which we came of age, all this was bound to occur. For too many years, the church seemed to have a bizarre preoccupation with sins of the flesh so unrelenting that, to this day, people will ask if the nuns taught me that patent-leather shoes reflect up. (No.) The enforced celibacy of the male priesthood, an invention only of the faith's second millennium, taught a clear lesson: eschewing human sexuality was the greatest glory of the highest calling. ("Our idea is not to experience desire at all." — Clement of Alexandria, saint.) The ban on contraception taught that sex could be countenanced only when it could lead to pregnancy. There was no passion or pleasure, only procreation and punishment.
>
> We didn't understand, some of the bishops say now about the pedophiles among them, moved from parish to parish, with fresh choirboys to importune and then hush. We thought they could change. We thought they could be cured.

The bishops gathered wood for this current conflagration every time they turned away from the human condition to emphasize wayward genitalia. They must be amazed at how harshly they are now judged after all those years of deference, when they were allowed to make their own laws. Perhaps they sense that they are being judged with the ferocity of those accustomed to being judged harshly themselves. The judgment of divorced Catholics reborn in good marriages ordered not to go to communion. The judgment of women up all night with sick babies lectured about the sanctity of life. The judgment of hardworking, devoted priests who have watched the hierarchy cover up the dirt that sullies them, too. The judgment of now grown children who have taken to drink, drugs, domestic violence, because of the shadow that Father's wandering hands have cast over their lives.

It is about a pathology deep and wide, a pathology that allows blindness to continue as long as the Sabbath is observed.[27]

Missing the point has become the stock-in-trade of many who lead the world's Catholics, agonizing over how this could have happened. Perhaps they might want to ask ordinary Catholics who have been too little consulted by the high-handed hierarchy.

The truth of the matter is that the only voices that have kept justice and compassion at the center of the Christian message in the last decades are precisely the marginalized voices of liberation theologies. Those who have articulated their challenges are most often dismissed with invective and contempt. It is staggering to consider what Christian commitment to social justice and public policy in the last half century would look like without the contributions of the civil rights movement, black theology, the women's movement and feminist, womanist, and mujerista theologies, and the many voices who give primacy to the poor. In the wake of churchly complacency and fear, liberationist readings of Christianity have continued to be voiced, and concrete efforts at neighbor love have been shaped amid gross injustice and violence. To some extent, the substance of Christian spiritual practice has had to be lived out in active opposition to the very churches who claim to speak for God.

It should be clear by now that the dream of a world freed of homophobia and gender violence can be realized only as part of a wider incarnation of justice and a recovery of concrete longing for caring community. The ecstasy of intimacy and deep connection—the real experience of love—depends on our breaking the bonds not only of sex-phobia, but also of "whiteness" that cannot embrace the many-hued beauty of all creation and of class and cultural arrogance that leads to contempt for all who differ. The resurrection of a decent liberality in Christian spirituality, then, requires far more than better education in sexuality, though improvement on that score would do no harm. What is needed is a conversion away from the blinding worship of the Market God, who is the chief rival for the souls of Christian people and the world we inhabit.

Fortunately, the way forward toward greater spiritual depth also involves a recovery of embodied passion and the deepening of our capacity for joy and pleasure in struggling for abundant life. It has taken a long time for Christian people to place the image of *justice* as right-relatedness at the center of our vision of *love*. We should not play fast and loose with connecting the two—the true legacy of liberal theology—for our world needs both as never before.

Staying on the path of what we feminists call a "hermeneutic of suspicion," rather than becoming sidetracked by a denominationally centered piety, is urgent as we move forward. It was only because many have learned to see the full face of gender injustice that some progress has occurred. However, serious work against white racism and the full facing of anti–working-class bias as aspects of liberal failure are still needed. A reluctance to critique the past and the desire to cling to certitudes about the profundities of Christian tradition are no substitute for truth about our complicity in evil. Many have claimed that all liberalism needed was more biblical ardor and certitude or a more Americanized cultural style. To the contrary, what is required is a new passion for respectful multicultural (including interreligious) learning and more awareness that our wealth has accelerated global poverty and contributed to the destruction of noncapitalist cultures.

The realization of our complicity in violence can be liberating. Loyalty to tradition is obfuscating without the willingness to resolutely face mistakes in the moral practice of the Christian past and in the wrong-headed theologies *that indecent practice generated.* It is time to be uncompromising: Where a concern for justice does not guide, Christian theology does not illumine, and our spiritual vision remains, at best, distorted and, at worst, complicit in evil.

As I have insisted, the pilgrimage back to a more critical rereading of the Christian past is not simple, especially when more modesty and less triumphalism about the presumed adequacy of Christianity's "great" traditions are required. Of course, clarifying conceptual mistakes is never an end in itself. Its purpose is for the sake of clearer-eyed contemporary practices of neighbor love. Valorizing earlier "theological greats" without a consciousness of our own spiritual mistakes carries serious risks to our spiritual health. Whatever carries the mark of "profound tradition" also carries the imprimatur and the power of self-evident truth, and with that aura, genuinely critical thinking dies. The integrity of Christian communal speech always depends every bit as much on truth-telling about the *failures* of our Christian communal past as it does on celebration of past profundities.

Endless liberal theological talk about the importance of critical thinking does not produce such thinking. Living out justice-love requires the active seeking of truths we have not yet heard, and those truths come only from others that we have treated with contempt, those "spiritually poor" in our eyes. It is learning behind the "rhetoric of elites" and the recovery of a passion for "the common wealth" of shared community that are needed. Additionally, our understanding of neighbor love must come to include all who share our earth-space, including, of course, the innumerable non-blathering species of those we have not yet really be-neighbored.

Notes

1. Lewis C. Daly, *A Moment to Decide: The Crisis in Mainstream Presbyterianism,* Denominational Study Series (New York: Institute for Democracy Studies, 2000), 11ff.

2. The term used here is borrowed from the outstanding report to the 1991 General Assembly, "Keeping Body and Soul Together: Sexuality, Spirituality, and Social Justice," which among other things recommended that the denomination reverse its condemnatory policy toward gays and lesbians and embrace an

uncontested norm of justice-love in teachings about sexuality. Because it stressed compassion and justice, it was, of course, rejected.

3. Maggie Kuhn, as she was affectionately known to justice-loving Presbyterians, was a longtime staff member of the Board of Christian Education of the former United Presbyterian Church USA. After retirement she founded the Gray Panthers advocacy network, which was militant in calling for justice for seniors, and traveled the country developing strategic responses to the needs of older persons.

4. Robert McAfee Brown, one of Presbyterianism's most stellar interpreters of justice-centered faith, brought wit and clarity to the theological task. His St. Hereticus column was published in the pages of the journal *Christianity and Crisis*. His death in 2001 was an incredible loss to the cause of maintaining compassionate spirituality.

5. Professor Williams was singled out for attacks following the Re-Imagining Conference in Minneapolis in 1995. A doctored tape that elided two incomplete sentences was used as evidence that she was a Christological "heretic." Professor Williams and other speakers at the conference did indeed raise questions about Blood Atonement doctrines, but so have many other liberal theologians in the twentieth century. The result of this strategy of targeting a leading African American scholar was to mobilize prominent African American leaders of the denomination to protest the mean-spiritedness and obsessive "homosexual" preoccupations of the denomination's leadership. See "A Letter of Concern from Black Presbyterians." See also Delores S. Williams, *Sisters in the Wilderness* (Maryknoll, N.Y.: Orbis, 1993).

6. Though many interpreters read the current burgeoning of self-proclaimed fundamentalism as a *return* to a familiar position rooted in biblical inerrancy and the specific doctrines stressed in the early part of the century by those objecting to Darwinian theories of evolution, much of today's fundamentalism is of quite a different ilk. Little emphasis is placed on doctrine or on separation from the secular realm, and much emphasis is placed on obedience to a nationalistic vision of salvation. Much of the new fundamentalism is shaped by national corporations, such as Focus on the Family. Its high-tech religiosity is quite different from the culturally separatist fundamentalism of the past. On the old fundamentalism, see R. A. Torrey, *The Fundamental Doctrines of the Christian Faith* (New York: George H. Doran, 1918).

7. The major recruitment device of the new fundamentalism is through radio station ownership and propaganda. Various networks of Christian radio abound, and while some are explicit in their convictions, many offer so-called news and cultural commentary without crediting sources. The level of disinformation is astonishing, and in the region where I live, reporting often features White House press releases read without attribution.

8. I prefer the term "old line" to the more frequently used "mainline" because in the last thirty years the massive shift of Protestant membership has been toward those denominations that do not have concrete historical connectedness to churches that had their origins in Europe. Today, the growth in Protestantism is in denominations founded in the United States. Protestants are increasingly indigenized, and historical awareness is not cultivated, which may account for the fact

that many Baptists, at one time the "inventors" of the separation of church and state, today enthusiastically embrace the idea of a Christian America analogous to the German Christianity of the Third Reich.

9. Consider, for example, the major study of theological education in the 1950s, H. Richard Niebuhr, *The Purpose of the Church and Its Ministry: Reflections on the Aims of Theological Education,* in collaboration with Daniel Day Williams and James M. Gustafson (New York: Harper, 1956).

10. The term "conjure," used here to describe the imaginative task of the theologian, is borrowed from womanist theological writing and black women's literary criticism. *Conjuring: Black Women, Freedom, and Literary Tradition,* ed. Marjorie Pryse and Hortense J. Spiller (Bloomington: Indiana University Press, 1985).

11. I think it is important to recognize the *novel* features of the evangelicalisms being constructed in contemporary society. The claim of the new Christian Right, that what is happening is a rebirth of conservatism, is simply false. The New Christian Right is highly creative at packaging a new species of Christian piety.

12. Beverly and Tim LeHaye have been particularly successful in packaging the new fundamentalism, she through organizing affluent "Neo" women to stand adamantly and sexily for traditional female roles, her husband, Tim, through popularizing the Rapture novel, which enables readers to "know" what the Bible says without having to read it. Needless to say, these novels are truly fictional. For an early work, see Tim LaHaye, *The Battle for the Family* (Old Tappan, N.J.: Fleming H. Revell, 1982).

13. Harvey Cox, *The Secular City* (New York: Macmillan, 1965). This theological bestseller of the 1960s turned out to be a wee bit premature, but the ways in which secularizations of various sorts have affected us still need revisiting.

14. The term "Market God theology" I also owe to Harvey Cox in his recent writing.

15. Many of liberal theological persuasion have been astonished at the tenacity and virulence of efforts aimed to force churches such as my own to roll back pro-choice positions adopted earlier by our once liberal denominations. It should be remembered that the efforts to do so make sense only within a perspective that situates neoliberalism and neofundamentalisms squarely within the deeply embedded patriarchal misogyny of Christian tradition. See my *Our Right to Choose: Towards a New Ethic of Abortion* (Boston: Beacon, 1983).

16. My own earliest political engagements came from undergraduate experiences working in the first congressional campaign of Eugene McCarthy, whose campaign chair was Robert McAfee Brown. Living through events that forged a strong progressive party in Minnesota by overcoming historically imbedded antagonisms between Protestants and Catholics was for me a transformative spiritual and political experience, which also led to a genuine commitment to ecumenical Christianity and interreligious solidarity. Such sentiments no longer characterize the relations between liberal Protestant and official Catholic stances since the Catholic hierarchy's war to make compulsory pregnancy the law of the land.

17. Mariana Valverde, *Sex, Power, and Pleasure* (Toronto: Women's Press, 1985).

18. Bertram Gross, *Friendly Fascism: The New Face of Power in America* (New York: M. Evans, 1980).

19. See above, note 9. See also Daniel Day Williams, *The Spirit and the Forms of Love* (New York: Harper & Row, 1968).

20. See for example, "Christianity and the Industrial Classes," *Theological Magazine of the Evangelical Synod of North America* 57 (1929): 12–18.

21. James Gustafson, *Ethics in a Theocentric Perspective* (Chicago: University of Chicago Press, 1981, 1984). Some have observed the close similarity between Gustafson's dispassionate deity and Stoicism.

22. Paul Tillich, *The Socialist Decision,* trans. Franklin Sherman (New York: Harper & Row, 1977). The importance of political context to Tillich's work is also apparent in *Against the Third Reich: Paul Tillich's Wartime Radio Broadcasts into Nazi Germany,* ed. Ronald H. Stone and Matthew Lon Weaver (Louisville: Westminster John Knox, 1999).

23. An excellent introduction to German critical theory is Trent Schroyer, *The Critique of Domination: The Origins and Development of Critical Theory* (New York: George Braziller, 1973).

24. The most serious neoliberal misreadings of Reinhold Niebuhr include those of Richard Neuhaus and Michael Novak.

25. It is important to recognize that Niebuhr's attacks on Christian pacifism were based on misreadings of the positions discussed.

26. John Coleman Bennett, *The Radical Imperative: From Theology to Social Ethics* (Philadelphia: Westminster, 1975). Bennett should be remembered as one of the most underestimated and too soon forgotten figures of the twentieth-century liberal Christian tradition. He remained a trenchant theological critic of public policy until his death at the age of ninety-two.

27. A brilliant analysis of why the Roman Catholic Church is in such difficulty around priesthood and sexuality is Anna Quindlen, "Patent Leather, Impure Thoughts," *Newsweek,* April 1, 2002.

2

Authority, Resistance, and Transformation

Jewish Feminist Reflections on Good Sex

Judith Plaskow

The effort to develop feminist accounts of good sex within the context of patriarchal religious traditions raises a host of methodological problems. The very formulation of the project recognizes the tensions between feminism as a social movement committed to the liberation of women from all forms of oppression, and the direction and intention of traditions that have contributed directly and indirectly to women's subordination and marginalization in religion and society. The "Good Sex" project begins from the reality that women have rarely participated in the formulation of sexual norms and values in the major world religions, and that religious sexual values have seldom been conducive to the health or well-being of women.[1] In bringing together a group of women connected to different traditions, the project seeks to create a space in which the participants can "think new thoughts," reflecting on sexuality from the perspective of the concerns and experiences of women in our cultures. At the same time, it assumes that these new thoughts will somehow remain in relation to the religions being transformed and will possibly authenticate themselves through connection to neglected or dissident strands within those religions.[2] The project thus immediately

---

Editors' note: This essay was written as part of a feminist interreligious and international colloquium sponsored by the Religious Consultation for Population, Reproductive Health, and Ethics. The "Good Sex" colloquium had as its mandate to explore two central questions: What is good sex under conditions of globalization at the beginning of the twenty-first century, and what do feminists from diverse religious traditions have to contribute to the understanding and enactment of good sex?

becomes entangled in fundamental questions about how feminists argue for and make change, especially when the changes envisioned may radically challenge central elements of tradition.

Defining the questions

My interest in this essay is not so much in defining good sex from a Jewish feminist perspective as in examining how to think about the issue. As a Jewish feminist theologian, I find that the task of transforming Jewish sexual norms raises questions about authority that I must sort out before I can begin to think substantively about the characteristics of good sex. The Jewish feminist movement in the United States has flourished in the context of a decentralized, remarkably diverse Jewish community, in which there are many competing visions of the nature of Judaism and many opportunities to shape Jewish life in new directions. In a situation in which the great majority of U.S. Jews have rejected or are redefining elements of traditional Jewish belief and practice, the issue of authority is crucial and has implications well beyond the area of sexuality.[3]

The question of how to ground and argue for criticisms or constructive reworkings of religious tradition is pressing for any theology or group that does not simply assume the validity of traditional sources of authority, such as Scripture, revelation, or centralized religious leadership.[4] Yet, because sexual control of women is such a key element in broader patriarchal control, the topic of sexuality raises the issue of authority with particular vividness and urgency. On what basis can feminists advocate particular visions of sexuality in ways that will prove intelligible and convincing to others?

The problem of authority arises for feminists as soon as we begin to challenge any aspect of the status and role of women. Once we acknowledge the possibility of deeply questioning any element of tradition, we seem to undermine the hope of religious certainty at a level that goes far beyond the specific issue at hand. However narrow the grounds for particular criticisms—and feminist criticisms of the treatment of women and religious sexual values are in fact deep and wide-ranging—rejecting any element of tradition throws all the rest into question. This is because, however much feminists still may value certain insights and perspectives we glean from our traditions, we no longer value them simply because they are there. Rather, we are confronted with having to self-consciously appropriate and re-appropriate from the conflicted strands within every tradition those that make sense and bear fruit in our own lives, finding ways to explain our choices in ways that make sense both to ourselves and to others. Logically, we cannot "have it both ways." We cannot both deny the authority of religious tradition where it negates our feminist values and, at the same time, build on that authority where it seems to support those values.

A lot of recent scholarship on Jewish attitudes towards sexuality intensifies this issue of authority in that it highlights the tensions and disagreements within Jewish tradition, denying the reality of any unitary perspective.[5] Such a move is enormously helpful in deconstructing fundamentalist appeals to religious authority in that it makes clear that *all* claims to authority involve selectivity and that Jewish tradition by no means speaks on sexuality with a self-evident, unambiguous voice. This scholarship is also useful to feminist reconstructions of religion in that it surfaces minority or dissident viewpoints in the Jewish past that may counter dominant perspectives on issues of sexual values. At the same time, however, in dissolving the purported unity of Jewish tradition into a series of dissonant and ever-shifting strands, it increases the difficulty of arguing for the priority or authority of one strand over any other. Jewish tradition—like all religious traditions—is characterized by continuing contestation of key issues, which issues are in turn continually redefined in different geographic locations and different historical contexts. Notions of authority are also continually reinterpreted in accordance with the outcome of such contests. Claiming the authority of a specific strand, then, is not a matter of identifying the essential and authentic voice of *the* Jewish tradition. Rather, it is part of a contest in our own time over which voice claiming to speak for tradition will prove compelling to a significant proportion of the Jewish people.

The complex and contradictory nature of Jewish teachings on sexuality, moreover, points to another problem in privileging neglected, positive themes within Jewish tradition. All too often in feminist discussion, highlighting the liberating elements of a tradition as its authoritative voice involves disregarding the strands that have been oppressive. The troublesome aspects of a tradition do not disappear, however, simply because we ignore them, but are left to shape consciousness and affect hearts and minds. Thus, appealing to the first creation story, in which male and female are made in God's image, and ignoring the second, in which woman is made from man, leaves intact the latter account to be used by others as a continuing justification for the subordination of women. Similarly, appealing to those elements in Judaism that honor the importance of married sex as a value in its own right apart from procreation, while neglecting the ways in which even married sex is restricted and controlled, allows the sexual control of women to continue unexamined as part of the fabric of Jewish marriage. If one does acknowledge and attempt to grapple with the oppressive aspects of a tradition, the question inevitably arises as to the grounds on which its nonoppressive elements can be considered more fundamental.

A final problem relating to authority concerns the sources that are relevant in thinking about the subject of sexuality. Given that any reconstruction of tradition necessarily selects from the conflicting voices on a particular issue, still, what is even germane to a consideration of this topic? It is striking that, when issues of sexuality are discussed in religious contexts, a handful of texts are often cited and argued about over and over, as if they were the only sources relevant to shaping norms around sexual behavior. In the Jewish community, debates around homosexuality have often revolved around two verses in Leviticus and rabbinic commentary on them, while Christians add to the scanty resources in the Hebrew Bible a third verse in Romans. This approach ignores the host of other injunctions in the Bible and rabbinic tradition about forming ethical relationships, creating community, and ensuring social justice. It fails to view sexuality as just one dimension of human relationship, embedded in a constellation of familial, interpersonal, and communal connections that shape, support, or deform it. Instead, sexuality is seen as a peculiar problem for ethics, a discrete and troublesome domain requiring unique regulation. In addition to confronting problems around grounding sexual values, therefore, feminist accounts of sexuality also need to locate the issue in a larger social context. Building on the early feminist insight that "the personal is the political," feminists need to insist that "good sex" on the interpersonal level is possible only in the context of just social, political, and economic relations.[6]

Thinking about compulsory heterosexuality

I would like to illustrate the ways in which some of these issues concerning authority come into play in relation to a particular dimension of sexuality by reflecting on compulsory heterosexuality within the Jewish tradition as a barrier to good sex. I choose to focus on a central oppressive element in my tradition rather than on some emancipatory theme, because I believe that it is the negative aspects of tradition that most profoundly shape women's current sexual situation and most require attention and transformation. In my view, the starting point for feminists in thinking about good sex must be resistance. Feminists must begin by examining and dismantling the institutions that stand in the way of women even imagining fully our needs and desires.

The concept of "compulsory heterosexuality," which Adrienne Rich placed on the U.S. feminist agenda through her well-known essay on the topic, refers to the complex social and political processes through which people learn how and are made to be heterosexual.[7] The first and simplest way in which heterosexuality is made compulsory is that other modes of sexual expression are forbidden on pain of punishment or death. Such a prohibition on male/male anal intercourse appears in Leviticus 18:22 and 20:13 and forms the starting point for all Jewish discussion of homosexuality — as well as Jewish gay and lesbian resistance to traditional attitudes toward homosexuality. Although lesbianism is not mentioned explicitly in the Bible, the rabbis find a reference to it in Leviticus 18:3, "You shall not copy the practices of the land of Egypt... or the land of Canaan." They interpret the practices in question as a man marrying a man and a woman marrying a woman. Both the Palestinian and Babylonian Talmuds also contain brief discussions of whether women who " 'rub' with each other" are considered to have committed an illicit sexual act and are therefore forbidden to marry a priest.[8] The rabbis' consensus that such acts are "mere licentiousness," that is, not real sex, and therefore not disqualifying, reveals another weapon in

the arsenal of compulsory heterosexuality: rendering sex between
women invisible by defining it as impossible.[9]

While contemporary Jewish debates about homosexuality generally revolve rather narrowly around these verses in Leviticus and
the few rabbinic sources interpreting them, I find this material less
useful for understanding heterosexuality as an institution than the
pervasive assumption in biblical and rabbinic texts that heterosexual
marriage is the norm for adult life. In getting at this larger context
of Jewish attitudes towards marriage and family relations, Genesis 3:16 — "Your desire shall be for your husband and he shall
rule over you" — is far more revealing than Leviticus 18 and 20
because it names the connection between gender complementar-
ity, compulsory heterosexuality, and the subordination of women.
Gayle Rubin, in her classic essay "The Traffic in Women," argues
that, in traditional societies, the social organization of sex is built
on the links between "gender roles, obligatory heterosexuality, and
the constraint of female sexuality."[10] Gender roles guarantee that the
smallest viable social unit will consist of one man and one woman
whose desire must be directed toward each other, at the same time
that men have rights to exchange their female kin and control their
wives in marriage that women do not have either in themselves or
in men.

Genesis 3:16–19, which describes God's punishments of Adam and
Eve for eating the fruit of the tree of knowledge, offers a remarkably condensed and powerful statement of the connections laid out
by Rubin. In increasing Eve's pain in childbearing and punishing
Adam with having to sweat and toil to gain his bread, God as-
sumes/ordains differentiated gender roles and, at the same time,
defines them asymmetrically. Eve's (heterosexual) desire for her husband will keep her tied to childbearing despite its painfulness and
will allow him to "rule over" her. My point is not that compulsory heterosexuality as a Jewish institution is rooted in this story, but rather
that this myth of origins provides a lens for examining interrelation-
ships that are spelled out at length in Jewish narrative and law. In
the Jewish case, as in the traditional societies Rubin discusses, rigid
gender roles support the channeling of sex in marriage. A man who
is not married (the texts speak from a male perspective) is seen as
less than whole, for only a man and woman together constitute the

image of God. The extensive laws regulating women's sexuality and placing it under the control of fathers or husband ensure that women will be available for marriage to men who can be fairly certain that their wife's sexuality belongs only to them.

In a context in which "good sex" is defined as sex that is under male control, the question of what constitutes good sex from women's perspectives simply cannot be asked within the framework of the system. For the Bible and for the rabbis, "good sex" is sex that supports and serves a patriarchal social order. The so-called divinely ordained laws concerning marriage and divorce, adultery, rape, and so on allow for the regular and orderly transfer of women from the homes of fathers to the homes of husbands or, if need be, from one husband to another. Women's fears, desires, and preferences, their efforts to find meaning in or resist this legislation, are non-issues and "non-data" that are also non-sense in the context of the rabbinic worldview.[11] As Rachel Adler points out in a powerful article about women's role in the Jewish covenant community, the categories of a system of thought determine the questions it can ask, allowing it to pile up huge amounts of information on certain questions while rendering others invisible. The problems that receive extensive attention in Jewish law are the "status problems of marriage, desertion, divorce, and *chalitzah* [levirate marriage] which the tradition itself created and from whose consequences it now seeks to 'protect' women, since by its own rules they can never protect themselves."[12] Insofar as the rabbis do attempt to "protect" women—by trying to find ways to get a husband to divorce his wife if she so desires, for example—they indicate some awareness of the limits and injustices of the system they have created and, in this sense, offer some resources for criticism. But insofar as they are willing to address these injustices only within the framework of the system that gives rise to them, they close off any possibility of women entering as subjects and reframing the issues in genuinely new terms.

As Rubin's analysis suggests, however, control of women's sexuality is just one dimension of the institution of compulsory heterosexuality, which is also spelled out in *halakha* (Jewish law) in terms of property rights, work roles, and religious obligations and exemptions. In her book on the construction of gender in Roman-period Judaism, Miriam Peskowitz examines a Mishnaic passage that shows the rabbis in the act of extending a husband's power over the property his wife acquired before marriage, so that while the wife may continue to own property, the husband controls it and is entitled to the profits that flow from it.[13] In their ensuing debate about the validity of this legal innovation, the rabbis involved presuppose that a man has authority over his wife. What they need to determine is the extent of that authority in the sphere of property ownership, much as in other contexts they will discuss a husband's power over his wife's sexuality. The conversation, Peskowitz argues, reveals that there are many nodes "in the construction of sexual difference," sexual control constituting only one area in which marriage allows a man to "rule over" his wife.[14]

The Jewish division of religious labor also presupposes and helps construct a social structure in which heterosexual marriage is the norm. The exemption of women from positive time-bound commandments—in particular, set times for daily prayer—assumes that they are involved in household obligations that are their first responsibility and priority. In caring for small children, observing the rules of *koshrut* (dietary laws) and preparing for holy days by cooking special foods and making their homes ready, women free men for their own prayer and Torah study and enable them to observe the dietary laws and the Sabbath and holidays fully. For their part, women need men to take the ritual roles in the home that they themselves are neither obligated nor educated to assume. In other words, the whole series of laws that exclude women from public religious life, laws that Jewish feminists have analyzed and criticized from the perspective of women's spiritual disempowerment, are also part of the system of compulsory heterosexuality. That system is not just about sex, but also about the organization of daily life around gender role differentiation and the power of men over women.

Because compulsory heterosexuality is interstructured with a whole network of sexual, social, economic, and religious relations in Jewish law, creating the preconditions for good sex cannot end with questioning the few biblical and rabbinic passages on same-sex relationships. The material on such relationships is scanty and specific, so that those advocating expanded rights for gays and lesbians have been able to challenge it from a number of directions. Are other forms of male sexual interaction, other than anal intercourse,

forbidden by Leviticus?[15] Did the Torah or the rabbis have any concept of homosexuality as an orientation, or were they condemning
homosexual acts performed by heterosexuals?[16] While such critical
questions are important and useful in trying to gain acceptance for
gays and lesbians within the framework of Jewish law, they never
step outside that framework to confront the broader system of compulsory heterosexuality. That system controls and marginalizes all
women, whether or not they are heterosexual, and whether or not
they are married. It also makes illegitimate any sexual or life choice
outside of heterosexual marriage, so that self-pleasuring, celibacy,
singleness, cohabitation without marriage, et cetera, all constitute
forms of resistance to compulsory heterosexuality.[17]

Once one begins to see the relationship between compulsory heterosexuality and sexism in its myriad forms, however, the questions
about authority that I raised in the first part of this essay return in all
their power. How does one question this central aspect of Jewish tradition and still remain in relation to the tradition? Are there voices
in traditional Jewish texts that dissent from or reveal fractures in
this system, and on what basis can they be mobilized? Where do I,
where does any contemporary feminist critic stand in even raising
these questions?

Starting points

I would argue that the feminist critic must begin not by allying herself with dissenting voices within her tradition, but by questioning
the authority of tradition, resisting any framework that leaves no
room for women's agency, and then proceeding to transform tradition by placing women at the center.[18] Feminism begins in resistance
and vision, a resistance and vision that are not simply personal but
are rooted in "communities of resistance and solidarity" that are
challenging specific forms of oppression out of concrete experiences
of alternative ways of being in the world.[19] Thus, the feminist and
lesbian, gay, and bisexual movements have allowed women to feel
the power and potential of bonds between women; to experience an
intimacy, sexual and otherwise, that often has been trivialized or
undermined; and to claim our power as agents to participate fully
in society and religious communities on terms that we define.

This experience of the power of being, as Mary Daly early described it, over against the institutions that have consigned women to nonbeing, does not of itself threaten these institutions or render them harmless, but it does provide starting points for imagining a different future and criticizing the forces that stand in its way.[20] To my mind, *this* experience, rather than any dissident strands within patriarchal religion, is the authoritative foundation of resistance and transformation because given the conflicting voices within any normative text, the decision to claim such strands must come out of some experience of their greater power to support fullness of life for a larger group of people. Out of participation in a community of resistance and transformation, one then looks for and consciously claims the resistive elements in a particular tradition in order to mobilize them toward a different future.[21]

What does this mean and not mean in relation to compulsory heterosexuality? Beyond the dimension of critique, which I see as central to a feminist appropriation of tradition; there are several ways in which feminists can find resources for resistance and transformation within our religious traditions. One is by deliberately allying ourselves with the self-critical strands in texts that have been understood as normative. In her early and influential reinterpretation of Genesis 2–3, Phyllis Trible pointed out that the explicit statement in Genesis 3:16 that a woman's "desire shall be for [her] husband, and he shall rule over [her]" occurs in the context of divine punishment for disobedience. Remarkably for a patriarchal society, the story does not depict women's subordination as natural and divinely ordained, but as a perversion of the created order that is a result of sin. Trible thus reads this story not as *pre*scribing male supremacy but as *de*scribing it, not as legitimating but as condemning it.[22] For her, the insight that male supremacy is a distortion of creation constitutes the true meaning of the biblical text, which thus stands over against patriarchy.

Given that the description of compulsory heterosexuality is part of the same passage, one could make a similar move, arguing that this aspect of social life too appears under the sign and judgment of sinfulness. But aside from the fact that such an approach would ignore Genesis 1, in which male and female together constitute the image of God, there are deeper problems with claiming to have found the true meaning of any biblical text. Just as every text was written in a specific historical, social, and religious context, so texts are interpreted in particular contexts that give rise to particular exegetical needs.

The current desire to find an underlying nonsexist or nonheterosexist vision in Scripture comes out of a political and religious situation in which various forms of fundamentalism are on the rise all over the globe and are attempting to tighten control over every area of women's lives. In the United States, the Christian right has claimed the mantle of Christian authenticity, equating authenticity with control of sexuality and women, and the same dynamic is taking place within Judaism. As contemporary Judaism has become increasingly diverse and fragmented, issues of sexuality and women's roles have become the battleground for arguments about Jewish legitimacy. In a religious context in which the reactionary side of an increasingly heated debate claims divine authority for its position, it is tempting to argue that the essence or fundamental core of the tradition supports a progressive stance. However, this is finally to get into an irresolvable shouting match in which each party claims God on its side. It also means that feminists accept in principle the authority of texts that are at many points antithetical to women's power and agency and that can be used against the feminist cause as easily as for it.

Although the difference may be subtle, I see the claim to have discovered the authentic meaning of a tradition as different from self-consciously drawing on the dissident voices within it, while grounding oneself in a community that is actively working to create a Jewish future in which women are full Jews and full persons. For the purposes of resistance, it can be strategically useful to point to the contradictions or moments of self-criticism within normative texts, showing how opposing positions can be justified on the basis of the same sources. Yet it is not useful to debate which position is finally more authentic. From the perspective of the texts, the question of authenticity has no meaning; the texts encompass genuine disagreements.

The argument over texts is in reality an argument over competing social visions. Whose version of the future will hold sway? Who will have the right to determine the distribution of society's goods and resources, to say whether a given social or religious system meets basic human needs? Precisely because this is the real issue in question, however, it is important to highlight the dissident strands within a sacred text in order to crack open or challenge dominant religious and social perspectives and thus enlarge the space for change. From this point of view, it is useful to notice that women's subordination is conjoined with heterosexuality in the context of punishment for sin, not because this renders invalid two thousand years of sexist and heterosexist readings, but because it helps us to imagine an alternative future.

A second way to mobilize resources for resistance and change is to look at Jewish sources with an eye to the historical possibilities that they simultaneously conceal and reveal, so that one can make visible the existence of "forbidden" sexual practices or transgressive gender relations.[23] Thus, for example, the same rabbinic passages that can be read as denying the possibility of sexual activity between women can also be seen as acknowledging the existence of such activity, but regarding it as inconsequential. When the rabbis discussed the question of whether a woman who "rubs" with another woman is permitted to marry a priest, they may have been aware of the female homoeroticism amply attested in Roman sources, but may not have seen it as worth punishing.[24] From this perspective, the relative silence of Jewish tradition regarding both female and male homoerotic behavior may be construed as a form of permission. To take this view is not to deny the importance of heterosexuality as an ideology and an institution, but it is to suggest that behavior that did not threaten heterosexual marriage may not have been regarded with much seriousness.[25] Reading Jewish texts in light of what we know of cultural attitudes and practices at the time they were written begins to uncover the complex historical reality masked by an exclusive focus on official prohibitions. In doing so, it also broadens the sense of historical possibilities on which feminists can draw in seeking to transform the tradition in the present.

Still a third strategy of resistance and transformation that is especially important in dealing with issues of sexuality involves broadening the context of teachings on sexuality by looking at them through the lens of attitudes toward social justice. Rabbi Lisa Edwards, in a sermon on the Torah portions that contain Leviticus 18 and 20, argued as follows:

We are your gay and lesbian children: "You must not seek vengeance, nor bear a grudge against the children of your people" (Lev. 19:18); we are your lesbian mothers and gay fathers: "Revere your mother and your father, each of you" (19:3); we are the stranger: "You must not oppress the stranger. You shall love the stranger as yourself for you were strangers in the land of Egypt" (19:34).[26]

In reading the prohibitions against male/male sex in the context of surrounding injunctions about just social relations, Edwards risks getting drawn into arguments about which is the more fundamental or essential dimension of the tradition. By focusing on broader social justice themes, however, she also makes the critical point that any choice of sources in a debate about the meaning and intent of tradition always involves selecting from conflicting perspectives. Moreover, she places the biblical passages on homosexuality in the context of the gay and lesbian community of resistance, focusing on the interconnections between sexual ideologies and social injustice rather than on private sexual behavior.

Resistance and transformation

I began this essay by raising issues of authority and tradition, and the authority of tradition in thinking about good sex. To what extent can we ground ourselves in the positive resources in our traditions in thinking about good sex? How do I justify the choices that I make as I lift up certain strands within Jewish tradition and repudiate others? I have argued that the authority for singling out the self-critical and dissident elements in our textual traditions comes not from the traditions themselves, but rather from the new possibilities envisioned and created by the particular communities of solidarity and resistance in which we participate.

As I reflect on the "Good Sex" group itself as one such community, I am struck by the extent to which our initial work together provides us with methodological clues for approaching our common project. Brought together to think constructively about good sex from our perspectives as women, we found ourselves focusing again and again on the ideologies and institutions that stand in the way of good sex in our different cultures. We began, in other words, from a stance of resistance, realizing that the first task in creating a space for good sex is addressing the many injustices that make good sex unimaginable for many of the women in the world.

We also spoke of resources in our own experiences, in our cultures, and occasionally in our religious traditions that provide us with glimpses of a sexuality and sensuality that we would like to make more possible, both in our own lives and the lives of others. We repeatedly return to these glimpses, I would argue, to authorize ourselves as we seek to find our way between what is most women's sexual reality and what we hope will be. Struggling with this gulf, both in our social institutions and our religious traditions, we look for energy and insight not only, and not primarily, in the positive strands of our religious traditions, but in our communities of resistance and transformation.

Notes

1. Mary E. Hunt, "Good Sex: Women's Religious Wisdom on Sexuality," *Reproductive Health Matters* 8 (November 1996): 97–103.

2. Ibid., 97.

3. Only 50 percent of U.S. Jews are affiliated with any particular religious movement within Judaism. Of that 50 percent, 80 percent are non-Orthodox. This means that, to varying degrees, they accept the notion of Judaism as an evolving tradition that must adapt itself to changing historical and social circumstances.

4. Judith Plaskow, *Standing Again at Sinai: Judaism from a Feminist Perspective* (San Francisco: Harper & Row, 1990), 18–21.

5. I have in mind such works as Daniel Boyarin, *Carnal Israel: Reading Sex in Talmudic Culture* (Berkeley and Los Angeles: University of California Press, 1993) and *Unheroic Conduct: The Rise of Heterosexuality and the Invention of the Jewish Man* (Berkeley and Los Angeles: University of California Press, 1997); Howard Eilberg-Schwartz, *People of the Body: Jews and Judaism from an Embodied Perspective* (Albany: State University of New York Press, 1992); Mark Biale, *Eros and the Jews: From Biblical Israel to Contemporary America* (New York: Basic Books, 1992); and Michael Satlow, *Tasting the Dish: Rabbinic Rhetorics of Sexuality,* Brown Judaic Studies 303 (Atlanta: Scholars, 1995).

6. This was a central and recurrent theme in all our "good sex" conversations, as seen in many essays in the published volume, *Good Sex: Feminist Perspectives from the World's Religions,* ed. Patricia Beattie Jung, Mary E. Hunt, and Radhika Balakrishnan (New Brunswick, N.J.: Rutgers University Press, 2001).

7. Adrienne Rich, "Compulsory Heterosexuality and Lesbian Existence," *Signs: Journal of Women in Culture and Society* 5, no. 4 (1980): 631–60.

8. The Talmud is a compendium of Jewish law and lore, taking the form of a commentary on the Mishnah, a second-century code of Jewish law. Since the Mishnah was the center of study at rabbinic academies in both Palestine and Babylonia, there are two Talmuds. The Babylonian Talmud is fuller and is considered the masterwork of rabbinic Judaism.

9. For some introductory material on these issues, see Rachel Biale, *Women and Jewish Law* (New York: Schocken Books, 1984), 192–97, and Rebecca Alpert, *Like Bread on the Seder Plate: Jewish Lesbians and the Transformation of Tradition* (New York: Columbia University Press, 1997), 25–34.

10. Gayle Rubin, "The Traffic in Women: Notes on the 'Political Economy' of Sex," in *Toward an Anthropology of Women,* ed. Rayna R. Reiter (New York: Monthly Review, 1975), 179–80.

11. Mary Daly, *Beyond God the Father* (Boston: Beacon, 1973), 12.

12. Rachel Adler, "I've Had Nothing Yet So I Can't Take More," *Moment* 8, no. 8 (September 1983): 24.

13. The Mishnah is a second-century code of Jewish law that forms the basis of the Talmuds. See note 8.

14. Miriam B. Peskowitz, *Spinning Fantasies: Rabbis, Gender, and History* (Berkeley and Los Angeles: University of California Press, 1997), 35.

15. Saul Olyan, " 'And with a Male You Shall Not Lie Down the Lying Down of a Woman': On the Meaning and Significance of Leviticus 18:22 and 20:13," *Journal of the History of Sexuality* 5, no. 2 (1994): 185f.

16. Bradley Artson, "Gay and Lesbian Jews: An Innovative Jewish Legal Position," *Jewish Spectator* (winter 1990–91): 11.

17. It is remarkable how little has been written criticizing Jewish insistence on marriage from other than gay and lesbian perspectives. See Laura Geller and Elizabeth Koltun, "Single and Jewish: Toward a New Definition of Completeness," in the first anthology of Jewish feminist work, *The Jewish Woman: New Perspectives,* ed. Elizabeth Koltun (New York: Schocken Books, 1976), 43–49. Also the section "Being Single" in Rabbi Debra Orenstein, ed., *Lifecycles: Jewish Women on Life Passages and Personal Milestones* (Woodstock, Vt.: Jewish Lights, 1994), 99–116.

18. I am very grateful to the group conversation at the "good sex" meeting in Amsterdam for pushing me to be clearer about the ways in which Jewish feminists have moved beyond simply "resisting" women's traditional roles to creating new forms of practice, identity, and community. Mary Hunt's concept of imagination in her "Just Good Sex: Feminist Catholicism and Human Rights" in *Good Sex* (158–73) is a helpful way of naming this dimension of feminist method and practice.

19. Sharon D. Welch, *Communities of Resistance and Solidarity* (Maryknoll, N.Y.: Orbis, 1985).

20. Daly, *Beyond God the Father,* chapter 1.

21. See Daniel Boyarin, "Justify My Love," in *Judaism since Gender,* ed. Miriam Peskowitz and Laura Levitt (New York: Routledge, 1997).

22. Phyllis Trible, "Eve and Adam: Genesis 2–3 Reread," in *Womanspirit Rising,* ed. Carol P. Christ and Judith Plaskow (San Francisco: HarperCollins, 1979), 80.

23. This theme of concealment and revelation kept coming up in our "good sex" conversations in relation to recovering women's history and experiences in many traditions.

24. Alpert, *Like Bread on the Seder Plate,* 29–34; Bernadette Brooten, *Love between Women: Early Christian Responses to Female Homoeroticism* (Chicago: University of Chicago Press, 1996).

25. Alpert, *Like Bread on the Seder Plate,* 33.

26. Lisa A. Edwards, "A Simple Matter of Justice," sermon, April 29, 1993.

3

How to Read What We Read

Discerning Good News
about Sexuality in Scripture

Johanna W. H. van Wijk-Bos

How do we read what we read?

> Philip drew up and on hearing him read the Prophet Isaiah asked: "How do you read what you read?" (Acts 8:30).[1]*

Uncertainty in the face of Holy Scripture is nothing new. Three illustrations highlight that one method or way of reading does not suffice for all times and places.

In the story of the encounter between the apostle Philip and an Ethiopian court official (Acts 8:26–40), Philip is guided by the Spirit to meet a foreigner who is friendly to Judaism and is reading the prophet Isaiah on his travels. Philip asks whether he understands what he reads. Since the traveler acknowledges a need for guidance, the apostle uses this opportunity to "proclaim the good news of Jesus" to a receptive listener.

In a time prior to Philip's evangelization, a lawyer had asked Jesus what he should do to gain eternal life. To this question Jesus replied with another question: "What is written in the law? How do you read?" Out of the exchange between the questioner and Jesus, eventually a parable unfolds, the so-called parable of the Good Samaritan. With this parable Jesus interprets the commandments to love God and the neighbor and sends the lawyer away with the admonition to act as a neighbor.[2]

---

*Translations of biblical texts are by the author unless otherwise noted.

A long time before Philip and the Ethiopian, before the time of Jesus, turmoil occurred in the small kingdom of Judah of the seventh century B.C.E., when temple and court officials located a scroll they considered of possibly great significance. The text went from priest to court secretary to the king, who sent a delegation to find out from the highest authority, the Holy God of Israel, what it was all about. When the delegates consulted the prophet Huldah, she verified that this was indeed a word from God and that the future would hold great adversity for the inhabitants of Judah on account of God's anger. Huldah authorized the text and interpreted it.[3]

Three different occasions elicit three different ways of reading. The Deuteronomy text, with its warnings about the consequences of disobedience, is interpreted quite literally by the prophet and applied directly to the time of King Josiah. In the case of the lawyer and Jesus, a question about action is referred to the text. The lawyer asks what he must *do;* Jesus in return asks, "How do you *read?*" When the lawyer expresses bewilderment, it is explained to him how he should read by means of a parable that transposes love for God and neighbor into a recognizable contemporary situation of Jesus' day. For Philip it is clear that the section the Ethiopian is reading from Isaiah applies directly to Jesus and, therefore, should not be interpreted literally. The Isaiah text thus opens up an occasion for proclaiming "the good news of Jesus." Inevitably, once holy *words* become holy *text,* issues of authority and interpretation arise.

The distance between the biblical text and us is great. When we open the pages of the Bible, we are literally reading a different world. The more than two thousand years of interpretation that lie in between make the matter only more complex. Yet, in considering current predicaments, people of faith turn to the Bible as the foundation for what to believe and how to act. Because so many of the conflicted issues of our day result in an impasse over arguments about the Bible, when it comes to Scripture and sexuality, it seems appropriate to begin with our own fundamentals for reading, or interpreting, the Bible.

My own interpretation of Scripture proceeds from both a feminist perspective and faith in the possibility of the text as mediator of God's guidance for our lives today. The Bible as a religious text has exercised and still exercises strong influence on the lives of the faithful in two major religious groups, Judaism and Christianity. My feminist biblical scholarship is done in the context of a Christian Reformed Protestant belief in the authority of Scripture. It is thus not my intent to erase the influence and authority of the Bible by uncovering the prejudices that undergird much of biblical writing but rather to lay a renewed claim to biblical authority by understanding the text to exceed the sum of its patriarchal parts and by searching for a biblical hermeneutic that itself exposes these prejudices as opposed to the core of biblical teaching.[4]

Therefore, I suggest that inquiry into Scripture and sexuality be guided by the following basic principles:

1. There is *not one way* of reading the Bible, as the Scripture itself testifies (see the examples above). Moreover, there is *not one thing* we read in the Bible. Whether we are literalists or nonliteralists, we read the Bible selectively.[5]

2. We need a principle of interpretation, a hermeneutical "key," on which to base our selectivity, rather than letting issues of the day solely determine what we count as important and what we ignore. This hermeneutical key needs to be consistently biblical, i.e., consistent with the overall themes of both the First and Second Testaments.[6]

3. Because we take the historical context of the Bible seriously, we take seriously the distance between ourselves and Scripture, between our world and the world of the Bible. Only as we try to understand as clearly as possible what the biblical world was like can we make the connections to our own world.[7]

Reading the world of the Bible

When faced with the texts of Holy Scripture we are confronted with not one but many worlds. The Bible as a written record reflects a history of more than a thousand years, a period of great change on all levels, social, political, and religious. Were we to sketch the biblical record of the history of the people that gave birth to the Bible from the time of their beginnings up until the time of Jesus, it would look as follows: A kin-group of herders and tent-dwellers migrated from Mesopotamia to the small habitable area on the Mediterranean coast called Canaan. This group expanded slowly and finally was forced by famine to migrate to Egypt for their survival. In another period, after the kin-group in Egypt had expanded considerably and their members were put to work at forced labor, the group escaped and trekked through the Sinai peninsula back to Canaan, where they eventually settled. The kin-groups lived in a loose federation in Canaan until the times required a centralized form of government.

The loose federation of groups became a more organized nation during the tenth century B.C.E. What we call ancient Israel fell apart by the end of the century, and two realms came into existence, one in the south and one in the north, each with its own central administration. Both kingdoms were vulnerable to outside attack, beset by powerful, expansive empires to the southwest (Egypt) and the northeast (Mesopotamia). At times the kingdoms were also at war with each other; thus, peaceful times were rare for ancient Israel.

In the last quarter of the eighth century, the northern kingdom succumbed to the Assyrian empire; about 150 years later, around 590 B.C.E., the same fate overcame Judah in the south as Jerusalem fell to Babylon. Persia followed Babylon as the reigning power in the area, and after fifty years of exile, a decree from the Persian king made it possible for those from Judah who wished to do so to return "home." Then followed two centuries of rebuilding and restoration, but Judah remained a province of the large empire of which it had become a part, first Persia, then Greece, and finally, in the days of the New Testament, Rome. This reality colored the lives of people until the days of Jesus and afterwards. Dependence, heavy taxation, hard labor, and frequent occupation by foreign armed forces were all part of the normal routine. Instability and oppression provided much of the context for the texts comprised in the Bible, especially the First Testament.

Women and men in the world of the Bible

In such an unstable world, how did women and men live together, and what rules governed sexual relations? The mode of social and economic life of the loosely organized tribal federation during the early periods was that of a small-scale, self-sustaining agricultural society. Historically, we are speaking of the Late Bronze and the

Early Iron age (1600–1000 B.C.E.), when survival of these groups depended on their ability to produce enough healthy offspring to guarantee an ongoing population. War, famine, epidemics, and endemic parasitic diseases were a constant threat. For most women, bearing children in sufficient numbers to insure a surviving population left them weak and more vulnerable than men to such threats. The obsession with biological productivity, which is clear from many biblical narratives, should be understood within this context. Regulations of sexual relations should be viewed likewise.[8]

During the period of the monarchies, agriculture continued to secure sustenance and well-being for extended families or kin-groups outside of the two main cities, Jerusalem and Samaria, neither of which probably had populations that ever exceeded thirty thousand people. The practice of intensive agriculture required women to spend as much as five hours in the fields next to men. In this social matrix, a *functional* equality between women and men prevailed even if, conceptually, the status of females was lower than that of males.[9] Daily life was centered on what can be called the family household, an economic as well as a biological unity. In producing most of what it needed to sustain itself for survival, the household was the determinative location for most women, men, and children. This is where women lived and sometime exercised considerable authority, an authority we may deduce from Proverbs 31:10–31 and other texts.[10] In the culture of city life, with its governing male bureaucracy and market-oriented economy, women's contributions were less valued, and their more restricted social roles would eventually become *ideological* rather than functional.[11]

After the Babylonian exile, with the return to Judah and restructuring of life in postexilic times, renewed anxiety about biological productivity came to the fore. Because of greatly reduced numbers, chances of survival once again hit an extremely low point, and an emphasis on reproduction was instituted with renewed vigor. Very possibly, the priestly lawgiving in the book of Leviticus, with its strong concerns for the maintenance of familial and other boundaries, dates from these times. Similarly, family life took on greater importance in terms of the exercise of religious function, a development that may have accentuated the role of women in the household and the importance of the female.[12]

In view of the high mortality rate of women and children, the regulations that governed the sexual relations of women and men were, understandably, intended to further biological productivity in all biblical periods. Generally speaking, boundaries around sexual relations arose from concerns about orderly family relations and maintaining the greatest biological productivity possible. Intimacies that threatened order and productivity within heterosexual marriage, including adultery, incest, prostitution, and homosexual relations, were forbidden.[13] Other sexual intimacies, such as polygyny, brother-sister marriage, and concubinage are found without penalty in the Bible.

The ancient world of the Bible was structured in a patriarchal way, and it should not come as a surprise that laws regulating sexuality reflect male power to set the boundaries for acceptable sexual relations. The 1991 Presbyterian study, "Keeping Body and Soul Together: Sexuality, Spirituality, and Social Justice," correctly identified as patriarchal the dominant sexual code in our own culture, a code that "legitimates male gender privilege and sanctifies heterosexual marriage as the exclusive pattern for well-ordered sexual expression."[14] Similarly, dominant patriarchal models prevailed in biblical times. Given the overwhelming need for biological productivity, as discussed above, biblical codes legislating sexuality were constructed as either contributing to or taking away from this productivity. However, the Bible does not ground the relations between women and men as unequal theologically. In all areas, including sexuality, women and men are viewed as created equal by God, exactly as stated in Scripture:

> Then God created humanity in God's image,
> in God's image God created it,
> male and female God created them. (Gen. 1:27)

Sexual inequality enters into the garden with human disobedience:

> To the woman God said:
> I will multiply, yes multiply
> the pain of your pregnancy
> in pain you will bring forth sons;

to your man will be your desire
and he will rule over you. (Gen. 3:16)

This Genesis 3 text does not reflect dominant-subordinate gender relations as willed or designed by God, but rather describes what has ensued for their relationship as a consequence of their act of disobedience in eating from the tree of the knowledge of good and evil. Patriarchy is recorded in the First Testament of the Bible as a *descriptive* rather than *prescriptive* reality. No theological construct guides or justifies this reality.[15]

Today, by God's grace, women and men are in the process of delivering an ongoing challenge to patriarchal structures and ideologies. Religious women and men do not find faith warrants for the inequalities that exist in both their social and their religious world. Christians ground their convictions about women's "newly cherished human dignity and equality" in their strongly held faith in the God of Jesus Christ, the God who desires the enactment of justice and love on the earth, and in the insight that patriarchal systems fly in the face of this desire.[16]

The disconnection between our world and the world of the Bible thus resides in new insight gained with the help of the biblical text and in very different social realities. The mandate in favor of biological productivity, so much a part of the biblical social world dictating most sexual mores and rules, is gone from our social world. In fact, we face a reverse problem: a world with too much biological productivity and in many places situations of scarcity, poverty, and general deprivation.

Reading sexual intimacy in the Bible

What is the biblical vocabulary of sexual intimacy, and how do we read it?[17] No word exclusively denotes sexual activity, and verbs take on sexual meaning in the context of activity. One word that occurs frequently for sexual relations, used in relation to Adam and Eve, is the verb "to know."

And the human being *knew* Chawwa, his woman,
and she conceived and gave birth to Cayin. (Gen. 4:1)

"To know" with a sense of sexual intimacy is used mostly with a male subject, but can also occur with a female subject, as that of a virgin who has "not known" a man.

Another common expression is "to go into." In Genesis 6:4, the sons of God are said to "go into" the daughters of humanity. This verb, for obvious reasons, is used only with a male subject. There is little question here of a reciprocal sexual act. A frequent sequence is "he saw, he took, and he went into." Once more quoting from the story of the sons of God who copulate with human women:

> The sons of the gods *saw* the daughters of humanity
> for they were good-looking
> and they *took* for themselves women
> from all they chose...
> when the sons of the gods *went into*
> the daughters of humanity. (Gen. 6:2, 4)

In the story of Judah and Tamar in Genesis 38, we read that Judah "saw" a Canaanite woman, "took her," and "went into her."[18] Similarly, Onan "went into" Tamar, as later did Judah (38:9 and 18).[19]

Potentially more reciprocal are the terms "to lie with" and "to approach." The first verb is used when the daughters of Lot have sexual relations with their father (Gen. 19:32–35). Ironically, the more reciprocal verb "to lie with" is used of Shechem and his rape of Dinah (Gen. 34:2).[20] "To come near" or "approach" is used in Exodus 19:15 to proscribe sexual relations by male members of the covenant community before they "come near" to the presence of God at Sinai.

In the context of some of these sexual encounters, the word "love" is used but almost always originating with the male. Nowhere in the ancestral stories is a woman said to love a man, although in the David narratives Michal, Saul's daughter, is said to love David.[21] Nor are women recorded as "loving" women, with the striking exception of Ruth, who is said to *love* Naomi (Ruth 4:15). As Brenner observes, "It seems that Hebrew Bible female figures do not excel as 'loving' agents—of the legitimate divine male figure (completely absent), their children (rare), other women (apart from Ruth, who loves Naomi), or men."[22]

The only biblical text that presents a picture of mutual love and equal sexual relations is the Song of Songs (The Song of Solomon).

Phyllis Trible views these poems as the counterpoint to the story of Genesis 2 and 3, which she entitles "A Love Story Gone Awry."[23] Here we find a celebration of sexuality as a part of God's good creation in a completely shared, unabashed mutuality of male and female. Here is a paean of praise for sexual love, with both male and female giving full voice to longing, joy, and pain. Here the woman exclaims, "I am my beloved's, and to me is his desire" (Song 7:10) in contrast to the divine declaration of Genesis 3:16. Although the Song of Songs forms an exception, its presence in the Bible testifies to the possibility of breaking through the nonmutuality exemplified by the rest of the Bible.

How do matters evolve in New Testament times? For the early Christian community, in trying to establish and maintain itself in the far-flung Roman empire, it seems to have been a matter of some urgency to regulate sexual and conjugal relations into "normal" patterns. The number of passages that deal with these matters is relatively high.[24] While an analysis of these passages lies beyond the scope of this discussion, it may be sufficient to note here that the verb "to love" does not occur with a woman as subject in the context of the wife-husband relationship. Where husbands are mandated to love their wives, as in Ephesians 5:21–25 and Colossians 3:18–19, the required posture on the part of women is not love but submission. The one text that pushes the conjugal relationship in a more reciprocal direction, 1 Corinthians 7:1–4, uses a word that points to obligation. The notion of love is absent.[25] Because the Corinthians passage is the only one that can be assigned with any certainty to Pauline authorship, it is likely that in early Christianity the impulse was strong to conform male-female relations to traditional cultural norms of the day.

What are we to conclude from this brief overview? As women and men who in faith have issued a challenge to patriarchal structures and ideologies, how do we read this biblical vocabulary in which the heterosexual male gender sets the norm?[26] Clearly, faithful people today are not called to repeat the norms and patterns of sexual relations observed here. Otherwise, we might as well try to construct a church building by following the instructions given by God for the construction of the Tabernacle in Exodus! Prescriptions for and descriptions of sexual conduct, including those for same-sex conduct, were determined by the cultural patriarchal norms of biblical times and by high anxiety about biological productivity. The testimony of the biblical text itself to the equality of male and female in the image of God (Gen. 1:27) stands in stark contradiction to the sociosexual arrangements that prevailed in biblical times.

The practice of justice

Thus far, we have found ways of reading that point to a disconnection between our world and the biblical world, between our manner of conceiving and living human relations and sexuality, on the one hand, and the biblical manner, on the other. Such exploration is necessary in order to recognize clearly how literal interpretations and applications of biblical norms and practices with regard to human sexuality lead into a world of behaviors and relationships that, in faith, we know to be unloving, oppressive, and against God's will for human creatures. Is there a way to "read what we read" so our path of faith connects with that of the Bible?

The 1991 Presbyterian study "Keeping Body and Soul Together" identifies the great divide not as one "between men and women or between heterosexual and homosexual persons." Rather, it argues, "The great moral divide is between justice and injustice."[27] At first blush, the category of justice may not seem to offer a way to connect with the Bible on norms for human sexuality, especially if we experience justice as a limiting, even constricting designation rather than a freeing one. When we consider the word on biblical grounds, however, we discover that biblical justice, *mishpat* in Hebrew, is far from a mechanistic, legalistic concept. The people of the Bible, bound to God in Sinai covenant or Christ covenant, are required to pattern their actions and perceptions after those of the God who is in covenant with them. As they are attentive to God's presence with them, they are called to pursue justice with their neighbor. Justice is fulfilled in deeds of mercy and love to those who need it most. God's justice is equated with God's love for the poor, the widow, the orphan, and the stranger. God's heart is said to burn with a passion for justice. A people become God's covenant people as they practice this kind of justice, and in so doing, they may be called a *holy people.*[28]

The requirement for ancient Israel to be a *holy* or a *dedicated* nation is rooted in the covenant-bond with God and in God's holiness (Exod. 19:6 and Lev. 19:2, for example). The people's holiness consists in their modeling themselves on God. God's holiness can be understood, of course, as God's otherness, a contemplation of which causes human awe and adoration.[29] We may think of the proclamation of the Seraphim in the book of Isaiah: "Holy, holy, holy, Holy One of Hosts, filled is the earth with God's glory!" (Isa. 6:3) On the other hand, the Bible also states that God is "in the midst of the people" as the Holy One: "For I am God and not a man; in your midst the Holy One; I will not come in anger" (Hos. 11:9).

According to biblical scholar Baruch Levine, God's holiness is intended to describe not God's essential nature but rather how God is manifest. In Hosea 11, God's holiness is made manifest through God's forgiveness. Levine observes that God's holiness becomes clear because God acts in holy ways. For Israel the way to holiness was to model its practices on God's attributes. If we follow both these insights, it means that the community's holiness manifests itself insofar as it emulates God's passion for justice.

The prophet Micah laid down the essential requirements for the covenant community. After running through hypothetical requirements of faithful behavior (Mic. 6:6–7), the prophet phrased it thus:

> [God] has told you, human being, what is good.
> And what does the Holy God seek from you
> but the doing of justice,
> the love of loyalty
> and walking modestly with your God. (Mic. 6:8)

The Hebrew word I have translated as "love of loyalty" is *hesed,* indicating the love and loyalty between covenant partners. English translations often render it as "kindness" or "loving-kindness." Two verbs of action and movement, "doing" and "walking," surround a verb of orientation, "love." Two expressions of orientation, "love of loyalty" and " modesty," amplify a word of action, *justice.* In this text, action and perspective are woven into a tight fabric; to loosen one makes the entire fabric unravel.[30]

The medieval Jewish commentator known as Rashi observed that the final requirement in the Hosea text, of walking with God, does not mark a shift from ethics to piety, from human relations to relations between people and God. "On the contrary," observed Rashi, "walking modestly with your God is a description of doing justice and extending mercy to one's neighbor. It is our conduct and disposition in the world, the attitudes which we strike with our fellow human beings, which are the acid test of the nature of our relation with God."[31]

In the Torah, the most frequent articulation of this concern for justice is found in the required behavior toward the stranger. A stranger was a person without the rights and privileges that belonged to full members of the community. Strangers were those who lived vulnerable lives in constant need of protection, since potentially, they were all marginalized people. Laws protecting the stranger are the ones most frequently cited and the ones most extensive in scope, ranging from the prohibition to oppress to the requirement to love, with a host of specific behaviors cited in between.[32] Neither the status of the stranger nor the character of oppression has changed radically from biblical times until today. Strangers are those different from the dominant group who are not accorded the same rights and privileges that full members of the community have.

The requirement to practice justice, specifically in the shape of love toward the stranger, does not suffer from the time-bound nature we observed in biblical family structures and sexual relations. Moreover, it is a consistent biblical theme that receives a prominent place in the Torah, is developed in the Prophetic writings, and occurs significantly in the rest of biblical literature.[33] In the Gospels, the theme is incorporated in the parable of the Good Samaritan (Luke 10:25–34) and in that of the Great Judgment, where Jesus is identified with the stranger (Matt. 25:35 and 43).

This justice theme thus serves as a hermeneutical key with which to unlock biblical texts that are constrained by time-bound norms. There can be no doubt that in patriarchal systems and ideologies, women are constructed as the "other," take up the status of strangers, and are deprived of full equality with men in the image of God. Male regulatory power in sexual relationships makes strangers of those who do not fit the unequal heterosexist paradigm of sexuality. Called by the "good news of Jesus," we must denounce such practices of estrangement as contrary to the practice of justice demanded from those who consider themselves in covenant relationship with God. In the practice of justice, as covenant partners with the God of justice, we are required to love the stranger as we love ourselves (Lev. 19:34). In so doing, we love both God and neighbor, the two directives on which "hang all the law and the prophets."[34]

When Huldah interpreted the Torah scroll, she pointed to the idolatrous practices of the community that had angered God (2 Kings 22:17). Injustice toward the vulnerable neighbor, on the basis of human-made, time-bound, patriarchal rules, constitutes a practice of idolatry in elevating cultural norms to the status of divine commandment. When the lawyer asked Jesus his questions, the parable Jesus told led in the direction of practicing justice as love extended to the one in need, the stranger who has a claim on his *hesed,* his covenant loyalty. When the Apostle Philip interpreted the Bible to the Ethiopian, he did so in a way that proclaimed "the good news of Jesus." We do not know more of what Philip told the Ethiopian than that.

How do we discern good news about sexuality in Scripture? For us, in facing our own uncertainties when reading the biblical text, the "good news of Jesus" at least means that in Christ, the God of the Jews of ancient Israel has entered into covenant with outsiders. Within this covenant the requirements for a faithful life are not different from those expected of the original covenant community. The practice of justice is to be applied to all our relationships. All relationships, especially those in which traditionally unjust paradigms hold sway, are answerable to the rule of covenant loyalty.

Notes

1. Acts 8:26–40. Philip's question in verse 30 contains a pun not easily rendered in English so most translations provide a version of "Do you understand what you read?" The two verbs used are forms based on the Greek verb *ginoosko.* It is possible, however, to use "read" for both verbs, understanding the first to be the kind of reading that equates understanding. Hence, for this phrase I propose the translation, "How do you read what you read?"

2. Luke 10:25–37; see also Matthew 22:34–40 and Mark 12:28–34.

3. 2 Kings 22:8–20. Although no one knows the exact contents of the document referred to in 2 Kings 22, many scholars agree that the Torah scroll referred to here is most likely a part of Deuteronomy. Deuteronomy as a whole makes the blessings of land and produce contingent on obedience to the covenant and the commandments. These commandments include a prohibition of idolatry but also the requirement to love God and treat vulnerable categories of people with compassion and love (see, for example, Deut. 4:25–31; 6:4–9, 14–15; 7:1–26; 10:12–22; 24:17–22). The prophet Huldah points to practices of idol worship as the cause of God's anger (2 Kings 22:17).

4. Not all feminist scholarship approaches the Bible in this way. Compare my intent with that of Athalya Brenner, for example. For Brenner, the task of "uncovering" and "defusing" the influence of the Bible is in itself an important, if not the most important, task of feminist biblical scholarship. See Athalya Brenner, *The Intercourse of Knowledge: On Gendering Desire and "Sexuality" in the Hebrew Bible* (New York: Brill, 1997).

5. It is interesting to note that a section of Leviticus, a book which in the view of many Christians has little useful or instructive to say, has taken on renewed significance in regard to the emphasis on Jubilee, especially in terms of forgiving debt to countries that are sliding more and more deeply into indebtedness on account of loans granted by the World Bank and the International Monetary Fund. Selectivity in choosing to highlight certain biblical texts is often driven quite legitimately by a contemporary issue or need.

6. This fundamental principle implies, for example, that one Testament does not stand in judgment over the other. The words of Jesus, even if we knew exactly what they were, are not more important than the testimony of Scripture elsewhere. Neither is the Second Testament as a witness to God's gracious involvement with the world superior to, or truer than, the witness of the First Testament. This error is not a part of the Reformed tradition but stems from deeply embedded anti-Judaic and anti-Jewish attitudes in the Christian tradition and present communities. In the Reformed stream of the Christian tradition, the entire Bible testifies to the same God who was incarnate in Jesus Christ.

7. Only such a reading will grant the text its authenticity and preserve some boundaries of its meaning. In terms of the First Testament, a reading within a historical context leaves intact not only the authenticity of the original composers and receivers of this text, but also that of their direct inheritors, the Jews. I do not mean to imply by this remark that the Bible "records history," for neither in subject matter nor in style of writing does the text conform to a modern idea of historiography. In its narrative parts, the Bible tells the story of God's engagement with ancient Israel, from its earliest ancestral beginnings, through the time of the monarchy and beyond the exile. The story is obviously related to historical facts but does not reflect a modern need to "have all the facts," or to record "true facts."

8. Whereas men's life expectancy was somewhere around forty years at this time, for women this would be put more realistically at thirty. Childbirth itself weakened a physical system that had to sustain many threats. See Carol Meyers, "The Roots of Restriction: Women in Early Israel" in *The Bible and Liberation: Political and Social Hermeneutics,* ed. Norman K. Gottwald (Maryknoll, N.Y.: Orbis, 1983), 289–304. Athalya Brenner, in analyzing reports from burial grounds that

date back to the early Roman periods, more than a thousand years after that researched by Meyers, puts the average age of mortality of women at twenty to twenty-five years of age. Brenner, *The Intercourse of Knowledge*, 65.

9. Meyers, "The Roots of Restriction," 289. See Carol Meyers, "Everyday Life: Women in the Period of the Hebrew Bible," in *The Women's Bible Commentary*, ed. Carol A. Newsom and Sharon H. Ringe (Louisville: Westminster John Knox, 1992), 244–51.

10. Although the description of the "powerful woman" of Proverbs 31 is idealistic, to be effective it must comprise elements that fall within a recognizable world. The woman of this poem not only works hard, she has the authority to buy and sell (vv. 16–18, 24); she not only provides but also teaches (vv. 20–26). One also has the impression that her husband basks in her renown (v. 23).

11. Thus Meyers: "the former socioeconomically *functional* significance of women's restricted roles was perpetuated and hardened into fixed practice based on *ideological subordination* of women to men. This theologized endorsement of an older functional necessity was passed along to later Jews and Christians as normative tradition and behavior" ("The Roots of Restriction," 289).

12. For example, see the modest suggestions made by Claudia Camp: "One might speculate that, as autonomy and decision-making authority flowed back to the collocation of families from the ruined central power structure, the community-wide authority of women in their on-going role as managers of their households also increased." See Claudia Camp, *Wisdom and the Feminine in the Book of Proverbs* (Sheffield: JSOT, 1985), 261.

13. For various prohibitions, see Leviticus 18 and 20; also Deuteronomy 27:20–23.

14. "Keeping Body and Soul Together: Sexuality, Spirituality, and Social Justice," the report produced by the Special Committee on Human Sexuality of the Presbyterian Church (U.S.A.), was brought to the 203rd General Assembly in 1991. This document, contrary to many reports, was never as such brought up for a vote before the Assembly. The quotation can be found on page 31. One of the great merits of this report was the linking of patriarchal structures and ideology with homophobia. See also Ilona N. Rashkow, *Taboo or Not Taboo: Sexuality and Family in the Hebrew Bible* (Minneapolis: Fortress, 2000).

15. Such theological constructs do occur in the Second Testament. We may perhaps understand such guidelines as provided in 1 Corinthians 14:34–35, Ephesians 5:22, Colossians 3:18, Titus 2:5, 1 Timothy 2:9–15, and 1 Peter 3:1 from the perspective of a once functional inequality developed into an ideological one. See note 11. In this case the weight of testimony from the Second Testament needs to be corrected by that of the First Testament.

16. The expression about women's dignity and equality is from Elizabeth Johnson, *She Who Is: The Mystery of God in Feminist Theological Discourse* (New York: Crossroad, 1992), 6.

17. For a full discussion of all relevant terms, see Brenner, *The Intercourse of Knowledge*.

18. The New Revised Standard Version obscures the sequence by translating the verb "to take" with "marry": "There Judah saw the daughter of a certain Canaanite whose name was Shua; he married her and went into her" (Gen. 38:2). See

also Genesis 28:6–9, where the Hebrew uses the verb "to take" and the NRSV translation renders "marry."

19. The sequence of these three verbs does not in itself indicate wrongdoing, but ambiguity is at work, and the resulting events may not be exactly sound morally. In the case of the rape of Dinah, it is noteworthy that the sequence is "see," "take," "lie with," and "force." This sequence is not clear in the NRSV where we read: "When Shechem, son of Hamor the Hivite, prince of the region, saw her, he seized her and lay with her, by force" (Gen. 34:2). The Hebrew has four verbs and only the last one is negative: "saw her, took her, lay with her and forced her."

20. For other examples of "to lie with" see Genesis 30:15, 16; 35:22; 39:7, 12, 14; Exodus 22:15; Leviticus 15:33; 19:20; Deuteronomy 22:22, 23, 28, 29; 1 Samuel 2:22. For a complete list see Brenner, *The Intercourse of Knowledge*, 24.

21. Isaac is said to "love" Rebekah (Gen. 24:67), Jacob "loves" Rachel (Gen. 29:18 and 30). For the story of Michal and David, see 1 Samuel 18:20 and 28. In addition the verb has a general female subject in Proverbs 7:18; 8:17, 21.

22. Brenner, *The Intercourse of Knowledge*, 23.

23. Phyllis Trible, *God and the Rhetoric of Sexuality* (Philadelphia: Fortress, 1978), 144–65.

24. See 1 Corinthians 7:1–4, Ephesians 5:21–33, Colossians 3:19, 1 Peter 3:1–7, and Titus 2:4–5.

25. The NRSV reads "conjugal rights" in 1 Corinthians 7:3. In Titus 2:4, the writer requires that older women teach young women to be *philandrous,* literally "man-loving."

26. See Brenner, *The Intercourse of Knowledge*, 179: "There is no female sexuality in the H[ebrew] B[ible] for women of any class apart from whores, although there is female sexual desire and diminished capacity to love. By comparison, the admittedly limited sexual autonomy or agency accorded to free adult males looks like a huge privilege. If sexuality is requisite for constructing gender, then the one truly normative gender in the H[ebrew] B[ible] is the M[ale] gender."

27. The writers of the report eased the starkness of the word "justice" by pairing it with *love* and wrote of "justice-love" and "right-relatedness." "Justice-love or right-relatedness, and not heterosexuality (nor homosexuality for that matter) is the appropriate norm for sexuality" (*Presbyterians and Human Sexuality 1991* [Louisville: Presbyterian Church (U.S.A.), 1991], 20).

28. In this direction we may understand the words of Exodus 19:6: "And you yourselves shall be for me / a royal realm of priests / and a holy nation." For Baruch Levine, "The statement that God is holy means...that God acts in holy ways; God is just and righteous." For ancient Israel, "the way to holiness...was...to emulate God's attributes." Baruch Levine, The Excursus on Holiness," *The JPS Torah Commentary: Leviticus, The Traditional Hebrew Text with the New JPS Translation, Commentary* (Philadelphia: Jewish Publication Society, 5749/1989).

29. For further discussion of this concept, see Johanna W. H. van Wijk-Bos, *Re-imagining God: The Case for Scriptural Diversity* (Louisville: Westminster John Knox, 1995), 31–33.

30. The translation "modestly," instead of "humbly," as the NRSV renders it, may also be read as "carefully" or "attentively." Paying careful attention to the

need of the neighbor is the requirement here, rather than being loud and certain about the sins of others and one's own righteousness.

31. As quoted in William McKane, *The Book of Micah: Introduction and Commentary* (Edinburgh: T. & T. Clark, 1998), 190.

32. Some of the more important texts are Exodus 22:20–23; 23:9; Leviticus 19:9–10, 33–34, Deuteronomy 10:17–19 and 31:12. See also Jeremiah 7:6 and 22:3. For the Second Testament, Matthew 25:35. Unfortunately most English translations, including the NRSV, do not render the Hebrew word consistently in English, so that the Hebrew word *ger* sometimes reads "stranger" and many other times "resident alien." The category of *ger* is thus often veiled in the English text. For a full discussion of these and other biblical texts, see Johanna W. H. van Wijk-Bos, "Solidarity with the Stranger," in *A Journey to Justice* (The Presbyterian Committee on the Self-Development of People, Presbyterian Church [U.S.A.], 1993).

33. The entire book of Ruth concerns itself with the contributions made by a "stranger" to the well-being not only of an ancient Israelite local community but also to the house of King David. See also Psalm 94:6 and 146:9 for articulations of lack of care for the stranger as a testimony to wickedness and of God's care for the stranger.

34. See Matthew 22:40 and Luke 10:25–37.

4

We're Here, We're Queer

Teaching Sex in Seminary

Carter Heyward

> I had to prepare for this and
> not just by reading Lorde and Weeks and Raymond
> or my own stuff
> I had to do more than think
> about "sexuality" "theology" "ethics"
>
> in order to come to this
>
> I had to connect with you
> through memories fantasies humor
> and struggle
> sometimes touching
> often amazing
> always worthy of respect[1]

Many years ago, the great black queen of soul Aretha Franklin topped the charts with her song "R-E-S-P-E-C-T," which still today causes bodies of all colors to shake and jive. Somehow you know, with Aretha, that when you dance to the music, there's nothing more important to a human life well lived than "respect." This is why, over the last thirty years, increasing numbers of theologians and ethicists, biblical scholars and pastoral care teachers have been teaching sex in seminaries as part of the theological education of lay and ordained ministers. Somehow we know, like Aretha Franklin, that respect for self and others is an underpinning of justice and peace and is also a primary human expression of the love of God. Moreover, we know that self-respect and respect for others are moral capacities born of well-integrated human lives in which sexual integrity is foundational. Hence, my insistence in the poem, part of which is quoted above, that communicating about sexuality — through the pages of a book, in a classroom, in the kitchen, or in bed — necessitates an awareness, certainly on the part of the teacher, that all of us, all students and teachers, are "always worthy of respect."

Next spring I will teach a course on queer theology at the Episcopal Divinity School in Cambridge, Massachusetts, where I've been on the faculty for nearly thirty years. This will be, as I figure it, the twelfth time I've taught a course on sexuality at EDS and about the twenty-fifth course on sex that I've participated in teaching in seminaries and other theological centers in the United States, Australia, the United Kingdom, Switzerland, and Germany. In this essay, I will be focusing on how, in my pedagogical experience, teaching sex in seminary has evolved over the last three decades.

Before moving into this discussion, however, I want to say something about how odd, in a way, it has seemed to some of our critics and, indeed, to many of us who are seminary professors that here we are doing this work—trained academics in religion, seldom with any background in sex education, and often without much professional experience in parishes or other arenas of pastoral care giving.

Who are we to be teaching seminarians about sexuality? Clearly we are not "experts" in the realm of sexuality, whoever such experts might be. We are not, for the most part, well versed in social studies, biology, or psychology; nor are we sexologists. We are theologians, folks with some expertise in, and often passion for, making connections between, on the one hand, the religions and spiritualities of communities and individuals and, on the other, many other realms of human experience, such as sexuality. So our expertise is in shaping theological critique and construction in which, always with the help of others past and present, we try to understand how our human lives are connected with one another and with the life of God. Moreover, since we are sexual beings ourselves, our own stories and those of our communities have led us to questions and often more questions about how, and under what circumstances, our sexual and spiritual energies converge, merge, dissipate, separate, and are mutually "instructive" to us.

Perhaps those of us who teach sex in seminary are a bit like the Clergy and Laity Concerned group that formed in the 1960s and 1970s in response to the war in Vietnam. They were not experts on war; if they were experts, it was in peacemaking. In a culture of war, Clergy and Laity Concerned represented a counterculture. Similarly, we theological educators who teach about sexuality usually share a commitment to helping build communities, religious and other, in which people can be at peace with themselves and others *as sexual beings.* Holding this goal, we have often found ourselves at odds with our denominations and other church bodies, who seem too often bent upon perpetuating sexual ethics and teachings based largely on fear, ignorance, control, and (even in some liberal religious traditions) fundamentalist readings of Scripture. In this fear-based ecclesial culture, those who teach sex in seminary have often embodied countercultural energies and hope.

Teaching sex over three decades

Looking back to the early 1970s, it seems to me that there are four distinct, though overlapping, periods of how we have taught sex in progressive Christian seminaries like the Episcopal Divinity School.

Period one: feminist theology (1970s)

Without the women's movement of the late 1960s, we *still* wouldn't be talking about sex, in seminary or anywhere else. Oh, we'd be "doing it" all right, but it would be in fear, shame, and secrecy. The current sexual abuse crisis in the Roman Catholic Church and the cardinals' (and pope's) inability to understand what is happening and why illustrates stunningly the sexual and spiritual pathos of an institution that has taken pride in being untouched by the feminist movement. It was a Roman Catholic scholar and feminist, Mary Daly, who in the late 1960s began to warn her church about the cost of continuing to disempower Christian women.[2] In the early 1970s, Mary Daly's name became almost synonymous with Christian feminism, a movement that the Roman Catholic Church chose to ignore, preferring to feed off of its unexamined patriarchal mythos, which could lead nowhere good in the realm of human sexuality.

Meanwhile, in some Protestant seminaries as well as among Roman Catholic and other women in extraecclesial movements and groups, thanks to such outspoken Roman Catholics as Mary Daly and Rosemary Radford Ruether and such Protestants as Letty Russell, the women's movement was taking hold among still small but growing numbers of Christian women seminarians.[3] It was in this context, in the hallowed halls of theological educational institutions, that many of us began to talk about sex for the first time in our lives. In the early 1970s, the setting for these conversations was often a "consciousness-raising group" of six or eight women in seminary. These "cr" groups met once a week to discuss such questions as, "When did you first realize how women get pregnant?" "When did you become aware of your clitoris?" "When did you first masturbate?" "Talk about how you felt about your body when you were ten years old, and when you were fifteen."

While most of our male professors at the time would have been totally baffled by what these kinds of questions could possibly have contributed to our theological education, it was sharp and clear to our generation of women students and to the men in our lives who were paying attention. It was about power—sexual power or, in Kate Millett's famous feminist words, "Sexual Politics."[4] Who holds what kind of power over whom, and to what effect? Our best teachers were also getting clear, with themselves and us, that these power-questions moved seriously into the very core of theology, ethics, biblical interpretation, historical readings, and pastoral care. (Even today, more than thirty years later, many seminary professors and students are still unclear how these power-questions shape liturgy, but that is another, albeit related, story!)[5]

In 1975, as a young, recently (and irregularly) ordained Episcopal priest, I joined the faculty of the Episcopal Divinity School to launch a professorial vocation of teaching "systematic theology." Through my student work at Union Theological Seminary in New York City and the movement for the ordination of women in the Episcopal Church, I landed at EDS as a committed feminist. Within a year, I knew that I both needed and wanted to learn how to teach sexuality as a theological issue. Christian feminism had shown me already that the historic power dynamics between Christian men and women — Christianity's sexual politics — were continuing to shape Christian life, values, behavior, and the world itself. It was clear to me that sex (short for "sexuality") was, and is, not only a feminist issue, but also a Christian issue.[6]

Like other feminist theologians in the 1970s, I began teaching sexuality by teaching feminist theology mainly, though not exclusively, to women students. Our focus in the mid-to-late 1970s was not as much on genital sex per se as on the power relation between men and women, though we knew—from experience as well as feminist literature (most of it secular) — that there is a connection between power and sex, always.[7]

The most important development during this period, when sex was being taught in seminary as a component of feminist theology, was that students and faculty alike were becoming increasingly aware that we could not make a clear distinction between Christian theology's historical treatments of women and sexuality, because most of the theologians revered within mainstream Christianity have treated both women and sexuality with contempt and, often, hatred. The most astute feminist theologians and ethicists — my own beloved companion Beverly Harrison comes to mind—realized this very early in the evolution of feminist theologies and began to insist that misogyny — the hatred of women — festers at the root of Christianity's fear-based sexual ethics.[8]

Period two: theology of sexuality (late 1970s to the 1980s)

Thanks to the feminist movement, by the late 1970s the Christian churches had become arenas of another, closely related activist movement: the struggle among gay and lesbian Christians for affirmation and full inclusion in the life of the church. Wittingly or unaware, gay men and lesbians, who in the late 1970s had begun to "come out" in increasingly large numbers, represented the church's opportunity to begin making radical changes in how the Christian community understands itself biblically, historically, theologically, ethically, pastorally, and liturgically. Ironically, there were then some gay and lesbian seminarians who harbored no personal desire to "represent" anything other than their own interests in being ordained, getting married, and/or experiencing a basic acceptance of who they are. These men and women seemed to believe that because the church "ought" to be a just and decent organization, they shouldn't have to be "political" (read: upset folks) in order to be accepted for who they are. They, of course, were right up to a point: the church "ought" to be a realm of God, an arena of justice-love, hope, and gratitude. However, real life cannot be lived simply on the basis of how things ought to be. We cannot simply be idealists, certainly not if we are teaching sex in seminary.[9]

This second period of teaching sexuality was launched by the widespread "coming out" among gay men and lesbians already in seminaries or on their way. Like feminism, coming out belonged to the wider culture. It was happening everywhere! Lesbians and gay men were popping out of closets to name ourselves and take up the space in life we believed we deserve simply as brother and sister humans. Much of this began to take place on seminary campuses in the mid-to-late 1970s, and this momentum spurred on courses designed to study and celebrate the spirituality of sexual energy that "seeks" to come out, find a voice, and experience a new freedom.

During this period, most gay men seemed to assume that we're all born gay or straight or maybe bi. Whatever we are, it's "by nature." Many, perhaps most, lesbians—especially those who identified as feminists—assumed, to the contrary, that most of us are "polymorphously perverse," to quote Freud, meaning that we are capable of a wide range of sexual-identity experiences, from within which we "choose" the best fit for ourselves.[10] During the late 1970s and early 1980s, the liberal Protestant churches began to accept the "essentialist" or "naturalist" position that was being offered by gay men like Troy Perry (founder of the Metropolitan Community Church) and Father John J. McNeill (a Jesuit priest with a special ministry to gay and lesbian Christians). In Troy Perry's words, "The Lord is my shepherd and He knows I'm gay."[11] These men and others like them had great integrity. They were beacons of personal courage, and their ministries were and continue to be resources of hope and blessing for countless queer Christians. Nonetheless, by their proclamations that homosexuality and heterosexuality are essentially unchanging and unchangeable, theologians like Perry and McNeill unwittingly made it difficult for progressive Christians to understand sexuality as, often, a more nuanced dimension of our life together, a dimension that is at least partly constructed culturally. Feminist theologians and other feminist theorists had begun to put forth a "social constructionist" view of sexuality that assumes sexual identity is related to how people experience power in the world, especially power relations between men and women.[12] As the Roman Catholic Church had ignored the feminist movement within its ranks, so too now the Protestant churches began to ignore the lesbian feminists whose lives and understandings of our sexualities had little or nothing to do with having been born that way and everything to do with the mysterious and mutual interactions of "nature" and "nurture," birth and choice, simplicity and complexity.

This was the context in which students began to ask to study sexuality from a theological perspective. In other words, keeping sexuality front and center meant asking what we can learn about it from the Bible, from historical theology, and from other resources like psychology. The assumption beneath courses on a "theology of sexuality" was that, like any other human interest — e.g., war and peace, friendship, the earth, parenting — sexuality could be studied in relation to how we and others understand God. These courses signaled a breakthrough in education for ministry: no longer, in many theological seminaries, were studies of sexuality taboo, although to this day in the more effete corridors of academia, sex is still dismissed as a queer notion.

Period three: sexual theology (mid-1980s to mid-1990s)

The most interesting to me, and challenging, of the four periods came next and was ushered in by two forces: the HIV/AIDS crisis, in its early years thought to be a disease afflicting primarily white gay men, and a renewed concern about social power relations in response to an indifference to these matters by the Reagan administration and, increasingly, the general public.

We may recall that, in the early 1980s, most people associated AIDS with sexually active gay men in the United States. Subsequently, HIV/AIDS would show itself to be indiscriminate in relation to sex and gender and would develop into a major world health crisis that is currently threatening the entire world, especially sub-Saharan Africa. But in the 1980s, gay men in seminaries and elsewhere in the United States were struggling against the toll this terrible disease was inflicting on their communities of friends and lovers. Lesbian women were often among the primary support networks of gay male

friends and loved ones. The effect of this difficult period on theological education was significant. Seminarians in general, gay men
in particular, wanted like Job to interrogate God: what was going
on, and why? Increasingly during the 1980s, teaching about sex in
seminaries gave way to studying God through the prism of sexual
experiences, including the linking of sex with death.

During this period of time, another force was at work among seminary students and faculty. Remember that the first ten or fifteen
years of sexuality studies in seminary—like the women's movement
of the 1960s and 1970s — had been largely undertaken by white
middle-strata women (lesbian and heterosexual), who were joined
in the 1980s by openly gay men who were studying theology. Along
with the AIDS crisis, which necessitated putting sex in perspective,
the mid-1980s brought a challenge to the whiteness of the theological interest in sexuality. This challenge came from two arenas in
which greater racial/ethnic diversity had been building for a number
of years—the seminary faculties and the leaders of the denominations. Why were theological discussions of sexuality so white? women
of color began interrogating their white feminist colleagues. Why
were the students and faculty who engaged in this work nearly always white? When, if ever, did these white people intend to look at
the racism of their studies and of the gay and lesbian movements in
the churches?

Interestingly, the combination of the AIDS crisis and the insistence
that white lesbian and gay folks examine our whiteness, not just our
sexual identities, as a location of theological significance helped reframe the focus of our sexual studies in seminaries during the late
1980s and 1990s. James B. Nelson, whose works on sexuality had
been formative for many Christian seminarians during the 1970s
and 1980s, suggested in the late 1980s that those seriously interested in liberation should be doing "sexual theology," not merely
"theologies of sexuality."[13] In other words, we need to be setting our
theological eyes on God, not sexuality, as the centerpiece of our work
as students and teachers of theology and sexuality — even if some
of us discover, in this process, that "our unalienated erotic power" *is*
God. That is to say, even if in setting our attention on God rather than
sex, we find that the two are one much more often than Christian
tradition suggests.

The AIDS context had already begun to clarify for many gay men and their friends the wisdom in this shift. For white lesbian feminists, the shift was also critical, though many of us came at it from a different direction. With our attention riveted toward the lives and stories of "other" women — women of color, poor women, women of other faith or spiritual traditions, disabled women — many of us found ourselves in the role of listener. For some of us — especially erudite professors and eloquent, prolific students — this was a rather new role in theological education. Ten and fifteen years earlier, the most vital roles we could play were to speak, name, claim our power, and, if lesbian, come out. By the late 1980s, many white feminist Christian theologians, lesbian and heterosexual, had begun to realize that one of the most potent theo-ethical abilities is to be able to listen to others. In learning to listen and in hearing a multiplicity of voices, sometimes very unlike our own on matters of sex and God, we began to see that theology is a vast terrain. In truth, we are hearing, studying, and constructing sexual theologies (plural). As we do so, a multiplicity of sexualities (cultural as well as personal sexual identities) gives us many different sexual windows into Sacred Power.

One of the most precious, yet to some extent fleeting, gifts of this period was the notion of "identity politics," in which we began to understand the moral, pastoral, social, and political integrity of acknowledging our own and others' "identities" or "social locations" as basic to theological and ethical work. It made a difference, because of cultural assumptions and disparities of power and privilege, whether an assigned essay about God and sex was by an African American man or a Native American woman, an Anglo lesbian or a heterosexual Asian man.

As sexual theologies proceeded to be debated and discussed, another intellectual movement with political implications was beginning to impact theological studies — queer theory, a postmodern philosophy that dismisses "identity" as too fixed a notion for the fluidity, change, and "transgressive boundaries" that are the stuff of real life.

Period four: queer theology (mid-1990s to early 2000s)

Queer theory, U.S. version, was a product of the economic growth and exuberance of the 1990s, reflected by the election and popularity of Bill Clinton, together with the emergence of transgenderism and with postmodernism as its theoretical underpinning. In the postmodern world, there is no such thing as a fixed gender or a "right" way of being a man or a woman, a Christian lesbian or a gay Jew, a capitalist entrepreneur or the president of the United States. Whoever we are, we are. Whatever we do, we do — and, of course, whatever we do should be done in a spirit of justice and compassion. This is the gist of a postmodernist populism. For all practical purposes, it's a libertarianism that depends for its morality on the strength of each individual's conscience and her or his commitments to social justice and personal integrity. Queer theory is an intellectual methodology (origins in the work of Michel Foucault), not a populist movement or system.[14] In the United States, however, and especially in the church and religion, queer theory denotes an interest in sexual populism together with a highly abstract understanding of what sex is (for example, an exchange of power or a performative ritual).

Enter feminist liberation theology. One of the most intriguing pedagogical and intellectual "meetings" I've experienced as a teacher of theology has been between queer theory and feminist liberation theology, which is basically the feminism we teach at the Episcopal Divinity School. While queer theory is individualistic and idiosyncratic, feminist liberation theology is communal and strives to reach consensus. While queer theory is highly abstract, feminist liberation theology seeks to be embodied and concrete. Beginning in the mid-to-late 1990s, I began teaching seminars in "queer theology," encouraging students to bring together the best of queer theory and feminist liberation theology.

As a course, it has seemed to work fine, yet I sometimes ask myself (and am asked by others): Is there too great a disparity between feminist liberation theology and queer theory for the two to be held together in one course? Are we trying to weld — or simply study — two perspectives? From a feminist liberation perspective, is "queer theology" an oxymoron?

If teaching queer theology were simply a way of wrestling with a contradiction in terms, I'd have to wonder if all efforts to teach sex in seminary, to bring sex into theological discourse and theological reflection to sexual matters, were for naught. I say this because

it seems to me, as a liberation theologian and a feminist, that the
point of doing theology is to bring questions of value and judgment
to all human experiences, including the "experience" that we meet
under the rubric of "queer theory." This means that, at least at the
Episcopal Divinity School, to do queer theology is, in fact, to explore
queer theory—such as Judith Butler's concept of gender as "performance"[15] — from feminist liberation theological perspectives, which
are rooted in justice commitments and a "bias" for the standpoints
of marginalized and oppressed peoples. Thus, most queer theorists
would find queer theology too mired in the politics of queer identity, just as most feminist liberation theologians find queer theory
too apolitical to be very useful in this world in which surely even the
stones cry out for justice. Still, we are doing queer theology these days
in seminary.

So what is "queer"? The term, as we use it in queer theology,
has four different histories and meanings: (1) "queer" is a syn-
onym for gay, lesbian, bisexual, and transgender, e.g., "I'm queer";
(2) "queer" denotes a political movement in the churches and society
on behalf of gender and sexual justice, e.g., "Act-Up" and "Queer Nation"; (3) "queer" denotes a postmodern movement with roots in the
work of French philosopher Michel Foucault, in which the emphasis
is on the transgressive, performative qualities of sex; and (4) "queer"
can be used to describe any group, movement, or people who are
publicly in solidarity with gay, lesbian, bisexual, and transgender
people.

Teaching queer theology, I always say that anyone who wishes
to be queer can do this theology. I often suggest that my octoge-
narian heterosexual mother is the "queerest" member of my family
because she speaks out publicly so forcefully on behalf of her lesbian
daughter. At the beginning of the semester the last time I taught this
course, in 2001, I gave the class a "teaching exercise" as a piece of
homework:

Que(e)rying your lives: A teaching exercise

1. What is your first memory of being a girl or boy? (Choose the
   one that most closely fits how you see yourself today. If neither
   fits, choose another image.)

2. How did your race/culture/ethnicity and your class location as a child help shape this memory?

3. Have you ever felt that you'd like to be the "other" sex/gender identity? Yes or no, discuss this.

4. What lessons did you learn as a child about your sex/gender identity from (a) your parents, (b) the church, (c) teachers, (d) peers?

5. When do you remember imagining yourself as straight or as gay-lesbian? Think of an early memory and try to describe it.

6. Have you ever been afraid of being hurt because you are known or assumed to be queer?

7. Do you feel personally safe today in the United States? Who or what do you think will protect you? Think about this in terms of your race, class, sex/gender identity, sexual identity/orientation, age, religion, and life-situation (work, family, etc).

8. What is most compelling to you about queerness? What is most frightening?

9. What does any of this queering have to do with God, as you understand God?

List five queer characteristics of God. List five queer characteristics of yourself, regardless of how you describe your sexual identity/orientation.

The 2001 seminar was built around films and discussion, beginning with several documentaries on gay and lesbian youth, queer senior citizens, transgenderism, and connections between race and gender politics. It ended with the class watching and doing group projects around three full-length popular movies, which many of the students had seen on the big screen: *Priscilla, Queen of the Desert; Boys Don't Cry;* and *The Women of Brewster Place.* Requirements for course credit included (1) a short paper on criteria for queer theologies, and (2) participation in a working group, its presentation to the class on one of the popular films, and its queer theological response to the film. Each group was required to include in its presentation a consideration on how the film might be studied in a parish or other context of ministry. Two of the groups wrote papers that included questionnaires for parishioners and workshop proposals. The third group created a PowerPoint presentation for use in local congregations. I did not attempt to build into the course a plan for follow-up to see if and how the projects actually were put into use in communities beyond the course.

Several recurrent theological themes were explored through the group presentations and class discussions:

Creative/Sacred Power: We can re-image power as neither above nor beneath us but rather as our creative, liberating energy in relation to life, others, world, and God (who is this Power).

Identity: We can work to destabilize identities. We can resist naturalizing identities—gender, sexual, other identities—as fixed and unchanging. We can seek ways of speaking these truths without dismissing or trivializing the queer identities that so many sisters and brothers have discovered and are naming for the first, second, or third time.

Transgression: We can welcome the opportunity to be "transgressive" theologians, seeking ways to respectfully and mutually cross boundaries, that is, to connect in a struggle for right mutual relation—boundaries not only of gender, culture, race, religion, age, but also of species, for example, in efforts on behalf of environmental justice and animal rights.

Marginalization: We can "prefer"—choose—the margins over the centers of our collective life in the world (the "centers" being where power-over, or power-as-domination, is revered and exercised). We can come to realize that liberation theologians always work on the margins, either by history, by choice, or both.

Performance: We can be "performative" theologians—artistic, ritualistic, musical, silent, spacious, moving about, delighting in God—and respectfully, prayerfully play with images of God, sex, ourselves, one another, and the world.

Courage: We can cultivate shared capacities for risk-taking in a world and church that value stability (which we can rattle a bit) and conformity (which we can undercut simply by being ourselves).

Perspective as good humor: As queer Christians, we can help one another learn to take ourselves lightly in a church that often takes itself (its doctrines and identity) far too seriously—and we can take ourselves (or others) seriously in contexts in which we (or they) are being trivialized or otherwise hurt.

Perspective as ability to be critical (and criticized): As Christians, we can be critical of "queerness" wherever it does not do justice or love mercy; and as queer folk, we can be critical of Christians whose visions of God, Christ, and church are narrow and exclusive.

Challenging pedagogical issues

Over the years, as the teaching of sexuality in progressive seminaries has evolved, some pedagogical issues have remained more or less constant. They should be mentioned here, because each continues to demand the serious attention of those of us who teach in this area. I will comment briefly on three such issues:

1. the challenge of engaging thoughtfully and compassionately the special vulnerability—openness to growth and change, but also to fear and hurt—of many students who take courses on sexuality;

2. in the context of oppressive structures such as racism, sexism, and heterosexism, the challenge of teaching members of oppressed and oppressor groups in the same class; and

3. the pastoral challenge created by the disjuncture between queer theology and most of the churches' teachings on sexuality.

Student vulnerability. One of the most hopeful and delightful aspects of teaching sex in seminary is that it tends to attract those who are ready to grow and change as students of God and the world, men and women who are vulnerable—open—to Sacred Power and to their sisters and brothers, those who bring open minds and big hearts to bear on their experiences and those of others. Most students who elect to take a course in sexual or queer theology are ready for the course. In order to help make sure that students are ready, I often set certain prerequisites for the "sex courses." For example, I require students to have studied feminist or liberation theologies, so that they at least will not be shocked by concepts that often bump against religious assumptions that they have grown up with and may, in ways, still cherish.[16] Beyond prerequisites, if the course is going to be academically advanced or a small seminar, with twelve or fewer participants, I usually ask that folks "apply" for the course by writing a brief paper on why they want to take it and to indicate their readiness for it. (In recent years, Episcopal Divinity School has made available to students the syllabi for all upcoming courses prior to registration, which is helpful to those who are trying to decide if they want to take a particular course.) If, after reading the application, I have any question about the student's academic or emotional readiness, I will ask him or her to meet with me or, if this is impossible for some reason, to talk with me by phone.

Still, there are times, every several years, when someone enrolls in the course who, it turns out, ought not to be there. These students find it upsetting and sometimes their behavior is disruptive and upsetting to others. In such cases, it's my responsibility to encourage the student to get help. Seminaries have pastoral staff who can consult with faculty members and students and make referrals. Over three decades of teaching these courses at EDS to 250–300 students, there have been maybe a half dozen times when I've suggested to emotionally stressed students that they drop the course. In another three or four cases, I've had to ask disruptive students to drop the course. Once the administration of the seminary had to post a guard outside the door to make sure the student did not return.

Oppressed and oppressor together. Another splendid teaching resource is the presence in most of these courses of members of both oppressed and oppressor groups: gay men, lesbians, bisexual and heterosexual folks; younger and older men, women, and transgender students of different racial, cultural, class, and religious heritages. The more diversity among social locations and identities, the richer the educational experience *if the professor and students are able to use the tensions that inhere in differences as creative educational resources.* How is this done? The teacher can make clear, at the outset, that the diversity in the class is, in fact, a resource for learning if, and only if, the students are able to honestly acknowledge and explore their differences and the tensions they will certainly experience among themselves. The teacher must also stay alert to what is happening—in the silences as well as in what is spoken, to those absent as well as those present — and be willing to put a goodly amount of energy and time into honoring and respecting not only the differences in social power represented by the students but also the personal journey that each student is on. All students need to experience the course as a place in which they are honestly welcome, provided they show their respect for others by a willingness to listen and learn from others, especially those whose lives are most challenging to them.

Seminary and church. It is simply a fact: the progressive seminaries in the United States and Canada are at least two or three decades ahead of the Christian churches — including most parishes of even the most liberal Protestant denominations. So what does this mean for teaching sex in seminary? It means that we have to learn and teach folks to be bicultural — to learn and respect two distinct, often oppositional "cultures." On the one hand, the church historically is conservative on matters of sex and gender as well as its relation to issues of power and authority. This has not changed, and the better part of wisdom is not to expect it to move far or fast. On the other hand, we who are "queer and here" in the church are becoming increasingly radical not only on matters of gender and sex, but also in relation to social power and claiming the authority of our own experience, not as isolated individuals but as members of a number of sometimes overlapping communities. The church may be one such community, but so too are our queer networks, our political allies, our colleagues and comrades, and our circles of friends. With this in mind, we who teach and we who learn in seminaries — especially if we are involved in queer studies — have to hold simultaneously our commitments to our church "cultures" and our equally strong commitments to other arenas of our lives and work, our faith and values.

Queer theology invites Christian students to learn a new language of life without abandoning the old one. For all of us, teachers and students, this bicultural adventure, which often feels like juggling, is an opportunity to cultivate a high tolerance for ambiguity and tension as well as the spiritual gift of what Dorothee Soelle has named a "revolutionary patience."[17]

There is one other critical pedagogical issue for queer theology, which is also profoundly spiritual, and that is the matter of time. My students, colleagues, other friends, and I increasingly feel that we do not have enough time — to read, think, or even feel deeply in a sustained way. The most obvious villain is the technology that has given us countless gadgets to "help" us organize our lives but which, in fact, is giving us more things to do and to worry about not doing. We are living more fragmented and distracted lives today than ten years ago. What does this have to do with teaching sex in seminary? I believe it has everything to do with teaching sexual and queer theologies, because these theologies can help us discover and transform the real villain, which is not high technology, but rather the advanced capitalist deification of achievement and profit above human and creaturely connectedness, above our struggles for more deeply mutual relation, above the simple pleasures we are here on this planet to share: health, food, sleep, play, animal and human friendship, music and dance and other adventures in creativity, work we can enjoy, worship with integrity, prayer and meditation, the joys of real intimacy, the passion of good sex. The connectedness, the pleasures, the prayer, the play, and the struggle for the justice-love that threatens to transform the world: this is what teaching sex in seminary is all about.

Notes

1. Carter Heyward, *Touching Our Strength: The Erotic as Power and the Love of God* (San Francisco: Harper & Row, 1989), 1.

2. Mary Daly, *The Church and the Second Sex* (New York: Harper & Row, 1968). See also *Beyond God the Father: Toward a Philosophy of Women's Liberation* (Boston: Beacon, 1973), which has become a classic in the recent history of women's liberation and all matters of sex and gender.

3. Rosemary Radford Ruether, *New Woman, New Earth: Sexist Ideologies and Human Liberation* (New York: Seabury, 1974), and Letty M. Russell, *Human Liberation in a Feminist Perspective* (Philadelphia: Westminster, 1974). These were among the early books linking Christian teachings on sex and gender with human oppression and, thus, with the struggle for liberation.

4. Kate Millett, *Sexual Politics* (Garden City, N.Y.: Doubleday, 1970).

5. It has been my experience, as an Episcopal priest and seminary teacher, that significant liturgical change is far more difficult to "spark" than theological transformation in other arenas (classes, film, writing, poetry, and general table conversation). It's noteworthy, for example, how often folks will insist that the "gender of God" is not an issue for them — but will protest any attempt to include references to God as "Mother" in Christian worship. A splendid resource in the area of liturgy and feminist theology is Marjorie Procter-Smith's *Praying with Our Eyes Open: Engendering Feminist Liturgical Prayer* (Nashville: Abingdon, 1995). See also the liturgical resources at the end of my 1999 book, *Saving Jesus from*

Those Who Are Right: Rethinking What It Means to Be Christian (Minneapolis: Fortress, 1999).

6. "Sex" is a term used both for gender-designation ("It's a girl!") and for sexual activity ("having sex"). In common culturally shaped usage, "sex" as a term is either synonymous with, or connected to, "sexuality," which is usually a more formal reference to gender-related identity, gender-based activity, and/or gender-shaped feelings and behavior. For a brief piece on the control of sexuality in Christian history, see Carol S. Robb's essay on "sexuality" in the *Dictionary of Feminist Theologies,* ed. Letty M. Russell and J. Shannon Clarkson (Louisville: Westminster John Knox, 1996), 258–59.

7. For example, Millett's *Sexual Politics;* also Gerda Lerner, ed. *Black Women in White America; A Documentary History* (New York: Pantheon, 1972); Barbara Ehrenreich and Deirdre English, *For Her Own Good: 150 Years of the Experts' Advice to Women* (Garden City, N.Y.: Anchor/Doubleday, 1978); Del Martin and Phyllis Lyon, *Lesbian/Woman* (New York: Bantam, 1972); Susan Brownmiller, *Against Our Will: Men, Women, and Rape* (New York: Bantam, 1975); Shulamith Firestone, *The Dialectic of Sex: The Case for Feminist Revolution,* rev. ed. (New York: Bantam, 1971); Adrienne Rich, *On Lies, Secrets, and Silence: Selected Prose: 1966–1978* (New York: W. W. Norton, 1979); and Linda Gordon, *Woman's Body, Woman's Right: A Social History of Birth Control in America* (New York: Viking/Pilgrim, 1975). The list goes on and expands through the 1980s and into the twenty-first century, becoming more culturally diverse as it grows.

8. See Beverly Wildung Harrison's essay "Misogyny and Homophobia," in which she explores the connections between hatred of women and fear of same-sex love, in *Making the Connections: Essays in Feminist Social Ethics,* ed. Carole S. Robb (Boston: Beacon, 1985).

9. In the context of Christian community, I'm fond of pointing out that Jesus' disciples really *must* be "wise as serpents and innocent as doves" — pragmatist and idealist, strategist and visionary, each an important dimension of our Christian identities. The best way to help incarnate our visions of justice and compassion for all is to be smart and strategic in our struggle on behalf of the realm of God.

10. See my "coming out" pieces: "Theological Explorations of Homosexuality," *The Witness,* June 1979, and "Coming Out: Journey without Maps," *Christianity and Crisis,* June 11, 1979. These are published in my book *Our Passion for Justice: Images of Power, Sexuality, and Liberation* (Cleveland: Pilgrim, 1984).

11. Troy Perry, *The Lord Is My Shepherd and He Knows I'm Gay* (Los Angeles: Nash, 1972). This was one of the first published books written by an openly gay or lesbian Christian. See also John J. McNeill, *The Church and the Homosexual* (Boston: Beacon, 1976, 1993).

12. For a definitive feminist example of the "social constructionist" position as it was taking shape in the late 1970s and throughout the 1980s, see Adrienne Rich, "Compulsory Heterosexuality and Lesbian Existence," in *Powers of Desire: The Politics of Sexuality,* ed. Ann Snitow, Christine Stansell, and Sharon Thompson (New York: Monthly Review, 1983), 177–205. Other variations of constructionist understandings of sexuality in the 1970s and 1980s can be found in works of such secular social theorists as Michel Foucault, Jeffrey Weeks, and Gayle Rubin. In theological literature, see Beverly W. Harrison's *Making the Connections;*

Carter Heyward, *Touching Our Strength: The Erotic as Power and the Love of God* (San Francisco: Harper & Row, 1989); Anne Bathurst Gilson, *Eros Breaking Free: Interpreting Sexual Theo-Ethics* (Cleveland: Pilgrim, 1995); Marvin M. Ellison, *Erotic Justice: A Liberating Ethic of Sexuality* (Louisville: Westminster John Knox, 1996); and James B. Nelson and Sandra P. Longfellow, eds., *Sexuality and the Sacred: Sources for Theological Reflection* (Louisville: Westminster John Knox, 1994). A compelling presentation of the social construction of sexuality is Kelly Brown Douglas's *Sexuality and the Black Church* (Maryknoll, N.Y.: Orbis, 1999).

13. Writing in 1988, Nelson notes "a shift from 'theologies of sexuality' to 'sexual theologies.'" He continues: "Before the past two decades, the vast preponderance of Christian writers on sexuality assumed that the question before them was simply this: What does Christianity (the Bible, the tradition, ecclesiastical authority) say about sexuality? It was a one-directional question, moving from religious faith to sexual experience. Now we are also asking: What does our experience of human sexuality say about our perceptions of faith — our experience of God, our interpretations of Scripture and tradition, our ways of living out the gospel?" *The Intimate Connection: Male Sexuality, Masculine Spirituality* (Philadelphia: Westminster, 1988), 115.

14. Michel Foucault, *The History of Sexuality* (New York: Pantheon, 1978). See also Gayle Rubin, "Thinking Sex: Notes for a Radical Theory of the Politics of Sexuality," in *Pleasure and Danger: Exploring Female Sexuality,* ed. Carole S. Vance (Boston: Routledge & Kegan Paul, 1984), 267–319.

15. Judith Butler, "Sexual Inversions," in *Discourses of Sexuality: From Aristotle to AIDS,* ed. Donna Stanton (Ann Arbor: University of Michigan Press, 1992), 544–61, and "Against Proper Objects," in *Feminism Meets Queer Theory,* ed. Elizabeth Weed and Naomi Schor (Bloomington: Indiana University Press, 1997), 1–30.

16. For example, many folks are deeply attached, more than they often realize, to gendered images of God as masculine/male. Queer theology involves theological gender-bending, playing and praying with God in ways that most Christian students will not be familiar with, unless they know some feminist, womanist, other women-centered, and liberationist theologies. It can be very disorienting for a student deeply attached to a particular image of God to feel that this image is being undone or trivialized while in fact the image is only being relativized — placed in relation to many other images and experiences of the Sacred.

17. Dorothee Soelle, *Revolutionary Patience,* trans. Rita and Robert Kimber (Maryknoll, N.Y.: Orbis, 1974).

Part Two

Sexualities

5

Black Body/White Soul

The Unsettling Intersection
of Race, Sexuality, and Christianity

Kelly Brown Douglas

> Within Western Christianity... there is an influential tradition
> of radical asceticism, calling for the denial of bodily pleasure
> and expressing fear of sex.... Body-alienation and deep suspi-
> cion of eros and passion are pervasive aspects of our religious
> heritage.[1]

> It is very important to remember what it means to be born in
> a Protestant Puritan country, with all the taboos placed on the
> flesh, and have at the same time in this country such a vivid ex-
> ample of a decent pagan imagination and the sexual liberty
> with which white people invest Negroes — and then penalize
> them for.... It's a guilt about flesh. In this country the Negro
> pays for that guilt which white people have about flesh.[2]

The disturbing tradition forged by Christianity's alliance with Pla-
tonic/Neoplatonic dualism is well documented. When the early
church fathers accepted the Hellenistic divide between the perfect
immaterial world and the flawed material world, they provided the
theological foundation for centuries of church sanctioned tyranny.
This platonized Christianity suggested an antagonistic relationship
between the perfect soul (a reflection of the immaterial world)
and the imperfect body (a reflection of the material world).[3] The
soul was divinized while the body was demonized. The body was
condemned as a source of sin. Bodily sin was soon equated with
sexual pleasure. A "sacred" disdain for the sexual body pervaded

the Christian theological tradition and, thus, oftentimes allowed the church to tolerate a violent disregard for particular human bodies and a vilification of entire peoples.

Inasmuch as certain people are sexualized, and inasmuch as the soul and not the body is revered, then to enslave, attack, or oppress particular human bodies becomes theologically justifiable, if not acceptable. This is evident in an "influential" Christian tradition that has variously sanctioned chattel slavery, patriarchal oppression, and heterosexism.

The 1991 Presbyterian report on human sexuality judiciously examines the legacy of human injustice perpetuated by Christianity's adoption of a Platonic dualism that counterposes the body and soul, and hence sexuality with spirituality. This report clarifies that dualistic paradigms inevitably generate other antagonistic dualisms that subsequently produce injustices such as sexism and heterosexism.[4] It correctly suggests that if the church is to promote gender and sexual justice, it must rethink its theology of the body/sexuality, abandon its allegiance to dualistic paradigms, and construct a new sexual ethic. This new ethic will promote "justice-love," where the "gift of sexuality and God's gracious call to be in loving, caring, mutual relations with [all] others" is nurtured and celebrated.[5]

Notwithstanding the thoroughness of the Presbyterian report, it fails to fully appreciate the magnitude of human injustice created by Christianity's embrace of Platonic dualism. This failure is due, in large measure, to the inadequate attention given to the problem of white racism. While this report certainly recognizes and denounces "white power and privilege," it does not probe, as it does with sexism and heterosexism, the complicity of dualistic Christian thinking in relation to racial injustice. By not examining the racial factor more completely, the report easily misses the subtle, though perhaps more insidious, impact of platonized Christianity on human lives. If the church is ever to espouse a sexual ethic that truly compels justice and affirms "the marginalized and oppressed" in their struggles for freedom, then the coherence between "influential" Christian theology and racist ideology cannot be overlooked. Specifically, the unsettling intersection of race, sexuality, and platonized Christianity demands attention. This essay will attempt, therefore, to examine this intersecting reality by probing the complex relationship between

Christianity and black sexuality. The prescient insights of James Baldwin will help to facilitate this inquiry.

Platonized Christianity, white culture, and black sexuality

No one has done more to expose the beleaguered state of black sexuality than literary genius and social critic James Baldwin. He is unparalleled among the first contemporary black voices to shatter the silence concerning black sexuality. In works such as the novel *Go Tell It on the Mountain* (1953) and the drama *Amen Corner* (1954), Baldwin, shaped by the rich and creative complexity of the black faith tradition, passionately reveals how cultural and religious convictions have anathematized black sexuality, thus virtually robbing black people of their very humanity.[6] Specifically, Baldwin properly indicts white culture *and* "white" Christianity for denigrating black sexuality to such a degree as to disrupt black life and well-being, if not distort black spirituality. He stridently proclaims, "The Negro pays for that guilt which white people have about the flesh."[7]

Baldwin's incisive proclamation points to the troubling, but often ignored, compatibility between white cultural assumptions and platonized Christianity. Both alienate black people from their sexuality. Even more disconcerting, the "influential tradition" of platonized Christianity provides a tacit "sacred canopy" for the white attack upon black people. The end result is that black women and men are left with the hapless choice between acceptability/holiness and freedom/wholeness. ("Wholeness" as used here broadens the notion of freedom. It suggests not simply that the black community is physically, politically, and socially free, but that all black men and women are whole, that is, healed of the emotional, psychological, and spiritual wounds inflicted by their profound oppression.)[8] A closer look at the white cultural assault upon black sexuality will help us especially to recognize Christianity's collusion with white racist presuppositions in obstructing black freedom/wholeness.

To reiterate, James Baldwin provides a rare and revealing literary view into the complex assault upon black sexuality. In *Go Tell It On the Mountain,* he effectively does this through the portrait of one black woman. He describes her this way:

When [black] men looked at Deborah they saw no further than her unlovely and violated body. In their eyes lived perpetually a lewd, uneasy wonder concerning the night she had been taken into the fields. That night had robbed her of her right to be considered a woman. No man would approach her in honor because she was a living reproach, to herself and to all black women and to all black men.... Since she could not be considered a woman, she could only be looked on as a harlot, a source of delight more bestial and mysteries more shaking than any a proper woman could provide. Lust stirred in the eyes of men when they looked at Deborah, lust that could not be endured because it was so impersonal, limiting communion to the area of her shame.... Reinforced in Deborah [was] the terrible belief... that all men were like this, their thoughts rose no higher, and they lived only to gratify on the bodies of [black] women their brutal and humiliating needs.[9]

Deborah was raped by a group of white men. The fact of her rape indicates white cultural assumptions about black people. The consequences of her rape disclose the profound impact these assumptions have had on black people's relationships to their own black body selves. Let us first look at the implications of her actual rape.

Deborah's rape witnesses to the history of black women's violation at the hands of white men. It further suggests the white cultural view of black people that fosters such violation. In an effort to dehumanize them, white culture (that culture which protects and secretes white supremacist notions and practices) depicts black women and men as hypersexual, lustful, and passionate beings. White cultural rhetoric claims that black people are over-sexualized and governed by their libidos. Black men are considered rapacious predators — "mandigo bucks." Black women are regarded as promiscuous seductresses — "Jezebels." To depict black men as sexual predators provided a justification for lynching, castration, and other crimes committed against their bodies. To label black women Jezebels allowed white men to rape them with impunity.

In the illogic of white culture, white men were considered the victims of black women's seductive nature. Thus, black women were left to navigate the danger of being cast as Jezebels. Unfortunately, the fictional Deborah, like so many actual black women, was not able to avoid the sexual danger associated with being black and female. She subsequently suffered the debilitating stigma of white culture's sexualized violence. She felt guilty about the rape. She became ashamed of her own body. She became detached from her female sexuality. Eventually, she was able to see herself only through the prism of white culture and as a sexual object. This self-image subsequently impacted her relationships with black men. She viewed them as lustful predators—unwittingly agreeing with white culture's sexualized image of the black male. At the same time, black men looked upon Deborah as a harlot—again a view consistent with that of white culture. The end result was that Deborah was left with a distorted self-image and without an intimate loving relationship.

Essentially, through an event in the life of one female character, Baldwin concisely discloses the complex white cultural assault on black sexuality. As a part of its dehumanizing efforts, white culture demeans black women and men by over-sexualizing them, and then subsequently penalizes them on the basis of this sexualized caricature. The impact of this white cultural onslaught on black life is multidimensional, as seen in Deborah's life and about which more will be said later. For now, it is important to note the imprint upon black spiritual life. It is in looking at this that we can discern how Christianity has conspired with white culture in compromising black freedom/wholeness. Again, it is through a description of Baldwin's character Deborah that the spiritual impact is clarified:

> What better woman could be found? *She* was not like the mincing daughters of Zion! She was not to be seen prancing lewdly through the streets, eyes sleepy and mouth half-open with lust, or to be found mewing under mid-night fences, uncovered, uncovering some black boy's hanging curse! No, their married bed would be holy, and their children would continue the line of the faithful, royal line. And, fired with this, a baser fire stirred in him also, rousing a slumbering fear, and he remembered...that Paul had written: "It is better to marry than to burn."[10]

This description of Deborah represents the thoughts of a black preacher, Gabriel, as he contemplates the merits of marrying her.

In his mind, Deborah is redeemed from the disgrace of rape because she has remained sexually inactive since that attack. She is
pure as long as she denies her sexual impulses. A sexually repressed
Deborah is, thus, suitable for marriage. Gabriel further reasons that
marriage is a redemptive act for him as well as for Deborah. Just as
it would free Deborah to *properly* express her sexuality for reproductive purposes, it would allow him to act on his sexual urgings without
jeopardizing his salvation.

Gabriel's reflections clearly suggest a platonized Christian influence, which Baldwin describes as "Protestant Puritanism." To repeat,
within this tradition sexuality is seen as evil. "Sexuality and spirituality are viewed as opposites. . . . Persons can be either sexual or
spiritual, but not both in any meaningful, integrated way."[11] For
Gabriel, the way to integrate sexuality and salvation was within
the bounds of marriage, a view again consistent with Protestant
Puritanism. Thus, Gabriel did resolve to marry Deborah, presum-
ably saving himself even as he redeemed her. Ironically, in the end,
Gabriel's marriage to Deborah would prove destructive for both of
them as it denied Gabriel sexual pleasure.

Throughout Baldwin's novel, his characters wage war against
their sexuality in an effort to secure their salvation. They struggle
with the temptations of masturbation, intimate pleasure, adolescent desire, and homoerotic passions. They believe that giving in to
their sexual desires, for purposes other than procreation within wed-
lock, might please their body but jeopardize their very soul. Baldwin
goes on, however, to uncover a tragic truth surrounding this kind of
black church spirituality: the "price for the 'redeeming' ticket" is far
too costly. He dramatically points out that to safeguard one's salvation by denying one's sexuality is to forfeit personal and intimate
relationships, and hence happiness and well-being. He explicitly
shows this in a dialogue between two characters in his play, *Amen
Corner:*

> LUKE: Margaret, once you told me you loved me and then you
> jumped up and ran off from me like you couldn't stand the smell
> of me. What you think *that* done to my soul?
>
> MARGARET: I had to go. The Lord told me to go. We'd been living
> like — like two animals, like children, never thought of nothing

but their own pleasure. In my heart, I always knew we couldn't go on like that—we was too happy. . . . We hadn't never thought of nothing but ourselves. We hadn't never thought on God![12]

What Baldwin captures in the struggles of his fictional characters, as illustrated by this dialogue, is in fact a prominent belief within a significant part of the black faith tradition, the part most influenced by "Protestant Puritan" (i.e., evangelical) theology. It is the belief that things of the "flesh" are evil, antithetical to God and barriers to one's salvation. While such a belief has certainly served a positive function by promoting a certain set of moral values, family stability, self-regard, and perhaps saving black lives,[13] in highlighting this aspect of black faith (an aspect that Baldwin had to contend with in his growing up), Baldwin poignantly discloses what can happen when a platonized Christian tradition shapes black life—a life already put upon by sexualized racist ideology. In effect, platonized Christianity conspires with white culture to disable black health and well-being, that is, wholeness. Let us examine more closely this conspiratorial relationship.

White culture asserts that blackness is synonymous with unrestrained sexuality. Platonized Christianity argues that sexuality is a cauldron of evil and opposes the human connection to God. By arguing the "evilness" of sexuality, Christianity implicitly provides a theological justification for any claims that a people governed by sexual desires are innately evil. Christianity, especially when it does not challenge the sexualized depictions, in effect vindicates white culture's vilification of black people. Platonized Christianity and white culture thus become de facto allies in demonizing an entire race of people.

What we too often find in relation to black church people is, in fact, a twofold sexualized condemnation of their humanity. In this regard, the interaction between white culture and "platonized" Christianity is almost lethal. What is at stake is not simply the sinfulness of the body, but also the vileness of blackness. This double burden of sin fundamentally forces black men and women to develop an intransigent attitude toward sexuality, all in an effort to at least sever the tie between it and their blackness. Practically speaking, black peoples' hope for social acceptance and salvation is contingent on one pivotal requirement: a radical rejection/denial of sexuality. Such a rejection potentially disproves white characterizations and promises divine affirmation. With one radical act of sexual denial, black people can affirm their humanity and redeem their soul. Again, it should also not be forgotten that such a sexual denial has surely saved black lives. Given the continuous history of black men being attacked, maimed, and executed because of presumed sexual activity, sexual denial becomes a viable survival tactic.

This sexual rejection/denial is most typically manifest in a refusal to discuss or acknowledge matters of sexuality. Sexuality is treated as a taboo issue within the black church community. In many black churches influenced by this view of sexuality, congregation members are restrained from dressing in certain ways or engaging in particular activities (i.e., dancing, attending movies) that might ignite sexual energy. As philosopher Cornel West has prophetically observed about the black church and other black institutions:

> These grand yet flawed black institutions refused to engage one fundamental issue: *black sexuality.* Instead, they ran from it like the plague. And they obsessively condemned those places where black sexuality was flaunted: the streets, the clubs, and the dance-halls.[14]

The consequences of this avoiding silence, its positive value notwithstanding, have perhaps been more deadly than "saving," particularly in more recent history.[15] For instance, it has contributed to the black church community's slow response to the HIV/AIDS crisis even though this crisis has had a particularly devastating impact upon black life.

Another form of sexual rejection/denial has been the black community's tendency to be hypercritical in regard to behaviors considered sexually atypical or abnormal. Such sexual scrupulousness attempts to protect black people from the charge of being sexually deviant. For example, in a heterosexist society where nonheterosexual expressions are considered abnormal, the black church community is typically uncompromising in its disapproval of any form of homoeroticism. Some have asserted that homosexuality itself is incompatible with black life.[16] Some black scholars have gone so far as to pronounce homosexuality a "white thing," based on the erroneous claim that it was not a part of black people's African heritage, but was introduced by Europeans.[17] Baldwin acknowledges the strident homophobic sentiment of the black church in *Go Tell It on the Mountain* through the main protagonist's struggles with his own sexual identity.[18]

What is important to note, overall, is that black women and men are oftentimes burdened by *both* white incriminations and Christian judgments in regard to their sexuality. The end result is a radical response of sexual denial that commonly fosters sexual silence and sexual discrimination, as well as unhealthy self-regard and strained intimate relationships. These problematics are profound, but there can be a more subtle and harmful result of Christianity's collusion with white culture.

The mutuality of platonized Christianity and white culture makes black people vulnerable to another profoundly disturbing rejection: a rejection of their very black selves. This occurs in at least two ways. First and most obviously, by rejecting their sexuality they are in effect rejecting that which allows them to love themselves and love others like them. They are rejecting that which compels men and women to be in "communion and community" with themselves and others. Baldwin points to this disquieting consequence of sexual denial through the life of the aforementioned character Gabriel. Gabriel's radical denial/rejection of his own sexuality effectively alienates him from his family and community.

The second form of rejection nurtured by the collusion of Christianity and white culture is more penetrating but perhaps more difficult to discern. It occurs through attempts to escape the sexualized stereotype associated with being black. Such attempts can result in not simply a rejection of sexuality, but an unwitting rejection of one's blackness. Essentially, black men and women actually acquiesce to the white depiction of blackness. Specifically, they try to separate themselves from that depiction by adopting an ascetic sexuality. This adoption results in at least two things. First, it sets them apart from those black people who perhaps foster the sexual stereotype by finding pleasure in non-procreative sex. Such persons become a part of the "unsaved," "the unredeemed," and "the unholy," while those who practice an ascetic sexuality are a part of the "saved." Black people basically fall prey to placing a judgment upon one another similar to that which white culture places upon them, only in this instance the defining categories are holy versus non-holy as opposed to white versus black. Once again, as noted in the Presbyterian report, one unjust dualistic paradigm generates another.

The second possible consequence of adopting an ascetic sexuality is perhaps even more unsettling. Such an adoption lends itself to black men and women, in effect, rebuffing their own black selves. That is, they try to offset their "blackness" by adopting a "white" model of sexual purity. They atone for their *black* body by maintaining a "white" soul. While not actually denying their racial identity, their holiness, not their blackness, becomes the mark of their very humanity and the gateway to their salvation. Their blackness is at best downplayed and at worst overcome. "Holiness," therefore, does not necessarily signal wholeness. Rather, it may portend a sexually racialized self-loathing. Baldwin points to this insidious dynamic in a description of his father. He said of him:

> He was defeated long before he died because, at the bottom of his heart, he really believed what white people said about him. This is one of the reasons that he became so holy.[19]

This dynamic is also reflected in an evangelical hymn that black church people often sing when confessing the redeeming power of Jesus' blood:

> Oh! precious is the flow
> that *makes me white as snow* [italics mine];
> no other fount I know
> nothing but the blood of Jesus!

Once again, Baldwin's observations are born out: black people do pay a high price for white people's views toward the "flesh, [especially black flesh]."[20] As our discussion has shown, platonized Christianity is a perfect partner to white culture. They cooperate in destroying black life and well-being in multiple ways. Left now for us to discern are the theological implications of this disastrous collaboration as we move toward a sexual ethic of justice.[21]

Toward a new sexual ethic

An examination of platonized Christianity in relation to black sexuality clarifies some significant theological problematics concerning Christianity's adoption of a dualistic paradigm that condemns sexuality. Fundamentally, this adoption makes Christianity's collusion with unjust power almost inevitable. As was the case with patriarchalism and heterosexism, Christianity's cooperation with white culture is nothing less than cooperation with unjust power. The question becomes, why does a platonized Christianity invariably result in an unholy alliance with power? It is here that the late French philosopher Michel Foucault is helpful.

"How is it that in a society like ours," Foucault asks, "sexuality is not simply a means of reproducing the species, the family, and the individual? Not simply a means to obtain pleasure and enjoyment? How has sexuality come to be considered the privileged place where our deepest 'truth' is read and expressed?"[22] Foucault argues that this is so because sexuality is integral to power. It is the axis where the human body and reproduction come together. Power can be exerted over a people through careful regulation of their bodies, their perceptions of their bodies, and their reproductive capacities.

Foucault further notes the importance of sexuality to maintaining power, especially inequitable power. He argues that sexuality is a mechanism by which distinctions can be made between classes and groups of people. To question or impugn the sexuality of another bolsters one's claims to superiority as it suggests another group's inferiority. An attack upon a people's sexuality becomes important, then, because sexuality involves one's humanity. Therefore, to malign a people's sexuality is to call into question their very humanity and thus to challenge their capacity to exist without legal and extralegal if not ecclesiastical restraints.

If we understand the role of sexuality in maintaining power, it becomes clear how Christianity's demonization of sexuality predictably leads to its collaboration with unjust power. To reemphasize a point made earlier, it provides sacred justification for the vilification and subjugation of a sexualized people. The Presbyterian report is thus right to call for a rejection of such dualisms, particularly as they lead to this unholy alliance with unjust power.

The report appropriately argues that whenever Christian churches find themselves siding with power, they are opposing the movement of God in history. It makes clear that God's revelation in Jesus discloses God's unambiguous solidarity with the powerless and oppressed in human history. As liberation theologian Gustavo Gutiérrez suggests, there is a divine "preferential option for the poor."[23] Therefore, whenever the church implicitly or explicitly conspires with power, it alienates itself from God.

A just sexual ethic is compelled to maintain God's preferential option for the powerless, while it simultaneously denounces the church's relationship with unjust power. It must also unambiguously reject any dualistic paradigms that harbor such a relationship. There is still, however, an even more basic reason for rejecting Christianity's embrace of any dualistic schema, and that is the Christian confession that God is triune.

Christianity's trinitarian doctrine not only points to something very crucial about the nature of God, but it also exposes platonized Christianity as heretical. To claim that God is trinitarian is to profess a God that is internally and eternally relational. Such a God is one that does a "perfect dance" with God's self, as implied by the Greek word *perichoresis,* used by the Cappodocians during the fourth-century debates to describe God's trinitarian nature. As theologian Christopher Morse explains, "The fullness of God's being...is to be thought of as dancing equally throughout the three inseparable distinctive ways that the one God is God."[24] God's perfect dance is one where the three aspects of God as creator, redeemer, and sustainer exist or dance in a relationship of mutuality and reciprocity. It is this trinitarian view of relationship that provides the foundation for the way human beings are called to relate to one another, that is, in nonhierarchical relationships of mutuality and reciprocity. The trinitarian doctrine thus precludes at least two things: Christianity's embrace of any viewpoint that opposes or diminishes the sanctity of loving, intimate human relationships, and Christianity's adoption of dualistic thinking. Such thinking unquestionably violates trinitarian ways of knowing and living. A just sexual ethic is one that renounces any form of platonized Christianity not simply because of its susceptibleness to unjust power, but chiefly because it contradicts the belief in a triune God. Dualistic perspectives are inevitably antagonistic and thus are incompatible with trinitarian thought that is inherently complementary.

It should always, if not first and foremost, be noted that dualistic perspectives that negate the sanctity of the body are incompatible with an incarnational faith. Jesus Christ, the incarnate one, suggests the inherent contradiction between Christianity and any form of dualism that places the soul and body in an innately antagonistic relationship. The message of God's embodiment in Jesus is unambiguous: the human body is not evil, but rather an instrumentality for divine presence. It is the medium by which God is made "real" to humanity, through which God interacts in human history. To accept that Jesus, the first-century Jew from Nazareth, is God incarnate is to recognize that the human body is not an impediment to divinity, and thus the soul and body should not be set against one another. The body, in this regard, is not the enemy of the soul but rather the home of the soul making possible the human connection to God. In view of Christianity's central confession, that Jesus is God incarnate, platonized forms of Christianity are exposed not simply as heretical but as anti-Christ.

An exploration of platonized Christianity from the perspective of race makes something else perfectly clear: white culture is a sin. It is evil as it secretes racism *and* most especially as it vilifies black sexuality in particular and nonwhite sexuality in general.[25] The manipulation and denigration of nonwhite sexuality is characteristic of white culture. This is a culture that exists primarily as it is contrasted with that which is nonwhite. It is maintained by white racist ideology while at the same time it secretes this ideology. Critical to white culture is its ability to avow white superiority by asserting—seemingly "by any means necessary"—the inferiority of nonwhite peoples (be they Hispanic, Native American, Asian American, or African American). As Foucault firmly argues, there is no better way to impugn the character and humanity of a people than by maligning their sexuality. In this regard, a just sexual ethic is required to be as unrelenting in its opposition to white culture as it is in its stance toward patriarchal and heterosexist culture. This ethic is obligated to identify the ways in which white culture defiles the sexuality of nonwhite peoples and to clarify the role of platonized Christianity in this defilement. Essentially, a just sexual ethic cannot avoid condemning white culture for demonizing that which it holds as sacred: human sexuality.

Finally, a just sexual ethic must call the church to account for its complicity in protecting and perpetuating white culture. Only when the church names and takes responsibility for its collusion with white cultural oppression will it be able to repent and change its way of acting. Until such time, it will continue to perpetuate a tradition of tyranny, anchored in a platonized Christianity that serves only to destroy black lives. If the church is ever to be a true advocate for the marginalized and oppressed, then it cannot continue to ignore the unsettling intersection between race, sexuality, and Christianity.

In the end, James Baldwin's searing observations provide a profound theological challenge. It is in understanding how the "Negro carries the burden of white guilt about the flesh" that we can begin to appreciate the complex problematics of a platonized Christianity. Ultimately, a just sexual ethic is compelled to affirm that dualistic perspectives on the world and humanity invariably lead to sinful structures and unjust human relationships and thus are antithetical to Christian faith.

Notes

1. *Presbyterians and Human Sexuality 1991* (Louisville: Presbyterian Church [U.S.A.], 1991), 1.

2. "Studs Terkel Interview 1961," in *Conversations with James Baldwin,* ed. Fred L. Standley and Louis H. Pratt (Jackson: University of Mississippi Press, 1989), 8–9.

3. I have adopted the term "platonized Christianity" to suggest that part of the Christian theological tradition is prominently influenced by Platonic dualistic thinking and paradigms.

4. The Presbyterian report identifies two other problematic dualisms, a gender dualism between men and women and a dualism between freedom and accountability. For further discussion of these dualisms, see *Presbyterians and Human Sexuality 1991,* 14–16.

5. Ibid., 29.

6. It should be noted that this essay affirms the Presbyterian report's understanding of human sexuality as a "gift from God," which compels our relationships and connections to ourselves, others, and God.

7. "Studs Terkel interview, 1961," 9.

8. I have adopted the term "wholeness" from Alice Walker's definition of a womanist as one who is "committed to the survival and wholeness of entire

peoples." For this definition, see Alice Walker, *In Search of Our Mothers' Gardens* (New York: Harcourt Brace Jovanovich, 1983), xi.

9. James Baldwin, *Go Tell It on the Mountain* (New York: Modern Library edition, 1995; original copyright 1952), 86–87.

10. Ibid., 135.

11. *Presbyterians and Human Sexuality 1991,* 1.

12. James Baldwin, *The Amen Corner* (New York: First Vintage International Books, 1998; original copyright by Dial Press, 1968), 57–58.

13. Again, it must be noted that black people, especially black men, were lynched because of their sexuality.

14. Cornel West, *Race Matters* (Boston: Beacon, 1993), 86.

15. For an in-depth discussion, see Kelly Brown Douglas, *Sexuality and the Black Church* (Maryknoll, N.Y.: Orbis, 1999). Note especially the introduction, where this issue is first raised.

16. See, for example, the argument made by black ethicist Cheryl Sanders in "Christian Ethics and Theology in Womanist Perspective," in *Journal of Feminist Studies in Religion 5,* no. 2 (fall 1989): 90. See also Nathan Hare and Julia Hare, *The Endangered Black Family: Coping with the Unisexualization and Coming Extinction of the Black Race* (San Francisco: Black Think Tank, 1984).

17. See *Sexuality and the Black Church,* especially chapter 4 for a discussion of "Homophobia and Heterosexism in the Black Church and Community."

18. The homoerotic struggles of *Go Tell It on the Mountain* are found in the unspoken tensions and play between the main protagonist, John, and the teenage church organist Elisha. See especially the wrestling scene and the conversation that follows in part 2, chapter 1.

19. James Baldwin, "My Dungeon Shook: Letter to My Nephew on the One Hundredth Anniversary of the Emancipation," in *The Fire Next Time* (New York: First Vintage International Books, 1993; original copyright by Dial Press, 1963), 4.

20. See the epigraph, p. 99.

21. While beyond the scope of this essay, the specific implications and challenges for the black church and community are discussed in *Sexuality and the Black Church.*

22. Quoted in James Miller, *The Passion of Michel Foucault* (New York: Doubleday, 1993), 293.

23. See, for instance, Gustavo Gutiérrez, *A Theology of Liberation* (Maryknoll, N.Y.: Orbis, 1973) and *The Power of the Poor in History* (Maryknoll, N.Y.: Orbis, 1984).

24. Christopher Morse, *Not Every Spirit: A Dogmatics of Christian Disbelief* (Valley Forge, Pa.: Trinity Press International, 1994), 131.

25. It should be noted that given the significance to white economic power of black people as initially free labor and later cheap labor, coupled with the stark contrast in color and physiognomy between black and white people, white culture has paid inordinate attention to black sexuality. For more on this see *Sexuality and the Black Church.*

6

Bisexuality

Variations on a Theme

Susan Halcomb Craig

In the field of music composition, one popular form is that of a theme with variations. An initial theme is stated that is generally strong and simple, moderate in tempo, and brief. This theme is followed by any number of variations which, while maintaining the harmonic and melodic structure of the original, may alter rhythm, tonality, texture or embellishment in a myriad of exciting and colorful ways.[1]

Transposing this form analogically to the field of human sexuality, it is important to note that for much of the twentieth century, the theme of sexuality was assumed to be *heterosexuality,* with homosexuality presenting its variations in the lives of lesbian women and gay men. Almost certainly this was the view of members of majority faith traditions in the United States.

One of the most significant ways in which the Presbyterian study "Keeping Body and Soul Together" broke new ground was that it moved heterosexuality from this dominant position and instead put *human sexuality* in the place of undergirding theme. The study then named heterosexuality as one variation on the theme of human sexuality, intrinsically valued no more and no less than the same-sex variations of gay men and lesbians. In doing so, battle lines were drawn for denominational struggles continuing into the present.

What a difference this change of theme made for those seeking sexual and gender justice, not only in society but also in religious and spiritual domains. Perhaps the Presbyterian report pushed as far as it could for its time, referring to bisexuality here and there without developing its distinctiveness within the theme of human sexuality. Sadly, therefore, a minority of readers, among them bisexual people of faith, read the report with some disappointment, aware that our variations had yet to be fully included. It was time for those of us claiming bisexuality — as a distinct sexual orientation in the larger constellation of queer variations on a theme — to begin composing for ourselves.[2]

In the early 1990s the secular press was already publishing books and articles on the topic of bisexuality.[3] In the religious field, the magazine *Open Hands* of the Reconciling Congregation Program of inclusive churches within the United Methodist Church dedicated its fall 1991 issue to "Bisexuality: Perceptions and Realities."[4] But the topic of bisexuality was too hot for mainstream presses of mainstream denominations. John Carey, chair of the Presbyterian Special Committee on Human Sexuality, writing in *Christianity and Crisis* in August 1991, listed five areas difficult to discuss in "middle-class religious communities," and then four more "virtually *impossible* for the church to tackle."[5] Bisexuality was the first on his "impossible" list.

It took twenty-five years, or until 1995, for the word "bisexual" to appear on the official T-shirts of the San Francisco Pride March. Now just a few years later, it is a pleasure to be included in the full composition. Let the music begin!

Double variations: exploring bisexuality

There is no one way of being bisexual. Bisexuals are women and men who differ in the same ways that people of all orientations do. We are people of many faiths and no faith, and we claim no common moral code. Our sexual orientation is not a unifier of our experience. So instead, we say that within bisexuality lie further variations. In musical terms, variations within a variation of this sort are named double variations.

Nevertheless, there exist a few summary definitions that are by now generally accepted.[6] Bisexuality is located on the continuum of sexual orientations linking exclusive homosexuality at one pole to exclusive heterosexuality at the other. Whether the space between these poles is linear or is fluid and dynamic, a range of bisexualities lie all along the continuum. Many of us are attracted more to persons of one sex than another, and that may change over time. Most of us are attracted to persons with little regard to sex or gender and instead focus on personality traits and the quality of a developing relationship. The imperfect designation "bisexual" refers to persons who experience the capacity for sexual, emotional, or affectional attraction to those of same or different sex, whether or not the attractions are physically acted out. As with persons of all orientations, sexual orientation is a function of who we are, not of our sexual behavior. In addition, bisexual persons are those who choose the name for ourselves, as descriptive of our experience.

Recent research has moved beyond binary categories of male and female, gay and straight. Fields like gender and queer studies, queer theory, biology, psychology, and sociology open up dualistic boxes and offer wide-ranging discussion on the origins of sexual orientation and gender identity. To date there are few sure answers. How does one become bisexual? Pragmatically for now, bisexuals suppose one becomes bisexual in the same way that one becomes heterosexual, a gay man, or a lesbian. Is it a choice? We assume no more or less so than for any orientation, preference, or gender.

But one thing is sure: there are a lot of us. In its one substantive reference to bisexuality, the Presbyterian report states that "research on sexual behavior indicates that very few, if any, of us are either exclusively heterosexual or homosexual. There is a whole spectrum between the two, including the phenomenon of bisexuality."[7] It is this phenomenon that engenders fear in the hearts of many who prefer an either/or world.

Biphobia is the irrational fear or hatred of persons who are bisexual and is similar to the phenomenon *homophobia*. Biphobia is fueled by a misunderstanding of bisexuality and by the myths that arise from lack of accurate information. One such myth is that bisexual persons are promiscuous, requiring at least two differently sexed or gender-identified partners simultaneously. Another is that we are "really gay" but don't know it, either because of immature sexual orientation development or because we are "confused," or that we are gay, but are posing as heterosexual in order to "pass" in a heterosexist world. A third is that we are "really heterosexual," but are experimenting with same-sex sexual expression inauthentically. And a last is that we are half hetero- and half homosexual, a myth perhaps springing from the split or implied "twoness" in the word "bisexual."

All these myths are demeaning and inaccurate, resting as they do on a lack of knowledge and a fear of difference. Buried deeply within the hearts of their creators may be the fear of difference within themselves, as well as of that without. Regardless of what has given these myths birth, however, it is important to greet them with accurate information and to accept what bisexuals say of ourselves: that bisexuality is a true sexual orientation like heterosexuality and homosexuality, and that it is one of the family of queer variations on human sexuality's theme. Bisexual women and men may be single or in committed relationships, celibate or sexually active, just like everyone else. Bisexual people of faith also believe that a comprehensive religious ethic calls us to covenantal fidelity within our relationships.

Textural variation: bisexuality and the Bible, theology, and spiritual practice

In musical variations on a theme, one common form of variation is textural. In the textural variation, the theme may be transposed to a lower voice while new countermelodies appear in higher voices to accompany it. By altering the texture, the theme may be obscured or highlighted, muffled or accentuated. Most excitingly, it will be heard in wholly new ways.

In like manner, bisexual people of faith experience our variation to include new songs of the Sacred. Like people of every orientation, when bisexuals listen to and follow the voice of the Spirit of God, we can be forever changed. We learn from the inside out that our sexuality and spirituality are intertwined and indivisible. Let those who have ears hear! We learn that the sounds and sensations of our bodies are holy. And as we tune our ears to the frequencies God employs, meaning is revealed in the midst of our everyday lives. Bisexual persons of faith are not unique in these powerful experiences, but are part of a larger sacred harmony.

It might be said that bisexuals are left out of the Bible. Certainly there is no direct mention of us by name in Hebrew or Christian Scriptures. Others might assume that we are intended or included in the few biblical texts they interpret to condemn *homo*sexual persons. Instead, we simply take our place, sure that a divine Creator includes us all, irrespective of orientation, in the human family. We affirm that we were there when "God created humankind in [the divine] image," and when "God saw everything that [God] had made, and indeed, it was very good" (Gen. 1:27, 31). We are there today, in full membership in the colorful and complex community God created. To Jesus' repetition of God's command to "love your neighbor as yourself" (Lev. 19:18, Matt. 22:39), we assert that there are no boundaries to God's neighborhood and that, yes, bisexuals make fine neighbors! As we affirm our God-likeness and our goodness, we also claim our place in the wideness of divine sexuality.

Just as God revealed the divine name "I AM WHO I AM" to Moses (Exod. 3:14), and as John's Jesus also chose the name "I AM" (John 6:35 ff.),[8] humans of all orientations, including bisexuals, are given gifts to live into over time, each becoming more and more "who I am" in relation to God's call on God's image within. Faithfully to be who each is created to be in all fullness includes sexuality; then each of us may hope to "lead a life worthy of the calling to which [we] have been called, with all humility and gentleness, with patience, bearing with one another in love, making every effort to maintain the unity of the Spirit in the bond of peace" (Eph. 4:1–3).

When bisexual women and men search for biblical ancestors, we reflect on those whom people of other orientations also claim. This occurs because of the paucity of detail in scriptural texts, biblical authors' rudimentary understanding of human sexuality, and the possibility of movement between sexual orientations during the course of lifetimes. For example, perhaps Ruth and Naomi, one or both of them, were bisexual, loving each other deeply and also marrying in different periods of their lives.[9] Perhaps the same was true of David and Jonathan, one or both of them.[10] Since there can be no certainty, there is room for openness and reexamination.

Most interesting among our possible ancestors, however, is the figure of Jesus himself. In him we have a consistent boundary breaker, who bowed neither to conventions nor to stereotypes of his time. As an incarnation of Wisdom/*hochmah*/*Sophia*, he may be said to have embodied a female, as well as a male, persona in the body of a male.[11] We know him, emotionally, to have been tender and tough, questioning and strong, to have wept passionately and burned with the fire of just anger. Healing, he touched and was touched by women and men. Doing the work of justice, he crossed religious and political borders. In his loving, he was moved by men and by women. From biblical inference[12] or scholars' supposition,[13] Jesus might be termed bisexual in orientation, if not necessarily in behavior. Or theologically speaking, incarnate as Jesus and resurrected as the Christ, he might be said to model the fullness of all divine and human sexuality, and thereby to include bisexuality.

In addition to biblical and theological melodies in our variation, bisexual women and men listen for spiritual disciplines and practices. Since many of us cannot predict the sex or gender of those who will attract us and are drawn instead by the "rightness" and quality of developing relationships, bisexuals may experience a fine appreciation of the movement of God's Spirit in our lives, "blowing where it chooses...but [we] do not know where it comes from or where it goes" (John 3:8).[14] Releasing our expectations and presuppositions, we may encounter instead a sense of wonder, even awe as God's Spirit chooses us and others to be in intimate relationship.

The practice of letting go and giving space to a Higher Power, as twelve-step programs attest, is rich and freeing and faith-filled. Once bisexuals are relieved of the burden of ego's insistence, we can discern our path to the true nature of Love, that "love is patient; love is kind; love is not envious or boastful or arrogant or rude. It does not insist on its own way" (1 Cor. 13:4–5). Even to know our orientation as bisexual may require holding off on its naming, observing the passage of eros in our attractions, dreams, and relationships over time, in order to discern the Spirit's patterning in our lives.

Another spiritual practice we hold in common with our gay, lesbian, and straight brothers and sisters is that of believing in ourselves and trusting in God in the void of social scientific, biological, or psychological evidence defining who we are in terms of our sexuality or explaining how we got that way. Some of us will not live long enough to see conclusive data, and those who do will decide on its importance, if any. But "for now we see in a mirror, dimly" (1 Cor. 13:12) and practice being and doing, faithful as we are able to be to the love, justice, and compassion that is our calling.

A third spiritual practice for all queer friends is that of coming out—to selves, families and friends, congregations, and workplaces. This is and should be a self-affirming, deep, and sacred time when intimate and important truths are shared with others. Because not everyone can yet be open about sexual orientation, however, all of us can choose to work toward a world in which all will be safe and free to come out.

But coming out can be especially challenging, even dangerous, for bisexual women and men. Because of biphobia, our self-disclosures may be greeted by a lack of comprehension or by downright hostility, from both gay and straight communities. We often need to educate others in the process of coming out as bisexual and hope that by "putting a face" on bisexuality, biphobic reactions will gradually cease. For gay, lesbian, and bi youth planning to come out to parents and friends, many schools and universities now have mentoring and support groups that can be very helpful when adverse reactions are expected. Although youth today are generally less biphobic and homophobic than earlier generations, the spirituality of coming out is still often compromised for queer persons of faith.

It is also further complicated for bisexuals when friends assume our sexual orientation based on the sex of our partners: we are thought to be gay or lesbian if we have a same-sex partner, and straight if not. In addition, others often place bisexuals in hetero- or homosexual boxes, on the basis of stereotypes regarding lifestyle, personal characteristics, or appearance. In all these instances, open bisexuals have the responsibility to speak up and actively to come out, both because of the importance of being who "I AM," and also of naming who we are. We may hope in this way to do our part in making the world a safer place for people of every orientation to come out.

A fourth spiritual practice belongs to individual bisexuals, as well as to our communities of faith. Since all sexuality is a gift from God, all are meant to use it well in ways that benefit ourselves and others. Bisexuality may not be the gift we expected or one we know much about. It surely may come as a surprise—and an unwelcome one— to our faith communities. Bisexuals can take the responsibility to educate ourselves, to find mentors and partners to accompany us, and to engage in prayer, journaling, meditation, spiritual direction, or other spiritual practice as we come to discern the best use of God's gift of bisexuality for each one of us. This is work we do for our whole lives, as circumstances change and as we pass from stage to stage in our own maturing.

The community, and especially the faith community, also has a role to play. Congregations are meant to aid in the discernment of members of all orientations, correcting, affirming, and walking on a common path of discovery and faith. Sadly, there are few congregations in most denominations willing to accompany openly gay men and lesbian women on their journeys of faith, and fewer still to take a stand with openly bisexual members. So it falls to bisexual people of faith and to like-minded persons of all orientations to create supportive communities of friends, not unlike that surrounding Jesus in his day, who are willing to make covenant together so all of us may discern and follow God's intent for our lives.

Lastly, in every historical period all persons are encouraged to adopt the practice of justice-love through action for social and spiritual change, seeking improvement in community and world. People of every orientation may be called to lobby for federal or state legislation regarding partner benefits or the right to marriage for all people. Some may engage in "ecclesiastical disobedience" within denominations, so that all will be able to serve and be ordained to office or pastoral ministry, in accordance with God's gifts. It may fall to others to work for inclusivity with regard to language, so that publications read, "lesbian, gay, bisexual, and transgender" instead of "gay and lesbian." Any or all of us may be called to interrupt a bi- or homophobic joke or to educate a colleague. What's important is that all share in the work.

Bisexual persons of faith participate in these spiritual disciplines, realizing the interwoven nature of the web of oppressions. We join hands with those who suffer because of sex or age, race or ethnicity, ability or nationality, class or orientation in order to say, "No more closets! No more war! No more oppression!" And we do so grounded in the strong vision of One who created humanity out of love and longing for relationship, to live together as one body, one world family.

Continuous variations: the ground of bi/sexual ethics

In continuous variations, a musical phrase is played over and over again in the lowest, or bass, line of a piece, with varying melodies played in the upper voices. This bass line is often called the "ground."

In most cases, it is constant throughout a composition, and its harmonic structure remains unchanged.

A progressive religious sexual ethic is constructed in the same way, positing a single sexual ethic for all people, "one tune" as the strains of a common ground playing through all human variations. As early as 1991, "Keeping Body and Soul Together" asserted that "the Church must lift up a normative vision of sexual integrity that applies in an inclusive manner to the whole Christian community, irrespective of gender, sexual orientation, or marital status" that will "operate with a single moral standard."[15] Simple and elegant, this ethic was and is grounded in love of God, neighbor, and self and is based on the moral values of commitment, fidelity, and integrity.

The thought that there could be a single sexual ethic for persons of all sexual orientations came as a surprise to some, especially those who had supposed that the only sexual expression to be countenanced morally or spiritually was heterosexual and married. An ethical double standard evolved that was consistent with this view, blessing sexual expression only among married heterosexuals and requiring celibacy or abstinence for all lesbians, gay men, and bisexual and transgender friends, single or in relationship, as well as for single heterosexuals. It was a standard that gave greater value to the *form* of a sexual relationship than to its *substance*.

Yet it is the substance, not the form that matters, as many battered, heterosexually married persons can testify. The Presbyterian report's "Christian Ethic of Empowerment for Wholeness and Responsibility" values the goodness of sexuality, sexual and spiritual wholeness, and mutuality and consent.[16] Such an ethic is committed to reclaiming eros and passion, to guaranteeing bodily integrity and self-direction for every person, to taking responsibility for decisions and actions, and to fidelity in relationships. Like the more recent interfaith "Religious Declaration of Sexual Morality, Justice, and Healing,"[17] the Presbyterian report calls for full inclusion of persons of faith of every sexual orientation in religious institutions, and for such institutions to advance sexuality education, to make ordination standards fully inclusive, and to bless commitment services and holy unions.

Bisexual women and men of faith can readily affirm such a progressive sexual ethic as common ground that includes and challenges us all. Such an ethic also assists bisexual persons in responding to one of the more persistent myths raised about us: that bisexuals require two partners simultaneously, one same-sex and one different. This myth may be generated by inaccurate suppositions that we are half hetero- and half homosexual and that we, therefore, "need" biologically complementary and different sexual expression at the same time. It may spring from a simplistic sex-based understanding of difference.

Yes, it is true that bisexual persons experience attraction to friends of different and same gender identity and sex. However, contrary to the myth of promiscuous bisexuality, there is no evidence that bisexual persons also experience a greater *number* of sexual relationships than persons of other orientations. In addition, since bisexuals tend to demonstrate mixed ["masculine" and "feminine"] gender identity and acculturation, we experience no "lack" or need for pairing with one or another biological sex. Rather, we fall in love, as other persons do, with an other, and we make moral, relational decisions and commitments that adhere to the same spiritual and ethical criteria available to all.

Bisexual persons of Christian faith and character are called to live in "right relationships" of sexual intimacy marked by mutuality, by equal power and vulnerability, by respect and consent, responsibility and fidelity, and grounded in love and justice — just like everyone else. All Christians are inspired in their loving by the biblical model of a covenant-making God who calls us through the person of Jesus Christ. Our understanding of fidelity is based, as its derivation from *fides* reveals, on the Reformed concept of faithfulness — to one God, to one's self, and to others. In a relational sense, fidelity stands for steadfastness, for staying-with-another, and for commitment for the long haul, as God is faithful to God's people.

Fidelity is a relational value that marks connections to friends and mentors, families and professional colleagues, faith and community members and guides, as well as to committed life-partners. The shape fidelity takes will differ from relationship to relationship, but it should include honesty and mutuality, conversation and negotiation, and openness to growth and change. A relationship characterized by fidelity should not only do no harm to another, but it should also seek the happiness, the best interest, and the fullest flowering of the other.

Over the course of our lives, the narratives of bisexual persons of faith will demonstrate that we have been attracted to and, in many cases, will have been in faithful relationship with both women and men. In this sense, our relational histories may look different from those of our serially monogamous heterosexual friends or of our gay male brothers and lesbian sisters, but they will probably not be quantitatively different. God's Spirit in her infinite Wisdom is everywhere surprising persons of all orientations with *eros,* to which our fitting response is "Thank you!" or "God is good!"

All who honor God's goodness and delight in God's presence need also to honor God's image in each person. Christian women and men of diverse orientations are subject to the same ethical command in this regard. In every age, there will be those, among them people of faith, who argue that fidelity in relationship need not require sexual monogamy. There will also be those, among them people of faith, who argue for fidelity as sexual exclusivity within committed partner relationships. Speaking personally, as well as from conversation with Christian bisexual women and men over the years, there are many like me who choose this latter form of exclusivity as the better way to express fidelity within our intimate relationships. We do so for reasons of faith and because we are persuaded that this way enables us to follow most closely the religious and ethical values of right relationship. Other heterosexual, gay, lesbian, and bisexual women and men will choose relationships with life partners in which sexual exclusivity is not a requirement of fidelity. However, there is nothing particular to bisexuality that predicts or necessitates this latter choice. Learning to live ethically responsible lives means that all of us will need to greet with gratitude the sparks of *eros* in each other while making holy and wise decisions about whether or not to act on them sexually.

Rhythmic variations: the blessings of bisexuality

Since God created humanity and named it good, making all people in the divine image, it follows that all possess gifts necessary for the whole. Bisexual women and men affirm that our variations are as important to the full human harmony as are those of all others. Like others, we have gifts unique to us that are meant to be used both for church and society. Though as bisexuals we may "march to a different drummer," we take our place and bring our distinctive rhythms to contribute to the composition of the whole.

In religious institutions still riven by Western dualisms, the "either-ors" that lead to stereotyping and demeaning others, bisexual men and women by our nature bring a holistic view of interconnection that can help span divisions. In faith communities that have in the past valued men over women, mind over body, spirit over earth, white over rainbow, transcendent over immanent (the list is long), bisexuals resist false polarizations within and outside of ourselves in which only one of an opposing pair can be good and right. We speak from our embodied selves to the spectrum, to gradations, and to plural possibilities. We know there are always more than two choices, and that "winning" or domination is a destructive concept. As bisexuals seek to name our special gifts without claiming superiority over those of others, we speculate whether:

- in a political climate characterized by conflicts between good and evil, us and them, bisexual persons may be reconcilers, those who can imagine mixed solutions to intractable problems;

- in academic environments tuned to specialization, we may be able to bridge two or three disciplines—or to create a synthesis that may be redemptive;

- in a global reality dissected by oppressions of ethnicity and nationalism, class, sex, and more, bisexuals may see the large shape of domination and the abuse of power, considering the effect of the complex of oppressions as a whole, rather than singling out one or two;

- in societies increasingly peopled with bi- and tri-racial friends and persons of mixed religious backgrounds, the bi- and tri-among us may possess an embodied ability to affirm unity and embrace diversity that is sorely needed;

- in spiritual realms, bisexual persons may serve as healers in the times of interreligious conflict. We may be gifted to sense

the common pulse, to affirm multifaith world reality and to
understand the overarching unity that permits and includes
our particularities.

There is something in the bodies and beings of bisexuals that urges
us to unite what is so often sundered. And we believe that this urge
can be healing for the planet. Surely if humans are to survive as a
species and to heal our many rifts, humanity will need to learn a
language of "in-between," of "both-and," of interconnection, and of
multiplicity. So bisexual women and men affirm that our gifts are
required for reconciliation and for peace, together with those of all
others in God's good creation.

The 1991 Presbyterian report "Keeping Body and Soul Together"
may largely have left out bisexual women and men of faith, but we
rejoice in our inclusion today. To be able to join the composition as
beautiful variations on the theme of human sexuality has been our
hearts' desire. We pray for the transformation of religious institutions and communities, so that all may be honored and all voices
heard in God's one grand and sacred harmony. Let the performance
begin! Or, in the words of Orsino, duke of Illyria, in Shakespeare's
most gender-bending comedy *Twelfth Night,* "If music be the food of
love, play on!"[18]

Notes

1. Willi Apel, ed., *The Harvard Dictionary of Music,* 2d ed. (Cambridge, Mass.:
Harvard University Press, 1972), 892–95. I am indebted to Krysta Close and Travis
Stevens, undergraduate students in the Thornton School of Music of the University
of Southern California in Los Angeles, as well as to many other friendly readers
of this essay for their assistance.

2. For the last fifteen years I have identified as a bisexual woman. I have read
and written about bisexuality, created and led workshops about it, counseled and
been in conversation with those who name themselves bisexual as well as with
friendly others in queer and straight communities. While the majority of my conversation partners are Euro-American people of faith, also present in the dialogue
are African American, Hispanic, and Asian friends. Although I am female, white,
privileged, ordained, from "the North," and now sixty years old, a significant
number of my friends in conversation are current university students and those
from past campus ministries. In the chapter that follows, the "we" that I refer to
is the complex of folk with whom I've been and remain in conversation.

Transgenders, transsexuals, intersex friends, and others were not included in
the 1991 Presbyterian report. Because my experience is as a bisexual woman of

faith, and because I am aware that transgender realities will be included in the current volume, I will limit my contribution to bisexuality.

Before receiving my master of divinity degree, being ordained as minister of word and sacrament in the Presbyterian Church (U.S.A.) and beginning pastoral ministry, I was employed as a college chapel director of music and choral conductor. In this essay I bring artistic, spiritual, and sexual identities together.

3. See, for example, Fritz Klein and Timothy J. Wolf, eds., *Two Lives to Lead: Bisexuality in Men and Women* (New York: Haworth/Harrington Park, 1985); Thomas Geller, ed., *Bisexuality: A Reader and Sourcebook* (Hadley, Mass.: Common Wealth Printing Co., 1990); Loraine Hutchins and Lani Kaahumanu, eds., *Bi Any Other Name: Bisexual People Speak Out* (Boston: Alyson Publications, 1991); Eva Cantarella, *Bisexuality in the Ancient World* (New Haven: Yale University Press, 1992); and Elizabeth Reba Weise, *Closer to Home: Bisexuality and Feminism* (Seattle: Seal Press, 1992).

4. "Bisexuality: Perceptions and Realities," *Open Hands: Reconciling Ministries with Lesbians and Gay Men* 7, no. 2 (fall 1991), a publication of the (then) Reconciling Congregation Program, a network of United Methodist local churches.

5. John Carey, "Sexuality: What We Couldn't Say," *Christianity and Crisis* 51, no. 12 (August 19, 1991): 259. The italics are Carey's. It is worth noting that the word "transgender" wasn't even mentioned.

6. Much of the material that follows is summarized in "More Light on Bisexuality," a noncopyrighted publication of More Light Presbyterians that was developed in large conversation and passed by the MLP Board in 1999. It can be accessed at *www.mlp.org* and freely duplicated.

7. *Presbyterians and Human Sexuality 1991* (Louisville: Presbyterian Church [U.S.A.]), 54. Continuing the quotation, "On the whole this report has not dealt with bisexuality and we do not have the space here to do so. It does, however, remind us of the complexity of sexual orientations, and cautions us about being too simplistic when we categorize and label persons as sexual. The key point in an ethic of mutuality is to promote justice and right-relatedness in any loving relationship."

8. In addition to John 6:35 are the following Johannine references: 6:41, 51; 8:12, 24, 28, 58; 9:5; 10:7, 9, 11, 36; 11:25; 13:19; 14:6, 10; 15:1, 5; and 18:5.

9. See the book of Ruth, especially 1:16–17; 3:6–18; 4:13–16.

10. See 1 and 2 Samuel for the lengthy story of love between Jonathan and David.

11. Although many writers are addressing this subject, Sharon Ringe's *Wisdom's Friends: Community and Christology in the Fourth Gospel* (Louisville: Westminster John Knox, 1999) is perhaps the most accessible and comprehensive. See especially page 62, and background sections beginning with pages 30, 36, and 60.

12. Mary, Martha, and Lazarus of Bethany are the only named disciples whom Jesus is said to have *loved* (John 12:4, 5). In addition, tradition points to Jesus' love of the "beloved disciple" (John or Lazarus?) and Mary Magdalene.

13. Conversation in queer Christian communities has long engaged the topic of Jesus' sexuality. For a constellation of references positing that he might have been bisexual, see William E. Phipps's *The Sexuality of Jesus* (Cleveland: Pilgrim, 1996), 71 and notes, where he quotes Rosemary Radford Ruether, James Cone,

and Bill Johnson. Nancy Wilson also comes to this conclusion in *Our Tribe: Queer Folks, God, Jesus, and the Bible* (San Francisco: HarperCollins, 1995), 147ff. It is not important to me personally that Jesus "be bisexual," but rather that he embody the inclusion of all sexual orientations and gender identities present in human community.

14. Note that the same Greek word in this passage means both *wind* and *Spirit*.

15. *Presbyterians and Human Sexuality 1991*, 19–20.

16. Ibid., 19. More Light Presbyterians' position paper "More Light on Sexual Ethics" also takes the same approach and derives from the same conversations and authors. As with the More Light paper on bisexuality, the ethics paper is not copyrighted and is available on the website *www.mlp.org* for downloading and duplicating.

17. This statement was developed by the Sexuality Information and Education Council of the United States (SIECUS). It is also not copyrighted and may be duplicated. It is printed on one side of the "More Light on Sexual Ethics" statement, and is available also at *www.siecus.org/religion/reli0001.html* or *www.religionproject.org/declaration.html*. As of February 2002 it has been endorsed by 2110 religious leaders or clergy and continues to accept endorsements.

18. William Shakespeare, *Twelfth Night, or What You Will*, 1601, line 1, in *The Oxford Shakespeare: The Complete Works*, ed. Stanley Wells and Gary Taylor (Oxford: Clarendon Press, 1988), 693.

7

Sexuality and Aging

"Young Love" and "Old Love"

Chris Glaser

Last night I attended a performance of *Romeo and Juliet* at the Shakespeare Tavern in Atlanta. I have read and seen the play so many times that I anticipated scenes and could have recited some of the lines with the actors. Yet, given that I intended to begin work on this chapter on aging and sexuality today, I viewed the romance between the leads as if for the first time. And I was struck that they fell in love at first sight and their entire romance occurs over the course of a few days.

The first production of the play that I recall seeing is Franco Zeffirelli's cinematically lush 1968 rendition. I was seventeen years old, the age of the actor who played Romeo. I completely comprehended his sudden and passionate feelings, though mine would have been directed at him rather than Juliet. I empathized deeply with their star-crossed romance as one whose own romantic feelings would also be unacceptable if known. I played the record album of key scenes so frequently that it is quite worn.

Now, at the age of fifty-one, I view the "instant" romance quite differently, a contrast between my experience in youth and that of middle age. Perhaps my young love was more instinct, a biological predisposition to mate at all costs, attraction based mostly on appearance, and its drive hormonally enhanced because the survival of the species demands healthy progenitors as soon as possible. If I were heterosexual, that would mean children. Though my sexuality would never produce children, I shared that urgent instinct to mate with appealing bodies as quickly as possible.

129

Today I find that my sexuality is more art than instinct, more
an act of the will than an act of ungoverned eros, broader in its
acceptance of suitable mates by appearance, narrower in its definition of suitable mates by character, and more willing that "time will
tell." I better understand the friar who performed Romeo and Juliet's
marriage when he dissuaded Romeo from suicide at his banishment:

> Thy wit, that ornament to shape and love,
> Misshapen in the conduct of them both,
> Like powder in a skitless soldier's flask,
> Is set afire by thine own ignorance.
>   (*Romeo and Juliet,* Act III, Scene III)

Of course this foreshadows the tragedy that will take place later in
the play when Romeo, his wit "misshapen" and too quick to act, takes
poison, mistakenly thinking Juliet is dead. In essence, the friar warns
that we lose our wits, move too swiftly, and endanger ourselves when
the passion to merge with another, the passion of eros, takes charge.
Before performing the marriage between Romeo and Juliet, the friar
warns Romeo about young love:

> These violent delights have violent ends,
> And in their triumph die, like fire and powder,
> Which as they kiss consume. (Act II, Scene VI)

Unleashed energy is the grand power of young love. Yet as I heard
the line delivered, I contrasted it with the Psalmist's prophecy that

> Steadfast love and faithfulness will meet;
> righteousness and peace will kiss each other. (Ps. 85:10)

Though the Psalmist is describing the relationship of God to Israel, it
may serve as a model for all loving relationships and better reflects
my experience of "old," or what some would call "mature," love.
A developed or cultivated love includes steadfastness and faithfulness, righteousness (justice) and peace (a harmonizing of the chaos
of eros).

Let me quickly say I don't want to suggest a hierarchy of love nor
align "young" love automatically with youth or "old" love automatically with age. I am using the terms "young" and "old" to avoid
terms like "immature" or "mature" because of the latter's negative

contrast. (To non-ageist ears, both young and old sound good.) Each serves the purpose for which it is intended, and each is good. An older person can experience a "young" love while a younger person can experience an "old" form of love. I want to avoid "presentism," which means judging the past by contemporary standards. Personally, I want to avoid my youth judging my age and my age judging my youth.

Just as I learned different eating habits with each decade, so my sexual expression has changed over the years. Things I could eat with impunity in my teens I had to eat measuredly in my twenties and rarely in my thirties to prevent gaining weight, ensure my health, and extend my life—as far as possible. At the same time, my culinary pleasure increased as I learned to like more foods, to taste exotic flavors, and to savor the dining experience. Though I still love fast food, I more often enjoy a leisurely dinner carefully created with an eye to presentation and taste, accompanied by appropriate music and stimulating conversation.

You can see where this analogy is going. Though I still like "quickies," moments when passion (or a tight schedule) seizes me and my lover in the kitchen and we end up on the floor between appetizers and the salad, I more often enjoy a leisurely evening of lovemaking with attention given to mutual pleasuring of all parts of our bodies, carefully dressed and undressed with an eye to erotic inspiration, occasionally and playfully incorporating exotic fantasies discovered over the years, accompanied by appropriate music and stimulating speech.

"What planet do you live on?" I can hear some readers saying. Yes, of course, the stereotype of age is that erotic desire falls off or that lovers get into a rut that goes right to "the act" without much pleasure. That to me is not the aging process, but the routinization process.

Let me return to my dining analogy. (This analogy undoubtedly brings smiles to readers' lips, but I use it intentionally. Mary Hunt, a contributor to this volume, once said that she cherished the day when we would be able to casually throw condoms into our grocery carts along with milk and eggs. Of course, the term "condoms" is only a metaphor for the inclusion of the erotic in our everyday lives.)

I love to cook, but I keep changing menus. Just as the ancient philosopher was not able to step into the same river twice, I can't "step into" the same risotto twice or the same configuration of foods. I may repeat with variations something that turned out well, but eventually I move on to other menus and return to old ones for variety. The same is true for restaurants. I have a few that are favorite haunts, but I enjoy trying different places, and I like it when my usual places change their menus or have specials.

Again, you know where I'm leading. The reason sex gets "old" or rather "stale" is because we don't devote enough creativity to it. A new candle or a different scent or method of seduction can make all the difference. I know I'm not to write a "How to Make Your Sex Life Exciting" chapter, but aging has given me both perspective and experience from which to write.

When sexual expression becomes routinized, there's the temptation to dine at other restaurants, so to speak. For some, this is where my analogy begins to turn. For others, it confirms their predilection or addiction to "young" love, finding ever-fresh sexual partners to break the routine. Again, my experience is that true lovers improve their pleasuring of one another the longer they remain together. Old lovers are not only in bed with one another; they are embedded with memories of their earlier love—not all peaches and cream of course, but their struggles as well. For them, even what others would call routinized sex may be fraught with pleasure and joy.

Years after my father's death, I was helping my mother change the sheets on her bed, a small double bed in which my parents had slept nearly every night of their fifty-one and a half years together. I pointed out to her what I took to be undissolved detergent on the bottom sheet, and rather demurely she explained that it was my father's talcum powder seeping through. She put it on the mattress pad so the bed always smelled like him. I discovered, in addition, that she slept with a shirt he had worn under one pillow and his pajama top under another because they retained his scent. I remembered the visitation at the mortuary, when my mother stood with one of her widowed church friends beside my father's open casket, remarking, "I know this is just his earthly body—but oh, I loved it so!" One could say that she continued her erotic relationship with my father until her own death on that same bed years after. My brother found her lying peacefully on top of the bedspread with her eyes gazing toward the foot of the bed. Given her insistence on staying in the house because she felt my father's presence there, we comforted ourselves with the thought that she had seen Father standing at the foot of the bed beckoning her to join him in God's eternal realm.

What would keep someone erotically connected for so long? I believe it was an intense experience of young love that they allowed to age as a fine bottle of wine. After Mom's death, I took from her house letters my parents exchanged during their times of separation. High school sweethearts (he was the editor of their school paper, she served as its treasurer), they were separated first by his temporary job at a meatpacking facility in Omaha, then by his move to California to drive trucks in the Sierras for a bread company, and finally, after their marriage and move to California together, during his service in the occupying U.S. forces in Japan at the close of World War II. She wrote less often and more briefly. His letters were written almost daily and ran as long as twenty pages of small script. They are filled with passion and promise. I am certain that their passion and promise saw them through later financial and emotional struggles rearing three children in southern California.

From conversations I learned, sometimes obtusely, that their sexual life had been conventional, and yet, when they were my present age, I overheard my father say to my mother how vital sexuality was to their relationship. When I was in college and the subject of homosexuality first came up in conversation, I remember being surprised when my father said to my mother, "If they feel for each other what I feel for you, then I can understand why they want to be together." Young love had never left my parents even as old love blessed them.

How does "the kiss of fire and powder" become the "the kiss of righteousness and peace," "the kiss of justice and peace"? By strict definitions of "right relation," my parents had an unjust relationship, as my father was head of the household, at least in theory and often in practice. There are those who would define sexuality itself as mutuality, but I believe at heart that's an attempt to define "good" sexuality over against "bad" sexuality. I believe sexuality itself is amoral. Sexuality spills all over the place. It can't absolutely be controlled, regulated, categorized, or tamed. It is libertarian by nature. It is promiscuous by nature. The sex researcher Alfred Kinsey is credited by Gore Vidal with a magnificent line, to the effect that promiscuous is what you call someone who's having more sex than you are.[1] Sexuality is something we experience in every relationship, even when being celibate or chaste. It is the erotic component to all touch, whether groping someone in a movie theater or participating in the laying on of hands. Yes, I wrote that deliberately to shock you.

To make you feel better, as well as to complete the picture, I will also say that spirituality also is amoral. Spirituality, too, spills all over the place. It can't be absolutely controlled, regulated, categorized, or tamed. It is libertarian by nature. Spirituality is promiscuous by nature. To paraphrase Kinsey, charismatic is what you call someone who has more spiritual experiences than you do. Spirituality is something we experience in every relationship, no matter how carnal or ascetic, violent or peaceful. It is the spiritual component of all touch, whether groping someone in a movie theater or participating in the laying on of hands.

All of this is to say that I believe there are no absolutely moral parameters inherent in sexuality or spirituality. They are merely the media by which we play out our lives, the paint on the canvas by which we execute a self-portrait, the words on the paper with which we write out our stories. Sexuality and spirituality are both fueled by eros, that passion to unite in sexual or spiritual communion, what I call "the urge to merge." That's why either can be violent, grasping, controlling, and deadly. I'm afraid I part ways with those who say rape is more about power than sexuality. Is it not true that for the rapist, violent power serves as the ultimate aphrodisiac? For the pedophile, the necrophiliac, the parent who molests his or her child, and the person who engages in bestiality, aren't control and dominance (forms of power) at least part of what turns them on? More often (and socially more acceptably), such sexual violence has been ritualized as the "naughty boy" or "naughty girl" who wants to be spanked by "daddy" or "mommy," or other sexual fantasies that are played out involving rape, sadomasochism, discipline, bondage, and master-slave relationships. Each of these may or may not include genital contact or orgasm, but each reflects the many ways in which sex and power may be linked.

To put in perspective this shadow side of sexuality, let me say that I believe something similar of spirituality. Spirituality, the erotic passion for spiritual communion, has led to Crusades, Inquisitions, "holy" wars, jihad, burning of heretics and witches to save their souls, bondage to orthodoxy, excommunication (ironically a product of wanting unity *absolutely*), and more. Spiritual violence has also been ritualized in socially acceptable ways, from our dying to our old selves in baptism, to Christ sacrificed in the breaking of the Communion bread.

Aging has taught me that what must govern the eros of both sexuality and spirituality is love, specifically agape, the Christian adaptation of the Greek concept of benevolent, unselfish love. "Love is the willingness to extend one's self for one's own or another's spiritual growth," as Scott Peck defines love in *The Road Less Traveled*,[2] a good definition of the New Testament understanding of love, a love to be visited not only on one's self and one's neighbor, but on one's enemy.

Despite everyone from Jesus to the Beatles affirming that "love is all you need," the excellent 1991 report of the Presbyterian Special Committee on Human Sexuality, "Keeping Body and Soul Together: Sexuality, Spirituality, and Social Justice," concludes "justice-love" should guide all relationships, including sexual ones. The committee sought to emphasize the close connection between the themes of justice and love, explicitly departing from any kind of sentimentalized notion of love apart from the demands of justice, which requires a fair sharing of power. I despaired, as should we all, that "love" had become so disassociated from "justice" and "justice" from "love" that the hyphenated word was now necessary! God's covenant relationship with the Jews had always included both righteousness (justice) and mercy (the forgiving nature that we call love). The marriage of righteousness and mercy, or the marriage of justice and love, as the committee attested, is certainly a superior paradigm for sexual relationships rather than marriage alone, which includes inequalities and injustices between partners and, at the same time, presently excludes same-gender couples.

Beyond the surface controversies surrounding the committee's critique of patriarchy and marriage and its affirmation of homosexuality, the deeper waters were no less disturbing. I believe Presbyterians didn't like romantic love being deconstructed—deromanticized, as it were. They did not appreciate the truth that the personal is the political, and vice versa. In my analysis, they wanted to hold on to "young love" at all costs, requiring denial, blinders, and stunted growth to hold on to the illusion that love can solve all things. Love can indeed solve many things, but only with a component of justice, which I define as "agape institutionalized." A benevolent love that wishes everyone's well-being becomes laws that protect the rights and privileges of women, children, gays, lesbians, and so forth, in a world that generally assumes the rights and privileges of men (at least white and straight men).

Yet since the 203rd (1991) General Assembly of the Presbyterian Church (U.S.A.) rejected the report, I've come to realize that though we may love justly (old love), there is often no justice in love (young love). We hope that "justice is blind," meaning indiscriminate in its application, but we despair that "love is blind," meaning again, indiscriminate in its application. However, that nondiscriminating love is what Jesus calls us to exercise, becoming mature in love even as God is mature, causing the rain to fall and the sun to shine on the just and unjust. We are called to love justly even in the face of injustice. Because we are called to love ourselves properly so as to better serve others, as both ancient and contemporary Christian theologians have understood the second great commandment,[3] I believe that the face of this love does not always turn the other cheek. It has been suggested that that method would put the victim's nose squarely in the way of a second hit, meaning a more destructive blow that might shame the perpetrator and call forth his or her decency not to inflict it. While some consider this effective for nonviolent political demonstrations (though I have my doubts even about this), it is surely ineffective in coping with sexual abuse, in or outside of marriage. "Turning the other cheek" is young love in action, eros ungoverned by agape. Agape, old love in action, requires love for the self as well as for the perpetrator, a love that would resist putting either in the place of receiving or giving the violence.

At the same time that I believe there are absolute boundaries to be preserved between violence and vulnerability, there is a narrow threshold between pleasure and pain. Little bites on the neck can be as erotically stimulating as little kisses, for example. Though I believe that a relationship in which one partner always dominates at the expense of the other may be judged spiritually (and in other ways) unhealthy, in the day-to-day erotic dance one partner may lead at one time and follow at another. The one who dominates now may submit later on, or one who dominates in one instance may submit in another. This temporary imbalance is both necessary (because one usually initiates a sexual encounter, an act of vulnerability as well as an act of power) and delightful (giving oneself vulnerably to another may be as much a turn-on as receiving another's vulnerability).

All these interactions may occur within the parameters of agape institutionalized as justice. This is where the community plays a role in the most personal of relationships. Let me give an example. I attended a talk by gay theorist Eric Rofes, who supports the right of an individual to have unprotected sex with someone infected with HIV. I was sitting with Daniel Helminiak, a former Catholic priest who has authored several books about sexuality and spirituality, including the best-selling *What the Bible Really Says about Homosexuality.*[4] Daniel was growing more restless by the minute because of Eric's assertions. He muttered to me (and later said in the public forum) that he was tired of individuals who claimed their "rights" without regard to their communities. "If that person gets sick, he's going to expect the community to help in his care, pay his medical bills either directly or indirectly through higher insurance premiums and taxes, volunteer to bring him meals-on-wheels and clean his apartment, and expect me to hold his hand. He must consider how his personal behavior affects his community." Thus, the community has not only the right but also the obligation to institutionalize boundaries of agape (justice) around a couple's expression of eros. The desire of "young love" for mergers regardless of risk must be guided by "old love." That's why the community has not only the right but also the obligation to provide information and support to avoid sexually transmitted diseases, as well as pregnancies that will not be carried to term and unwanted children who will be neglected or abused. There are many forms of risky sex whose consequences will require the services of the community. Again, "old love" must guide "young love," just as "young love" fuels "old love."

Finally, I imagine that many readers will have expected of this chapter a pathetic description of old people vis-à-vis sex. "Keeping Body and Soul Together" testifies truthfully to the disregard this society often has for older people, to society's desire to view them as "broken" sexually (a view seriously modified by the introduction of Viagra since the report) or as asexual, and to families and retirement institutions discouraging their sexuality and sexual relations. The report explores the positive experience of "pleasuring" that many seniors enjoy but that does not necessarily include genital activity, and ends with a caution that our era tends to unnecessarily equate human fulfillment with sexual satisfaction (an insight for *all* ages). Everything in the report's chapter on "Older Adults" I find to be true and enlightening, and to repeat it here, other than in this summary, seems unnecessary.[5]

That many younger and middle-aged people project their fears of mutability and vulnerability onto older people does not diminish the positive dimension of aging to be found in "old love." Aging is a lifelong process, and at any stage our sexual expression may be impeded by accident, circumstance, or a change in our psychological or physiological health. To use old age as a kind of dumping ground for our anxieties does a disservice to the people who have survived and thrived all this time to get to their advanced age, an accomplishment in and of itself. "Aging ain't for sissies," the adage goes, and older people have greater inner resources for handling sexual changes than we give them credit for.

I have written instead of the perspective on sexuality that aging may bring. Because I am not in the oldest category, I have much to learn. But I have noticed the trend from "young love" to "old love," the interplay of eros and agape, the pervasive and permissive natures of both sexuality and spirituality, and the integrity of love and justice. These features can be had or ignored at any age.

Notes

1. Gore Vidal, *Palimpsest: A Memoir* (New York: Penguin Books, 1995).

2. M. Scott Peck, *The Road Less Traveled* (New York: Simon & Schuster, 1978), 81.

3. See Paul Ramsey, "Non-Preferential Love and Duties to Oneself," in *Basic Christian Ethics* (New York: Charles Scribner's Sons, 1950), 157–66.

4. Daniel Helminiak, *What the Bible Really Says about Homosexuality* (Tajique, N.Mex.: Alamo Square Press, 1994, 2000).

5. *Presbyterians and Human Sexuality 1991* (Louisville: Presbyterian Church [U.S.A.], 1991), 58.

8

Teens and Sex

Just Say... What?

Debra W. Haffner

In the summer of 2002, the General Assembly of the Presbyterian Church (U.S.A.) once again debated its sexuality education curriculum for youth. Once again, a group submitted a minority report urging the General Assembly to vote to stop using *God's Gift of Sexuality* and prepare more conservative resources.[1] Once again, people opposed to the curriculum raised objections to its content. According to a press release from the General Assembly, Ginny Garrard, a youth advisory delegate from Flint River Presbytery, said she'd examined the materials and found "many things which shock me." She said that one part of the current curriculum contains "a half-page about masturbation and only a couple of lines about abstinence" and that a Presbyterian curriculum on sexuality "should begin and end with the Bible."[2]

Fortunately, once again, people concerned with the sexuality needs of all the denomination's youth prevailed. Rev. Laura Fleetwood, of Arkansas Presbytery, who said she has used the PC (USA) curriculum for twenty years, countered that it is "biblically based and theologically grounded" and does emphasize that sexuality is appropriate only "in the context of the intimate relationship of marriage."[3] The General Assembly affirmed *God's Gift of Sexuality,* requested an updated list of resources, and approved an overture affirming "the importance of offering high-quality and affordable PC (USA) curriculum for ages preschool to adult... that is affordable, adaptable, user-friendly and appealing to congregations."[4]

The Presbyterian Church (U.S.A) has debated the content of sexuality education for adolescents since the publication of the curriculum in 1989. Such debates are not unique to the Presbyterians and have occurred in many mainline denominations and in school systems across the country. According to Leslie Unruh, the director of the National Abstinence Clearinghouse, adolescent sexuality "next to abortion is probably the most controversial subject today."[5]

Adolescent sexuality is often the focus of controversy because of adults' confusion about their own sexuality and their discomfort with their teenage children's developing sense of a sexual identity. The United States is moderately erotophobic: we are relaxed enough about sex to have it, but fearful of its power and the accompanying guilt, shame, and negative experiences too many adults carry. Our teenagers are often caught in the crossfire: the culture that adults produce for them by way of movies, music, magazines, and television all give the message that "everyone is doing it" while the official message is "just say no." Even the most progressive of parents and programs adopt a "just say later" or, at best, a "don't ask, don't tell" philosophy.

The 1991 Presbyterian report "Keeping Body and Soul Together" offers young people "a fresh word about sexuality — one that we trust may break through the jaded cultural messages with good news for a meaningful life."[6] The report heartily endorsed the then two-year-old *God's Gift of Sexuality* and called for increased attention in particular to the needs of young people who had experienced sexual abuse, as well as to gay and lesbian adolescents. It called on Presbyterians to "take an active role in assuring that schools in their communities provide sexuality education, including discussions of sexuality appropriate for pre-teenage children."[7] The report called for a sexual ethic that challenged young people to "recognize and abide by the wisdom of postponing having sexual relations until they have the maturity to integrate the ethic of right-relatedness in their lives."[8]

In reviewing the 1991 report, it is interesting to note the societal changes that have occurred in the last decade that may affect young people's experience of their sexuality and their decisions about sexual behaviors. In 1991, the risk of HIV/AIDS to young people received one line in the report. Bisexual and transgender young people were not on the radar screen of even the most progressive advocates. Date rape drugs did not exist. The Internet's emails, instant messaging, and chat rooms were unknown to teenagers and adults alike.

Schools were just beginning to implement HIV/AIDS education, and abstinence-only education programs were taught for the most part only in a few conservative community agencies and churches.

Despite dire media predications to the contrary, teenagers in the United States have become more sexually responsible in the decade since the 1991 report. The teenage birth rate in 2000 was 48.7 per thousand, compared to 62.1 in 1991, a 22 percent drop in nine years. Birth rates declined for all age groups of teens and for each major race and ethnicity group. In 2000, there were 497,067 births to teenagers, a 10 percent decline in the number of teen births as compared to 1991.[9]

The reason for the decline in teenage births can be explained by a decline in the proportion of teenagers who have had sexual intercourse and by an increase in the proportion of teenagers who use effective methods of contraception and condoms. In 1993, 53 percent of high-school-age teens in grades nine to twelve had had sexual intercourse; by 2000, that number had decreased to 45.6 percent. Nearly two-thirds of young people who had had voluntary sexual intercourse had used a condom at first and last intercourse,[10] a dramatic increase from the 45 percent who did so in 1988.[11] According to researchers at the Alan Guttmacher Institute who looked at rates in 1986 as compared to in 1996, "Roughly one-fourth of the drop in the teenage pregnancy rates between 1986 and 1996 resulted from increased abstinence...and approximately three-fourths from decreased pregnancy rates among sexually experienced teenagers."[12] Notably, the abortion rate actually declined from 38 percent to 35 percent and did not account for any of the decline in teen birth rates.[13]

Although encouraging, these trends should be put into context. The United States still has one of the developed world's highest birth rates; only Armenia, Moldavia, Georgia, and the Ukraine report rates as high.[14] Additionally, comparison reveals a teenage birth rate in the United States that is at least five times higher than the teen birth rate in Spain, France, Italy, and Japan.[15] Teenage girls have the highest rates of chlamydia and gonorrhea of any age group of women, as do young adult males aged twenty to twenty-four.[16] Half of all new HIV infections in the United States occur to young people under the age of twenty-five.[17]

By and large, the public schools are failing young people's need for sexuality education. In 1991, the Sexuality Information and Education Council of the United States (SIECUS) estimated that only 5 percent of U.S. children and youth received comprehensive sexuality education in kindergarten through twelfth grade.[18] Since 1996, the federal government has funded programs that have as their "exclusive purpose, teaching the social, physiological, and health gains to be realized by abstaining from sexual activity."[19] These programs are required to teach eight points, including that "a mutually faithful monogamous relationship in the context of marriage is the expected standard of human sexual activity" and that "sexual activity outside of the context of marriage is likely to have harmful psychological and physical effects."[20] Nationwide in 2002, the government spent a remarkable $100 million on these abstinence-only programs, and President Bush asked for a one-third increase in funding in 2003.[21]

The federal abstinence-only program has changed the landscape of sexuality education in the United States. According to a study by the Alan Guttmacher Institute, by 1999 one-quarter of high school sex education teachers taught abstinence as the only way to prevent pregnancies and sexually transmitted diseases, compared to 2 percent who did so a decade earlier. Every state except for California has developed abstinence-only programming in schools, media, community-based organizations, and faith-based institutions using these federal funds.

These programs are based on political desires, not public health data about adolescents or, indeed, adult sexual behavior as criteria for effective sexuality education programming. They simply choose to ignore that the vast majority of Americans have first sexual intercourse outside of marriage, that the average age of first marriage is over twenty-five, and that some people are gay and lesbian and cannot marry. Nor do these programs help young people abstain from sexual intercourse until marriage.[22] Indeed, one study suggests that they may actually put young people at risk of pregnancy and disease because young people who participate in the program are *less* likely to use contraception and condoms when they do become sexually active.[23] These programs are also theologically unsound. According to "An Open Letter to Religious Leaders about Sex Education,"

Young people need help in order to develop their capacity for moral discernment and a freely informed conscience. Education that respects and empowers young people has more integrity than education based on incomplete information, fear, and shame. Programs that teach abstinence exclusively and withhold information about pregnancy and sexually transmitted disease prevention fail our young people.[24]

For a number of reasons, religious institutions have a unique role to play in reaching children and youth with sexuality information. After all, religious institutions serve more teens than any other agency in a community except the public schools, and they are the only ones specifically empowered to offer values-based education to children outside of the home. As schools become more restricted in what they can teach, religious institutions may be able to provide more comprehensive information in a values context. More than eight in ten teens say that religion is important in their lives, and more than half attend religious services weekly.[25] More than six in ten teens participate at least once a week in a program at a church or synagogue other than a worship service.[26]

Participation in a religious setting may actually protect young people against premature involvement in sexual behaviors. In a review of more than fifty studies of the impact of religion on sexual behavior, Dr. Brian Wilcox and colleagues concluded that "more frequent religious attendance is associated with later initiation of sexual intercourse for white males and for females across racial/ethnic groups [and] more conservative sexual attitudes and a decreased frequency of sexual intercourse."[27] Sexually active African American teenage girls who attend church frequently, pray, and partake in other religious activities are less likely to engage in sexually risky behaviors than their less religious peers. Religious teen females were 50 percent more likely to wait to have intercourse and 80 percent more likely to have used a condom the last time they had sex than their less religious peers.[28] Teens are twice as likely to cite their "morals, values, and religious beliefs" as affecting their decision about whether to have intercourse than any other single factor.[29] In a study of more than six hundred congregations, youth from congregations that include information about contraception as part of the religious education curriculum report virtually no instances of pregnancy. Almost all Jewish youth who are having sexual intercourse use a contraceptive method.[30]

Religious youth who did not engage in adolescent sexual intercourse shared characteristics beyond their simple involvement in a religious institution. According to a statistical analysis of more than six thousand young people who participate in religious institutions, those who are least likely to have intercourse:

- attend religious services one or more times a week;
- pray daily;
- are engaged in at least one other congregational activity besides worship;
- say that the teachings of the congregation and/or Scripture have a lot of influence on their sexual decision-making and that they learned these teachings from the congregation;
- feel a strong connection with congregational leaders and other youth in the congregation;
- feel that adults who work with them portray sexuality in a healthy and positive manner;
- say their congregation encourages abstinence from intercourse for high school–aged teens.[31]

Encouraging abstinence is only one factor in this portrait of sexually abstinent young people. Unfortunately, most studies also indicate that religious youth are less likely to use contraception. Disappointingly but perhaps not surprisingly, only 6 percent of teens say that ministers, rabbis, or other religious leaders influence their decisions about sex.[32] Only 14 percent of clergy say that their congregation offers a reasonably comprehensive approach to sexuality education while 37 percent say the congregation does almost nothing. Fewer than one in six religious youths say that their faith-based institution offers them significant information on birth control, STD prevention, HIV prevention, rape, or homosexuality.[33]

Teens and clergy disagree about the sexuality education that is being offered. Although 73 percent of clergy said that their congregation portrays sexuality in a positive and healthy way, only

46 percent of the teens in those same congregations agreed. While clergy and religious advisers rate their sexuality education programs as fair to good, youth in these programs rate them as poor.[34] The good news is that three-quarters of adults and teens believe that churches and other faith communities should do more to help prevent teen pregnancy.[35] Many denominations have made a commitment to sexuality education for young people. Several have passed policies that encourage their congregations to include sexuality education in the religious education program. These include American Baptist Churches in the U.S.A., the Central Conference of American Rabbis, the Christian Church (Disciples of Christ), the Episcopal Church, the Mennonite Church, the Presbyterian Church (U.S.A.), the Unitarian Universalist Association, the United Church of Christ, the United Methodist Church, and the United Synagogue of Conservative Judaism.[36] Indeed, more than thirty years ago, the National Council of Churches' Commission on Marriage and Family, the Synagogue Council of America's Committee on Family, and the United States Catholic Conference called upon churches and synagogues to become actively involved in sexuality education within their congregations and their communities.

Many denominations have produced sexuality education curricula; the majority are aimed at adolescents. Many could easily be adapted for other faith communities. There are also national organizations that have produced curricula for use in an interfaith setting. (See the end of this chapter, p. 153, for a list of curricula for adolescents developed for use in faith communities.)

The leaders of sexuality education programs in religious institutions need specialized training in teaching the curricula and responding to the sexuality needs of the young people. Several of the denominations provide specialized training along with their curricula although the training is often only a weekend workshop. If such training is not available, a program may consider using volunteers from within a congregation who already have professional backgrounds and experience working with young people, e.g., health educators, teachers, psychologists, and social workers. Teaching sexuality education requires professional skills that are not easily developed in short courses. Supervision of new educators is essential, as well as policies to safeguard children and adolescents from sexual abuse and sexual harassment.

Sexuality education programs in religious institutions have a unique opportunity to teach values within the theological commitments of the denomination. Although each congregation or denomination, depending on polity, will seek to develop a curriculum consistent with its own tradition, certain values transcend denominational frameworks. A colloquium of theologians convened by the Religious Institute on Sexual Morality, Justice, and Healing identified that any sexuality education program should:

- emphasize responsibility, rights, ethics, and justice;
- affirm the dignity and worth of all persons;
- teach that sexuality includes physical, ethical, social, psychological, emotional, and spiritual dimensions;
- complement the education provided by parents and faith communities. Parents should be asked to give written permission before a program begins, and homework assignments can encourage parent-child communication;
- explicitly identify the values that underline the program;
- teach that decisions about sexual behaviors should be based on moral and ethical values, as well as considerations of physical and emotional health;
- affirm the goodness of sexuality while acknowledging its risks and dangers;
- introduce with respect the differing sides of controversial sexual issues.[37]

Many congregations and denominations may not be ready to adopt a comprehensive sexuality education program, kindergarten through high school. Still, there are less intensive activities that a congregation can offer to support the sexual health and development of youth. These include:

- Using an outside consultant periodically from the health department, local AIDS organization, or local Planned Parenthood to speak with youth groups about sexuality issues.

- Facilitating youth group members' participation in community activities that relate to sexuality issues. For example, young people can volunteer at a family planning clinic, AIDS organization, children's hospital, adoption agency, or hotline for young people.

- Providing support groups for young people, including groups for those whose parents are going through divorce and for those dealing with sexual orientation, eating disorders, and body image issues. Leaders of "drop in" programs should have experience and training to handle teen sexuality issues.

- Including pamphlets about sexual health services in youth center spaces and hanging posters for young people from such organizations as the National AIDS Clearinghouse, the National Campaign to Prevent Teenage Pregnancy, and PFLAG (Parents and Friends of Lesbians and Gays).

- Training members of high school youth groups to provide education about peer pressure on dating, drugs, drinking, and sex to middle school students and preadolescents. Modeling safe behaviors will benefit both groups.

- Having movie nights with such themes as relationships, coming-of-age stories, marriage, friendships, and sexual orientation. These can be intergenerational evenings that include discussion between youth and adults after the movie.

- Providing small group sessions or worship services for high school and middle school youth that focus on such issues as body image, peer pressure, relationships with parents, and friendships. Young people should be given opportunities to talk among themselves and with trained leaders about the pressures they face.

- Providing a Bible study group for teens that focuses on texts with sexual themes and issues.

- Offering programs for parents and middle school students on adjusting to the challenges of puberty and adolescence, as well as maintaining open lines of communication through the teen years.

- Working with youth ministers and religious educators from other congregations to develop community programming.

- Opening youth programming to young people in the surrounding community.[38]

The challenge of the 1991 Presbyterian report on sexuality has not been met either for adolescents or adults. In today's increasingly complex world, there is an even more pressing need for commitment to sexual health, education, and justice. The Religious Institute on Sexual Morality, Justice, and Healing has been formed to provide a forum for progressive religious leaders to join together to advocate not only for sexuality education for young people, but also for sexual justice in faith communities and the wider society. More than twenty-two hundred clergy, theologians, and religious educators from thirty-five denominations have endorsed the "Religious Declaration on Sexual Morality, Justice, and Healing" since it was published in January 2000. (The full text of the declaration appears below on pp. 151–152.) The declaration calls for a sexual ethic focused on personal relationships and social justice rather than on particular sexual acts or the age, marital status, or sexual orientation of the participants. The declaration urges religious leaders and faith communities to provide comprehensive sexuality education, to advocate sexual and reproductive rights, and to assure the full inclusion of women and sexual minorities in congregational life, denominations, and society at large.

After its release, opponents from the organized Religious Right and conservative religious leaders attacked the "Religious Declaration" vociferously. Richard Land, president of the Southern Baptist Ethics and Religious Liberty Commission, called the document "yet one further sign of the increasing paganization of our culture sexually."[39] R. Albert Mohler Jr., president of Southern Baptist Seminary in Louisville, Kentucky, said,

The arrogance of this Declaration is breathtaking. These self-appointed moral revolutionaries will reject the clear teachings of Scripture in order to justify sexual perversions and destructive behaviors. In utter arrogance they claim a religious mandate for their declaration. In a cloak of distortions they seek to overthrow biblical morality and put a humanistic ethic of sexual liberation in its place. The result will be ruined lives and devastated marriage, lost innocence, and broken hearts.[40]

Dr. Laura Schlessinger, a conservative radio talk-show host, wrote a column entitled "Declaration Cloaks Its Positions in Religion"[41] and did a three-hour syndicated radio program attacking the statement. The Family Research Council has also attacked it. The February 2001 Focus on the Family *Citizen Magazine* ran a cover story attacking the "Religious Declaration" and me personally. A group called Mastering Life's Mysteries has developed a counter "Religious Declaration" that begins by saying, "Human sexual (genital) behavior is intended by God to be expressed solely within the confines of heterosexual monogamous marriage."[42]

These attacks have not slowed down the impact of the "Religious Declaration." It has now been endorsed by nearly three times the original endorser network. The presidents of two national religious denominations have endorsed it, as well as the presidents and deans of eighteen seminaries. Bishops from the Episcopal Church, the United Methodist Church, the Community of Christ (formerly the Reorganized Church of Latter-day Saints), the Evangelical Lutheran Church in America, and the American Catholic Church in the United States have also endorsed it.

A major goal in creating the "Religious Declaration" was to begin a dialogue about sexuality and religion. This goal has been more than realized. According to the search engine *Google.com,* there are over 14,700 websites that mention the "Religious Declaration." There are message boards devoted to the "Religious Declaration" and references on multiple other websites that cover a broad spectrum of groups from the most conservative to the most progressive. The "Religious Declaration" has been used by clergy to design worship services and as the focus for sermons. It has been used by denominations as a template to develop their own sexual ethics policy. The network of endorsers has also been used as a way to identify progressive supporters in more conservative denominations. A new guidebook, *A Time To Build: Creating Sexually Healthy Faith*

Communities, provides guidance to congregations on how to implement the mandates of the declaration.*

There is a compelling need for religious voices to join together to
offer prophetic witness to God's good gift of sexuality to all people.
Our ministry is to heal the brokenness that so many experience
about their sexuality and to help people celebrate their sexuality
with holiness and integrity. We must be committed to helping young
people understand their sexual development and offer them the
skills for moral discernment and responsible decision-making. We
must offer both young people and adults the opportunity and the
ability to choose meaningful, intimate relationships that are based
on consent, mutuality, honesty, and responsibility. When the decade
review of *Body and Soul* is written, may we be able to smile and say,
"Look how far we've come."

Religious Declaration on
Sexual Morality, Justice, and Healing

(Reprinted with permission from
the Religious Institute on Sexual Morality, Justice, and Healing)

Sexuality is God's life-giving and life-fulfilling gift. We come from
diverse religious communities to recognize sexuality as central to our
humanity and as integral to our spirituality. We are speaking out
against the pain, brokenness, oppression, and loss of meaning that
many experience about their sexuality.

Our faith traditions celebrate the goodness of creation, including
our bodies and our sexuality. We sin when this sacred gift is abused
or exploited. However, the great promise of our traditions is love,
healing, and restored relationships.

Our culture needs a sexual ethic focused on personal relationships
and social justice rather than particular sexual acts. All persons have
the right and responsibility to lead sexual lives that express love, justice, mutuality, commitment, consent, and pleasure. Grounded in
respect for the body and for the vulnerability that intimacy brings,
this ethic fosters physical, emotional, and spiritual health. It accepts

---

*The guidebook can be ordered for $12.95 (including postage and handling) from the Reli-
gious Institute on Sexual Morality, Justice, and Healing, 304 Main Avenue, #335, Norwalk,
CT 06851. Bulk rates are $9.95 for more than ten copies. All orders must be prepaid.

no double standards and applies to all persons, without regard to sex, gender, color, age, bodily condition, marital status, or sexual orientation.

God hears the cries of those who suffer from the failure of religious communities to address sexuality. We are called today to see, hear, and respond to the suffering caused by violence against women and sexual minorities, the HIV pandemic, unsustainable population growth and over-consumption, and the commercial exploitation of sexuality.

Faith communities must therefore be truth seeking, courageous, and just. We call for:

- Theological reflection that integrates the wisdom of excluded, often silenced peoples, and insights about sexuality from medicine, social science, the arts and humanities.

- Full inclusion of women and sexual minorities in congregational life, including their ordination and the blessing of same-sex unions.

- Sexuality counseling and education throughout the lifespan from trained religious leaders.

- Support for those who challenge sexual oppression and who work for justice within their congregations and denominations.

Faith communities must also advocate for sexual and spiritual wholeness in society. We call for:

- Lifelong, age-appropriate sexuality education in schools, seminaries, and community settings.

- A faith-based commitment to sexual and reproductive rights, including access to voluntary contraception, abortion, and HIV/STD prevention and treatment.

- Religious leadership in movements to end sexual and social injustice.

God rejoices when we celebrate our sexuality with holiness and integrity.

Faith-Based Sexuality Education Curricula
for Adolescents

Reprinted with permission from Debra W. Haffner, *A Time to Build: Creating Sexually Healthy Faith Communities,* Norwalk, Conn.: Religious Institute on Sexual Morality, Justice, and Healing, 2002.

Dating: The Art of Respect
Debbie Eisenbise and Lee Krahenbuhl
A middle school and high school curriculum (Church of the Brethren and the Mennonite Church, 1998); $14.95; Faith & Life Resources, P.O. Box 347, Newton, KS 67114; phone: 800-743-2484; fax: 316-283-0454; website: *www2.southwind.net/~gcmc/flp.*

God's Gift of Sex
Carol Duerksen
A seven-session course for teenagers (Church of the Brethren and the Mennonite Church, 1998); $13.95; Faith & Life Resources, P.O. Box 347, Newton, KS 67114; phone: 800-743-2484; fax: 316-283-0454; website: *www2.southwind.net/~gcmc/flp.*

In God's Image: Male and Female
Patricia Martens Miller
A human sexuality program for grades five through eight. Teacher's manuals, videos, student and parent worksheets, and additional materials are available for each grade (Catholic, 1989); teacher manual, $10.00; call for pricing of additional materials; Flannery Company, 13123 Arrowspace Drive, Victorville, CA 92394; phone: 800-456-3400; fax: 800-284-5600.

*Keeping It Real: A Faith-Based Model for Teen Dialog
on Sex and Sexuality*
A seven-session program for teenagers developed by the Black Church Initiative of the Religious Coalition for Reproductive Choice. It consists of a facilitator's guide and a teen activity book. 2000; Religious Coalition for Reproductive Choice, 1025 Vermont Avenue, N.W., Suite 1130, Washington, DC 20005; phone: 202-628-7700; fax: 202-628-7716; website: *www.rcrc.org.*

Let's Be Real: Honest Discussions about Faith and Sexuality
Duane A. Ewers and M. Stevens Games, Editors
This nondenominational Christian curriculum is designed for adolescents in middle school and high school. It consists of six sessions that discuss anatomy, decision-making, relationships, contraception, and sexually transmitted diseases, as well as media and culture. A parent resource is included. 1998; $20.00; Abingdon Press, 201 Eighth Avenue S., Box 801, Nashville, TN 37202-0801; phone: 800-251-3320; fax: 800-836-7802; website: *www.abingdon.org.*

Love—All That and More
A program for high school and college youth that includes a six-session curriculum and three videos as well as separate facilitators' guides for Jewish and Christian youth. 2000; $285, Center for the Prevention of Sexual and Domestic Violence, 2400 N. 45th Street, Suite 10, Seattle, WA 98103, phone: 206-634-1903, website: *www.cpsdv.org.*

A Course of Study for Teenagers, Revised and Updated
Rebecca Voelkel-Haugen and Marie M. Fortune
This curriculum for teenagers covers sexual abuse and harassment (UCC). 1996; $8.95; United Church Press, 700 Prospect Avenue, Cleveland, OH 44115-1100; phone: 800-537-3394; fax 216-736-3713; website: *www.ucc.org.*

Some Body! Fast Lane Bible Studies for Junior High Youth
Steve Ropp
A middle school curriculum (Church of the Brethren and the Mennonite Church, 1998); $9.99; Faith & Life Resources, P.O. Box 347, Newton, KS 67114; phone: 800-743-2484; fax: 316-283-0454; website: *www2.southwind.net/~gcmc/flp.*

True Love Waits 2001: Pure Joy: God's Formula
An abstinence-only-until-marriage campaign for teenagers and college students (Southern Baptist, 2001); $4.95; Lifeway Christian Resources, Customer Service Department, P.O. Box 113, Nashville, TN 37202-0113; phone: 800-458-2772; fax: 615-251-5933; website: *www.lifeway.com.*

Our Whole Lives (OWL): A Lifespan Sexuality Education Series
OWL is a comprehensive lifespan sexuality education series developed jointly by the Unitarian Universalist Association and the United Church of Christ Board for Homeland Ministries. The series includes OWL Grades K through 1, OWL Grades 4 through 6, OWL Grades 7 through 9, OWL Grades 10 through 12, OWL Adults, a parent guide, advocacy manual, and accompanying guides on OWL and faith for each grade level. Information about the program is available at the website of the Unitarian Universalist Association (Unitarian Universalist Association and United Church of Christ). Call for prices for each level. Unitarian Universalist Association, UUA Bookstore, 25 Beacon Street, Boston, MA 02108; phone: 800-215-9076; fax: 617-723-4805; website: *www.uua.org.*

Notes

1. *God's Gift of Sexuality* (Louisville: Presbyterian Church [U.S.A.], 1989).

2. John Filiatreau, "GA Affirms 'God's Gift' Curriculum," *News:* 214th General Assembly (June 20, 2002), available at *www.pcusa.org/ga214/news/ga02108.htm.*

3. Ibid.

4. Ibid.

5. "Sex Education Stirs Controversy," *USA Today,* July 10, 2002.

6. *Presbyterians and Human Sexuality 1991* (Louisville: Presbyterian Church [U.S.A.], 1991), 43.

7. Ibid., 47.

8. Ibid., 48.

9. *Facts at a Glance* (Washington, D.C.: Child Trends, August 2000). The decline in the number of births was smaller than the decline in the birth rate because of the increase in the number of teenage women.

10. Jo Anne Grunbaum et al., "Youth Risk Behavior Surveillance—United States, 2001," *Morbidity and Mortality Weekly Report,* June 28, 2002, 51 (SS04), 1–64.

11. J. E. Darroch and S. Singh, "Why Is Teenage Pregnancy Declining: The Roles of Abstinence, Sexual Activity, and Contraceptive Use," *Occasional Report,* no. 1 (New York: Alan Guttmacher Institute, 1999).

12. Ibid.

13. Ibid.

14. *Facts at a Glance.*

15. Ibid.

16. Ibid.

17. Todd Summers, Jennifer Kates, and Gillian Murphy, *The Tip of the Iceberg: The Global Impact of HIV/AIDS on Youth* (Menlo Park, Calif. Henry J. Kaiser Family Foundation, 2002).

18. National Guidelines Task Force, *Guidelines for Comprehensive Sexuality Education* (New York: SIECUS, 1991).

19. U.S. Social Security Act, Sec. 510 (b) (2).

20. Ibid.

21. *A Call to Action For Religious Leaders* (Norwalk: Conn.: Religious Institute on Sexual Morality, Justice, and Healing, 2002).

22. For an in-depth analysis of abstinence-only programming, see D. W. Haffner, "What's Wrong with Abstinence-Only Sexuality Education Programs," *SIECUS Report* 25, no. 4 (April–May 1997): 9–13.

23. J. Jemott et al., "Abstinence and Safer Sex HIV Risk Reduction Interventions for African American Adolescents: A Randomized Controlled Trial," *JAMA* 279, no. 19 (May 20, 1998): 1529–36.

24. "An Open Letter to Religious Leaders about Sex Education" (Norwalk, Conn.: Religious Institute on Sexual Morality, Justice, and Healing, 2002).

25. National Campaign to Prevent Teen Pregnancy, *Faithful Nation* (Washington, D.C.: National Campaign to Prevent Teen Pregnancy, 2001).

26. Steve Clapp, Kristen Leverton Helbert, and Angela Zizak, *Faith Matters: Teenagers, Religion, and Sexuality* (Fort Wayne, Ind.: LifeQuest, 2002, 2003).

27. National Campaign to Prevent Teen Pregnancy, *Faithful Nation.*

28. "Risky Sex Less Likely for Religious Teens," Reuters health news release, October 29, 2001.

29. National Campaign to Prevent Teen Pregnancy, *Faithful Nation.*

30. Clapp et al., *Faith Matters.*

31. Ibid.

32. National Campaign to Prevent Teen Pregnancy, *Faithful Nation.*

33. Clapp et al., *Faith Matters.*

34. Ibid.

35. National Campaign to Prevent Teen Pregnancy, *Faithful Nation.*

36. Debra W. Haffner, *A Time to Speak* (New York: SIECUS, 1998).

37. "An Open Letter to Religious Educators on Sex Education."

38. This list is used with permission from D. W. Haffner, *A Time to Build: Creating Sexually Healthy Faith Communities* (Norwalk, Conn.: Religious Institute on Sexual Morality, Justice, and Healing, 2002).

39. Tom Strode, "Current Baptist Press News," January 19, 2000.

40. Ibid.

41. Laura Schlessinger, "Declaration Cloaks Its Positions in Religion," United Press International syndicate, February 23, 2000.

42. "Religious Declaration on Human Sexual Morality," *www.gospelcom.net/ mlm/declaration;* also see "Declaration Affirms Biblical Teaching on Sexual Morality," *www.layman.org/layman/news/news-around-church/declaration-affirms-biblical .html.*

9

Embracing God as Goddess

Exploring Connections between Female Sexuality, Naming the Divine, and Struggling for Justice

Rebecca Todd Peters

> I will praise God, my Beloved,
> for she is altogether lovely.
> Her presence satisfies my soul,
> she fills my senses to overflowing
> so that I cannot speak.[1]

Recently we were sitting at the dinner table when our two-year-old looked up and asked, "Who is God?" You would think that, as a feminist Christian ethicist, I would have prepared myself for this question. Indeed, over the past several years I have painstakingly searched for children's books about God that reflect (or at least do not contradict) my own theo-ethical beliefs. We have been reading a number of these to and with her since she was very young. I have played out different scenarios in my mind about how to talk with her about God. I guess I was expecting something more along the lines of "Where does God come from?" or "Why did God make mosquitoes?" But she caught me unawares. *Who is God?*

Even if I have come to some kind of understanding approximating an answer to this question, how am I to explain this to a two-year-old? I began to talk about God's relationship to us and about how God had created the world and all the things in it and how much God cares for us. Not missing a beat she queried, "Did he make the trees?" "Yes, she made the trees." "Did he make the bunny rabbits?" "Yes, she made the bunny rabbits." "Did she make my milk?" "Well, the cow made your milk, but God made the cow." "Did she make the table?" And so on regarding all the objects within her sight for the next ten minutes.

Here is a young child who assumes that God is male, even with parents who are committed to gender justice and inclusive language. Luckily, we have paid enough attention to gender in our household that when I switched to a feminine pronoun in response to her queries, she quite naturally followed my lead. It's not that I want to teach her that God is female rather than male, or do I? Gender is an important, and highly contested, factor in understanding who God is, even for a small child.

In the struggles for inclusive language over the past thirty years, feminists, womanists, mujeristas, and other justice-seeking people have strived to develop images and metaphors for God that expand our imaginations and allow us to experience the divine in wholly new ways.[2] However, most people, even those committed to inclusive language, shy away from using female names and pronouns to refer to God. Mother God is rarely used, and the thought of speaking of the divine as Goddess is anathema to most Christians. The juxtapositions of the very words—God and Goddess—illustrate how deeply gendered our language remains.[3] "God" is no more gender neutral than "man" or "mankind" is, and yet, resistance to changing the way we talk about God/ess runs deep.[4] Female metaphors and analogies are acceptable on occasion, but we strive mostly for gender neutrality. Why this reticence to embrace truly female images of God that can stand beside the clearly male images of God that have colonized our thought, language, and theology?[5]

One way to answer this question is to enter into the process of re-imagining the divine ourselves and to discover the sources of our own fear and resistance to speaking of the divine as Sophia or Goddess. In doing so, we need to be aware that this fear is about more than a reaction to female names for the divine. It is about resistance to the ethical implications such language unleashes. As Beverly Harrison points out in an essay examining the relationship between sexism and language in Christian ethics, "A working assumption of a feminist ethic must be that we critically assess all language for its moral effects."[6] The purpose of this essay is to explore the ethical implications of one such relationship, the connection between our sexuality and how we image God/ess.[7] In the process, we will try on new ways of thinking about the power and presence of the divine in our lives and world. Because sexuality, and particularly women's sexuality, is not something readily associated with the divine, this might entail discomfort or uneasiness for some. Indeed, connecting women's sexuality with the divine may be at the heart of anxiety about Goddess language. Nevertheless, I invite readers to stay with this God/ess imagery for a time: embrace it, experiment with it, and search out sources of resistance to knowing the divine in different ways. This exploration may well show how female bodies and sexuality can offer expanded knowledge of and expressions for God/ess.

Confronting resistance and fear

Reaction to the 1991 Presbyterian report, "Keeping Body and Soul Together," exemplifies the resistance and fear that often greet attempts to rethink sexual theology. Right-wing detractors immediately attacked a foundational claim of the study, namely, that a sexual ethic with an exclusive norm of heterosexual marriage is no longer adequate. In doing so, critics highlighted controversial issues like homosexuality and teen sex without ever offering any reasonable or persuasive argument that the traditional norm they were defending was still viable. The Presbyterian Church (U.S.A.) has no exclusive hold on this reaction, however, as right-wing organizations within many mainline denominations have capitalized on people's fears about homosexuality and on mystification of lesbian, gay, bisexual, and transgender ("LGBT") people in order to portray the current debates about sexual ethics as if they were only about ordaining queer clergy.[8] This strategy has preempted a deeper, more productive debate about sexual behavior and Christian ethics that would recognize the diversity and complexity of intimate relationships and move beyond the woefully inadequate standard of marriage as the normative defining relationship within which sexual intimacy ought to occur. The controversy over "the sexuality report" was second only to the uproar two years later surrounding the Re-Imagining event.[9]

The hostile reaction to the Re-Imagining gathering (which brought the Presbyterian Church to the brink of denominational split) is illustrative of the discomfort and misunderstanding often attached to feminist liturgical expressions that incorporate divine female imagery.[10] In November 1993, twenty-two hundred women and some men spent four days together celebrating women's lives, struggles, and moral wisdom in the context of their faith journeys. Shared rituals focused on worshiping the divine in a multitude of forms and with a variety of names. Women's embodied experience, including sexuality, was lifted up as not only divinely blessed, but as a window into our knowledge of God/ess. The ideas that were expressed and celebrated were not radically new within feminist circles. What was transformative and ultimately so threatening about the event was that feminist theological ideas of the last several decades were collectively embodied in liturgy and brought into the cultural and religious mainstream through widespread media coverage initiated, ironically, by conservative right-wing publications, including *The Good News* (United Methodist Church) and *The Layman* (Presbyterian). The extreme reaction of right-wing factions within these Protestant churches to the incorporation of female images of the divine into the liturgy at the Re-Imagining Conference speaks to the volatility of this issue and the vehemence with which it has been treated in mainline Christianity.

The accusation of pagan worship is levied against feminist, womanist, mujerista, and other liberationist theologians whenever they explore female images and embodiments of the divine. This sensationalizing rhetoric seeks to discredit rather than to dialogue about theological and ethical issues. The Religious Right has invoked stereotypes and misinformation about feminist theologies and sexual ethics in an effort to portray them as forms of heresy and witchcraft that threaten the core fundamentals of Christianity. The strategy of the right wing has been to obfuscate meaningful theological efforts to reexamine God language and moral norms for sexual behavior by quoting people and ideas out of context and by playing on people's fears of change and difference. As happened with Re-Imagining, this discrediting is accomplished through demonizing the Other (for the most part, feminists, womanists, and

LGBT people) and denouncing changes proposed by historically marginalized groups of Christians.

The fact that the terms "homosexuality" and "goddess worship" have become lightning rods for conservative and fundamentalist factions of mainline churches is not coincidental. (The mere mention of these terms sends dollars flying into the coffers of right-wing organizations.) Changes in these two areas of theo-ethical discourse — language about God and sexuality—will require an enormous paradigm shift.[11] A dialectical relationship exists between conceptions of divinity and sexual ethics that must be acknowledged and examined as we seek sexual justice in confusing times. Differently said, theology and ethics are intimately related. While neither is determinative of the other, they exist in a dynamic relationship.[12] What we think about God/ess and our relationship to her affects our ethical decision-making. If we believe that God disapproves of nonmarital sex, then that affects behavior in one of several ways: we do not have nonmarital sex; we have nonmarital sex and feel guilty and alienated from God; we think that such a God does not make sense in a world in which nonmarital sex is a positive aspect of life and thus we reject God; or we experience God's presence and love in the context of intimate relationship, which helps us rethink our relationship with God and our theology. While beliefs about God/ess can influence behavior, so, too, our experience of the world is an important window into how and what we know about God/ess.

Change is occurring within the Christian tradition. Faithful believers are praying to a female Christian God/ess and embracing ethical models of sexual behavior that differ from the historic stance that Christian churches have supported. Contemporary sexual discourse marked by justice, love, and right relation requires an alternative social order and reflects a theological conception of the divine that is fundamentally different from traditional male-stream theology.[13] However, none of what is happening is necessarily heretical or against the historic principles of the Christian faith tradition.

In my judgment, those of us living at the beginning of the twenty-first century are experiencing the continued revelation of God/ess and a continuing process of reformation. The Religious Right is wrong in its assessment that these changes are incongruous with Christianity. As Elizabeth Johnson points out, "Words about God are cultural creatures, entwined with the mores and adventures of the faith community that uses them. As cultures shift, so too does the specificity of God-talk."[14] Resolution of these issues will mark the future of both church and society. This theological conflict reflects present ethical conundrums that people are facing daily. The only way for churches to stay relevant is for theology and ethics to help people make sense of the world in which they live.[15] *Semper reformanda* or "always reforming" is an ongoing and a cherished legacy of the Reformed tradition.

Women's bodies as a starting point for theo-ethical reflection about God/ess[16]

Women's bodies might seem like an odd starting place when thinking about God/ess, especially because historically women's sexuality, as Ursula Pfafflin points out, has been seen as a hindrance to contact with God, not to mention women's ability to function as ordained ministers and priests.[17] In this light, women's sexuality has long been a topic of theological import! If women experience relationship with God in all aspects of life — as we are menstruating, having sex, or giving birth — then the barrier lies not between women and God, but in traditional theological attitudes rooted in male ignorance and ambivalence about women and female sexuality. Women's experience of sexuality can offer powerful means for thinking afresh about God/ess.

In a recent essay, Beverly Clack explores the relationship between human sexuality and the concept of God/ess.[18] She notes that "the messy, painful, and sometimes tragic business of procreation and life-giving has not been seen as appropriate for the God of order celebrated in the Western tradition. Better that God should create by his word than through the organic process of birthing!"[19] I agree with Clack that the changing nature of women's bodies offers important insights into understanding the divine. For example, over the course of an average lifetime, female bodies morph and shift in amazing ways. Adolescent girls gradually develop swelling breasts and hips that indicate their ability to bear and feed children. Cycles of menstruation are marked by ovulation, changes in vaginal fluid, and blood issuing forth where there is no wound. During pregnancy, women grow larger with swollen bellies and feel many changes as their bodies nurture nascent human life. In childbirth, the female body opens in almost inconceivable ways and allows new life to issue forth from existing life. In nursing, women's breasts become heavy with life-sustaining fluid so pure and perfectly attuned to the needs of their infants that commercial manufacturers have been unable to reproduce it. Through menopause women move, once again, into a new state of being manifested in their physical bodies by hot flashes and the cessation of menstrual activity. Female orgasms and sexual pleasure vary widely not only from woman to woman, but also within the sexual experiences of an individual woman.[20] In short, the very nature of female sexuality can only be defined as *changeable*.

If we start with women's bodily experience of sexuality as a window into the divine, its very mutability can offer insight into redefining the way we think about God/ess. Furthermore, as Clack observes, "It is not only women who change: while there is less obvious physical evidence, men's bodies change too."[21] This is also important to consider in developing insights into the concept of divinity. Opening up our understanding of God/ess to the possibility of change can resonate profoundly with men as well as women.

Historically, the Western Christian tradition has emphasized God's immutability and impassability. Christian theologians have found comfort in viewing the divine as unchangeable in the midst of an unpredictable world. However, the concept of immutability is contradicted by actions of God/ess in the Hebrew Bible where we see God/ess changing her mind in negotiating relationships with particular figures. In Genesis, for example, we encounter a God/ess who thinks about her actions and discusses them with Abraham. Indeed, it is through her conversation with Abraham that she agrees to spare Sodom and Gomorrah if only ten righteous people can be found. Nevertheless, the idea of God/ess's changeless perfection has made deep inroads into the Christian imagination. While this image supposedly evokes God/ess's constancy and thereby comforts human beings by convincing us that God/ess is all that we are not, I find it a strangely dead image for a living faith. Theologically, the problem of understanding the divine as unchangeable becomes more complicated when combined with other attributes of God as "all good" and "all powerful." When this theological interpretation confronts very real evil and suffering in the world, the result is the classic dilemma of theodicy.

Given that tragedy and pain åre part of the human experience, a theology of an immovable God is woefully inadequate to help the majority of the world's people make sense of their lives. For people who experience lives of relative comfort and privilege, this theological construct may sometimes suffice. For those with a steady paycheck, a healthy family, a decent education, and the comfort and power to secure a First World existence, the image of God as all good, all powerful, and unchangeable can contribute to a personal sense of "blessedness" or well-being. It enables an interpretation of life circumstances as "blessings" that God has bestowed. As long as one remains inside that world, this theology may remain adequate.

What happens, however, when we think through the logic of this theology in the context of massive global economic disparity? Do First World white Christians really believe we are God's chosen people? That our power and privilege are divinely ordained? That we have more resources and physical comforts because *God loves us more?* Do we really believe that our consumption patterns and predilection for gas-guzzling cars and SUVs are morally neutral? Or that people the world over are living in poverty through some personal moral failing or because they have fallen into disfavor with God? Unfortunately, many U.S. citizens do believe these things, and a theology of impassability, beneficence, and omnipotence contributes to the isolationist behavior prominent among many First World Christians. In telling ways, mainline churches' preoccupation with arguing about individualized sexual ethics becomes a means to ignore the interconnections between androcentric theology and the structural sins of poverty, racism, and greed that underlie resistance to birthing a new social order.

Often, the theology of an immutable God fails even privileged, economically stable white Christians. How does one explain an unchanging, immovable God to a mother who has lost her baby or to a man diagnosed with incurable cancer? The emphasis on God's impassability and beneficence falls apart in the face of evil and tragedy. Our theological constructions of the divine must be large enough to help make sense of extreme poverty, random disaster and disease, and devastating violence. Faith is supposed to help make sense of the world. In moments of tragedy and despair, what kind of divine being can do that? An unchanging, changeless God generates self-blame and feelings of abandonment in the face of a changing, imperfect world. In contrast, a God/ess open to change is consistent with images of divine partnership with humankind, working together in the ongoing process of co-creation.[22]

Women as life-carriers, life-bearers, and life-formers know what it is like to be changed by our children and to weep with them in their pain, to be rejected by them and love them still, and to be aware of them even when they are not present.[23] Through our embodied experience, women have known the pains and joys of physical and emotional change. Our monthly cycles and experiences of puberty, childbirth, nursing, and menopause allow us to know change as a natural part of the cycle of life. However, I have no intention of idealizing, romanticizing, or essentializing these experiences. Many women experience debilitating pain on a monthly basis while others experience amenorrhea due to extreme malnutrition.[24] The majority of the world's women in labor face the very real possibility of death along with other dangers that accompany giving birth, and many women never experience pregnancy and childbirth. While motherhood can bring great joy, it is also often tedious, stressful, and boring. Nevertheless, the fact that most women share at least some of these experiences provides fertile ground for exploring possible insights that might expand our knowledge of God/ess. While the Genesis text tells the story that humanity was made in God's image, we know also that it is human to create the divine in our own image. A static image of God based primarily on male experience and articulation of the divine must be supplemented and reshaped in dialogue with female experience and knowledge of the divine.

The image of God/ess as creator, life-bearer, and ground of all existence has deep historical roots and resonates well with many of the world's women. In a world increasingly damaged by human behavior and hubris, many people are turning toward an image of humanity in partnership with a divine being who cares for the earth. As co-creators with God/ess, we can take comfort in the knowledge that she risks and weeps with us in the face of tragedy. Understanding God/ess as open to change can allow us to face tragedy without blaming the divine or feeling that we have been abandoned.

This way of thinking about God/ess also has bearing on how we construct sexual ethics. Images of the divine matter because our sexual ethics reflect our understanding not only of God/ess, but also of her relationship with humanity. It is this radical notion of the divine as Goddess as well as God as our partner and friend and as being-in-relation that was celebrated at the Re-Imagining Conference. It is also the divine image found at the heart of much contemporary discourse about sexual ethics.

Language about God/ess and sexuality

Thus far we have compared a traditionalist understanding of God with a liberationist understanding of God/ess. What relationship does the image of God/ess have with sexual ethics? Many theologians have made trenchant observations about how traditional, patriarchal theology affects the understanding of gender and sexuality. Perhaps most famously, Mary Daly wrote, "If God is male, then the male is God."[25] Clack has noted that "Just as power, knowledge, invulnerability, and steadfastness are privileged in an androcentric culture, so omnipotence, omniscience, and impassibility are central to the classical concept of God."[26] These androcentric notions of God have contributed to a social order in which control and order are highly valued and maintained. If God is imaged as a divine being "in control," then control itself becomes a desirable moral norm.

In the midst of such a theological climate, the control of sexual partnering, sexual expression, and sexual behavior become important social and ecclesiological tasks. However, sexual desire, attraction, erection, and orgasm are not experiences easily controlled. We do not necessarily choose the person to whom we will be attracted. While Western culture validates heterosexual desire, when it comes to same-sex attractions, many people insist that gay people should control their attractions in ways that heterosexual couples are never asked to do. Traditional religiocultural belief systems rooted in androcentric Christian theology have long held that homosexual behavior is wrong because it stands outside the social order of control so central to this theology. A double standard is created in which it is permissible for heterosexual people to fall in love and pursue relationships with the objects of their affection (provided they with-hold sexual coupling until after they are legally married), but same-sex attractions are denounced as deviant and sinful. Heterosexual people who accept this double standard may experience cognitive dissonance when they come face to face with gay friends and loved ones who are just as powerless as they are to decide or control to whom they are attracted. Inasmuch as many heterosexually identi-fied people become aware of their inability to exercise control over their feelings of desire and choice of a love partner, they can resonate with the experience of their gay, lesbian, bisexual, and transgender friends and family. It is in these complex feelings and choices of personal relationship and in the risks that people take to share their stories that transformation beyond homophobia takes place in church and society.

Human experience of erection and orgasm also witness to the mythic dimension of the belief that we can "control" our sexual-ity.[27] As many men are painfully aware, their ability to stimulate or inhibit an erection at will is not always something they are able to control. The popularity of drugs like Viagra that enable men to have erections supports the contention that we humans ought to be able to control sexual performance. (Even the language of "perform-ance," "impotence," and "frigidity" suggests deeply imbedded issues of power and control.) Additionally, most women and men are not able to "control" their orgasms. Mary Pellauer speaks of sexual en-counter as a journey that is different every time she and her partner meet. She describes approaching orgasm this way:

> To stop here is frustrating, incomplete; it leaves me with a sense that it is not over, that there is more....All I can do is to re-main open to the flaring guidance I receive from the impulses and feelings as they arise, little beaconlights summoning me forward.[28]

A certain amount of vulnerability, abandonment, or surrender is in-volved in giving oneself over to sexual ecstasy. These realities do not mesh well with theological and cultural values based on the glorifi-cation of power and control, but what happens to sexual experience and understanding when images of the divine shift?

Focusing on God/ess's graciousness and love, as well as her desire for justice and a flourishing creation, can generate a very different sexual ethic. These are precisely the theological foundations on which recent models of sexual ethics are grounded. The love and concern of God/ess for the wholeness of human experience is emphasized over against order and control. Rather than prescribing the form in which sexual activity should take place (heterosexual marriage), liberationist ethicists address the substance of the sexual relationship itself. Is it healthy? Is it harming anyone? Does it contribute to creating a more just world? A sex-positive "ethic of common decency," such as that offered in the 1991 Presbyterian report, affirms that God/ess celebrates and delights in our sexuality and that it is truly a gift given to enjoy, explore, and share within the boundaries of relationships that contribute to individual and communal well-being. This sexual ethic is not about eliminating boundaries or ethical mores as guides for sexual activity. Rather it requires redefining where those boundaries should lie and what occurs within sexual relationships. Images and beliefs about God/ess have direct bearing on how we discern those boundaries and moral norms. A God/ess open to change, vulnerability, and partnership exercises a nontraditional form of power rooted in relationality and reciprocity. These, then, can become the moral ground for ethical behavior in the world, including sexual behavior.

The very fact that many people experience the divine presence in their relationships with lovers, children, parents, and friends is witness to the power of transformation that exists in mutuality. In exploring the possibilities of knowing God/ess more fully, we need to "get into our souls" and realize the positive ways that women and men can experience divine relational power. Embodied knowledge of God/ess is new for some and threatening for others. One way to overcome fear of the unknown is to start by sticking a toe into the abyss. I invite you to experiment with these ideas, experience the movement and diversity they offer, and discover the joy they unleash. You might start by exploring female-gendered language for God/ess in your own prayer life and spiritual journey. How do these images of God/ess feel? How do they change your relationship with God/ess? Then examine language for God in worship. Has your church incorporated female images and language about God into liturgy or merely eliminated the male ones? Talk with people in your congregation, especially children, about their understanding of God. Is your congregation comfortable praying to God as Goddess? Are your girl and boy children growing up equally affirmed in the image of the divine?

Along the way we must remember that the experimental nature of this process is an attempt to gain insight and knowledge about something inherently ineffable. Ultimately, the divine remains a mystery. Exploring and utilizing female names and images for the divine is an attempt to know God/ess in new ways, ways that have deep personal resonance for many people. However, this epistemological insight into the divine should not be regarded as counterfundamentalism or an effort to replace traditional male images of God with female ones. Rather, expanding God/ess language in personal and corporate worship can reveal the divine to us in fresh and challenging ways.

Embracing the kin-dom: the challenge of a new social order

The use of inclusive (or rather expansive) language in worship, especially in speaking about God/ess, is often dismissed as "merely" semantics and a matter peripheral to the deeper concerns of faith and life. It is important to insist, again and again, that the issue of language is central because language both reflects and reinforces what we believe about God/ess, our relationship with her, and relationships between the entire human and nonhuman world. *Metanoia* is called for, a change of mind and heart. If genuine transformation does not take place, if we do not believe deeply in our souls that this matters, it becomes easier to acquiesce in the face of resistance or simply ignore the history of female imagery for the divine in biblical and Christian traditions. Certainly this is not the only issue communities of faith should be addressing, but success in our struggles for justice in other areas is related intimately to how we worship, the hymns we sing, the prayers we utter, and the images of God/ess that stir hearts and minds.

The language of worship, prayer, and the daily vernacular is never a fringe issue. It indicates the kind of social order that Christians embrace and live into in ministry, mission, and our life journeys.

Womanist scholars have long emphasized the link between songs, prayers, and language of the black church with a justice-oriented and liberatory theology that seeks "hope, salvation, and transformation."[29] As long as we continue to allow a male monopoly of language for the divine without balancing it with female language and images, we capitulate to the powerful privilege of male-dominated culture and replicate those structures in our very speech. It has been thirty years since Mary Daly's groundbreaking book, and yet we still have not moved "beyond God the Father." Until we are able to do so and embrace God/ess the Mother along with the many other female faces of the divine, we will fail to realize the social order of justice and equality that so many are striving to usher forth.

Re-imagining God in ways that incorporate female images is intimately connected to struggles for justice that address concrete, material oppressions in people's lives. To come full circle, I return to my daughter. As a two-year-old, she is at the beginning of discovering the world, including God/ess. I want her, as a womanchild, to know God/ess in ways I had to discover only as an adult, in ways that connect my embodied female self (and her embodied female self) to that which is divine. One gift that we gave her to help her on that path is her Christian name. In the first days of her life, as I held her in my arms, I felt the presence of the sacred and knew that this tiny infant would be a window into God/ess's wisdom for me in the years to come. Naming her Sophia was a personal act of reclamation of the divine as female. I also hoped that blessing her with a strong name and a personal connection to the female Christian traditions of the divine would offer her strength and wisdom for her own life journey.[30]

As the child of educated, white, U.S. parents, Sophia will undoubtedly live a life of relative privilege. What matters is how she is taught to understand and use her privilege. No one is exempt from the urgency of struggles for justice. Privileges are not blessings from God/ess but accidents of birth. First World Christians and particularly *white* First World Christians must remember that faith is about being in relationship with God/ess and the larger world. In the midst of privilege it is easy to focus exclusively on the first relationship, especially if we retain a traditional "God's-in-control-all's-right-with-the-world" image of divine power (and by extension, our own). The image of the divine as Goddess calls people of faith to live into the future beyond a mythology of control and with openness to change. With the voice of a mother, sister, and female friend, She calls us to a renewed sense of accountability, asking us to risk losing even our gender and other social privileges in order to further the work of justice.

Notes

1. Janet Morley quoted in Mary Grey, *Introducing Feminist Images of God* (Cleveland: Pilgrim, 2001), 15.

2. Mary Grey's *Introducing Feminist Images of God* is a wonderful overview of the history of these struggles and how different feminisms, including Jewish, liberationist, womanist, and Two-Thirds World women (African, Asian, and Latin American) have approached talking about God.

3. Virginia Ramey Mollenkott first brought this point to my attention at a Families 2000 conference sponsored by the National Council of Churches in 1991.

4. In this essay I refer to the divine as "God/ess" with the exception of particular contexts in which an exclusively male image of the divine is intended. In those cases I use the traditional "God."

5. Following Sallie McFague's advice, we must be cautious about broadening conceptions of God to include the "feminine" over against the "masculine" because this strategy has a tendency to reinforce culturally scripted stereotypes. Sallie McFague, *Models of God: Theology for an Ecological, Nuclear Age* (Minneapolis: Fortress, 1987), 98–99.

6. Beverly Harrison, "Sexism and the Language of Christian Ethics," *Making the Connections: Essays in Feminist Social Ethics,* ed. Carol Robb (Boston: Beacon, 1985), 24.

7. For an exposition of the ethical implications of the gospel lyrics "mother to the motherless" and "father to the fatherless" with regard to the topics of power and injustice, see Cheryl Townsend Gilkes, " 'Mother to the Motherless, Father to the Fatherless': Power, Gender, and Community in an Afrocentric Biblical Tradition," *Semeia* 47 (1989): 57–85.

8. The term "queer" denotes those who self-identify outside of a heterosexual identity, including gay, lesbian, transgender, and bisexual persons.

9. For a more detailed analysis of the Re-Imagining Conference, see Stewart M. Hoover and Lynn Schofield Clark, "Event and Publicity as Social Drama: A Case Study of the RE-Imagining Conference 1995 [sic]," *Review of Religious Studies* 39, no. 2 (December 1997): 153–71.

10. For a more thorough study of divine female imagery in the Bible, see Virginia Ramey Mollenkott, *The Divine Feminine: The Biblical Imagery of God as Female* (New York: Crossroad, 1983); Raphael Patai, *The Hebrew Goddess,* 3d ed. (Detroit: Wayne State University Press, 1990); and Asphodel P. Long, *In a Chariot Drawn by Lions: The Search for the Female in Deity* (Freedom, Calif.: Crossing Press, 1993).

11. This observation is not meant to be reductionist in the sense that these are the *only* two issues relevant or necessary for moving into a new justice-centered era, nor do I mean to imply that they are the most important. Racial justice, economic justice, and environmental justice are also paradigmatic of a justice-centered social order, but in this new era, we will need a much broader conception of God/ess along with a potent critique of compulsory heterosexuality.

12. In traditional theological parlance, this is often referred to as the herme-neutical circle.

13. As the purpose of this essay is to explore reasons that ethical formulations have been so difficult for the church to engage, I will not re-present their arguments here. Suffice it to say, I reject the traditional ethical model of marriage as the sole locus for sexual intimacy and assume that a sexual ethic must be grounded in right relation, justice, and love. See Carter Heyward, *Touching Our Strength: The Erotic as Power and the Love of God* (San Francisco: Harper & Row, 1989); Christine Gudorf, *Body, Sex, and Pleasure: Reconstructing Christian Sexual Ethics* (Cleveland: Pilgrim, 1994); Anne Bathurst Gilson, *Eros Breaking Free: Interpreting Sexual Theo-Ethics* (Cleveland: Pilgrim, 1995); Marvin Ellison, *Erotic Justice: A Liberating Ethic of Sexuality* (Louisville: Westminster John Knox, 1996); and Lisa Sowle Cahill, *Sex, Gender, and Christian Ethics* (Cambridge: Cambridge University Press, 1996).

14. Elizabeth A. Johnson, *She Who Is: The Mystery of God in Feminist Theological Discourse* (New York: Crossroad, 1992), 6.

15. This is not the same as capitulating to contemporary culture or adopting an attitude of "if it feels good do it." Far from it. Serious attempts at rethinking sexual ethics and language about God/ess are critical explorations into the biblical and social meanings of justice in our world today.

16. It is important to note that in discussing the female body and the insights it might provide in understanding God/ess imaginatively, it is not my intent to essentialize women or totalize women's bodily life experiences. Differences of age, race, economic status, culture, and other markers of vulnerability affect women's experiences of their bodies in distinct ways. In this brief essay I am drawing on the realm of my own experience as a white, heterosexually partnered, married, professional woman, and mother of a daughter. I invite other women to contribute to this discussion of how sexuality helps us re-imagine God/ess.

17. Ursula Pfafflin, "Mothers in a Patriarchal World: Experience and Feminist Theory," *Concilium* 6, no. 206 (1989): 16.

18. Beverly Clack, "Human Sexuality and the Concept of the God/ess," in *The Good News of the Body: Sexual Theology and Feminism,* ed. Lisa Isherwood (New York: New York University Press, 2000), 115–33.

19. Ibid., 118.

20. Mary Pellauer, "The Moral Significance of Female Orgasm: Toward Sexual Ethics That Celebrate Women's Sexuality," in *Sexuality and the Sacred: Sources for Theological Reflection,* ed. James B. Nelson and Sandra P. Longfellow (Louisville: Westminster/John Knox, 1994), 153.

21. Clack, "Human Sexuality and the Concept of the God/ess," 130.

22. This image of partnership resonates with contemporary womanist discourse about the divine that emphasizes God's relationship with humankind in

seeking liberation from oppression and strength for life's struggles. See particularly Kelly Delaine Brown, "God Is as Christ Does: Toward a Womanist Theology," *Journal of Religious Thought* 46, no. 1 (1989): 7–16; and Karen Baker-Fletcher, "The Strength of My Life," in *Embracing the Spirit: Womanist Perspectives on Hope, Salvation, and Transformation,* ed. Emilie Townes (Maryknoll, N.Y.: Orbis, 1997), 122–39.

23. While this is certainly not a universal description of all mothers, these represent common experiences of many women who are.

24. In the Two-Thirds World, this malnutrition is due to extreme poverty while in the First World it is more often the result of deeply troubled women seeking approval and acceptance through unrealistic and unhealthy standards of beauty.

25. Mary Daly, *Beyond God the Father: Toward a Philosophy of Women's Liberation* (Boston: Beacon, 1973), 19.

26. Clack, "Human Sexuality and the Concept of the God/ess," 119.

27. This should not be read as support of the idea that men (or women, for that matter) are unable to control their responses to their sexual feelings or desires. While people are capable of making responsible decisions about how they exercise and act upon sexual desire, we are not always able to "control" such physical aspects of sexual response as arousal, erection, and orgasm.

28. Pellauer, "The Moral Significance of Female Orgasm," 156.

29. *Embracing the Spirit: Womanist Perspectives on Hope, Salvation, and Transformation,* edited by Emilie Townes, is oriented toward connecting African American experience and the black church with these themes of hope, salvation, and transformation. Karen Baker-Fletcher in "The Strength of My Life" specifically addresses the topic of "God-talk." Delores Williams, *Sisters in the Wilderness: The Challenge of Womanist God-Talk* (Maryknoll, N.Y.: Orbis, 1993) also addresses the relationship between language about God, womanist and black liberation theology, and the struggle for justice; see particularly chapter 6.

30. For an exemplary development of contemporary Sophia theology, see Johnson, *She Who Is.*

10

Men, Male Myths, and Metanoia

Daniel C. Maguire

Nature has not provided a clear blueprint for gender definition, so culture steps in to fill the void. Before we are capable of critical thinking, we have already been typecast, shaped, and molded. Biology does provide the *x, y* chromosomal definitions of girls and boys, but it is culture that provides the *x, y* definitions of their personalities and attitudes. Lots of twisted messages have been absorbed into our psyches in that osmosis process called "growing up." Roles, self-images, and myths that tell us what we are lie in wait with the blue and pink blankets to assume control and turn us into the kind of man or woman this particular culture at this particular time has decided we should be.

Religions are big players in this socialization process. As religious ethicist John Raines says, "Religions are gendered entities, although often presenting themselves as something simply natural or God-ordained and therefore objective and universal."[1] The Abrahamic religions, Judaism, Christianity, and Islam, have a masculinized God who controls and commands. It is men who are specifically made in that male God's image, and so these religions feed into a macho culture that exalts all manner of male dominance. That is not the way with all religions, and indeed there are remedies for it within Judaism, Christianity, and Islam. Some religions have a head start on this. Taoism, for example, views ultimate reality as feminine and privileges gentle leadership and adaptability. A man growing up in a Taoist culture would have a different sense of self.

Praise be to those religions that dare to step into this briar patch and try to peel away the prickly macho overgrowth to see what stranglehold it has on our sense of ourselves. Presbyterians did this in their 1991 report, "Keeping Body and Soul Together." They recognized that their bold move was only a first step with an unending series of agonizing but liberating steps to follow.

Religions like to stay with old ideas that, like well-broken-in old slippers, provide a comfort we rely on. What could be more discomforting than scholars like Jack Miles in his book *God: A Biography*? He writes: "The God whom ancient Israel worshiped arose as the fusion of a number of the gods whom a nomadic nation had met in its wanderings."[2] That tears the cozy old slippers off believers who felt that God, at least, was secure from fallible characterizations. Bad enough we don't know what *we* are, but not knowing what *God* is shakes the foundations.

This is the can of worms opened by courageous Presbyterians when they undertook to look at sexuality in all of its dimensions and to look especially at how we imitated some bad images of God in deciding what we ourselves are. The "imitation of God" has always been a central category in the three Abrahamic religions. This presents a problem that requires some choices, however, precisely because of the contradictory descriptions of God in both the Jewish and Christian Scriptures. Jeremiah 31 shows a God who promises everlasting love and gentle care while Genesis 6 shows a God who regrets creating humankind and sets out to drown the whole bunch of them, except for a little ark full of chosen folks and animals. As Miles says, this is a God who is "not just unpredictable but dangerously unpredictable."[3] The Jesus of Matthew 11 is meek and humble of heart, but there is little of that ten chapters later in the Jesus of Matthew 21 who, in an epic of "disorderly conduct," tore up the temple, knocking over tables and verbally blasting and disrupting the temple staff. Obviously, deciding what is "God-like" requires scholarly guidance and good sense.

When we are told that we are made "in the image of God," the question arises: which God? If we want to use religious resources to rethink the corrupting notions of gender and sexuality that we have received uncritically from the culture, we have choices to make. Christians have always made choices and often played games with Scripture. Pacifist Christians went to Isaiah 2 to find their mandate to hammer their swords into ploughshares and their spears into pruning hooks, but Crusaders found in Joel 4 the explicit order to hammer their ploughshares into swords and their pruning hooks into spears.

The solution lies in good biblical scholarship. There is much in Scripture that is merely descriptive. It tells us what the culture was like in those harsh times. There was polygamy and brutal slaughter of innocent people in the Bible, but we don't take those as norms. We look amid all of the often confusing and obscure pages of the Bible in search of the norms that apply to today. Our goal is the light that shines through the biblical darkness and points to a new and liberating path.[4] That light is there.

Justice and peace are the two main goals and ideals of Judaism, Christianity, and Islam. Those images and stories in Scripture that point in that direction are the guideposts. When Paul tells women to cover their heads and be silent and to obey their husbands as though those husbands were divine, we see neither justice nor peace in those ideas. They are descriptive of how people thought and lived. They are not a norm for all time. But when Paul in Galatians 3:28 says that in the new perspective of the Jesus movement the usual hostile divisions between males and females, between Greeks and Jews, between slaves and masters are rejected and dissolved, we hear a new symphony, a fresh song of joy, that promises a new heaven and a new earth marked by justice and peace.

When the Song of Songs celebrates sexual pleasure as a supreme gift of God, we can feel our spirits cleansed of the neurotic sexual guilt that sinful Christian history heaped upon us in a supreme insult to our bodies. Scripture study is a search for the renewable moral energies, the real moral treasures that await us in that flawed classic called the Bible. The study of Christian history follows the same discerning path. Such selectivity, guided by the goals of justice and peace, is the hallmark of good theology.

The twisted images of sex

Let's face it. The religions of the world, including the Abrahamic three, have been dominated by men. We can say that, to a great extent, the scripts on all kinds of issues were written by men. The radically egalitarian call that shines through in texts like Galatians

3:28—a text that was probably a basic mantra of early Christianity—got muted. Patriarchy snuffed it out, even by the time the later New Testament was completed. The Jewish comfort with sex was also lost, and the worst of Greco-Roman influences snuck in and took over. Eventually we thought those alien influences, full of sexism and hatred of sexuality, were the word of God.

Sex, which is a blessing, came to be looked on as a blight, and interestingly, the men who dominated Christian leadership tended to blame it on women. This became a sorry legacy that Christianity bequeathed to the Western world. If you distort the notion of sexuality, you distort the concept of what a man is and what a woman is. If sexuality is despised and looked on as a pollution, there can be no healthy definition of gender. We are sexual beings, and when we falsify and degrade the meaning of sexuality, we warp our very selves. This is what happened. Women came to be thought of as identified with sex in a way men are not. This confused our sense of both male and female since both are equally and naturally sexual. Sexuality was seen as bad, and women came to be seen as implicated in sexuality in ways that men are not. Notice how women prostitutes are degraded and scorned, but the men who visit them are not, because in a sick macho culture men are not as defined by their sexuality as are women.

The inability to face our sexuality in Western culture is to a great extent religiously grounded, with historical Christianity bearing enormous blame. Augustine saw sexual passion as the conduit of original sin, so heinous and infectious that the passion of parents that leads to conception befouls the souls of newborns. Ambrose said the worldly marry but the children of the Kingdom of Heaven refrain from all fleshly lust. The Penitentials that regulated Christian life during the early Middle Ages ruled that during times of prayer and on religious feasts there must be no sexual activity. (Contrast this with the Jewish expectation that rabbis engage in sexual relations on the Sabbath.) Thomas Aquinas conceded that marriage was a sacrament, but he said it was the least and last of the sacraments because it had the least spirituality. Sexual pleasure, even in marriage, was long thought to be sinful. And the rule was the more pleasure, the more sin. William of Auxerre in the thirteenth century said that a holy man who has sex with his wife and finds it hateful and disgusting commits no sin. He added, with regret, "This, however, seldom happens."

The twelfth-century Petrus Cantor opined that sex with a beautiful women was a greater sin since it caused greater delight. His contemporary Alain de Lille disagreed, saying sex with a beautiful woman was less sinful "because he was compelled by the sight of her beauty," and "where the compulsion is greater, the sin is slighter." Taken to its logical extreme, this would justify the rape of overwhelmingly beautiful women. Catholicism decided that only celibate hands could administer the sacraments.[5] The message is clear: sexuality is incompatible with spirituality. Sex is dirty, spirituality sublime. And women are the cause of this. If they were not so attractive, this pollution would not enter men's lives. This poison is the legacy of much of Western culture. It's part of what is called "original sin," and we all inherited it to some degree.

One might think that this puritanical horror of sex has been dissipated in a culture where sex is used ubiquitously in the marketplace to promote sales and where frenzied pornography abounds. However, as Grace Jantzen observes, this obsession reflects the historical Christian obsession and is really "the same preoccupation, turned inside out."[6] The addiction to pornography is fueled by a discomfort with sex.

In men, this implicit but virulent hatred of sex translates into hatred of women and of gay men who are perceived to be womanized. The hatred of women (a term I prefer to the Greek "misogyny") and the hatred of gays live at the edge of violence and spill over with vicious frequency. The hatred of women is complex. Like all hatred it involves uneasiness with self and even self-hatred. There is a brilliant observation in "Keeping Body and Soul Together," where one respondent says, "After listening to the stories of countless women in shelters, and after sitting in on several treatment groups for violent men, I can only conclude that battering—at least in part—is a substitute for tears. As little boys, men are taught that 'big boys don't cry,' and that when threatened or hurt, they should learn to 'stand up and fight like a man.' Being deprived of human tears, they, in turn, victimize women as a means to live out this impossible cultural assignment to control the feminine within themselves."[7]

The anatomy of twisted men

As the old saying has it, "A man's got to do what a man's got to do." First on that list ought to be finding out what being a man means. The Hindus tell an insightful parable about a tiger cub called "the roar of a tiger." A pregnant tigress was ill and hungry when she came upon a herd of goats. She lunged at one, missed it, fell, and was mortally wounded. Her cub was born, and the mother died, leaving the poor cub standing helplessly by her side. The goats returned and took pity on the cub and invited it into the herd, teaching it how to eat grass and make goat sounds. A few weeks later a healthy tiger arrived on the scene, and the goats dispersed. The cub had no such instinct and continued chewing the grass and doing its imitation of goat sounds. The elder tiger was outraged and upbraided the cub for eating that stuff and making such feeble noises. It took him by the neck back to his cave where a half-finished carcass awaited. It forced the cub to get its first taste of fresh meat. As the nourishment filled him with a strength he never knew, he let out, for the first time, "the roar of a tiger."

The moral of this parable is this: many of us were socialized to think we were goats when in fact we are tigers. The parable does not say that everyone should act like a tiger. It says that you should find out what you really are. The Hindus thought you would need a mentor to do that, someone to take you to a new site and press you to eat and digest a new image of yourself.

Applied to men in our culture, the macho image tells us we are goats, not men. It makes us act like something we are not. It gives us tendencies that are unhealthy and can be changed. I would list five tendencies the culture presses on men. Not all men buy into them, and not all buy in to the same degree. These are tendencies, not stereotypes.

1. *Violence is prominent* in macho cultures. Most of the violence in our daily news media are reports of men killing while women and children run for cover. This does not mean that all women are gentle saints, but war and harsh violence are largely a male preserve. There was strong resistance to letting women in the military; there was a strong sense that it is not really their thing. The Amazons, after all, are creatures of myth. They didn't exist. When the government

building was blown up in Oklahoma, none of us said immediately: "I hope they find the women who did it." They found Timothy McVeigh. When you are walking down a dark street and discover that two people are following close behind, you turn and see two young men. You don't say: "Thank God, I was afraid it was two young women."

No, there is a violent strain that infects the socialization of men. Show me your metaphors, and I will tell you what you are. In the metaphors of male-dominated religions, God becomes a Mighty Fortress or a Lord of Armies. It shows up in business where you "wipe out" the competition, where "sharks" are out to destroy the competition, and bulls face off with bears. It shows itself in male sports. The ancients said: *Inter ludendum, mores se detegunt,* i.e., when we play, our morals show through. Boxing and football are not gentle, and again Bulls and Bears and Hawks compete for prey. Even gentle poetry has been called by men a "raid on the inarticulate." Even in male-dominated medicine, diseases are "defeated" not cured.

2. The second macho-masculine debit flows from the first. It is *the hierarchical imperative.* Violence and aggression seek not cooperation but dominance, and dominance is the opposite of friendship and community. Hence the macho-male tendency in state, church, corporation, and family is hierarchy and control rather than democracy, mutual empowerment, and communion.

3. *Pernicious abstractionism* also serves militaristic and violent agendas. Violence requires abstracting. How well the philosopher Jean Paul Sartre said that the worst evil of which we are capable is to treat as abstract that which is concrete. We can't talk with unforked tongue about the killing of children and other civilians in war. We don't dare look our victims in the eye or touch their bleeding flesh. Instead, we talk about "collateral damage." That's how civilian deaths in Vietnam, Afghanistan, and Iraq are described by Pentagon spokespersons. Timothy McVeigh agreed: that's how he dismissed the deaths of children in the Oklahoma explosion. Only a mind beguiled by abstraction can sustain a violent, nonrelational mode of addressing reality.

4. All these negative tendencies are born of the penchant for violence. This fourth, *bottom-line thinking,* has the same roots. The results are everything; how we get there has less importance. John W. Dixon is on to something when he writes in "The Erotics of Knowing" that

"engineering may be the model for the masculine as biology is the model for the feminine."[8] (This is symbolic and illustrative, not an attack on engineers.) Biology is all about linkages and interdependence; engineering goes for sturdy results. Bottom-line thinking, exalted in male-dominated business and government, tilts toward stressing ends over means. As the Russian philosopher Nicholas Berdyaev put it, our means are more important than our ends, "for they express more truly what our spirit is."[9] Building a profitable corporation is a noble end, but if the means involve sweatshops and ecological ruin, the enterprise is a moral failure. If stress on military ends distorts our budget so that schools, health care, and infrastructure suffer, intoxication with ends triumphs again. Concern for "defense" neglects what is worth defending.

5. The male *hatred of women* is sustained by hostility and disdain. One mark of operative hatred is exclusion. The form that sustained exclusion takes is monopoly. For two hundred years in the United States, we have operated on a rigid quota system that insisted on and got a 90 to 100 percent monopoly for white males in all the principal centers of power in government, business, church, and the professions, and in the competition for desirable jobs at every level. A monopoly implies the superiority of the monopolizers and the inferiority of the excluded. The American monopoly is comfortably still in place, and all efforts to ease it, like the Equal Rights Amendment and affirmative action programs, are resisted. Women have a constitutional right in the United States to choose abortion. Due to harassment and terrorism, over 80 percent of the counties in the United States have no such service, and this does not upset the male legal establishment. Anthrax scares have been arriving in clinics that serve women's reproductive health for over ten years, and we paid no attention to such scares until they started affecting men in Congress and the media. Hatred is a fair name for all of this.

There is no effort here to say that all men are corrupt and that women are sheer perfection. There is not one of the five debits above that is not shared by some women, and there are men who don't fit into any of those debit descriptions. But in a man-made world—and that's what we have since males have held most positions of institutional power—those five debits are glaringly present. It would be hard for the male aristocracy to plead innocence on all counts, and there is no man who shouldn't look to see if some of the above has not seeped into his soul.

A different twist: metanoia as men's resistance

Mark's Gospel is probably the oldest of the four, and it starts out with the challenge that is key to the whole ministry of Jesus. It is wrapped in the Greek word *metanoia.* This is usually translated as "repentance," but more basically it means a whole change of mind-set and outlook. Luke 3:3–6 tells us that *metanoia* is the whole reason for being baptized. Baptism is a "baptism of *metanoia.*" Luke spells out in poetic language what *metanoia* involves. It means entering into ourselves, seeing how messed up we are and how much we need to be transformed. The valleys of our minds need to be turned into mountains, and the mountains made into valleys. We have to be, in effect, reborn, to shake off the hostilities and coldness of spirit that we have inherited. This, Luke says, is what is meant by the "salvation of God." Compare this to the Hindu parable of the tiger cub acting like a goat. Both religious traditions recognize that we are confused people, victims of bad myths. We are challenged to face that and change.

The five debits that society pushes on men, starting right from their toddlerhood, are resistible. That in fact is the Good News. One thing all the world's religions agree on is that compassion is the antidote to violence, and all five debits are rooted in violence. Compassion is the ability to look at all flesh, black, white, brown, red, and yellow, to look at men and women whatever their nationality or sexual orientation may be, to look at all of the rest of nature from which we evolved, and to be able to say, "This is my body, this is my blood." There is no other way to expel the venoms of violence, incorporate relationships of justice, and get the full taste of that elusive phenomenon called peace.

Duane Elgin in his book *Promise Ahead: A Vision of Hope and Action for Humanity's Future* says that the human race can be said to be in its late adolescence. He says that "we awoke in the infancy of our potentials roughly thirty-five thousand years ago" when we began to devise tools and develop art in cave paintings. About ten thousand years ago, the move to farming villages marked the transition to humanity's childhood. The rise of the city-state civilizations five thousand years ago marked late childhood. With the scientific-industrial revolution three hundred years ago, we moved into our adolescence. The current scenario is dangerous, Elgin says, because the power we have is a real peril in the hands of adolescents.

Adolescents are rebellious, trying to prove their independence, as we have tried to do rebelling against nature. They are reckless regarding the consequences of their actions, concerned with status based on material possessions. Finally, they tend to gather in gangs or cliques in an "us versus them" posture. That's a scary mix of combustibles, but a wrecked earth bears witness to the aptness of this imagery.

Elgin's hopeful thought is that in this communications era we may be poised to enter into our early adulthood.[10] Early adulthood could inaugurate an age of peace—peace with nature and with "the other," whether that other be people of different color, gender, sexual orientation, or nation. Maybe the promise of adulthood for our species contains the now budding discovery that we are kith and kin with all of nature. Sweet breezes of tolerance and respect are blowing in all of these areas. That they could augur an Isaian age of peace may be but a dream, but to transpose the words of William Butler Yeats, tread softly if you would tread on dreams like that.

Notes

1. John C. Raines, in *What Men Owe to Women: Men's Voices from the World Religions,* ed. John C. Raines and Daniel C. Maguire (Albany: State University of New York Press, 2000), 1.

2. Jack Miles, *God: A Biography* (New York: Alfred A. Knopf, 1995), 20.

3. Ibid., 46.

4. I offer criteria for sorting out the prescriptive good from the merely descriptive bad in my *The Moral Core of Judaism and Christianity* (Minneapolis: Fortress, 1993), chapter 4.

5. In her textbook of Christian sexual pathology, Uta Ranke-Heinemann chronicles the sick, neurotic attitudes that suffused Christian history. *Eunuchs for the Kingdom of Heaven: Women, Sexuality, and the Catholic Church* (Garden City, N.Y.: Doubleday, 1990).

6. Grace M. Jantzen, "Good Sex: Beyond Private Pleasure," in *Good Sex: Feminist Perspectives from the World's Religions,* ed. Patricia Beattie Jung, Mary E.

Hunt, and Radhika Balakrishnan (New Brunswick, N.J.: Rutgers University Press, 2001), 3.

7. *Presbyterians and Human Sexuality 1991* (Louisville: Presbyterian Church [U.S.A.], 1991), 40.

8. John W. Dixon Jr., "The Erotics of Knowing," *Anglican Theological Review 56* (January 1974): 8.

9. Nicholas Berdyaev, *The Destiny of Man* (New York: Harper Torchbook, 1960), 89.

10. Duane Elgin, *Promise Ahead: A Vision of Hope and Action for Humanity's Future* (New York: HarperCollins, 2000), 1–5.

11

Crossing Gender Borders

Toward a New Paradigm

Virginia Ramey Mollenkott

Until several years ago, the vast majority of people in the Western hemisphere felt that we knew the gender landscape so well that we had no need for maps. We were sure there were two sexes, male and female, from which flowed "normal" masculine and feminine gender-identifications. That is, real men naturally preferred those appearances, pastimes, and attitudes our society labeled masculine. Real women were drawn to all things defined as feminine. Only "opposites" attracted. Anyone who did not match this binary gender paradigm (such as transsexuals like Christine Jorgenson, who floated on the periphery of our gender awareness) were simply the exceptions that proved the rule. They were not *real* men or *real* women.

We had never heard the term "transgender," and we did not ask ourselves an obvious question: if gender truly were such a clear-cut polarity, why did we need the adjective "real" to describe those who could comfortably conform? Was that adjective intended to dismiss nonconformists as unreal and therefore unworthy of attention?

Feminists and womanists had analyzed the ways in which the male-female binary oppressed women by assigning them to secondary public roles or (preferably) to unpaid or poorly paid private roles. "New men" had rebelled against distorted concepts of masculinity as consistently fearless, controlling, and dominant. But they were regarded as extremists. Most of us remained unaware that the gender arrangements of society appeared to work well only because they silenced or erased millions of people who did not or could not fit. Those who were not defined out of existence were effectively contained by a combination of compulsory heterosexuality, compulsory motherhood,[1] and the idealizing/idolizing of the nuclear family.

For decades Christian churches have embroiled themselves in arguments about whether or not their homosexual members deserve first-class citizenship in Christ's Body. Are otherwise qualified lesbian and gay men eligible for ordination, leadership positions, and rituals of holy union? Even as these debates have absorbed our attention, the entire gender landscape has been shifting under our feet. Only now are we beginning to hear from the many bisexuals among us. Only now are we starting to notice the presence of transgenderists as well.

Like the polarization of male versus female, the polarization of heterosexual versus homosexual sounds hollow when we allow ourselves to examine the way human beings and other creatures actually live their lives. Once we widen our perspective, we discover that the binary gender paradigm is wrong on every count: There are in fact more than two sexes or genders. Regardless of sexual orientation, there are many people who do not identify with the roles, interests, and attitudes society labels as appropriate to their maleness or femaleness. Furthermore, these gender role assignments vary from culture to culture. In fact, many men, women, and "in-betweens" are *not* attracted exclusively to the "opposite sex."

The human gender diversity we Christians are only beginning to notice extends throughout other species as well. Many birds, beasts, and creatures of the sea engage in same-sex coupling and even lifelong same-sex bonding. Many are able to shift appearance and behavior to look like the "opposite" sex; and some are both male and female (that is, intersexual).[2] It would seem that the Creator must enjoy diversity, including gender variance, whether or not we human beings are willing to recognize that diversity.

The transgender challenge to the church

Religious studies professor Christine E. Gudorf succinctly summarizes the challenge to the church: "We are [currently] seeing the waning of sexual dimorphism as the prevailing paradigm for interpreting human sexuality [because] the evidence of exceptions continues to mount." There's a tendency "to reject dimorphism in favor of polymorphism."[3] The emerging paradigm that Gudorf calls "sexual polymorphism," I have termed "omnigender."[4] Others prefer the term "sexual continuism."[5]

Scientific evidence that there are more than two human sexes or genders is found chiefly in biology, psychology, sociology, and anthropology.[6] The biological evidence comes in the form of millions of intersexuals, people who fit neither male nor female categories. The anatomical components of sex include six interrelated factors—chromosomes, hormones, gonads, internal reproductive organs, the brain, and external genitalia—but for intersexual people, these components do not mix together in conventionally male or female patterns. For instance, a child might be born with two X-chromosomes, oviducts, ovaries, and a uterus, but also with a penis and scrotum. Is that child a girl or a boy? Most doctors would say that the child is a girl because potentially she could give birth, and they would use surgery and hormones to enact what they had decided. But there are no absolute scientific guidelines for making such decisions. Anne Fausto-Sterling points out that contrary to popular belief, biological "facts" are wrapped up in political debates about sex, race, and nationality: "As our social viewpoints have shifted, so has the science of the body."[7]

In about 1.7 percent of all births, children are born as *both* male and female or as *neither* male nor female, depending on how we wish to describe intersexuality. However, most intersexuals are "disappeared" by doctors who rush them to the operating room for "corrective" surgery. For instance, a clitoris of more than 0.85 centimeters or simply one that impresses doctors as "too big," has been deemed medically unacceptable and has usually been surgically reduced, even though chances are good that the girl may never have erotic sensation for the rest of her life. A penis of less than 2.5 centimeters has often caused doctors to remove it and surgically create a girl child, despite the fact that the penis might have functioned "normally" and might have grown to a "normal" size at puberty.

Why all this medical intervention that is mainly cosmetic and causes much suffering for the intersexual person? To preserve and protect the binary gender paradigm, in other words, to perpetuate "deeply held beliefs about male and female sexuality, gender

roles, and the (im)proper place of homosexuality in normal development."[8] If instead of forcing intersexuals to disappear, our society
chose to allow mixed-gender bodies to become visible on our gender maps, gradually the rules of what is culturally intelligible would
shift. Our awareness of biological variations would enable us to con-
ceptualize in-between or anomalous bodies as natural, even though
they would remain statistically infrequent or unusual.[9] No longer
would we mistakenly equate statistical frequency with naturalness,
and naturalness with normalcy, and normalcy with goodness and
the will of God. To the degree that church people side with the
idea of liberty and justice for all, we should lend active support
to intersexual people and to organizations like the Intersex Society
of North America, a nonprofit dedicated to ending shame, secrecy,
and unwanted medical intervention for children born with intersex
conditions or atypical reproductive anatomies.[10]

Biological evidence of intersexuality is not the only indication that
the dimorphic gender paradigm is inaccurate and causing untold
human misery. There is also the psychological evidence offered by
the lives of transsexual people. These are people who sense a discor-
dance between their physical bodies and the gender identity at the
core of their self-awareness. For instance, one female-to-male transsexual said that as a child, "I didn't envy boys. I *was* one. I didn't
know until puberty that I wasn't....While I knew inside that I was
a boy, [at puberty] all the evidence was against me on that. My
breasts. My periods. I had nothing tangible to prove that I was male."
And a male-to-female transsexual described his parents' forcing him
into a tub of cold water as punishment for secretly dressing like a
girl: "Even before [they caught me] they were aware of my 'feminine
strangeness,' as they called it. Even though I felt great shame every
time I tried to be real, I had to go against tradition in order to go
forward."[11]

Eventually, many transsexuals feel so much pressure to achieve
inner-outer coherence that they opt for hormonal and surgical reconstruction of their bodies. Before surgeons will provide sex reconstruction, transsexuals are required to work with a psychologist for
a minimum of three to six months, and then to live full-time for
a year in the social role of the "genetically other sex."[12] The fact

that health care professionals recognize the need of many transsexuals for hormones and surgery indicates their conviction that it is easier to change a body than it is to change a mindset or a core gender-identity.

One forty-five-year-old father, transitioning to the female she'd always known she was, bemoaned the loss of her "magnificent marriage" and possible estrangement from her "wonderful child." (Many transsexuals lose their families, friends, and jobs as part of the high price of transitioning.) This father reasoned that if she failed to transition and stayed in her marriage by continuing to "fake it" as a man, she would be "showing my child that it is ok to bury one's personality to pacify society."[13] How long can a social abstraction, the binary gender paradigm, be permitted to shame people out of being true to what they know about themselves? How long can followers of Jesus the Christ continue to support a paradigm that forces people to bury their own personalities?

In addition to the biological evidence of intersexuals and the psychological evidence of transsexuals, the bankruptcy of sexual dimorphism is demonstrated by alternative sexual orientations. The very existence of lesbians, gay men, and bisexuals proves the emptiness of the assumption that only "opposite sexes" attract. And despite the claims of religious and political leaders in various developing nations, same-sex activity occurs everywhere and always has occurred in every historical era, although the naming, construction, or organization of the same-sex activity may differ. Many cultures tolerate juvenile same-sex play among children and youth. Some cultures sanction age-structured or intergenerational same-sex activity in which boys perform fellatio as part of their growth into manhood, or women form "mummy-baby" relationships with adolescent girls.[14] Other cultures sanction gender-bending or transgender same-sex activity, in which one of the men dresses and acts female or one of the women dresses and acts male. Some cultures sanction role-specialized homosexuality for certain people who perform specific ritual, artistic, or social functions. Some cultures may go so far as to classify those who engage in same-sex activity as a Third Sex or Gender.

Of course, one must carefully distinguish between theory and practice. For instance, a Muslim scholar from Nigeria points out that "in many Muslim communities, there has been a centuries-long history of quiet toleration of male same-sex relations (including sexual intercourse and forms of cross-dressing)." Such toleration has persisted despite increasingly strident denouncement of these behaviors as "unnatural" and "anti-Islam."[15]

The contemporary lesbian, gay, bisexual, and transgender (LGBT) movement in the United States differs from these other social constructions by emphasizing relationships between mutually consenting adults, deemphasizing role specialization, and making gayness into a self-affirming identity. (Many LGBT leaders would agree that a "homosexual" may be self-hating, but openly identifying as "gay," "lesbian," "bisexual," "transgender," or "queer" requires a degree of self-acceptance.) Thus, when certain Native Americans deny that there are or ever were any gay people in their traditional cultures, they speak truthfully. They did not construct homosexuality as a separate identity, and they accorded respect to their "Two-Spirit" or gender-variant people (sometimes called *berdache*), who therefore did not have to struggle to achieve and maintain self-respect.[16]

Because same-sex relational issues have been discussed at length elsewhere in this book, I will simply assert my conviction that it is vital for gay men, lesbians, and bisexuals to recognize our movement as *basically a transgender movement.* Because compulsory heterosexuality and motherhood undergird and perpetuate the binary gender paradigm, anyone who is known to have engaged in same-sex activity is automatically classified as gender-variant or queer, even if he is a macho male, even if she is ultra feminine. And the fact that the most effeminate gay men and the butchiest lesbians are the most endangered among us should alert us to the fact that society cares less about what we do in private than it cares about a challenge to its longstanding gender assumptions. Therefore, it is self-defeating for gay, lesbian, or bisexual people to ignore transgender issues on the theory that adding those to the mix will delay our progress toward social justice. To gender traditionalists, all LGBT people are queer; so we had better work in supportive solidarity with all those who are seeking their just and rightful place within society.

Another evidence of gender-dimorphic bankruptcy is the evidence of many heterosexuals who refuse to abide by traditional gender roles and attitudes because they consider them demeaning, distorted, unjust, or simply impossible. Most transvestites (men who dress like women on a part-time basis) are heterosexual, many of them married.[17] They jeopardize their family relationships and their own safety because the impulse to cross-dress is so strong they cannot circumvent it. There are also many heterosexual women who prefer politics or bungee jumping to a day at the beauty salon, and many non–cross-dressing heterosexual men who prefer childcare or knitting to watching the Super Bowl at the local sports bar. These people are also transgender, inasmuch as they transgress the rules of sex/gender dimorphism.

Add to these heterosexual transgenderists all the other transgender people of any sexual orientation, and you have a large majority of the population. The original and narrower definition of the term "transgender" was "transsexual," but recently the term has been expanded into an umbrella term for all those who cross the rigid borders dictated by society's male-female rules and roles. Although terminology is still mercurial, currently the term "transgender" would include not only intersexuals, transsexuals, homosexuals, bisexuals, cross-dressers, and nonconformist heterosexuals, but also people who identify as drag kings, drag queens, genderblenders, androgynes, masculine women, feminine men, Two-Spirits, she-males, Third Gender, or simply otherwise. Can Christianity continue to uphold a binary gender paradigm that diminishes, shames, and maims so many?

Biblical suggestions and solutions

Christine E. Gudorf has offered some suggestions to religious communities that seek to respond to the current "shift toward a more polymorphous concept of sexuality." Among her suggestions: We should decenter and resist defining sexuality, because neither Moses nor Jesus nor Muhammad made sexuality a focal point. We should historicize sexuality by recovering the various models of marriage and family and the diverse constructions of sexuality through different eras of Judaism, Christianity, and Islam. We should also protect the weak without further disempowering them. The latter would require that religious communities support lifelong age-appropriate sexuality education, including supportive information about gender diversities, sexual orientations, and ways of avoiding sexually transmitted disease.[18]

Although Gudorf does not say so, her suggestions are more in line with the imagery of the Hebrew and Christian Scriptures than most religious leaders have recognized. For instance, the opening chapters of Genesis emphasize that God created humankind in the divine image (1:26; 5:1-2). Since Judaism and Christianity are monotheistic religions, we may be certain that the God in whose likeness both male and female were created is understood to be one single Spirit who is the Source of all that is. That one all-inclusive Being must inevitably encompass both male and female, as well as all that the English language treats as neuter. Yet the language of synagogue and church has obscured God's all-inclusive gender by using exclusively masculine pronouns to refer to God and by rarely mentioning the Bible's female or nature imagery concerning God.[19]

Furthermore, the teaching of Jewish commentaries on Genesis is that "Adam was at first created bisexual, a hermaphrodite."[20] That is, the original Earth Creature was both male and female until God placed that creature into a deep sleep and divided him/her into the human male and female as we now know them. Therefore, instead of being one of God's mistakes that must be corrected by modern medical ingenuity, hermaphrodites or intersexuals are part of His/Her/Its original creative impulse!

Jesus is described in the Christian Scriptures as "the exact imprint of God's very being" (Heb. 1:3) and as the offspring of a Virgin (Luke 1:26-35). It took an evangelical biologist named Edward L. Kessel to point out the implications of a literal belief in the Virgin Birth of Jesus: all parthenogenetic (virgin) births result in offspring with two X-chromosomes.[21] Because Jesus apparently underwent a sex reversal to a male phenotype (as sometimes occurs in parthenogenesis), he appeared to function as a normal male. However, if the Scriptural account is read literally, then the fact is that Jesus was chromosomally female all his life. By this interpretation, Jesus is not a *male* Savior, but an *intersexual* Savior; so that even from a biological perspective, women "resemble Christ" just as closely as men, and transgenderists resemble Her/Him most of all!

The New Testament uses a great deal of transsexual imagery concerning the Body of Christ, the church. As church members, males are included among Christ's brides (Eph. 5:29–32), Christian women are included among Christ's brothers (Rom. 8:28–29), the whole (female) church is urged to "grow up in every way into him who is the head" (Eph. 4:15), cross-dressing metaphors are used in positive contexts (Col. 3:9–10; Rom. 13:14), and the male-female polarity is listed among the dichotomies that are to be overcome "in Christ" (Gal. 3:28).[22] Epimenides, a gay shaman from Crete (sixth century B.C.E.) was quoted twice in the New Testament, both times favorably (in Acts 17:28 and Titus 1:12–13).[23]

Perhaps nowhere else is the Bible's movement toward inclusiveness more dramatic than in its treatment of eunuchs. Today we would classify eunuchs as transgender, and specifically as intersexuals, such as the *hijras* of India, who must castrate themselves in order to qualify as genuine *hijras* and who cross-dress as servants of the goddess.[24] The Bible defines eunuchs literally as males who are castrated and figuratively as anyone who for any reason does not or cannot marry and beget children. According to Deuteronomy 23:1, eunuchs were not permitted to enter "the assembly of the Lord."[25] The Hebrew prophet Isaiah reversed that legislation, proclaiming God's blessing on those eunuchs who keep the covenant: "I will give in my house and within my walls a monument and a name better than sons and daughters; I will give them an everlasting name that shall not be cut off" (56:3b–5). Jesus also spoke well of eunuchs (Matt. 19:12), which may be one reason he attracted so many unmarried and childless people into his discipleship of equals. (The Rev. Tom Hanks points out that single people were sexual minorities in Jesus' place and time— and that most of the New Testament was therefore written by sexual minorities.)[26] Finally, the eunuch from Ethiopia was welcomed and baptized into the assembly of Jesus' followers (Acts 8:26–40).[27] Surely it is this biblical movement toward transgender inclusion that ought to be normative for today's church!

According to Isaiah, "Thus says God, who gathers the outcasts of Israel, I will gather others to them besides those already gathered" (56:8–9). Jesus said something similar: "I have other sheep that do not belong to this fold. I must bring them also, and they will listen to my voice. So there will be one flock, one shepherd" (John 10:16).

It seems to me that any Christian congregation that marginalizes its transgender members—or any other category of members, for that matter—is acting in defiance of God's insistent inclusiveness.

Transgender sex ethics

Because transgender people come in any and all sex, gender, and orientational combinations, relational ethics for Christian trans-genderists would be similar to ethics governing heterosexual, bi-sexual, lesbian, or gay relationships. Certainly there is some trans-gender discussion about whether fidelity in partnership requires sexual exclusivity, and exactly what such exclusivity might entail. There is no question that truthfulness, fidelity, mutual justice-love, and profound whole-life concern should characterize committed partnerships. Like bisexuals, many intersexuals would be able to respond to male, female, or other "in between" people. Some individual intersexuals who somehow evaded medical intervention would even possess the ability to make love as *both* male and female. However, none of that changes anything about the biblical imperative for partners to "be subject to one another out of reverence for Christ" (Eph. 5:21).

Perhaps, because many transgenderists contain and express both male and female components, we incur an increased responsibility to show concern for what tradition calls the "opposite sex." For instance, it does not seem fair for a masculine woman to enjoy the freedom of men's clothing or the clarity of linear discourse without developing profound empathy for the pangs and struggles of her brothers. Many American men have been duped into believing that real men are in control at all times, whereas in their hearts they know they cannot meet that impossible standard.[28] Similarly, it does not seem fair for a married cross-dresser to express his feminine component exclusively through cosmetics, wigs, dresses, high heels, and coffee klatches while rejecting the "women's work" of cleaning, cooking, and childcare, and while avoiding involvement in movements that seek justice for women. "Bear one another's burdens, and in this way you will fulfill the law of Christ" (Gal. 6:2) applies to Christian people of any sex/gender/orientation, but moving across traditional gender categories may serve to intensify that responsibility and that opportunity.

The binary gender paradigm with its male-female polarization has caused and continues to cause unimaginable misery all over the world. It has ensured that women and children are the poorest of the poor, the hungriest among those who hunger. It has excluded millions of people from the gender map because with no language that adequately describes their experience, their existence is culturally unintelligible. It has deprived millions of the privilege of pursuing happiness in whatever gender identity, roles, or performances feel most authentic to their souls. Therefore, it has deprived the Creator of the fullest, most complete expression of diversity as it was intended to be played out upon the stage of this world.

The musical universe would be impoverished if Amadeus Mozart had refused to be God's flute. Similarly, forcing people into sex and gender straitjackets has denied the gorgeous diversity of God's manifestations. To one degree or another, all of us have been diminished by the stark opposition of male and female within the dominant gender paradigm. Whether we call it sexual continuism, polymorphous sexuality, omnigender, or some other name, now is the time for people of faith to move toward a different, more accurate, more justice-oriented and egalitarian paradigm.

Notes

1. Wanda Deifelt, "Beyond Compulsory Motherhood," *Good Sex: Feminist Perspectives from the World's Religions,* ed. Patricia Beattie Jung, Mary E. Hunt, and Radhika Balakrishnan (New Brunswick, N.J.: Rutgers University Press, 2001), 96–112.

2. See Bruce Bagemihl, Ph.D., *Biological Exuberance: Animal Homosexuality and Natural Diversity* (New York: St. Martin's, 1999). *Kirkus Reviews* describes this book as "scholarly, exhaustive and utterly convincing" in its "refutation of the notion that human homosexuality is an aberration in nature."

3. Christine E. Gudorf, "The Erosion of Sexual Dimorphism: Challenges to Religion and Religious Ethics," *Journal of the American Academy of Religion 69* (December 2001): 870–71, text and note 11.

4. Virginia Ramey Mollenkott, *Omnigender: A Trans-Religious Approach* (Cleveland: Pilgrim, 2001).

5. Martina A. Rothblatt, *The Apartheid of Sex: A Manifesto of the Freedom of Gender* (New York: Crown, 1995); Anne Fausto-Sterling, *Sexing the Body: Gender Politics and the Construction of Sexuality* (New York: Basic Books, 2000).

6. Fausto-Sterling denies that sex is distinct from gender, because labeling someone as a man or a woman is a social decision based on beliefs about gender. See *Sexing the Body*, 3–29.

7. Ibid., 7.

8. Ibid., 31–22 and 48–61.

9. Ibid., 76.

10. For further information about intersexuality, visit *www.isna.org*. Also contact Emi Koyama at the Intersex Society of North America (*emi@isna.org*) or 503-288-3191.

11. These testimonies are quoted by Mildred L. Brown and Chloe Ann Rounsley in *True Selves: Understanding Transsexualism* (San Francisco: Jossey-Bass, 1996), 56 and 62–63.

12. Ibid., 102.

13. Quoted in ibid., 129–30.

14. Esther Newton, "Of Yams, Genders, and Gays: The Anthropology of Homosexuality (1988)," *Margaret Mead Made Me Gay* (Durham, N.C.: Duke University Press, 2000), 232–35.

15. Ayesha M. Imam, "The Muslim Religious Right ('Fundamentalists') and Sexuality," *Good Sex*, 26–27. See also Mollenkott, *Omnigender*, 148–53.

16. The term *berdache* is used by some Native Americans but is offensive to others; see Mollenkott, *Omnigender*, 158–59; and Leslie Feinberg, *Transgender Warriors: Making History from Joan of Arc to Ru Paul* (Boston: Beacon, 1996), 21.

17. Gianna E. Israel and Donald E. Tarvis, M.D., *Transgender Care* (Philadelphia: Temple University Press, 1997), 27; Vern L. Bullough and Bonnie Bullough, *Cross Dressing, Sex, and Gender* (Philadelphia: University of Pennsylvania Press, 1993), 293; and *About Cross-Dressers and Crossdressing* (Waltham, Mass., International Foundation for Gender Education, 1999), pamphlet.

18. Christine E. Gudorf, *Body, Sex, and Pleasure: Reconstructing Christian Sexual Ethics* (Cleveland: Pilgrim, 1994), 884–86.

19. See Virginia R. Mollenkott, *The Divine Feminine: Biblical Imagery of God as Female* (New York: Crossroad, 1983).

20. W. Gunther Plant, *The Torah: Genesis — A Modern Commentary* (New York: Union of American Hebrew Congregations, 1974), 24, 19. For further discussion and documentation, see Mollenkott, *Omnigender*, 90–95.

21. Edward L. Kessel, "A Proposed Biological Interpretation of the Virgin Birth," *Journal of the American Scientific Affiliation* (September 1983): 129–36.

22. For further discussion and documentation, see Mollenkott, *Omnigender*, 107, 110–14.

23. Tom Hanks, *The Subversive Gospel: A New Testament Commentary of Liberation* (Cleveland: Pilgrim, 2000), 182.

24. Serina Nanda, *Neither Man Nor Woman: The Hijras of India* (Belmont, Calif.: Wadsworth, 1999).

25. Others who were barred from God's assembly included "those born of an illicit union" and their children to the tenth generation (Deut. 23:2). So those who think that Jesus was the illicit son of a Roman soldier have placed Jesus among the outcasts of ancient Israel.

26. Hanks, *The Subversive Gospel*, 148–49, 177, 182, and throughout.

27. In *The Church and the Homosexual,* 4th ed. (Boston: Beacon, 1993), John McNeill remarks that Jesus' reference to "those who have been eunuchs from birth" is "the closest description we have in the Bible of what we understand as homosexual" (64); and "the first group of outcasts of Israel that the Holy Spirit includes within the new covenant community is symbolized by the Ethiopian eunuch" (65).

28. Susan Faludi, *Stiffed: The Betrayal of the American Man* (New York: William Morrow, 1999), 14–15.

Part Three

Pleasure and Health

12

Gay Erotic Spirituality and the Recovery of Sexual Pleasure

Robert E. Goss

> Our eroticism delineates the contours of our faith, in the same way that it colors the texture and shape of all other segments of our lives. —Donald Boisvert[1]

Historically, in associating sexuality with irrational instinct and pleasure, Christianity has coupled sex and sin. Many contemporary Christian churches still judge gay sexuality as unnatural and sinful because it does not fulfill a procreative norm and is pursued as pleasurable. In this essay, I propose to answer the charges commonly leveled at gay sexuality as narcissistically seeking only pleasure. To the contrary, gay Christians are reclaiming their sexuality as a gift from God, and churches need to develop a new theological language that validates sexual pleasure as an original blessing, one that connects sexuality to justice-love.

In ancient Greece, eros was associated with the irrational, the mad, and the uncontrollable. Michel Foucault delineated how the classical world failed to invest sex with positive values; rather, sex was constructed as fearful, contributing to an ethic of self-control and abstinence.[2] The years between the first generation of the Jesus movement and Augustine witnessed the transformation and a jettisoning of the Hebrew notions of the body and sex in favor of Stoic and Neoplatonic constructs of sexuality as negative, rebellious, and dangerous. Christian asceticism, in seeking union with God, took pleasure in controlling sexual desire. Augustine feared sexual passion and pleasure; for him, sexual passion was very powerful and hardly manageable, resulting often in the loss of rational control. For many early Christian writers, concupiscence accompanied marital sex even when the intention was to have children. For Pope Gregory the Great, it was not sex but the sensual pleasure accompanying sexual intercourse that was sinful. Married partners who engaged in sexual intercourse for pleasure and not for the procreation of children sinned mortally. Thomas Aquinas modified the view of pleasure as sinful, for pleasure was to be condemned only if it accompanied nonmarital or unnatural sex.[3] The charge of sexual pleasure and sinfulness was reserved for deviant sexuality.

The history of sex in early and medieval Christianity was a continuous campaign to undo the powerful affirmations of sexuality in the Hebrew Scriptures and to negate sexual pleasure by forbidding clerical marriage, regulating marriage as a sacrament, and prohibiting all forms of sexual expression outside of marriage and its procreative purpose. In 1546, the Council of Trent lessened the severity of medieval characterizations of sexual pleasure by declaring concupiscence the "tinder of sin."[4] Catholic moral theology was very slow in relaxing its view on pleasure in marital intercourse, and it was only in the 1960s that sexual pleasure was understood as inducement for procreation within marriage.[5] Hidden Catholic fears of sexuality are often present within a simplistic dichotomy between hedonism and God as if sexual pleasure and choosing God are necessarily exclusive paths.

The Protestant reformers modified the legacy of Christian suspicion of sexual pleasure. They looked positively on companionship and love, but not without warnings about the power of sexual desire and its ability to reduce humans to animals. For the Protestant reformers, marriage redeems lust or sexual passion since marriage prevents fornication. The Puritans went beyond many Protestant denominations by praising marital love for its ability to deter "ungodly pleasures" and hinting that marriage was as good as virginity.[6] Protestant Christians, in general, have redeemed sexual pleasure and desire, but only within the restrictions of heterosexual marriage.

Christian theologies have been predominantly fearful and negative toward human sexuality, often devaluing the body and demonizing sex. Through a regimen of shame and guilt, Christians have been taught to be suspicious of sex, especially non-procreative sex. If sex were no longer linked to procreation, Christian leaders feared, it would become less obvious why it should be restricted to marriage. Christian suspicion of sexual pleasure was translated into cultural regulations, such as sodomy statutes in the United States that prohibit non-procreative, nonmarital sex. These statutes were adapted from Christian regulations against non-procreative sex; they prohibited anal and oral sex, even between spouses. Their intent was to restrict sexual pleasure to procreative actions. The intention of sodomy laws today is generally thought to be to prohibit same-sex sexuality. In *Bowers v. Hardwick* (1986), the U.S. Supreme Court appealed to "millennia of moral teaching" to uphold the state of Georgia's restrictive sodomy law.[7] It denied to gay men and lesbians legal protection for the kind of loving relationships and intimacy that most heterosexuals take for granted as their inalienable right.

Human sexuality is distorted by theologies that restrict sexual pleasure to heterosexual marriage and thereby deny the right to sexual intimacy and pleasure to queers. Sexual pleasure remains at the heart of charges against same-sex sexuality.

For the majority of Christian writers, the sharing of pleasure is not widely seen as part of good sex. In fact, Christians have generally disparaged the consideration of pleasure and, in particular, discounted sexual pleasure as either a moral or spiritual resource. As gay theologian Mark Jordan notes,

> Theological shame has corrupted or determined the language of sex....It has subjected sexual utterances to a ruthless hermeneutic of suspicion, and then it has suspected sexual motivations in every kind of utterance. These categories cannot easily be made pristine.[8]

Jordan suggests that Christians need a more original language to speak about sex in order to move Christianity beyond theological shame. He examines four traditional calumnies against pleasure: (1) erotic pleasure is unclean; (2) it is original sin, implicated in the primal fall as both cause and effect; (3) as part of animal nature, it interferes with reason; and (4) it is powerfully selfish and blocks the development of the truly moral.[9] Jordan attempts to redeem sexual pleasure as a theological category by linking erotic pleasure to spirituality. In the tradition of Christian mystics, he couples the language of sex to prayer, even comparing prayer to masturbation, a traditional evil described as "self-pleasure." He notes that our intimacies with God through prayer are "the pleasurable intimacies of creatures with bodies."[10] Such affirmations have long been explicit in gay theological writings about the giftedness of gay sex, as well as very explicit within the gay culture at large. Gay men have understood that unless their sex is pleasurable, it cannot foster mutuality, express love, or build community. Along with Jordan, gay men on the margins of church and society are relying on sexual pleasure as a source of joy, sexual justice, and spiritual practice.

Gayness represented as unbridled sexual pleasure

In an interview with *Rolling Stone* magazine, Paul Cameron, the architect of the Religious Right's propaganda, states,

> Untrammeled homosexuality can take over and destroy a social system. If you isolate sexuality as something solely for one's personal amusement, and all you want is the most satisfying orgasm you can get — and that is what homosexuality seems to be — then homosexuality seems too powerful to resist. The evidence is that men do a better job on men, and women on women, if all you are looking for is orgasm.[11]

Cameron argues that marital, heterosexual sex tends to be boring and that it does not deliver the "kind of sheer pleasure that homosexual sex does." He goes on to compare same-sex orgasm to heroin: "It's pure sexuality. It's almost like pure heroin. It's such a rush. They are committed in almost a religious way."[12] Cameron believes that if not stopped, homosexuality will become the dominant form of sexuality within a few generations because it is more pleasurable than heterosexual pleasure. The category of "homosexual" represents within the minds of many conservative Christians a symbol of a dangerous person who rejects all of society's rules for the sake of pleasure. The irony of this is that religious people who scarcely deal with their own sexuality are apparently willing and eager to define gay erotic pleasures without ever consulting gay men about sexuality.

Paul Cameron's extreme claims that homosexual sexual practices pose a threat to society has been popularized by the Christian Right.

In the 1994 "Road to Victory" conference, the Christian Coalition featured Cameron and his books. In his pseudo-scientific writings, Cameron fuels hatred with irrational fears of disease, moral contagion, and plague. Homosexuals are represented as predators, molesting children and subverting youth. These themes of disease, contagion, and seduction are familiar ones recycled from anti-Semitic and racist discourses from the early part of the twentieth century in the United States, and they continue to contribute to irrational campaigns of political intolerance and discrimination.

Modified versions of Cameron's beliefs are repeated within neoorthodox Protestant and Catholic constructions of homosexuality. Both operate from an Augustinian legacy that identifies sexuality with fallen nature. Catholic magisterial theology, following John Paul II, describes love as a duty and identifies concupiscence with sexual enjoyment and lust.[13] Traditionally, Catholic moral theology has had difficulty in allowing for the original blessing of spontaneous sexual desire, even when restricted to marriage. It added the restriction of procreation to marriage in order to regulate and control spontaneous sexual desire, thus devaluing sexual pleasure and, at best, burying it within procreationism. Catholic moral theology has often designated masturbation as "self-pleasure" and characterized homosexual relationships as "self-indulgent," both actions motivated by pleasure but lacking the finality of procreation within marriage. Catholic moral theologian Benedict Ashley writes,

> Current [gay and gay-friendly] propaganda and the mistaken compassion of psychiatrists and theologians have encouraged many homosexuals to deny their disability by arguing that homosexuality is just a legitimate variation of human sexuality, or even that it is the will of God. But sex was not created only for pleasure or to provide companionship. Sex is for marriage only.[14]

Neoorthodox Christians within mainline denominations and evangelical and fundamentalist Christians also identify homosexuality with unadulterated pleasure, threatening the conventional Christian view of marriage and family and violating the procreative norm of marriage. Though historically more positive toward marriage than Catholic theology, conservative Protestant theology also identifies same-sex relations with fallen nature or sin. Conservative Protestants recycle modified versions of Cameron's declaration of a homosexual threat to marriage and have partnered with Catholics in support of recent ballot initiatives to restrict marriage to the union of one man and one woman, such as California's Proposition 22 and Nebraska's Initiative 416–I. Thus, the Protestant and Catholic Right have created a culture of resentment and violence by maintaining restrictive control over sexual pleasure while identifying homosexuality with unbridled lust and sin.

Through its social practices and theologies, Christianity has promoted a religious regimen of shame and guilt to interrupt bodily pleasure and identify sin with sexual pleasure. Christian erotophobia has promoted alienation from the body and denial of embodied pleasure. Conservative Christians seem willing to scapegoat queers with charges of unbridled sexual pleasure, depriving them to the right to be sexually intimate except within the confines of heterosexual marriage. Anne Gilson observes, "Lesbian women and gay men often serve as scapegoats for an eros—a sexuality in general—which appears to church leaders out of control."[15] What gay men represent is the unbridled lust of sexual pleasure, but underlying this representation of same-sex sexuality is a great amount of psychological projection and fear of human sexuality, especially when it is uncoupled from procreativity.

The impact of ecclesial scapegoating of queer sex has precipitated a counteraffirmation by gay men of sexual pleasure as an original blessing and as grace. Additionally, gay Christians are insisting that Christian theology take seriously gay men's sexual experiences and the full range of gay sexual pleasures.

Gay recovery of sexual pleasure

Gay cultural critic Michael Bronski observes, "Pleasure threatens how society is organized."[16] Queer sex with its wide range of erotic expressiveness offers a vision of sexual pleasure divorced from the regulatory model of procreative sex. Queer sex strikes at the heart of the heterogendered system, breaking down social and gendered conventions based on archaic patriarchal codes. It challenges both cultural and conservative Christian ideas about sex, gender rules, relationships, marriage, and families. The living out of queer life, however, is much more threatening than any particular sexual act, for it intentionally defines a pleasurable way of life and constructs cultural forms to support that way of life. These are not only attractive but also alternative pleasures. Queer sex and queer life create what Bronski describes as "erogenous zones in the cityscape, early identifiable as a source of pleasure."[17] Their visibility has also produced a phobic response from traditionalist and fundamentalist Christians against the creation of queer families and legal maneuvers to prevent recognition of queer unions.

Queer sexual pleasure has become a cultural force threatening the heart of archaic religious codes bolstered by irrational defenses and arguments to privilege heterosexuals and hetero-procreativity in a postmodern world. Claiming erogenous zones of sexual pleasure "against the odds" has even led some gay men to speak about the subversive potential of gay sex to critique and parody prevailing notions of cultural masculinity. At the same time, they also speak of the reintegration of sexuality and spirituality insofar as intense sexual pleasure allows gay lovers to shatter their individual subjectivities and experience communion. The *jouissance* of gay love, the pleasure in the midst of sexual orgasm, becomes an epistemological mode for recovery of the body as spiritual.

From a queer Christian perspective, sexuality becomes the capacity for giving and receiving bodily pleasure; it comprises a wide range of experiences that include comfort, mutuality, self-discovery, grace, and love. For many gay men, it brings a convergence of *jouissance* and spirituality, the ecstasy of human and divine encounters. Simultaneously, it is a convergence of pleasure, certainly with another human being, but also, and significantly, with God.

A number of gay writers outside Christianity have written of same-sex sexual acts as a source of spiritual revelation.[18] For many gay men, the erotic body is integrated into spirituality. Because the general perception within the gay male community is that Christianity is hostile to gay sexuality, many have sought alternative spiritual paths to integrate their sexuality and spirituality. At the same time, the neoconservative gay Catholic author Andrew Sullivan writes about his sexual experience as "almost a sacrament."[19] A few gay Christian sex practitioners, such as Joe Kramer, or spiritual directors, such as

Michael Kelly, have given retreats and workshops for gay men on integrating sexuality and spirituality.[20]

Gay theologians speak also of the giftedness of sexuality. Former Jesuit John McNeill identifies three stages of homosexual holiness: coming out, intimacy with one another, and a covenanted ritual of relationship.[21] Gay scholar Donald Boisvert writes, "Sexuality is a gift from God, and it is a gift because of its varied manifestations. Being gay is therefore a blessing."[22] Boisvert comprehends that the gay community has developed its own redemptive language and spirituality to counter traditional Christian identification of homosexuality with sin and immorality. He rightly observes that gay spirituality is incarnational while Christianity "stands in an unresolved neurotic paradox."[23] Gay spirituality reclaims the beauty and holiness of the body while institutional Christianity maintains its residual anti-body and erotophobic prejudices. Gay spirituality sacralizes the sexual body that conservative Christians demonize. For gay men the erotic is the site of sacredness and revelation while traditional Christianity condemns the unregulated, nonheterosexually married and erotic body. In a similar fashion, biblical scholar William Countryman and co-author M. R. Riley understand gay sexuality as the "God-given gift, affirming that we are not defective heteros."[24] Queers are not a failure of creation; rather, they are God's gifts of surprises within creation who challenge the normative roles of gender and sexuality. In *Jesus ACTED UP*, I developed my own description of queer sex as love-making and justice-doing in light of the concept of justice-love elaborated in *Presbyterians and Human Sexuality 1991*.[25] This theological reframing has allowed me to recover queer sex as grace-filled, even sacramental, and rescue it from narrow ecclesial theologies of sexuality that demonize or exclude it.

Sabbath sex: blessed sex

The recovery of sexual pleasure is foundational to justice-love because when the two are connected, they engender a passionate connection to creation, one another, and God. Marvin Ellison makes an insightful observation concerning the disparaging of sexual pleasure:

> Erotic joy is typically disparaged as a moral resource. Frequently, "ethics" is taken to mean strict rules without exception that keep people from doing whatever it is they really want to do. People learn that if an activity feels good to them, they probably should not be doing it, at least not without guilt....The ethical here is equated with the negative ("Don't do it!"). Pleasure and duty are seen as opposites.[26]

If it is pleasurable, it is wrong or selfish. For Ellison, a liberation ethic can be grounded in erotic delight and power, validating the original blessedness of creation and erotic bodies. What Ellison describes as an "erotic ethic" is precisely what gay Christians, I believe, can contribute to their churches by insisting upon, and assisting in, the holistic reuniting of sexuality and spirituality. For many gay Christians, the coming out process is not complete until they come out to God and begin the process of integrating their sexuality with their spirituality.[27] God is present in our love-making. Coming out to God is integrating the pleasure of sex with the pleasure of God. This state of spiritual experience nudges us beyond alienation, sexual guilt, and body shame.

Gay Christian spirituality contains two major embodied configurations: the integration of sexuality and the transgression of oppressive norms. It is a struggle to find a language of giftedness and grace within gay sexual experience precisely because many churches exclude or demonize sex outside of heterosexual marriage. It is difficult for many Christians, but especially gay Christians, to recover the original blessing of their own sexuality without transgressing the received messages that have abused them, pathologized them, and labeled them as intrinsically sinful. The Christian legacy of erotophobia and the politics of shame has deeply impacted and oftentimes hindered the faith development of gay men. My own local church, the Metropolitan Community Church (MCC) of St. Louis, routinely offers a six-week course on "Recovering from Homophobic Religion" to help gay men and lesbians recover from years of religious abuse and shame about their sexual identity. Shame and guilt have interrupted the capacity of gay men to enjoy sexual pleasures with their partners, but equally important, they have interrupted their capacity for taking prayerful pleasure in God.

Following in James Nelson's footsteps, feminists, womanists, and queer theologians have placed the recovery of body theology at the center of their attempts to recognize and reclaim sexual pleasure as a moral good. Creation-centered theologies with their Jewish roots and Christian incarnational theology provide the matrix for recovering sexual pleasure as a moral good and connecting it with justice.[28]

One possible trajectory for the recovery of sexual pleasure within a creation-centered spirituality is to recover the notion of making love on the Sabbath as "blessed." Very few Christians have ever heard clergy speak of love-making as blessed on the Christian Sabbath. When I speak to Christian groups about blessed sex on the Sabbath, it frequently triggers an erotophobic response from individuals who have experienced profound shame and guilt about their homosexual feelings. The recovery of Sabbath sexuality may prove to be a promising trajectory for overcoming sexual shame and guilt and reclaiming sexual experience as sacred and holy.

Lesbian elder of the Universal Fellowship of Metropolitan Community Churches Nancy Wilson writes, "Sexuality was made for humanity, not humanity for sexuality."[29] Her paraphrase of Jesus' Sabbath logion brilliantly reconnects sexuality to the creation account in Genesis 1 and to a constellation of theological notions of the Sabbath: Sabbath as re-creation, a time of play, procreativity, the renewal and creation of a just society, and much more. Wilson writes,

> Sexuality is about being made in the image of God, who is Creator, and who is still creating. Insofar as we are in touch with our sexuality, we are connected to our passions, to our love for life, to joy, pleasure, and to the work of creation. The gift of sexuality is the gift of the means of creative relationship, of a God who loves joy, fun, and pleasure.[30]

The Sabbath and human sexuality were made for human pleasure. Within the Hebrew biblical tradition, sexuality is one activity that is not forbidden on the Sabbath. In fact, sex on the Sabbath partakes in the blessings of creation. Jewish practitioners of Kabbalist spirituality in the Middle Ages understood their lovemaking on the Sabbath as an act of prayer and devotion.[31] Christian antagonism to sexuality during that same period resulted in priests advocating abstinence on the Sabbath and on religious holidays, so that these religious days would not be profaned by acts of marital sex. Medieval clergy admonished Christians not to engage in conjugal relations on Sunday because it was the day commemorating Christ's resurrection. Moreover, they warned people to abstain from sexual relations on the following days of the week: Thursday: the day Jesus was arrested; Friday: the day he died; Saturday: the Virgin Mary's day; and Monday: the day to remember the departed. In addition, the forty days before Christmas and Easter, the entire period of a woman's pregnancy, and the forty days after the birth of a child were times of required sexual abstinence.[32] These prohibitions effectively identified more than a half year during which time sexual relations were not to take place.

The Sabbath fundamentalists of Jesus' time wanted to understand that humanity was made for the Sabbath. Similarly Christian churches have argued that humanity was made for sexuality, in keeping with narrow procreative theologies. Wilson's paraphrase reverses the direction of this restrictive legacy by comprehending the rich intersections of creation-centered theology and human sexuality, as did the medieval rabbinic traditions. Sexual pleasure can lead lovers to a profound consciousness of their social and spiritual existence. They may come to appreciate sexuality as a gift from God who loves embodied joy and erotic pleasure in and through the establishing of relationships with partner, community, and the world. Sex is both creative and procreative in mirroring God's action within creation and realizing the giftedness of sexual relations.[33] A commitment of love—whether heterosexual or same-sex—involves going beyond self, desiring to sexually pleasure the other, celebrating the giving and receiving of pleasure, being grateful for the shared love, and recognizing God's presence in love-making. Profound delight is found in the pleasure of the lover whether the lover is God, a partner, or both. The recovery of Sabbath sexuality as spiritual practice places human sexuality with a creation-centered spirituality, insisting that God made sex good and pleasurable.

Too often, even when churches have affirmed sexuality as a gift, they have immediately qualified it and regulated it with restrictions, as Sabbath fundamentalists did in their opposition to Jesus. However, God's grace, like the giftedness of sexuality, cannot be regulated or contained. Churches need to teach that God made sex good, an original blessing to be celebrated and enjoyed. Perhaps churches will one day recognize gay sexuality not as unbridled lust but as *wild, erotic grace* that rejoices in the pleasure of lover and God. From the perspective of his creation-centered theology, Matthew Fox writes, "Every time humans truly make love, truly express their lives by the act of sexual love-making, the Cosmic Christ is making love."[34]

Sexual pleasure and "just good sex"

Gay recovery of embodiment and sexual pleasure has its dangers. It can lead to apathy or even a body fascism, which recovers bodily pleasure at the expense of social justice. Exclusive stress on sexual pleasure can blind gay men to racism, sexism, ableism, economic injustice, environmental injustice, and many other issues.[35] Sexual pleasure is not morally neutral, for it can be pursued for narcissistic gratification alone or in order to extend justice-love.

The Christian repression of sexual pleasure, I would argue, has led to a violent Christianity. James Nelson and James Prescott have noted a correlation between the suppression of bodily pleasure and a high incidence of cultural violence and, further, also observed that those cultures in which bodily pleasure is valued have a lower incidence of violence.[36] A middle course exists between the Scylla of hedonism and the Charybdis of violence. Both extremes are monstrous distortions of Christianity. An exclusive search for self-gratification leads to narcissism and social apathy. Violence destroys bodily interconnection with other people, species, and the environment. Christian efforts to limit erotic pleasure have contributed to its violent legacy against women, sexual minorities, indigenous peoples, non-Christians, and the planet. Both hedonism and violence distance their practitioners from a justice ethic and praxis.

Sexual pleasure can, however, become the foundation for moral discourse and justice work. The 1991 Presbyterian Special Committee on Human Sexuality wrote, "To embrace the erotic as a moral good is a noble calling for persons of faith, especially those convinced that a Christian life without a place for erotic passion is cold and lifeless."[37] In a similar fashion, Carter Heyward, Marvin Ellison, Beverly Harrison, Mary Hunt, and other contributors to this volume have expended much energy in linking sexuality to justice. They realize that embracing sexuality and sexual passion revitalizes a Christianity that has either denied or cordoned off the erotic.

Sexual pleasure connected to creation and Sabbath is also connected to the biblical notion of justice-love. Justice-love can gauge the appropriateness of a variety of sexual relationships, as well as their limits. This notion certainly allows for recognition of the sexual pleasures in same-sex relationships, but also in single sexuality as well as pair-bonded and communal relationships.[38] A variety of sexual expressions can communicate justice-love. The Presbyterian committee writes,

> To do justice-love means seeking right-relatedness with others and work to set right all wrong relations, especially distorted power dynamics of domination and subordination. Embracing the goodness of our sexuality, of our erotic desire for wholeness and connectedness is, therefore, a godly gift to us. Erotic power, rightly ordered, grounds and moves us on, gently yet persistently, to engage in creating justice with love for ourselves and all others.[39]

The theological notion of justice-love does not preclude erotic relationships other than pair-bonded, monogamous relationships, and yet, we should note, Christian exploration of single sexuality and polyamory is only at its ethical infancy.[40]

Once gay Christians have escaped their erotophobic heritages, they can view their embodied pleasures as intertwined with spirituality and erotic justice. The incarnation of God in our sexual experiences can embody justice in our mutuality and the joy of giving and receiving pleasure, building an ecclesial sexual community, and expressing solidarity with the oppressed. Justice-love begins with our partners, intersects with God in love-making, and extends to the world. In other words, when love-making is connected with justice-doing, our capacities to love expand beyond mutual pleasure into the pleasure of loving God in our neighbor and in the marginalized. Personally, I have found that I cannot be passionate for justice work without being a passionate lover, and vice versa.

Erotic connecting of bodies means that gay bodies are connected erotically and joyfully, producing and inventing pleasures. Gay indigenous ethics has often echoed the ethical norms of "safe, sane, and consensual" of the S/M subculture. While these norms may be useful for individual sexual encounters, they remain too narrow for gay Christians because they reduce sex to the realm of private pleasures. Good sex, although pleasurable, is not a sufficient end for a Christian, for good sex must be expanded beyond private pleasures to integrate justice. Many gay Christians and other gay men have realized the procreative potentialities of their love-making and extended their overflow love to the creation of families with children, volunteerism, and justice work.

Feminist theologian Mary Hunt stresses that good sex is "just good sex." She rightly adds the qualifier "just," connecting sexual love to justice, for just good sex is pleasurable, uncoerced, and community building:

> Just good sex...is community building as a specific antidote to the couples trap or other privatizing moves. Perhaps, the intuition that it was meant to be procreative is not entirely wrong, only partial in that just good sex is really part of creating a new network of relationships that emerge from all relationships.[41]

Sexual pleasure is something that should be oriented to the higher purposes of justice-love. For Mary Hunt, just good sex is connected to the pleasures of justice. She writes,

> I would include the pleasure of knowing that children are fed, the pleasure of creating meaningful work, the pleasure of providing care to all, the pleasure of living in a nuclear-free world, the pleasure of ending violence, the pleasure of stopping racism.[42]

Unfortunately, many gay Christians either closet their sexuality (and thereby impede their spiritual development) or seek out marginalized denominational support groups, perhaps even joining exilic churches, such as the Universal Fellowship of Metropolitan Community Churches (UFMCC). While the gay community provides space for affirming erotic relationships, only a few ecclesial "erogenous zones" are willing to include, much less celebrate, the holiness of gay sexuality. The ecclesial erogenous zones that exist provide urgently needed sites for resistance to a negative, negating Christian legacy that hates the body and tightly regulates bodily and spiritual pleasures. These precious sites of freedom and integrity are places in which body and spirit may be holistically connected. Whenever that happens, there is, indeed, a joyful noise both in heaven and on earth.

Notes

1. Donald Boisvert, *Out on Holy Ground: Meditation on Gay Men's Spirituality* (Cleveland: Pilgrim, 2000), 117.

2. Michel Foucault, *The Use of Pleasure,* vol. 2 of *The History of Sexuality* (New York: Vintage Books, 1990).

3. See Thomas Aquinas, *Summa Theologica* (New York: McGraw Hill, 1964), q. 41, ans. 3, and q. 49, ans. 4.

4. Peter Gardella, *Innocent Ecstasy: How Christianity Gave America an Ethic of Sexual Pleasure* (New York: Oxford University Press, 1985), 13.

5. John T. Noonan, *Contraception: A History of Its Treatment by Catholic Theologians and Councils* (Cambridge, Mass.: Harvard University Press, 1965), 491–94.

6. Daniel Doriani, "The Puritans, Sex, and Pleasure," in *Christian Perspectives on Sexuality and Gender,* ed. Adrian Thatcher and Elizabeth Stuart (Grand Rapids, Mich.: Eerdmans, 1996), 33–52.

7. David W. Purcell and Daniel W. Hicks, "Institutional Discrimination against Lesbians, Gay Men, and Bisexuals," in *Textbook of Homosexuality and Mental Health,* ed. Robert P. Cabaj and Terry Stein (Washington, D.C.: American Psychiatric Press, 1996), 765. Urvaishi Vaid, *Virtual Equality: The Mainstreaming of Gay and Lesbian Liberation* (New York: Doubleday, 1995), 134–35. David A. J. Richards, *Identity and the Case for Gay Rights: Race, Gender, Religion as Analogies* (Chicago: University of Chicago Press, 1999), 81–82.

8. Mark D. Jordan, *The Ethics of Sex* (Malden, Mass.: Blackwell, 2002), 152.

9. Ibid., 157–63.

10. Ibid., 168.

11. Robert Dreyfuss, "National Affairs," *Rolling Stone Magazine* (March 18, 1999).

12. Ibid.

13. Ronald Modras, "Pope John Paul II's Theology of the Body," in *The Vatican and Homosexuality: Reactions to the "Letter to the Bishops of the Catholic Church on the Pastoral Care of Homosexual Persons,"* ed. Jeannine Grammick and Pat Furey (New York: Crossroad, 1988), 121.

14. Benedict Ashley, "Compassion and Sexual Orientation," in *The Vatican and Homosexuality,* 105–6.

15. Anne Bathurst Gilson, *Eros Breaking Free: Interpreting Sexual Theo-Ethics* (Cleveland: Pilgrim, 1995), 37.

16. Michael Bronski, *The Pleasure Principle: Sex, Backlash, and the Struggle for Gay Freedom* (New York: St. Martin's, 1998), 220.

17. Ibid., 190.

18. Robert Barzan, ed., *Sex and Spirit: Exploring Gay Men's Spirituality* (San Francisco: White Crane, 1995); Jeffrey Hopkins, *Sex, Orgasm, and the Mind of Clear Light: The Sixty-four Arts of Gay Male Love* (Berkeley, Calif.: North Atlantic Books, 1998); and Christian La Huerta, *Coming Out Spiritually: The Next Step* (New York: J. P. Tarcher, 1999).

19. Andrew Sullivan, *Love Undetectable: Notes on Friendship, Sex, and Survival* (New York: Alfred A. Knopf, 1998), 57.

20. Robert E. Goss, "Finding God in the Heart-Genital Connection: Joe Kramer's Erotic Christianity," *Theology and Sexuality* (March 2002): 32–44; Michael Kelly, *The Erotic Contemplative* (video series), produced by EroSpirit, Oakland, 1994.

21. John McNeill, *Freedom, Glorious Freedom* (Boston: Beacon, 1995), 53–89.

22. Boisvert, *Out on Holy Ground*, 41.

23. Ibid., 46.

24. L. William Countryman and M. R. Riley, *Gifted by Otherness: Gay and Lesbian Christians in the Church* (Harrisburg, Pa.: Morehouse, 2001), 7.

25. Robert E. Goss, *Jesus ACTED UP: A Gay and Lesbian Manifesto* (San Francisco: HarperSanFrancisco, 1993), 119.

26. Marvin Ellison, *Erotic Justice: A Liberating Ethic of Sexuality* (Louisville: Westminster John Knox, 1996), 80.

27. Robert E. Goss, "The Integration of Sexuality and Spirituality: Gay Sexual Prophets within UFMCC," in *The Spirituality of Men: Sixteen Christians Write about Their Faith,* ed. Philip L. Culbertson (Minneapolis: Fortress, 2002), 200–220.

28. James B. Nelson, *Embodiment: An Approach to Sexuality and Christian Theology* (Minneapolis: Augsburg, 1978); *Between Two Gardens: Reflections on Sexuality and Religious Experience* (New York: Pilgrim, 1983); *The Intimate Connection: Male Sexuality, Masculine Spirituality* (Philadelphia: Westminster, 1988). See also Carter Heyward, *Touching Our Strength: The Erotic as Power and the Love of God* (San Francisco: Harper & Row, 1989); Elizabeth Stuart and Lisa Isherwood, *Introducing Body Theology* (Cleveland: Pilgrim, 2000); Elisabeth Wendel-Moltmann, *I Am My Body: A Theology of Embodiment,* trans. John Bowden (New York: Continuum, 1995); Kelly Brown Douglas, *Sexuality and the Black Church* (Maryknoll, N.Y.: Orbis, 1999). Other authors are included in James B. Nelson and Sandra P. Longfellow, eds., *Sexuality and the Sacred: Sources for Theological Reflection* (Louisville: Westminster John Knox, 1993).

29. Nancy Wilson, *Our Tribe: Queer Folks, God, Jesus, and the Bible* (San Francisco: HarperSanFrancisco, 1995), 266.

30. Ibid., 267.

31. David Biale, *Eros and the Jews: From Biblical Israel to Contemporary America* (San Francisco: Basic Books, 1992), 100–109.

32. Pierre J. Payer, *Sex and the Penitentials: The Development of a Sexual Code, 550–1150* (Toronto: University of Toronto Press, 1993), 23–28. James A. Brundage, *Law, Sex, and Christian Society in Medieval Europe* (Chicago: University of Chicago Press, 1987), 157–59.

33. On the procreativity of same-sex relationships, see Robert Goss, "Challenging Procreative Privilege: Equal Rites," *Theology and Sexuality* 7 (spring 1997): 33–55; "Queering Procreative Privilege: Coming Out as Families," in *Our Families,*

Our Values: Snapshots of Queer Kinship, ed. Robert E. Goss and Amy Adams Squire Strongheart (New York: Haworth Press, 1997), 3–20.

34. Matthew Fox, *The Coming of the Cosmic Christ* (San Francisco: HarperSan-Francisco, 1988), 172.

35. Goss, *Jesus ACTED UP,* 156–59.

36. See James Nelson, *The Intimate Connection: Male Sexuality, Male Spirituality* (Philadelphia: Westminster, 1988); James W. Prescott, "Body Pleasure and the Origins of Violence," *Bulletin of the Atomic Scientists* (November 1975): 10–20.

37. *Presbyterians and Human Sexuality 1991* (Louisville: Presbyterian Church [U.S.A.], 1991), 9.

38. See "Challenging Procreative Privilege," in Robert E. Goss, *Queering Christ: Beyond Jesus ACTED UP* (Cleveland: Pilgrim, 2002). For a range of sexual relationships, see Goss and Strongheart, *Our Families, Our Values.*

39. *Presbyterians and Human Sexuality 1991,* 9.

40. For example, see Kathy Rudy, "Where Two or More Are Gathered: Using Gay Communities as a Model for Christian Sexual Ethics," in *Our Families, Our Values,* 197–216. For an expansion of Rudy's thought, see Kathy Rudy, *Sex and the Church: Gender, Homosexuality, and the Transformation of Christian Ethics* (Boston: Beacon, 1996). Elizabeth Stuart has a very creative exploration of eschatology and queer sexual relationships in Stuart, "Sex in Heaven: The Queering of Theological Discourse on Sexuality," in *Sex These Days: Essays on Theology, Sexuality, and Society,* ed. Jon Davies and Gerard Loughlin (Sheffield: Sheffield University Press, 1997), 185–202.

41. Mary Hunt, "Feminist Catholicism and Human Rights," in *Good Sex: Feminist Perspectives from the World's Religions,* ed. Patricia Beattie Jung, Mary Hunt, and Radhika Balakrishnan (New Brunswick, N.J.: Rutgers University Press, 2001), 172.

42. Ibid. Ellison makes a similar point: "Good sex is good because it touches our senses powerfully but also because it enhances our self-worth and deepens our desire to connect more justly with others" (Ellison, *Erotic Justice,* 89).

13

Receptivity and Revelation

A Spirituality of Gay Male Sex

Scott Haldeman

I am becoming a gay man. This is a lifelong project and a large part of my work in this current phase of my life. Each day, each hour, each encounter, I must choose to be out or not, to be proud or ashamed, to be courageous or fearful, to "flame" or to "play it straight." Each day I must choose to face and fight the stigma of tradition, society, and church, or allow it to eat away a bit more of my energy, my life. Each day, while the seminary for which I work is committed to the full inclusion of sexual minorities in the life of the church and society, the homophobia of other institutions threatens the meaningful work and livelihood of both myself and my partner, and so I must choose how much to put us at risk, calculate who knows whom, choose discretion or openness.

Each day, under such circumstances, I practice my own version of a gay life. I demonstrate my affection to my lover, kissing him goodbye in the kitchen since the porch seems too exposed, reaching carefully for his hand lest the couple behind us in the theater notice, searching out safe places to be together, reveling in each other's bodies at home, seeking yet more intimacy, exploring yet unfound pleasures. Each day, as well, I think socially, politically, theologically, ecclesiologically, and liturgically in queer ways, from a margin. Each day, too, I do things like read, prepare lectures, exercise, wash dishes, commute, and get ready for bed.

In all these things I, like you, practice who I am becoming.[1] I practice being gay as I practice being a teacher, a scholar, a father, and a spouse. I practice these things in relation to the choices available and the constraints that impinge on those choices.[2] In some ways, I am confined by the meanings given to notions of being "gay," "male," "partner," "father," "liturgist," "white," "academic," and many other labels, which I claim with more or less comfort. I negotiate them, too, accepting, rejecting, or most often making some sort of compromise with these images, categories, and boxes that are available, here and now, to me and the mechanisms that enforce them. Laurel Schneider challenges us to turn from a natural law understanding of sexual identity to a queer one in which identity is understood as communal and the norms governing behaviors are more about relational effect than the protection of static identity categories. She puts the matter this way:

> So whether I *am* a lesbian or *choose* to be one is relevant only in terms of what I ultimately do in community with being one. How, for instance, does being lesbian [or refusing to be lesbian] make me a better, more whole person working toward a better, more honest and peaceful world? ... Does being a lesbian give me strength to love others more deeply and courageously? If the designation helps me with that—and in my case it does—so much the better.[3]

Therefore, we must consider our practices in terms of their effects and choose, without ignoring real constraints, what will make us better neighbors and friends, more attuned to the needs of others and our world.

I reflect here on a few things revealed to me while "on the bus." While recognizing the roots of my queer self in earlier days, I have been "in the life" for only a short while. In these few years of being "out," my eyes have opened to many new aspects of myself, of being human, of community, and of justice and faith. I focus here on one practice and, actually, on only one aspect of one practice, namely, sex. Because sexual practices are particularly significant to gay male identity and at the same time culturally despised, they function as a locus of debate. Sex with another man is also particularly meaningful to me in ways that oppose hegemonic interpretations and, thus, is a compelling topic for me. However, a few caveats are in order.

First, I consider sex only as I know it, meaning sex involving myself and another man. This is rather limited in scope, surely, but

necessary to keep as concrete as possible. In other words, I am not attempting to define revelatory aspects of sex generally, nor do I make
any claim to speak for other queer folk, the term I use as shorthand
for lesbian, gay, bisexual, and transgender people and other sexual
minorities in a heterosexist society. I make no claim of insight into
sex between women, sex between all men, or sex even of the other
person with whom I have had sex. I simply cannot tell you what sex
between men means, much less what sex in general means, but only
about what some sex acts have meant and are continuing to mean
to me, a white academic with leisure to think on such things, lately
out, once married to a woman, and now in a long-term relationship
with a man.

What I hope to accomplish by looking critically at my particular story is to encourage readers to reflect on their stories and
thereby engender mutual learning through dialogue. This is both a
methodological and an epistemological claim. In other words, first,
I contend that articulation of the particular leads not so much to
generalizations, but to conversations among those who bring their
particularities to voice. And, second, our knowledge, limited by
social location and perspectival horizon, is grounded in bodily experience and grows in analytical power only through recognition of
these limits and in joining with others in critically appreciative dialogue. In other words, I reject the opportunity to impose my insights
on others or define their experience. At the same time, I accept responsibility to consider the implications of my norms and values for
others in a social system that coerces many through physical and
social violence in order to protect the security and privilege of a few.

Second, as the title of this essay indicates, I believe sex is revelatory. By this I do not mean that when I am in bed, I regularly
experience theophanies, the sensible presence of the divine, as witnessed to in Scripture: God in a burning bush that is not consumed,
in cloud, fire, earthquake, and wind, or in the sound of sheer silence.
Nor in light of Romans 1:18–32, a central text used to keep queer folk
from ordination and full participation in the churches, do I consider
my human lover a god. What Paul condemns here is idolatry, a temptation as much for heterosexuals as it is for queers. As far as I can tell,
this has not been an issue in my own relationship, for as much as I
love my "husband," I do not associate him with God.

Revelation, instead, has come to me in a way that I would call sacramental. Material, embodied, sensory experiences that mediate, but do not delimit in themselves, particular, partial, and fragile aspects of divine reality, divine grace, and divine love. By sacramental experience, I am referring to something akin to an icon through which one sees, as through a portal, something of the attributes of God. In Christian tradition, material objects mediate God's presence as they are used communally and ritually to remember God's past saving activity and to imagine and rehearse God's promised future. Less traditionally but no less faithfully, in the commingling of bodies, I feel deeply and tangibly, yet fragilely and fleetingly, something of divine love. Sex as revelation is about mediated knowledge of God, about encountering God, in partial, momentary glimpses, through the act of encounter with my lover.

Third, my title indicates that I intend to outline a spirituality of gay male sex. Again, my claims are humble. My purpose is to evoke, not limit the reflections of others. But what is spirituality these days, other than a very slippery term? I like Don Saliers's definition that Christian spirituality is "living at full stretch,"[4] evoking Irenaeus's ancient claim, paraphrased as "the glory of God is a human being fully alive."[5] Spirituality means the sum of life in relation to God and neighbor, comprising how one lives in this world and not simply a yearning for something beyond it. This way of life is inescapably relational and directed toward life abundant both in history and in hope of God's coming reign.

Finally, what aspect of my sex life am I talking about? Shall I employ the language of romance and risk layering the topic with suffocating gauze? No, while seeking not to offend or discomfort, I want to be clear that I am speaking about what I have learned in moving in a sexual sense from top to bottom. Already there are problems of euphemism: these words may imply a static structuralism that I neither promote nor experience. Over four years ago, in a flash of emotional and relational chaos, I found myself in an unexpected place of receptivity, a place where I now feel at home as I have felt in no other place in my life. In bed with another man, I have found myself not as the Leviticus code defines it, "lying with another man as with a woman," but as one the authorities considered unworthy even of condemnation, the receptive partner in gay male intercourse (Lev.

8:22). Opening myself to receive another physically has revelatory—spiritual, ethical, and theological—value for me, even as it is also a new source of pleasure, a practice that deepens relationality, and an inversion of my former self-understanding. By continuing to practice receptivity in a sexual sense, I am forming and being formed as a new person. I am finding this person more and more to be the one I want, for moral and ethical reasons, to become.

Am I condemning, along with the Levites, those on top? By no means. Am I positing that this act, this role, has better moral quality than others? By no means. While eschewing complete moral relativism, I understand human thought and behavior as profoundly ambiguous, as both potentially life-giving and revelatory, a locus of grace if practiced in mutual love and respect and, if not, potentially destructive, divisive, and death-dealing. For this reason, all we do is in constant need of critical reflection and reform. My claim, then, is that playing the receptive role in sex can be healthy and healing, while it can also be destructive and harmful. Like other human practices, it involves risk. Andrea Dworkin sees penetration as colonization,[6] and I do not dispute that it can be for many women and some men, and yet it is not always so. It can also be a moral good even though condemned and rendered illegal in many locales inside and outside the United States. In addition, am I at risk for defining myself by this one practice, the dread of sodomy? Probably, but this is a risk worth taking in order to oppose the forces of hate and fear that threaten my living and loving and the lives and loves of countless others.

To return to the practice itself, I like playing the receptive role in sex. Moreover, on occasion, I experience it not so much as a desire, but as a physical need like hunger or thirst. As I receive and hold the other, I find myself feeling complete, whole, and yet yearning for more—more justice, more mutual respect, and more well-being for myself, my partner, communities near and far, and the whole world. For me, being receptive in sex is sacramental, and what sacramental occasions offer, in a proleptic sense, is fragile but real satisfaction and a promise of an ultimate, complete satisfaction of our deepest and best yearnings.

I would like to name and then expand upon four movements of anal intercourse. First, as I play with my lover, I begin to feel a sense of anticipation. He attends to me, and I to him. As he wraps around me, lays upon me, or comes up behind, his erection touches my body, and I shudder. I sense my permeability, abandon notions of self-protectiveness, and let him cross the membrane of my skin. He enters me. I am full of him, allowing him to touch me deep inside while holding him with my body. After we have rocked together, moved as closely as we possibly can, and found a rhythm that suits us both, he cums. I usually want him to stay inside me, hold me close, and share those final throes of orgasm, to partake and absorb him. Finally, in the moments and, on good days, for hours afterwards, I feel my openness, the stretching of my body to fit another, and be filled.

There you have an account of a despised practice. What religious traditions define as an unforgivable evil is an act in which I find life. How to explain the discrepancy? It is not enough to note it and move on. Too much is at stake: the vocations and very lives of my brothers and of my sisters, too.

For Leo Bersani, "the rectum is a grave."[7] In trying to understand society's revulsion toward anal sex during the escalating North Atlantic AIDS crisis, especially as it ravaged the population of men who have sex with other men, he notes how the victims of this scourge were portrayed as if they were killers. Anal sex was seen not merely as a risky behavior for transmitting a virus, but as the primary disease itself. Without subscribing to his ahistorical reading of anal sex, we can sense the threat felt in the larger culture about any man submitting to penetration in this "blame the victim" stratagem. Contrary to my own experience, opening oneself to receive a male lover threatens masculine identity, something evidently so fragile that it must be protected by force. This disdain for anal sex between men shows both the depth of misogyny and the cultural mandate to define men as those who penetrate rather than are penetrated. Although I reject equating the experience of women as receptive sexual partners with that of men, the notion is found in scriptural descriptions of the penetrated man acting "as a woman." Other cultural slights imply that he has "lost his manhood" and been "feminized." Such metaphors are longstanding and apparently devastating to many men, outside of and within the gay community. The fear of feminization has given license to the bashing and rape of gay men, similar to ways in which misogyny is enforced through the rape of women. Within the gay community, this stigmatizing of receptive (male) sex has led to the development of more or less static sexualized categories, such as "top" and "bottom," so that, perhaps, men may claim a more secure identity within a subculture of gender ambiguity that both reflects and subverts hegemonic definitions of masculinity.[8]

Better vocabulary for talking about sex and power is needed, and Susan Kippax and Gary Smith provide us help.[9] They recognize that phallocentric norms have deep-seated effects on contemporary Western society and on any cultural structures based on a static, hierarchical binary system of value: that penetration is power and the penetrated powerless, that one is either male or female, dominant or submissive, the inserter or the receptacle, active or passive — the latter in each dyad being, of course, also lesser. At the same time, Kippax and Smith have also found that in a major ethnographic survey in Australia gay men describe anal intercourse in ways that contest this static dualism. These men deploy new descriptors, such as active passivity, versatility, powerful receptivity, and pleasurable vulnerability.

Keeping this in mind, I seek interpretations of my own practices that contest the violence and disdain of heteronormativity, challenge static understandings of power, postures, and roles in sex and other human interactions, and help overturn phallocentric anthropologies. While acknowledging that I may find only what I am looking for, I seek complex, flexible, and ethically self-conscious ways of construing and criticizing my own behaviors. Without fostering naïve romanticism about the democracy of gay sex, my own sense of receptivity is not about being passive, but of fully participating in an act of mutual pleasuring. It is not about abandoning my maleness, but about reinventing it. It is not about surrendering control, but often about being very much in control, even while playing a supposedly submissive role. In any case, I understand control not as the exercise of power over the other, but about mutual care, intensity of sensation, and conscious role playing. Desiring and being desired, while practicing a healthy vulnerability, can be mutually pleasurable, as well as empowering and healing.

To gain a clearer understanding of how sexual receptivity contributes to spirituality, consider the phases of the sex act noted above. First, I assume a posture in which I can be entered. Second, the boundary of my skin is crossed. Third, I receive and am filled by another. Fourth, we commune in intimate embrace and movement, reaching toward ecstatic release. I take these four as spiritual values. They are touchstones for other parts of my life, as well. In other words, I am being formed in new ways by practicing this posture of openness and vulnerability, this permeability, this rhythm of emptying and being filled, and this regular, embodied communion. I will expand on each before concluding.

A posture of vulnerability

I am a student of ritual. As Ronald Grimes notes, ritual is embodied, so ritual studies must attend to posture. "A posture is not only one's manner of physical comportment (how one parks the body so to speak)," he writes, "but also one's attitude — one's manner or style in the world. Attitude denotes the spiritual component of posture."[10] Other practices sustained over time also shape our attitudes and spirituality. Grimes uses the language of sexual posture to describe two competing liturgical styles. I find in my own sexual postures a new sympathy for what he calls liturgical supinity, forms of worship and ritualization that arise from the ground and from human need as opposed to those imposed, as it were, from the sky as unquestionable, what Grimes calls "erect." Suspicious of forms that "render domination beautiful,"[11] I seek attitudes of prayer that tell the truth in all its complexity and stretch toward relationships of mutual respect and justice. So, too, I am suspicious of "sacred" forms that claim divine inspiration and thereby exclude styles of prayer based in local culture, discourage criticism, and serve to maintain unjust power relationships. I want to encourage the construction of rites that suit particular communities in dialogue with, but not in slavish imitation of, inherited tradition.

Supine myself, I tarry for my sisters and brothers, desiring that we construct together ways of ritualizing that empower holy acts, such as gathering, storytelling, washing, eating, anointing, giving thanks, and raising cries of want and need. Yet I do so as a man, a recognition made all the more necessary because of Grimes's own heavily gendered undertones. As a man, I place myself in the vulnerable position of supinity. I do so with a strong sense of security, based on the trustworthy relationship in which I practice this posture, but also on the privilege and power at my disposal that allows me to speak up and act for myself, should violation occur. Many who have had trust betrayed, who know about sexual and other kinds of violence, and who have been forced into supinity, may find such a posture too problematic to assume voluntarily.

I honor the need both for self-protection and for a wide variety of practices that may contribute to building human community. Yet, because I remain convinced of my own need for trust and vulnerability, I place myself at the other's disposal, including the community, in order to foster richer, more honest, and more transformative forms of rehearsing the reign of God together. All this takes place in the context of worship and as worship. As Grimes concluded before a group of mostly male liturgical scholars, "If you choose to embody and practice [the metaphor of supinity], it will stretch muscles you did not know you have. And you may be sure, you will be sore the next day."[12] Being supine can invite pain, literally and metaphorically, yet such a posture feels right and good to me. In it, I foster an attitude that avoids domination, engenders dialogue, and risks even the betrayal of trust in the hope of reconciliation and the increase of justice.

Permeability

Culturally considered, the anus is a place of dirt and discomfort. By allowing another person to approach this part of your body, you risk giving offense and being rejected as dirty, smelly, and ugly. Furthermore, opening to receive another into your body means risking pain and perhaps even harm. Such risks may also lead to pleasure, intimacy, and healing. Allowing another to come inside encourages me, in other places and times, to risk listening deeply to others across lines of difference, to touch and be touched in risky yet promising ways. No doubt there are other ways out of the trap of hypermasculine invulnerability, but living with permeable rather than rigid and unyielding boundaries is surely one. For instance, we may learn the value of risking peace rather than penetrating the enemy's defenses with smart bombs or to absorb the wisdom of others rather than to impose only irrefutable arguments upon them. Transgressing taboos against sodomy encourages me to reconsider the labels I paste upon others, denying them freedom to be truly themselves. Practicing permeability, I find myself more open and flexible as I try to live justly in communities of difference.

Of course, there are limits to risk-taking. I practice such permeability in a relational context of deep trust. While some may find pleasure in inflicting pain, even sadomasochism and bondage require establishing clear lines of communication, including signals of approaching boundaries between what is pleasurable and what is violation. With the rise of "bare-backing" (anal sex without condoms) among younger gay men, safe sex practices must again be encouraged, so that risk-taking does not lead to loss of yet another generation to AIDS. Adopting attitudes of permeability, while also being realistic about the possibilities of violation and transmission of a deadly virus, may encourage in us a fierce passion and yearning for abundant life, not a denial of suffering and death.

Emptying and being filled

The practice of being filled has helped me discover things about God. God's phallus as metaphor is not the problem it once was.[13] While the maleness of God remains central in Scriptures and so in theologies, it is now possible for me to relate in more playful and yet serious ways to these narratives. Ken Stone points out how the book of Hosea portrays God as the husband of Israel in ways that support sexist control of female sexuality, and yet this divine husband is also the cuckold. The power metaphor is broken, allowing space for queer images and, perhaps, queer lives.[14]

The Bible's almost exclusively masculine images for the divine present a lopsided and dangerous picture, one that many women refuse to accept as normative because it justifies their entrapment in second-class citizenship in church and society. Certainly we ought not confine ourselves to the tales of ancestors for knowledge about God. We must continue to imagine God in new language that allows her to escape any attempts to confine her divine freedom. However,

my delight in allowing my male lover to fill me allows me, analo-
gously, to delight also in the intimate approach of the God who is
imaged as male in Scripture. As Ted Jennings helps us see, this God
also delights in the seductive dance of his beloved, David.[15] I can delight in God as "he" melts, molds, fills, and uses me, as that most
hilarious of hymns, "Spirit of the Living God," puts it. At the same
time, I do not and cannot forget that God is *not* my male lover, does
not literally seduce me, and also delights in others who find their
pleasure and affirmation in different acts, bodily based analogies,
and relational metaphors. However, in practicing receptivity, I allow
myself the pleasure of being overwhelmed by God who delights in me
and wishes my good. This provides balance to other notions of God
that I hold dear, invites my attentiveness to God's presence in and
around me, and shatters the categories that have allowed keepers of
tradition to confine the divine for too long.

Communion

Finally, the deep physical intimacy of sex with my lover echoes and
deepens my understanding of communion. In bed, I give myself fully
to our embrace and synchronized movement. I take him in, hold him
deep, and partake of his touch and very being. This embrace has
little other purpose than mutual pleasure. Queer love, despised and
supposedly unproductive, is, in fact, often gratuitous and extravagant like the love of God in creation and redemption, like the kenosis
of Jesus in his sojourn with us and his torture and death, and like
the overwhelming love that graces the dead with new, incorruptible
life.[16] The church as the embodiment of God on earth is charged to
get on with discovering, celebrating, and living the promised era of
wholeness, peace, and justice. For that work, Jesus promises his presence as people gather about the table. As Augustine, paraphrased,
says about the table: "See there, it is you, you upon the table, you
the bread broken, the wine poured." In other words, we are what we
eat, this bread, this body. Communion is about ingesting, absorb-
ing, and assimilating self to other, other to self, very God of very
God, we, the Body of Christ. Communing in bed or at table, I become
more and more the lover and the beloved. I become more me, more
in union with my male lover, with my neighbors, with the stranger,

and with God. More and more love rises, melts, overflows. More and more love.

Conclusion

I practice receptivity in sex and also in life. It is shaping me, as other things I do also shape me, but as a condemned practice, to do this is to practice transgression. Still fire and brimstone have not consumed me, and although surely the Day of Judgment is coming, I feel confident of divine approval of my doing of this act. While I do not deny the possibility of self-deception, and although biblical and theological traditions give little support, the inward and outward dimensions of my life grow richer, truer, and more whole in ways I take as indications of rightness. Perhaps God is not a lover of static structure or of hierarchies of values and set orders. Looking from the margins, from below in a physical and a social sense, I see a divine self that is more playful and more serious, quite uninterested in notions of purity, and yearning to become a new thing among us, a communion in which all will dance a wild dance of joy and passion. Therefore, I plan to continue assuming a supine posture and to practice permeability, emptying and being filled, and communion, joining gladly in this impure dance of passion.

Do my reflections spark responses in you? If so, I have accomplished my purpose, to encourage not so much agreement as your own desire to reflect on your own practices, sexual and otherwise, in relation to the whole of your lives. Despite hypocrisy, rationalization, and brokenness, what we humans do remains the clearest indicator of who we truly are. All practices exist in relationship to every other, not in anything resembling coherence, and yet the full spectrum of our doing shapes who we are becoming. So, too, our practices are shaped by, and shape, our notions of self, community, and God. Through our practices we are revealed, just as God reveals her divine self in glimpses of uncontainable glory. So, too, our practices are becoming; they are flawed and in need of critique and reform. None of us has it perfect. While, as Tom Driver has written, "All my experience is Word of God for me,"[17] such words are partial, fragile, and not (yet) wholly trustworthy. They must be sorted out

in terms of their contribution to wholeness, justice, and truth. Therefore, we must find better, more honest, and more revelatory ways to
talk together about what we do and why we do it, as well as what we
condemn and what we value, if we are to "find and follow pathways
of freedom."[18]

Notes

1. A provocative discussion of the role of "practice" in human life comes from
Pierre Bourdieu, who proposes that human beings learn how to act with compe-
tence in their society through a complex system of practices that are defined and
constrained by a particular cultural field. He uses the term *habitus* to designate the
dispositions that enable people to know what to do in a variety of situations that
they encounter in life. This *habitus* does not determine one's choice since one can
act inappropriately or otherwise violate social norms, but it does shape deeply
one's self-understanding — body, mind, and imagination — so that the range of
choices available is defined according to the structures of the culture in which one
lives. See Bourdieu, *Outline of a Theory of Practice,* trans. Richard Nice (Cambridge:
Cambridge University of Press, 1977), 72–95.

2. In a critical assessment of Bourdieu's notion of *habitus,* Judith Butler writes
of the depth of coercion involved in enforcing particular interpretations of human
identity ("being called a 'girl' from the inception of existence is a way in which
the girl becomes transitively 'girled' over time") and of instances of resistances
to such habituations, such as using terms of insult (e.g., "black" and "queer")
as efficacious slogans for liberative social movements. See Butler, "Performativ-
ity's Social Magic," in *Bourdieu: A Critical Reader,* ed. R. Shusterman (Oxford and
Malden, Mass.: Blackwell, 1999), 113–28.

3. Laurel Schneider, "What If It Is a Choice? Some Implications of the Homo-
sexuality Debate for Theology," in "The Gilberto Castañeda Lectures, 1998–2001:
Countering Homophobia in Bible and Theology," *Chicago Theological Seminary
Register* 91, no. 3 (2001): 30–31.

4. Don Saliers, *Worship and Spirituality* (Akron, Ohio: Order of St. Luke, 1984,
1996), 1.

5. Irenaeus, "Against Heresies," in *The Ante-Nicene Fathers,* vol. 1, ed. A. Roberts
and J. Donaldson (Grand Rapids, Mich.: Eerdmans, 1989), 490.

6. See Andrea Dworkin, *Intercourse* (New York: Free Press, 1987). While her
critique of heterosexual intercourse as a means of reinforcing patriarchy is relentless and compelling to a degree, in her fourth chapter entitled "Communion," she
turns, I note with some surprise, to the novels and essays of James Baldwin in order
to describe this same act, but now between men, as an act of grace, "the intensity
and magnificence of violent feeling transformed into tenderness" (60).

7. Leo Bersani, "Is the Rectum a Grave?" in *AIDS: Cultural Analysis, Cultural
Activism,* ed. Douglas Crimp (Cambridge, Mass.: MIT Press, 1987).

8. I reflect upon some ways in which masculinity is practiced among gay men
in "Resistance and Replication: Gay Men, Male Gender Roles and 'The Chute,'"

presented at the 1999 annual meeting of the American Men's Studies Association at Vanderbilt University.

9. Susan Kippax and Gary Smith, "Anal Intercourse and Power in Sex between Men," *Sexualities* 4, no. 4 (2001): 413–34.

10. Ronald Grimes, *Reading, Writing, and Ritualizing: Ritual in Fictive, Liturgical, and Public Places* (Washington, D.C.: Pastoral Press, 1993), 39.

11. This phrase is inspired by the poetry of Adrienne Rich in *A Wild Patience Has Taken Me This Far* (New York: W. W. Norton, 1981), 3–5.

12. Grimes, *Reading, Writing, and Ritualizing*, 58.

13. While grateful for his insights on gender identity and worship of a lone male deity by male devotees, here I play on the title of Howard Eilberg-Schwartz's *God's Phallus: And Other Problems for Men and Monotheism* (Boston: Beacon, 1994).

14. See Ken Stone, "Lovers and Raisin Cakes: Food, Sex, and Divine Insecurity in Hosea," in *Queer Commentary and the Hebrew Bible,* ed. Ken Stone (London and New York: Sheffield Academic Press, 2001), 116–39.

15. See Ted Jennings, "YHWH as Erastes" in *Queer Commentary and the Hebrew Bible,* 36–74.

16. Xavier John Seubert discusses the generativity of homoerotic relations based upon the pure gift of self as a distinct yet parallel value to the traditionally recognized procreative generativity of heteroerotic relations. See "But Do Not Use the Rotted Names: Theological Adequacy and Homosexuality," *Heythrop Journal* 40 (January 1999): 71.

17. Tom Driver, *Patterns of Grace: Human Experience as Word of God* (San Francisco: Harper & Row, 1977), xiii. Available in reprint from the author through Union Theological Seminary, New York.

18. Tom Driver, *Liberating Rites: Understanding the Transformative Power of Ritual* (Boulder, Colo.: Westview, 1998), v.

14

Becoming "Possessed"

Toward Sexual Health and Well-Being

Sylvia Thorson-Smith

On the paper provided, draw a picture of your sexuality. (You will not be graded on the artistic quality of your drawing.) Then write a statement describing what you've drawn—how you see yourself as a sexual person. You do not have to describe all aspects of your drawing if you do not want to. Don't feel that you must write personal details about your sexuality. Think of sexuality in the broadest terms as you've learned in this class—your entire way of being sexual and gendered in the world.

So begins Part I of the final exam for the Human Sexuality class that I teach at Grinnell College. After a semester of studying a broad survey of research data on sexuality issues and examining the connections between the data and themselves, students are expected to create and describe a picture that reveals something that they have learned about human sexuality. Accompanying one drawing last year was this statement by a twenty-year-old African American woman:

The left side of my picture is daylight, and there is a sun in the right-hand corner. At the bottom is a box with a person hiding inside it, peeking out from the inside. Surrounding the box are these words: tolerance, sex roles, STD awareness, relationships, scripts, body image, sex, and love. On the right side of my picture, it is night. At the bottom of this dark starry scene is an open box with a person emerging from it and the words from the left side written *on* the person. I use this picture because my sexuality is multidimensional, as different as day is from night....The picture also symbolizes my growth in this class. At the beginning, I was more like the picture on the left. Now I am like the picture on the right: an emerging new being who is so knowledgeable about various sexuality issues that I have internalized them and made them a part of who I am.[1]

An invitation

While talking with this student about her picture at our final class session, I was reminded again of the power of language and visual imagery. A subtle but crucial feature of the description of her sexuality is found in the movement from day to night, light to dark. In the starry sky of night, this young black woman expresses the complexity and authority of her own identity. Like the woman in the Song of Songs who proclaims "I am black *and* beautiful" (over against other translations, such as "I am very dark, *but* comely"[2]), this student boldly expresses, in both art and language, the deep truth she has come to know in her body. Such an exquisite description of sexual *health* is made possible through her experience of sexuality education and by making the connections between what she knows and who she is.

For over twenty years and in a variety of circumstances, I too have experienced sexuality education as both student and teacher. Tentatively at first (and somewhat fearfully, as memory recalls), I stammered for words to discuss a classmate's research on breasts in a late 1970s graduate course titled "The Psychology of Women." With time and teaching experience, I was soon "having oral sex" (talking about it) more and more frequently, in many different settings.[3]

Even to write this essay on a topic as comprehensive as "sexual health," I realize that virtually everything related to constructive and destructive, individual and social experiences of sexuality could easily be "on the table." Furthermore, as a sexuality educator, I'm well aware of the dangers of selection. For too long and causing much too much damage, "experts" in this field have been primarily white men, doctors of various kinds and clergy, who have controlled the fields of research, defined the terminology, constructed the theories, established parameters of normalcy, and (even benignly) limited the field of vision and voices of experience that, if consulted, would create a fuller understanding of sexual health. My deep conviction is that anything one says about sexual health and well-being needs to be put forth in a spirit of humility toward the mystery of human sexuality—actually, human *sexualities*—and with an acknowledgment of the particularity of experience that shapes whatever is expressed as opinion and authority. Given this caveat, I and you the reader are invited to consider the question: What can be said and done to advance the human condition of *sexual health?*

Finding a language for sexual health and well-being

I've come to realize that the promotion of sexual health, in all its diversity of experience, has proved to be the premise and the goal of virtually every educational forum, advocacy position, and ecclesiastical involvement of the last two decades of my life, whether explicitly or implicitly. Healthy human sexuality is so thoroughly central to the totality of both personal and corporate well-being that it is advanced (or not) by everything that impinges on our lives and experiences. In one way or another, if we are educators, activists, change agents, or people who seek to integrate faith and life, we are about the project of sexual health. Sexuality is always central to who we are; we are never *not* sexual beings (regardless of how we do and do not act), and our sexual health must be located where it belongs, at the core of our humanity.

Responding to a different question on the previously mentioned final exam, another student turned my thinking about sexual health in a new direction when she wrote that we all need to "fully possess our sexuality and sexual decisions."[4] Reading this, I was struck by the possible interpretations implied in the language of "possession." What would it mean for each of us to fully possess, much less be fully possessed by, our sexuality? In addition to ownership and control, "being possessed" can convey madness, craziness, and even passion gone berserk. Religiously, possession can represent the embodiment of evil, for which exorcism or other purging typically is prescribed (by appropriate—read: male—clerical authority). How odd to think that possessing, and being possessed by, our sexuality could actually be healthy! Ponder the fright of it—the wonder of it.

Richard Blonna and Jean Levitan have entitled their textbook simply *Healthy Sexuality,* prefacing it with their conviction that "human sexuality is intimately tied to overall health and wellness. ...Essential to being healthy, people have to come to grips with themselves as human beings, to make sound sexual decisions and self-actualize their sexual selves."[5] They recall that "in 1947 the World Health Organization (WHO) defined *health* as 'the state of complete mental, physical, and social well-being, not merely the absence of disease.'"[6] According to Blonna and Levitan, the emergence of a holistic health movement in the 1960s attempted to expand this globally accepted but flawed understanding of health as a static state of existence. An early pioneer in the field, Halbert Dunn, preferred to view health as a continuum, in which maintaining a high level meant moving toward optimum functioning. Health, therefore, "is a conscious and deliberate approach to life and being, rather than something to be abdicated to doctors and the health-care system."[7] Halbert Dunn seemed to understand that there was something akin to *possession* in the regard for each person's conscious, deliberate maintenance of one's own life and health.

While general wellness has many different dimensions (physical, emotional, spiritual, social, intellectual, and environmental), well-being includes aspects of each of these dimensions that relate directly to our experience of sexuality. Regardless of the condition of our bodies, the relationship between our sexual and overall health is dynamic, not static. Every day we learn more and more about the integrated body-systems that give us life. New studies establish evidence, for example, that the risk factors for heart disease also may play a role in Alzheimer's disease, and that "what is good [or bad] for the heart may also be good [or bad] for the brain."[8] Our understanding of sexual health needs to reflect a similar assumption of reciprocity and holistic functioning: "Our level of sexual well-being contributes to our overall level of health. Conversely, our overall level of health influences our sexuality."[9]

1n 1991, the committee of Presbyterians who wrote the report "Keeping Body and Soul Together" grasped the importance of *wholeness* in framing a study on human sexuality. While not developing a specific chapter on sexual health, the report describes the challenge for Christians as, in part, affirming a call to "holiness as inclusive wholeness." Furthermore, wholeness is understood to frame sexuality in individual as well as communal terms: "This theological vision—of inclusive wholeness, of the well-being of all persons in full community with others—provides a powerful normative vision for sexual relations."[10]

In addition to providing a framework for "putting sex in perspective" with the changes, crises, and challenges of our time, the report includes ten "issue" chapters addressing men, women, adolescents, gays, and lesbians,[11] persons with disabilities, older adults, sexual violence, clergy sexual misconduct, HIV/AIDS, and reproductive technology. Each of these chapters provides strategies for how we can live into the possibility of justice and empowerment for wholeness and responsibility. Much was said in each of these chapters that had implications for sexual health; much was also unsaid. The diverse array of essays in this current volume is evidence of the continuing effort to frame discussions of sexuality in ways that lead to wholeness in personal and social well-being.

Crucial to our thinking about sexual health is, I believe, a recognition that not everything about us is healthy. There is much in our lives from which we need healing. Brokenness and harm are endured daily by millions of people in the form of disease, abuse, exploitation, dysfunction, harassment, hardship, injustice, discrimination, and the powerlessness to possess and be possessed by—to express and control—their sexuality. It is in facing the pain of sexual dis-ease that we can hope and work to construct ever new visions of wholeness and holiness, health and healing.

Obstacles and challenges to sexual health

The 1991 Presbyterian report challenges Christians to reclaim "a passionate spirituality of justice." However, because of the "church's difficulty in speaking a truthful and healing word about human sexuality," discussion of this challenge begins by citing the dedication from a book on adolescent sexuality:

> To the young people of this nation who must find their way to sexual health in a world of contradictions—where the media

scream, "Always say yes," where many adults admonish, "Just say no," but the majority just say...nothing.[12]

To some degree, ecclesiastical and cultural silence on human sexuality has been broken and replaced by a chorus of opposing voices contending for public and religious space on matters of sexuality. The Presbyterian Church (U.S.A.) and other religious communities have been embroiled, year after year, assembly after assembly, with debates about homosexuality, clergy sexual misconduct, reproductive rights and technology, sexuality education, and other issues. In 1991, the sexuality report identified "The Problem" in all of this as a "patriarchal model of gender inequality and its ethic of social control."[13] Evidence of the powerful grip that patriarchy and its sanctioned inequalities have on human sexuality is even more fully understood, I believe, in the decade since the report's distribution. Patriarchy distorts sexuality and mitigates against sexual health, not only by structuring relations of gender inequality and social control, but by interlocking them with complex patterns of racism, heterosexism, ecological destruction, economic hierarchies, and myriad practices involving power, privilege, and injustice. We have only just begun to break the silence on all of the hierarchical orderings that prevent us from being fully "possessed" by sexual well-being.

Years of teaching courses on gender have convinced me that replacing deeply institutionalized ways of living in the world with alternative patterns of behavior is neither quick nor easy. Many of us Second Wave feminists of the 1960s and 1970s naively thought that if we just pointed out the problem and made a rational case for doing something better, it would be done. Who would want to continue practicing sexism when shown how unjust and damaging it is? Why wouldn't everyone want laws (the ERA, for example) to make explicitly clear our democratic commitment to freedom and equality for women as well as men? Such idealists we were! As much as I still believe in lifelong commitment to social change, the sociologist in me tries to focus on the big picture and remember that the movement to *possess* personal and corporate health is a journey in which the path is part of the goal. The growth of wholeness requires constant care and tending in order to root out, again and again, the relentless tentacles of unhealthy history that still have a grip on the dominant cultural and religious construction of sexuality. These are not limited by, but would include the following:

1. The Pernicious Legacy of Dualism

Western culture, including Christianity, has been infected with the seemingly incurable disease of Platonic dualism, and its hold on us is one of the most tenacious obstacles to sexual health and well-being. Twenty-five years ago, James Nelson acknowledged that "the individual histories of our sexual alienation undoubtedly are as complex and varied as each of us is unique. Yet, there are two common threads: spiritualistic dualism and sexist dualism."[14] Spiritualistic dualism has its roots in the opposition between body and spirit, in our nagging suspicion that turning toward God means turning away from our body and our sexuality. Sexist dualism is a patriarchal consequence of body-spirit dualism, subordinating female to male as body is subordinated to spirit.

The 1991 report describes this well: "While maleness has been associated with superior rational and spiritual authority, femaleness has been regarded as inferior, in large part because of its primary association with the body, emotion, and sensuality."[15] Whenever and wherever we privilege the things of mind and spirit over the things of flesh and body, as well as all things regarded as masculine over all things regarded as feminine, we fail to function as fully integrated persons. We know authentic life in our spirited bodies, our embodied spirits; sexual health is known only in the unitary experience of wholeness.

2. Dualism Compounded in Categories of Difference and Privilege

Paula Giddings, in her essay "The Last Taboo," locates the late nineteenth century as the time in which differences would be seen in their most dualistic, binary oppositions.

> Such oppositions were effective means of social control at a time when the country was losing its sociosexual mooring in the face of radical and fundamental changes driven (like now) by a technological revolution.... Maleness was defined by its opposition to femaleness; whiteness by its opposition to blackness. The

same dualism applied to the concepts of civilization and primitivity, purity and pollutedness, goodness and evil, public and private. The nineteenth-century paradigm regarding sexuality tied all of these oppositions together.[16]

Never content to categorize human diversity simply as "different," patriarchal society invests power, reward, status, merit, and value in some categories over others. In a complex matrix of both personal and social relationships, our sexual lives are infused with virtually invisible and unexamined power dynamics. Furthermore, sexual health is narrowly defined according to the experiences and interests of dominant groups. Angela Davis and June Jordan contend that a comprehensive challenge to the normative framework of healthy sexuality is warranted:

> We cannot conceptualize healthy bodies, psyches, and communities without addressing problems that have always been taboo. This means that we must go beyond the civil rights framework that privileges men over women and the public sphere over the private. Now we have to raise hard questions about the relationship between our public and private lives.[17]

In particular, such questions would seek to understand and eradicate all forms of violence—disproportionately directed at women, people of color, sexual minorities, and all who are vulnerable—as a precondition for sexual health and well-being. The enforcement of race privilege, gender roles, heterosexual "normalcy," and innumerable patterns of hierarchicalism infect our sexualities and cause us much personal and social dis-ease. Thomas Harris had it right a few decades ago when he introduced some psychological slogans into the popular vocabulary: neither "I'm OK, you're not OK" nor "I'm not OK, you're OK" promotes health and wholeness; only "I'm OK, you're OK" does.[18] We have much to examine in our individual attitudes and social practices before we can rid ourselves of the legacy of dualism and its effects upon our sexual health and "not OK-ness."

3. A Shame-Based Notion of Sexuality

Compounding our experience of sexuality as bifurcated and split into hierarchical orderings of power-over and control, the shame we know in our bodies infects our sexual lives with dysfunction, depression, hiding, alienation, and all manner of compulsions and addictions. If we were to tell our stories truthfully, they would be filled with narratives of pain, isolation, loneliness, self-abuse, and deep feelings of unworthiness. Our denominational conflicts over matters of sexuality (primarily homosexuality) often mask underlying sexual agonies that individuals experience but often hide from in their lives and too often project onto those perceived as different (racialized others, "LGBT" persons) who thereby become sexualized and marked as inferior.

One of the defining experiences of the Special Committee on Human Sexuality that produced the 1991 Presbyterian report came when some members of the committee visited an adult Sunday School class in a city where we were meeting. When asked to identify issues about sexuality affecting their lives and troubling them directly, few people in the class spoke of their own experience and a few others commented abstractly about homosexuality (admittedly, without any first-hand knowledge of gay men or lesbians). Only later, in a hall outside the classroom, did a middle-aged woman share with a member of the committee that she was "a broken-hearted parent...full of guilt [and] convinced that she must have done something wrong" because her daughter was involved in sexual relationships that she didn't understand and from which she felt deep alienation. She went on to note that she was not the only one with such problems: "A good many members of this class are rearing grandchildren in their homes. We don't understand our children's lifestyles."[19]

Karen A. McClintock in her book *Sexual Shame: An Urgent Call to Healing,* identifies a *fault line* of shame in which congregations are embattled around a host of sexuality issues, such as abortion, adolescent sexual behavior, domestic partnerships, homosexuality, clergy sexual misconduct, and sex education. McClintock maintains that "these areas are often reinforced by individual and social shame, though they also hold the potential to be sources of grace."[20] Just as Adam and Eve hid in the Garden of Eden to cover the shame of their nakedness, so we know that such feelings of internal guilt and confusion are not the whole story. Earlier in the Genesis narrative, Eve and Adam were naked and *unashamed* at creation. Sexual health, our very humanness created in the divine image, is among the first gifts of a gracious God, delighting in our sexuality.

As distinct from guilt, which protects us by telling us we have done something wrong and violated our own values, shame is known in our sense of *being* and lies at the heart of self-worth. Awareness of the power of shame in our lives compels us to ask: Who are we as we stand before God? As we relate to each other? Persons of dignity and worth or persons in closets constructed of shame? Coming to health necessitates confronting the grip that shame has on our experience of sexuality and opening ourselves to grateful acceptance of our bodies and erotic capacity.

4. The Social Organization of Sexuality

Contrary to much scientific, religious, and popular thinking, sexual behavior is not purely an individual phenomenon. Our sexualities, including our patterns of health and unhealth, are actually organized and institutionally regulated by systematic social governance. The history of sexuality research is marked by examples of competing interests and conflicted struggles over the search for reliable knowledge about human sexuality. Alfred Kinsey, in the 1940s and 1950s, "openly and willingly challenged many basic societal beliefs" in order to "demystify discussions of sex as much as it was possible to do so. Sex, to him, became just another aspect of human behavior, albeit an important part." Though a Gallup poll found that 58 percent of men and 55 percent of women thought Kinsey's research was a good thing, many people attacked it, including the presidents of both Princeton University and Union Theological Seminary.[21] Upholding "traditional values" at the expense of discovering insights about optimum sexual health has meant that the well-being of people and society is frequently compromised by political, religious, and medical conflicts. Nevertheless, the particular methods that Kinsey and others have used to increase sexual knowledge deserve vigilant scrutiny and rigorous evaluation according to principles of human justice.

Of course, "advancements" in the field of sexual health must always be viewed critically with an eye toward the whole range of biases that affect the production of human knowledge. In the late nineteenth and early twentieth centuries, women were regarded as nymphomaniacs with thwarted femininity if they exhibited "too much" sexual interest in orgasm (particularly clitoral instead of vaginal); today, women may be perceived as "frigid" (or medically anorgasmic) if they aren't "sufficiently" orgasmic. Since the development of Viagra, marketers have inundated us with ads for the relief of male sexual dysfunction right along with promos for pizza, detergents, and soda pop, while female sexual dysfunction is under-researched and less entitled to medical intervention. It takes a "hermeneutic of suspicion," as well as thoroughgoing attention to all the ways in which society "discriminates," to detect which medical and legal strategies genuinely advance sexual health, and for whom.

Re-imagining sexual health and well-being

While I was working on a study of pornography for the Presbyterian Church in the late 1980s, it became clear to me that our culture is truly schizophrenic about sexuality. On the one hand, our obsessive-compulsive preoccupation with sex fuels our consumerism by marketing virtually every product with the enticement of sexual rewards, and on the other hand, internalized sex-negating voices shame us with finger-shaking moralisms and parental reprovals of "no no, don't touch." No wonder that capitalist entrepreneurs have found the perfect solution to such conflicted quandaries: if the sexuality that we possess (our own) is alienated from us, then marketers can dress everything up in its allure and sell it back to us for a hefty profit! As Elizabeth Fox-Genovese has observed: "Pornography is . . . obscene, not so much because it exposes naked flesh, but because it exposes our society naked."[22]

Where does one go to find good news about sex when "good sex"—healthy sex—is almost an oxymoron? What resources are available for escaping the ping-pong circus of repression-exploitation? The project of developing and experiencing sexual health is not bereft of strong theological and historical precedents. If we look closely, we can find good news in many places, even within our religious traditions—a good word that could overcome centuries of hostility toward human bodiliness and sexuality.

James Nelson's *Body Theology* offers one of the most hopeful perspectives for breaking the grip of dualistic thinking and practices of alienation and inequality that prevent us from becoming healthy sexual persons. In a brief but illuminating historical review of Judaism and Christianity, he answers the question "Where Are We?" with "Seven Sinful Problems and Seven Virtuous Possibilities." Says Nelson: "This ambiguous mix of the creative and the destructive in religion is particularly evident when it comes to religious dealings with human sexuality. That is because the dynamisms of human sexuality give it particular power for both good and ill."[23] Therefore, he contends, we must examine our traditions for the "perversions of their own central teachings" that have given rise to all manner of sexual alienation, *and* likewise we must pay heed to the virtues or positive resources in these same traditions for nurturing sexual wholeness. Both the Jewish and Christian traditions offer resources for sexual health in

1. the unity of bodyself rather than spiritualistic dualism;
2. the divine mandate for justice and human equality rather than patriarchal dualism;
3. the radical affirmation of every person, rather than heterosexism and homophobia;
4. the justification of self-acceptance and self-love (including masturbation) rather than self-rejection and condemnations of self-love;
5. ethical decisions predicated on love rather than legalistic rules without regard to meaning or context;
6. a sensuous, body-embracing "sexual spirituality" rather than a "sexless spirituality" of bodily mortification and pain; and
7. an understanding of sexuality as both personal and public rather than a strictly privatized sexuality.

The seventh of Nelson's "virtues" is particularly compelling. As long as we see sexuality and sexual health in only private, individual, and personalized terms, we will fail to make the connections between our sexuality and social institutions that affect the well-being of all.

Thus, the bedroom cannot be confined to the bedroom. Justice issues for the sexually oppressed, sexual abuse, reproductive choice, population control, exploitation in commercialized sex, adequate sexuality education — these, among others, are now obviously public issues. Yet we are only beginning to understand that there are important sexual dimensions to other vast social issues that previously we had not recognized. Social violence is a case in point. Whether it is crime on the streets, or the arms race, or economic oppression, or the assumptions behind our foreign policies in Vietnam, Central America, or the Persian Gulf, such violence has important sexual dimensions.[24]

All forms of social violence and alienation must be understood in relation to our personal experiences of sexual violence and alienation. Conversely, all forms of social health and well-being are intimately related to our personal experiences of sexual health and well-being. We must, therefore, seek health and wholeness not only in ourselves personally and privately, but corporately, in our public institutions and social norms.

Kelly Brown Douglas, with her womanist perspective in *Sexuality in the Black Church*, provides an important reminder that we also need to look beyond white cultural sources for theological and experiential frameworks that embrace connection between spirituality and sexuality. Many African cultures, for example, have resisted dualistic distinctions between the sacred and the secular, the soul and the body.

> There is no radical break in most African traditions between the spiritual and fleshly realms: all that is of the earthly realm is God's and is sacred.... The human body and the entirety of the human being are viewed as part of the sacred, as part of the divine, including the human being as a sexual and relational being. This is why many African cultures did not view sexual intercourse as bad or evil, but celebrated this sacred part of life.[25]

In spite of its rejection by the Presbyterian Church (U.S.A.), "Keeping Body and Soul Together" continues to offer good news about human sexuality and sexual ethics. Again and again, the Special Committee that wrote the report was commended for developing a tradition-centered, sex-positive, justice-seeking, embodied spirituality, including "an ethic of common decency." Contrary to those who think the report borders on heresy, I still believe that this proclamation of good news about sexual health is entirely faithful to the best of our tradition:

> Envisioning a Christian ethic of sexual wholeness, of justice-love as right-relatedness, and of sexual responsibility is authorized by a biblical vision of possibility. We are called to be a faithful people, committed to the doing of justice in response to God's own passion for caring justice.... The realm of God's shalom is not patterned according to the patriarchal values of kingly rule, of domination and subordination, but according to God's love for justice, for right-relatedness, and for reconciliation.[26]

"Keeping Body and Soul Together" not only speaks a fresh word about sexual health as integral to human well-being; it challenges the church to "address people's real life needs truthfully and with grace," redirecting "ethical attention toward enhancing moral substance in sexual relations." Furthermore, this must be done by lifting up a "vision of sexual integrity that applies in an inclusive manner to the whole Christian community, irrespective of gender, sexual orientation, and marital status."[27] Operating as a single standard of "justice-love" (mutual caring and right relationship in personal and social dynamics), our moral obligation in sexual relationship is one that values:

1. the goodness of our created sexuality,

2. sexual and spiritual wholeness,

3. commitment to reclaiming eros and passion,

4. mutuality and consent,

5. commitment to guaranteeing the bodily integrity and self-direction of every person,

6. commitment to taking responsibility for our choices and actions; and

7. commitment to fidelity in our relationships.[28]

"Keeping Body and Soul Together" was not (thankfully) the last word on religious statements promoting healthy sexual ethics. Many religious bodies have developed studies and constructive ethical statements. Particularly noteworthy among recent denominational and interfaith resources (for its explicit "health" agenda) is *A Time to Build: Creating Sexually Healthy Faith Communities,* written by Debra W. Haffner (a contributor to this volume) under the auspices of the Religious Institute on Sexual Morality, Justice, and Healing. In the context of much suffering due to the "sexual dis-ease" plaguing America,[29] this publication calls on religious communities to understand sexuality as a sacred gift with potential for health as well as potential for harm in patterns of domestic violence, sexual harassment and abuse, homophobia, adolescent pregnancy, sexism, and sexual exploitation.

Sexual health is something to be sought and possessed by faith communities as well as individuals. Therefore, healthy religious bodies are marked by the presence of leaders trained in understanding sexual issues, sexuality education classes for children and youth as well as programs to support the needs of adults, policies against sexual exploitation and harassment, and the welcome of all kinds of people and families into full membership within the community. Because "the great promise of our traditions is love, healing, and restored relationships," faith communities are called to be "truth seeking, courageous, and just" while advocating "sexual and spiritual wholeness in society."[30] Given the legacy of "bad news about sex" in our religious traditions, the "good news about sex" may well be that so many people of faith and religious leaders are re-imagining (what a lovely notion!) sex and creating a chorus of alternative messages:

- that "the joy of sex" is not merely a popular slogan but a religious principle,
- that human flesh is not a corrupted vessel in which divine spirit may deign to dwell but the unitary, breathtaking embodiment of the Creator's very likeness and image, and
- that the condition of sexual health is predicated on social justice and relationships of mutuality, integrity, respect, caring, and compassion.

Conclusion

In an essay delightfully entitled "Sex in Cahoots with the Sacred,"[31] Rich Heffern spells out some of the messages contained in sex education at his Catholic high school: "Don't trust your body. Your sexuality is shameful. Females are deeply suspect. In the hot-air balloon of spiritual ascending, you need your genitalia like you need 500 pounds of lead." Bodies do not lie, however, and when he later "fell into a serious infatuation" with a woman who "spoke French, knew how to wear good scents, read Salinger and Camus, listened to Mose Allison and Miles Davis, and drove a British sports car," this is what happened:

> One winter night at a party, made bold by some Chablis, we snuggled, touched, groped, kissed—and I remember being completely *ensorcelled,* enchanted. My head swam with the smell and feel of her, the taste of wine on her breath, the warm texture and yield of her embrace. In one fell swoop, we had entered territory I had been warned about....I remember going home that evening feeling as though I were walking on air.[32]

What Heffern experienced was "so intoxicatingly heady" that he realized he had discovered something very mysterious from time immemorial, fraught with "possibilities and perils." He concludes that between the two ends of the cultural spectrum—shame and sensationalism—lies a middle ground of "sustainable sex" where we can find communion with other human beings and all of life. Indeed, Heffern believes that healthy sexuality has the power to sustain us and even the web of life because "our yummy bodies are the real paradise where generosity begins, the true cradle of our love and care for others." As a sexuality educator, I am convinced that condemnation of sensual and erotic pleasure is one of the saddest, most debilitating consequences of our body-denying, sex-negating religious history. What would it mean to dust off the Song of Songs and proclaim the erotic love of God to set free and empower us for life? Might we not become healthier if we created safe places in which to touch, taste, smell, hear, and see the "yumminess" of our bodily senses and one another?

We live in a time and culture deeply suspicious of pleasure and yet insatiably thirsting for it, in products and experiences that offer to quench the human longing for intimacy, sensual delight, and sexual meaning. In her book *The Birth of Pleasure,* Carol Gilligan maintains that

> when pleasure threatens an order of living that has come to feel both essential and stifling, the dangers of pleasure are conjured up and magnified, so that pleasure comes to connote chaos and riot. But there is nothing intrinsically chaotic in pleasure. It has its own rhythms and cadences; finding and losing and finding again. It is the music of love. From Hannah Arendt we know that the enemy of freedom is not structure but totalitarianism, which sets out systematically to destroy freedom, co-opting voice and confusing language in a public enactment of terror. . . .
>
> Leaving patriarchy for love or democracy sounds easy, even inviting, but it is psychically as well as politically risky; at least at first, it seems to mean giving up power and control. Hope is the most dangerous emotion: it invites us to imagine an escape from tragedy, it tempts what we have come to think of as fate. The hope of the new, the nakedness of standing without a frame heightens our awareness of vulnerability and, with it, the temptation to return at whatever cost to the known. The birth of Pleasure, like any new life, is an invitation to creativity.[33]

Possessing our sexuality and becoming possessed by it is a risky venture that begins with the birth of pleasure and love in our bodies and moves forward in freedom to promote justice and reciprocity in personal and social interactions. Given the extensive ways in which our sexual desire is constructed to be sparked by the attraction of "opposites" and relations of dominance and submission, the eroticization of equality, reciprocity, and mutuality is truly a radical notion of pleasure, love, and all that makes for life. What we yearn for most is not a shallow, Madison Avenue notion of sexual health, but a sense of well-being grounded in the theological conviction beautifully proclaimed by Carter Heyward:

The divine presence is incarnate—embodied—in our relational selves.... The justice of God, alive in us insofar as we are true to ourselves, is reflected by the mutuality in our relationships with one another, which in turn enable us to sustain creatively the tensions in which the Sacred is at home among us. To know this deeply within ourselves is serenity.[34]

Notes

1. Latrisha Chattin, May 2002. Used with permission.

2. New Revised Standard Version, 1990: "I am black and beautiful, O daughters of Jerusalem"; Revised Standard Version, 1952: "I am very dark, but comely, O daughters of Jerusalem" (Song of Solomon 1:5a).

3. I would like to pay tribute to Jim Nelson for teaching me this expression as he led a workshop and invited participants to an "experience of oral sex—we're going to talk about it!"

4. Allison Barrett, May 2002. Used with permission.

5. Richard Blonna and Jean Levitan, *Healthy Sexuality* (Englewood: Colo., Morton, 2000), iii.

6. "Constitution of the World Health Organization," *Chronicles of the World Health Organization* 1 (1947): 29–43, in Blonna and Levitan, *Healthy Sexuality*, 11.

7. Blonna and Levitan, *Healthy Sexuality*, 12.

8. "A Healthy Heart May Thwart Onset of Alzheimer's," *Des Moines Register,* July 18, 2002, 11A.

9. Blonna and Levitan, *Healthy Sexuality*, 15.

10. *Presbyterians and Human Sexuality 1991* (Louisville: Presbyterian Church [U.S.A.], 1991), 7.

11. See other essays in this collection (Susan Halcomb Craig and Virginia Ramey Mollenkott) for discussion of the brief mention of bisexuality and total absence of transgenderism in the Presbyterian report.

12. Peggy Brick, "Toward a Positive Approach to Adolescent Sexuality," *SIECUS Report* 17, no. 5 (May–July 1989): 1, cited in *Presbyterians and Human Sexuality 1991*, 6.

13. *Presbyterians and Human Sexuality 1991*, 14.

14. James B. Nelson, *Embodiment* (Minneapolis: Augsburg, 1978), 45.

15. *Presbyterians and Human Sexuality 1991*, 14.

16. Paula Giddings, "The Last Taboo," in *Race-ing Justice, En-gendering Power,* ed. Toni Morrison (New York: Pantheon Books, 1992), 447–48.

17. Angela Y. Davis and June Jordan, "Foreword," in *Body and Soul: The Black Women's Guide to Physical Health and Emotional Well-Being,* ed. Linda Villarosa (New York: HarperPerennial, 1994), xi.

18. Thomas A. Harris, *I'm OK, You're OK: A Practical Guide to Transactional Analysis* (New York: Harper & Row, 1969).

19. *Presbyterians and Human Sexuality 1991*, 1–2.

20. Karen A. McClintock, *Sexual Shame: An Urgent Call to Healing* (Minneapolis: Fortress, 2001), 9.

21. Vern L. Bullough, "Alfred Kinsey," in *Speaking of Sexuality*, ed. J. Kenneth Davidson Sr. and Nelwyn B. Moore (Los Angeles: Roxbury, 2001), 32, 35.

22. Elizabeth Fox-Genovese, "Pornography and Individual Rights," transcript of a lecture at Grinnell College, Grinnell, Iowa, February 18, 1987, 29.

23. James B. Nelson, *Body Theology* (Louisville: Westminster/John Knox, 1992), 29–40.

24. Ibid., 39–40.

25. Kelly Brown Douglas, *Sexuality and the Black Church* (Maryknoll, N.Y.: Orbis, 1999), 84. See also, in this volume, Douglas's essay "Black Body/White Soul: The Unsettling Intersection of Race, Sexuality, and Christianity."

26. *Presbyterians and Human Sexuality 1991*, 19.

27. Ibid., 19–20.

28. Ibid., 19–23. For sources that informed this "ethic of common decency," see Beverly Wildung Harrison, *Making the Connections: Essays in Feminist Ethics* (Boston: Beacon, 1985), and Carter Heyward, *Touching Our Strength: The Erotic as Power and the Love of God* (San Francisco: Harper & Row, 1989). For an expanded presentation of the framework of the 1991 Presbyterian report and an ethic of common decency, see Marvin M. Ellison, *Erotic Justice* (Louisville: Westminster John Knox, 1996).

29. Debra W. Haffner, *A Time to Build: Creating Sexually Healthy Faith Communities* (Norwalk, Conn.: Religious Institute on Sexual Morality, Justice, and Healing, 2002), 9.

30. Ibid., 2.

31. Rich Heffern, "Sex in Cahoots with the Sacred," *National Catholic Reporter,* December 17, 1999, 14–15.

32. Ibid., 14.

33. Carol Gilligan, *The Birth of Pleasure* (New York: Alfred A. Knopf, 2002), 233.

34. Heyward, *Touching Our Strength,* 33.

15

AIDS in a Globalized Economy

A Religious Reality Check

Mary E. Hunt

Bishop Rainy Cheeks, an HIV-positive religious leader from Washington, D.C., put the matter bluntly at an August 2002 conference on Women and AIDS sponsored by CLOUT (Christian Lesbians Out): "The church is responsible for the spread of HIV/AIDS."

"If the Catholic Church does not change its teaching on the use of condoms to prevent the spread of AIDS, it should be held responsible for the deaths of thousands of AIDS victims," Joanna Manning, a Canadian religious writer, proclaimed at the opening of the Vatican-sponsored World Youth Day in Toronto, July 2002.

"I hope that all of you gathered here, and those you represent, want to break the silence barrier, that you are going to be ready — responsibly, urgently and in an engaging way — to speak and teach people about sex, about reproductive health," urged Desmond Tutu, Anglican Archbishop Emeritus of South Africa, addressing religiously affiliated African health organizations in 2000 at the Thirteenth International AIDS Conference held in his country.

"Unfortunately and shamefully, the church has been somewhat asleep on this issue, and maybe it's because of the social stigma," said the Reverend Franklin Graham, son of evangelical preacher Billy Graham. Despite his tradition's insistence on heterosexual, monogamous married sex, he asked: "How can people who have different opinions at least work together to help the people who are dying? How can we provide hope? That's my heartbeat right now."

"Some leaders are still afraid of them. They don't want to touch them," said the Reverend Jane Nuthu, a pastor of the Assemblies of God in Kenya who works with street children in Nairobi. "We take

any kid that is desperate. And we don't judge them," she claimed as a little girl whose mother had died of AIDS clung to her.

"A powerful missing ingredient has been the voice of the churches, the mosques, the temples — the entire religious constellation," indicted Stephen Lewis, special advisor on AIDS to Kofi Annan, UN secretary-general. "Dare I say that the voice of religion has been curiously muted?" he asked at an interfaith conference on religion and AIDS organized by the World Conference on Religion and Peace in Kenya in June 2002.

As HIV/AIDS becomes a global pandemic, these powerful challenges emerge from diverse segments of the Christian tradition and beyond. They stand in stark contrast to the ambivalence that characterized so much of the early reaction from Christian churches to a disease that will soon have taken more lives than all of the armed conflicts of the last century. Perhaps such tremendous loss is necessary to awaken the sleeping giant that organized religions have been in the early decades of the HIV/AIDS pandemic. Such frank talk may even put religious people in the vanguard of those who seek prevention and a vaccine. More to the point, it may catalyze those seeking to restructure the economic, social, and religious frameworks that ground an increasingly globalized world in which HIV/AIDS acts as a mirror reflecting injustice.

My starting point as a white, middle-stratum, and U.S. Catholic feminist compels me to focus where I live, on the religious communities that border my own. The Presbyterian report "Keeping Body and Soul Together" provides initial impetus for this reconsideration of HIV/AIDS in light of a decade of change in the pandemic. Since publication of the report in 1991, developments have been marked by decidedly mixed blessings from Christian churches.[1] Focus has been almost exclusively on sexual morality, construed in the most privatized way, to the exclusion of globalized, systemic analysis of the conditions that ground the pandemic.

To its eternal credit, the "majority report" ("Keeping Body and Soul Together") includes an excellent section on HIV/AIDS.[2] Perhaps this content contributed to the rejection of this innovative study by the Presbyterian Church, since the writers chose to look realistically at a health care emergency only worsened by homophobic and heterosexist assumptions. Acknowledging differences and difficulties with regard to sexuality, they wrote—unfortunately prophetically — that "It may be difficult, also, to listen to others whose values and opinions we do not share.... In a society in which strong taboos about sexual behavior predominate, and even discussion of sexual mores is often avoided, this constitutes a significant test of our openness to one another. Yet because of the link between HIV/AIDS and its sexual transmission, we do not have the option of remaining on the periphery of this discussion, either as individuals or as a church."[3] Would that this view had prevailed.

Indeed, the "minority report" of this Presbyterian project provides a classic example of what is unhelpful. In a model of theological reflection on sexuality that perpetuates a spiritualized, Scripture-focused approach, these pages are devoid of any mention of HIV/AIDS. Even the accompanying Study Guide is hopelessly out of touch with the reality of contemporary sexual activity, given its concern for such inane questions as "Why Did God Make Two Sexes?" (current sexology admits to several more) and its rhetoric about loving parents who would redirect their children's homosexuality to celibacy and their ministerial callings to nonordained functions.[4] In a world in which economic, racial, and sexual differences all but determine mortality and morbidity, theological attention must be paid to these fundamental issues despite differences over homosexuality that can function as a smokescreen to cover up indifference.

In this essay I will follow the good lead of the majority reporters and sketch the current contours of the HIV/AIDS situation as outlined at the Fourteenth International AIDS Conference held in Barcelona, Spain, in July 2002. In essence, the call is to examine AIDS in a globalized economy, not simply as a disease affecting one country or one group, as previous privatized analysis has tended. The face of the disease is changing so quickly that statistics and trends of ten years ago, even five years ago, are hopelessly dated. I am especially concerned to broaden the religious reflection as the epidemic changes from its early presentation as a seemingly gay male disease to one that now infects mainly poor women and their dependent children. I am, of course, deeply concerned about the well-being of gay men, especially young gay men who may not choose safer sex practices, but I want to place this concern within the larger context so as to have a realistic picture of the problem as it is growing around the world. Thus, I will turn to the religious issues as they now constellate not so much around issues of sexuality as around issues of power. My conclusion will focus on what religious people can do to be helpful as the epidemic moves into what may well be its most virulent stage.

The difference globalization makes

More than twenty years ago the earliest reported cases of AIDS in gay men occurred when the world was far more compartmentalized than it is today. It is fair to say that globalization has made all the difference in the world! "Globalization is a phenomenon that has remade the economy of virtually every nation, reshaped almost every industry and touched billions of lives, often in surprising and ambiguous ways," states *New York Times* editorial writer Tina Rosenberg.[5] From computers to Coca-Cola, nothing has "benefited" more from globalization than the spread of disease. Indeed, 20 million people have died; 40 million are currently living with the HIV infection. Moreover, how they live, how long they live, and why they live at all with HIV/AIDS is not a mystery or a case of luck, but now a predictable phenomenon that can be eradicated in time and managed in the meantime. This is the current medical consensus despite grim statistics and painful problems for each and every person who is infected.

What was first noticed in 1981 as a strange set of symptoms found in a number of urban-dwelling gay men in the United States is now one of the most complicated and far-reaching pandemics in human history. Dr. Peter Piot, Director of UNAIDS, the United Nations and World Bank agency with specific concern for the disease, states, "We are only at the beginning of the AIDS epidemic in historic terms."[6] Africa is renowned for the high level of infection in countries such as Botswana, where 45 percent of pregnant women served in city prenatal clinics (and 39 percent of the adults in general) are infected. In Zimbabwe and Swaziland a third of the adult population is infected. The Reverend Dr. Sam Kobia, a World Council of Churches official, has observed, "HIV/AIDS in sub-Saharan Africa is a plague of genocidal proportions. No other calamity since the slave trade has depopulated Africa as AIDS has."[7]

The Caribbean is not far behind, with Haiti and the Bahamas suffering high infection rates. However, the really large numbers lie ahead, when India, China, and Indonesia's huge populations begin to feel the impact of their rapidly rising rates of infection. China, for example, is a great unknown since data are hard to come by in rural areas. What is ball parked as a million people infected may indeed be 6 million or more. The Chinese government has finally acknowledged the seriousness of the problem and is threatening to copy some of the available therapies if prices are not lowered by their Western manufacturers.[8] Such numbers are almost incomprehensible in that they represent not only those who are likely to become ill, but also their children who will likely be orphaned and the jobs that will need to be filled. A cultural revolution of another kind is happening in a globalized economy that is increasingly feeling these kinds of ripple effects.

Despite these numbers, the fastest growing rate of new infections is in parts of the former Soviet Union, especially in the Russian Federation, where the loss of industrial jobs results in poverty. Prostitution and intravenous drug use, breeding grounds for the infection, are poverty's accompaniment. In short, it is not so much a matter of sexual mores, as some misguided U.S. Christians would have it, but of economic, racial, and gender considerations that determine the ever-changing aspects of HIV/AIDS.

Consensus at the Barcelona meeting was that, if prevention and vaccine are not on the horizon soon, more than 68 million people will die of the infection in the next two decades. Earlier projections for southern Africa, for example, turned out to be 30 percent lower than what actually happened. Those infected are well beyond the cohort of those first considered at high risk, namely, IV drug users and those who have sexual relationships with infected men, so that now the general populations of these countries are at risk. This is a significant change that underscores the need for broad-based education and social change. The task is to diminish risk factors such as being illiterate, being a woman in a male-dominated society, being a male who has sex with males in a homo-hating culture, and being a person of color in a racially stratified society.

If there is good news out of Barcelona, it is that in some parts of the world the rate of infection is dropping. As Dr. Piot reports, "Nations with accelerating epidemics must move quickly to adapt proven responses from countries that have succeeded in turning the epidemic around. The essential elements for reversing the disease's spread are frank, widespread HIV prevention, including access to voluntary counseling and testing, leadership at the highest levels of government, and access to care for people infected and affected by AIDS."[9] Countries such as Australia and Poland have done remarkable jobs of keeping the problem at bay. Interestingly, one reason given for Poland's success was the appointment of a priest to head the government's AIDS office, which has urged condom use and drug treatment for those most at risk. The overwhelming factors shaping the pandemic seem to be economic, not moral. Jobs and egalitarian mores work, not sexual sanctions and quarantines.

In the United States, what began as a white gay male disease is increasingly a disease of African American women and their dependent children. Shockingly, 90 percent of African American gay male teens, 70 percent of their Hispanic counterparts, and 60 percent of white gay male teens who have been tested and found to have HIV had no idea that they might be infected.[10] In addition, from 1994 to 2000, 55 percent of the new cases, as reported in twenty-four states, were African Americans despite their making up only 12 percent of the population.[11] What this means is that prevention efforts and access to advanced treatments, which may soon make HIV a chronic but survivable disease for many gay men, are simply not available now where they are most needed. With so many people having no access to the health care system, and even more without the rudimentary information on the disease, it is time to distribute prevention materials well beyond gay bars and baths and take them to the street corners, grocery stores, neighborhood churches, and soup kitchens.

A new drug, T-20, helps many patients who have developed resistance to other antiretroviral treatments. However, even those who have access to the best medical care and support systems live with enormous problems. Recent studies indicate that the protease inhibitors, once hailed as wonder drugs for keeping infected people alive and healthier longer, are showing links to increased risk for heart disease. All of this bodes poorly for those most at risk.

Women and children join gay men

Women and children are most at risk in a globalized economy that sanctions sexism and leaves most child rearing to women. Like gay men, who were among the earliest infected, they are considered marginal. Nowhere is this more evident than in the projection from Barcelona that by 2010, more than 20 million children will be orphaned in Africa because of AIDS, 5 million in other parts of the world.[12] In some of the hardest hit African countries, by 2010 one in seven children will have lost one or both parents. The impact of such loss is staggering on children's well-being, on economic means to sustain families, and indeed on a nation's abilities to develop. It bears repeating that the worst is yet to come.

Happily, one new initiative unveiled at Barcelona is MTCT-Plus, a short course antiretroviral medicine designed to prevent the transfer of the virus from mother to child (MTCT). For the first time in the history of this disease, women have benefited first from a new therapy and not in some derivative way. The effort has received an initial $50 million in funding, a good start but hardly enough to handle the millions of lives that potentially might be saved. In the United States, African American women are the fastest growing cohort of newly infected. Racism and poverty combine to make that the case and to keep their well-being from public scrutiny.

Another newly identified, women-related issue is the difficulty faced by transgender persons. One study revealed that one-third of all male-to-female transgender persons in Washington, D.C., are HIV-positive; of those, two-thirds are African American.[13] In addition to the usual risks, transgender persons are at risk from prostitution, invasive cosmetic therapy by nonprofessionals, exploitation because of their transgender status, and high incidence of alcohol and drug abuse. This is a community whose needs have never been taken seriously by Christian churches, but whose reality is now part of our common concern.

Given how most Christian churches have treated gay men, it is no wonder transgender people are pessimistic. Gay men, especially young gay men of color, face virulent opposition from many Christians with regard to their sexual choices, whether these men are infected or not. What began as a personal, religious objection to anal-receptive sex by men with men now translates into condemnation by the same people because such high-risk practices contribute to the spread of HIV. However, the result is the same — a wholesale dismissal of the goodness of gay men's lives and undue focus on their sexuality.

Some gay men are intentionally choosing to engage in barebacking, that is, anal-receptive sex without condoms, for reasons of deeper connection to another person, pleasure, intentional risk-taking, and spirituality.[14] This is a complicated matter, balancing private choice with communal well-being, personal proclivity with public consensus. For example, if health care were socialized (which it is decidedly not in the United States), the decision to put oneself at increased risk would have a growing social component. Moreover, the homophobic focus some churches have placed on certain sexual practices, while passing over the fullness of gay men's loving lives, does not instill confidence that the well-being of these men is at the heart of the matter. To the contrary. Listening to them on their terms, even if one disagrees, is the first step toward changing the conditions that create alienation, despair, and discrimination. Otherwise, churches remain significant barriers to welcome, inclusion, and celebration of gay men in the larger culture.

Funding remains the most contested aspect of the HIV/AIDS crisis. United Nations Secretary-General Kofi Annan emphasized the need for a fund of $7–10 billion *annually* to stem the tide.[15] He made clear that September 11 and its aftermath have only intensified the call for the world we want, one in which "a child does not die of AIDS every minute," as is now the case.[16]

In his 2003 State of the Union address President George W. Bush surprised many by announcing a five-year $15 billion program to provide global relief for AIDS with special focus on African countries and the Caribbean. While this is far more in line with the urgent requirements of the pandemic than the several million that have been spent each year to date, even this remains far short of what U.N. experts say is the $10 billion required each year. On the domestic front, there is a proposed 7 percent increase in government spending for HIV/AIDS services in the 2004 budget, but there is also a cut of $4 million on the prevention side. This reflects the failure of the administration, both nationally and globally, to support the most reliable preventive strategies, including condom usage.

The president did announce the approval by the Food and Drug Administration of a rapid HIV test, one that gives results in twenty minutes instead of several weeks. It is clear that when funding is forthcoming, so too is progress. However, right-wing, anti-sex ideologies regarding contraception and disease prevention work against holistic efforts to address this global challenge. Available funding goes a long way. Contemporary studies indicate that HIV/AIDS prevention is not as difficult as it might seem although compliance is far harder than expected. In fact, the know-how is at hand even when the money is lacking. Steps include what experts have been saying from the beginning, namely, that improving women's social and economic well-being, making condoms available and their use normative, offering counseling and frequent testing, and improving educational offerings, especially sex education, for young people and workers will go a long way toward reversing the trends.[17] While the consensus is less solid on needle exchange, it too appears to be a significant factor in lessening transmission. In the absence of a vaccine, and knowing how difficult developing a vaccine will be, this public health approach seems the wisest course in the short run.[18] However, gearing programs to specific populations and getting access to women and children, for example, in settings where men dominate, can be next to impossible. This is where churches can be helpful, though many choose not to be.

Religious issues

In 1991, there might have been an excuse for the way in which religious communities, especially Christian churches, narrowed their gaze at the HIV/AIDS pandemic to the sexual and especially homosexual modes of transmission. In an increasingly globalized world, however, that is no longer acceptable. Thus, when a catalogue of religious concerns is developed, I suggest that issues of sexual morality, specifically gay male sex, be considered only when all other issues have been aired. I urge this because of the disproportionate amount of religious energy that has gone into debating adult same-sex consensual behavior, which in my view needs no more scrutiny than any other form of adult consensual sex. To do so is to distract from the myriad issues for which religious insights, in my case from the Christian tradition, may be very useful.

Among the many possibilities for U.S. Christians, I would prioritize three that might have far-reaching implications: economic globalization, pharmaceutical morality and economics, and sex education and access to reproductive choice. These issues constitute the broadest rubric for understanding and eradicating the HIV/AIDS pandemic.

Economic globalization, as Tina Rosenberg argues, is at best a mixed blessing. Trade is essential to growth, and growth is key to raising living standards, but treaties such as NAFTA (North American Free Trade Agreement) and other World Bank/International Monetary Fund solutions systematically privilege the rich and use the labor and resources of those from poor countries to fund it. For example, the sex trafficking of women and children in prostitution that accounts for the spread of HIV/AIDS in many countries is a "logical" by-product of such a system. Likewise, the collapse of the Soviet economy and the now astronomical numbers of people in that region who are HIV-infected have a cause-and-effect relationship.

Thus, I urge religious people, especially Christians who claim gospel-based values such as love and justice, to forsake their worries about homosexuality and focus their attention and resources on the very economic system that grants their privilege. A critical analysis of the racist, sexist, and colonialist dimensions of contemporary capitalism and of its transnational caretakers, such as the IMF, would keep Christians busy for years to come. Such an exercise would, I believe, take us much closer to the root causes of HIV/AIDS in the social sphere than any comparable expenditure of energy on sexuality. The results of previous efforts to deal with sexuality have been disastrous. Methodists, Presbyterians, Episcopalians, and other so-called mainline Protestant churches have come scandalously close to schism on these matters. Gay men and lesbian women have been subject to shockingly uncharitable discourse that has had real consequences in hate crimes, job loss, and custody battles. My strong recommendation in the absence of any consensus is a moratorium on such discussions until capitalism is thoroughly and critically deconstructed.

Another related religious issue is the morality of pharmaceutical companies that have a lock on so many of the HIV/AIDS drugs. While there is no doubt about the miraculous strides that have been made in the development of drugs that will prolong and enhance the quality of life for those living with HIV/AIDS, when it comes to equitable distribution, the end is nowhere in sight. In fact, the routine treatments in developed countries are still out of reach of those in the poorest countries. Encouragingly, some countries like Zimbabwe have moved to sidestep patent requirements in order to import substitute generic compounds.[19] This move, in the spirit of Act-Up and other activist groups, shows an ethical way for a country to take in response to an acute problem that has infected upwards of a quarter of its adults.

The question is, how has such inequity developed so that the same disease can be a quick death sentence for one and a treatable chronic illness for another? More to the point, what can be done about it? I urge churches to take on the pharmaceutical industry in all of its moral and scientific complexity. This means not vilifying those who work in it, but assuming that they are partners in the provision of health care who want to act ethically. This applies both to treatment drugs and to any potential vaccine yet to be created. Both need to be distributed with the same concern for patient well-being.

Fundamental to this discussion is a Christian ethical reflection on how much profit is acceptable in the face of death since so much of the argument on the part of pharmaceutical companies is the need to keep profits for research and development of future drugs. Another important matter to consider is why racial disparity is found in so many AIDS clinical trials.[20] For a disease that is increasingly prevalent in so-called racial minority communities, it seems extraordinary that African American and Hispanic people living with HIV were only half as likely as their white counterparts to be part of trials involving treatment drugs and only half as likely to be among those who receive experimental drugs. Who knows about this pernicious form of racism, and why is it countenanced in the medical/scientific community? These are the pressing theo-ethical questions of the day.

None of these questions is easy to answer, and fruitful discussion will require massive doses of good will on all sides. Nevertheless, I predict that these will be the more productive questions to wrestle with in terms of human life than the now tired, polarized, and divisive discourse on homosexuality. For a change, church people will really sink their ethical teeth into a topic worthy of their best theological consideration.

A third priority issue is the highly polarized matter of reproductive health care both for people living in the United States and for those whose care is compromised because of U.S. political decisions to defund programs that might include abortion services. In fact, sex education is one of the most effective means of preventing sexually transmitted infections (STIs), including HIV. Family planning courses, including radio, television, and print media, that begin to shape public consciousness about the needs and rights of women and are communicated in language and images appropriate to the target population are crucial, especially for young people who are at the heart of this pandemic. Yet these issues, not to mention easy availability of condoms, remain well beyond the scope of most churches' concern. I submit that conservative religious efforts to couch reproductive health matters in moral terms are a major contributing factor in the rise of HIV/AIDS because they gloss over the life-threatening aspect of unprotected sex.

Catholics for a Free Choice, a nonprofit human rights organization, is engaged in a global effort to get out the message that "Banning Condoms Kills" through billboards and subway ads, as well as through newspaper and Internet outlets. As CFFC president Frances Kissling states forthrightly, "The Vatican and the world's bishops bear significant responsibility for the death of thousands of people who have died from AIDS. For individuals who follow the Vatican policy and Catholic health care providers who are forced to deny condoms, the bishops' ban is a disaster. Real people are dying from AIDS. Real bishops are silently acquiescent. We can no longer stand by and allow the ban to go unchallenged."[21] Her words take on even more vigor in light of the Catholic Church's pedophilia and cover-up scandal.

Catholics are not the only ones who have work to do on reproductive health as it relates to HIV/AIDS. The Religious Coalition for Reproductive Choice launched a solidarity effort in South Africa by sharing its "Keeping It Real!" sex education dialogue model in an effort to prevent the spread of HIV/AIDS. Material of this kind needs to be distributed in the United States, where sex education is considered largely a private family matter and where church and school discussion is dictated by the use of abstinence-only curricula. It is now obvious that such a head-in-the-sand approach must end.

Religious strategies

A clear-eyed reading of the "signs of the times" indicates that the tip of the HIV/AIDS iceberg is all we have seen. As the huge populations of China, India, and Indonesia begin to cope with the impact of a devastating public health disaster, it is obvious that the face of the disease—and, therefore, of the world—will change. Unfortunately, those who will bear the brunt of its fury will be women and children of color, the throwaway people whose lives are often expended in the service of maximizing globalized economic privilege for others. Even in the United States, the most deeply affected population is African American women whose place in the pecking order is low. This is an abomination. Creation is one for all. Anything less is a perversion. How might U.S. Christians respond? Better, how *must* they respond?

First, I suggest we keep the wide-angle lens on our ethical cameras and frame all of our analyses and proposed solutions in a global context. I have tried to do so in this essay by broadening any focus given to U.S. concerns to include what is happening elsewhere. Otherwise we persist in the pattern that puts our well-being ahead of all others. Our issues, no matter how urgent locally, must not take on disproportionate importance or distract us from paying close attention to what is happening throughout the global arena.

Second, we need to consciously declare a moratorium on sexual ethical debate, especially on homosexuality, until we have made good faith efforts on other major concerns, especially economic and racial matters. This is not to say that sexual ethics are unimportant. Rather, it is an acknowledgment of their ability to eclipse other issues and distract from a broader analysis, serving the purposes of those who would uphold the status quo. The reality is that religious conservatives seduce progressives into debates that lead nowhere because we do not share the same worldview on such fundamental matters as how many sexes there are, much less how they should behave. Debates that skirt those basic issues are pointless and can be destructive, especially of the lives of those gay, lesbian, bisexual, and transgender persons who are objectified in the process. I suggest that instead of continued discussions like ships passing in the night, we covenant to stop the deaths with concrete actions, such as condom distribution, and at least temporarily let the other issues take a back seat. Perhaps after a decent interval we can return to sexual matters per se, but for now I strongly urge action to prevent infection and to seek a vaccine. Surely we can all agree on those needs.

Third, I urge a systematic rethinking of the relationship between church and state or, better, religion and politics. It is at this level that so many decisions are made, whether on funding overseas population programs or same-sex marriage, without full disclosure as to sources, evidence, and limits of belief. I see this as the only way to break the political logjam that keeps funding for HIV/AIDS low and political capital for those who oppose it high. If the likes of Jesse Helms and Franklin Graham can see their way to support some funding for HIV/AIDS out of their religious convictions, perhaps there is hope after all. Indeed, there are many people well beyond the Christian community—Jews, Buddhists, and certain New Age groups, to name just a few—whose exemplary efforts Christians would do well to emulate when it comes to medical, pastoral, and social work related to HIV/AIDS. Frank disclosure of our faith-based starting points can only help.

Ten years from now, I suspect we will need to rewrite the text on HIV/AIDS and religion because the situation will have changed dramatically. I strive to change it on two scores—to eradicate the disease and its underlying social, economic, and political causes, and to turn this dastardly disease into a vehicle for globalized interreligious dialogue on what it means to share the planet creatively with people from a variety of faith starting points. That might be one of the few good things HIV/AIDS will ever produce.

Notes

1. *Presbyterians and Human Sexuality 1991* (Louisville: Presbyterian Church [U.S.A.], 1991).

2. Ibid., 74–81.

3. Ibid., 77.

4. Ibid., 107, 129.

5. Tina Rosenberg, "The Free-Trade Fix," *New York Times Magazine* (August 18, 2002): 28.

6. Peter Piot, quoted in David Brown, "Report on AIDS Offers Dire Prognosis," *Washington Post,* July 3, 2002, A3.

7. Sam Kobia, World Council of Churches press release, Geneva, Switzerland, November 23, 2001.

8. Elisabeth Rosenthal, "China Now Set to Make Copies of AIDS Drugs," *New York Times,* September 7, 2002, A1.

9. Peter Piot, quoted in Lawrence K. Altman, "UN Forecasts Big Increase in AIDS Death Toll," *New York Times,* July 3, 2002, A1.

10. Lawrence K. Altman, "AIDS Study Finds Many Unaware They Have Virus," *New York Times,* July 8, 2002, A1.

11. Ibid.

12. Lawrence K. Altman, "By 2010, AIDS May Leave 20 Million African Orphans," *New York Times,* July 11, 2000, A10.

13. "Washington Transgender Needs Assessment Survey, 1999–2000," brochure funded by D.C. Department of Health, HIV/AIDS Administration.

14. Robert E. Goss provides a thought-provoking perspective on this controversial matter in "Is There Sex in Heaven?" in *Queering Christ: Beyond Jesus Acted Up* (Cleveland: Pilgrim, 2002), 70–85.

15. Kofi Annan, "No Letting Up on AIDS," *Washington Post,* November 29, 2001, A33.

16. Ibid.

17. Lawrence K. Altman, "Modest Anti-AIDS Efforts Offer Huge Payoff, Studies Say," *New York Times,* July 5, 2002, A9.

18. For the story of the vaccine efforts, see Patricia Thomas, *Big Shot: Passion, Politics, and the Struggle for an AIDS Vaccine* (New York: Public Affairs Press, 2002).

19. Henri E. Cauvin, "Zimbabwe Acts to Obtain AIDS Drugs at Lower Prices," *New York Times,* June 1, 2002, A3.

20. Sheryl Gay Stolberg, "Racial Disparity Is Found in AIDS Clinical Studies," *New York Times,* May 2, 2002, A24.

21. Frances Kissling, Catholics for a Free Choice press release (November 29, 2001).

Part Four

Pain and Violence

16

How Can We Sing Our Song, and Who Will Hear?

Violence against Asian American/Immigrant Women

Thelma B. Burgonio-Watson

What is the chief end of [humankind]?
To glorify God and enjoy God forever.

—Shorter Catechism

By the rivers of Babylon,
There we sat down and there we wept
When we remembered Zion.
On the willows there we hung up our harps,
For there our captors asked us for songs.
And our tormentors asked for mirth, saying,
"Sing us one of the songs of Zion!"
How could we sing the Lord's song in a foreign land?

—Psalm 137:1–4

You shall not wrong or oppress a resident alien,
for you were aliens in the land of Egypt.
There shall not be abuse of any widow or orphan.
If you do abuse them, when they cry out to me,
I will surely heed their cry.

—Exodus 22:21–23

Rather than difference itself, it is the response to difference that is the problem. Rather than diversity itself, it is the attitude about culture that is the problem. Rather then diversity

269

itself, it is the way in which major institutions have responded to culturally, racially, and ethnically diverse people and gender difference that is the major source of our condition of inequality.[1]

From where I write

I write this as a Filipina, an immigrant, and a Presbyterian. I am an ordained minister in the Presbyterian Church (U.S.A.). I am a product of mission, specifically of the American Protestant missionaries who were sent to the Philippines in the 1940s and 1950s, among them Presbyterians, United Methodists, and Evangelical United Brethren.

It has been more than a decade since the Presbyterian General Assembly in 1991 chose not to approve the sexuality study "Keeping Body and Soul Together: Sexuality, Spirituality, and Social Justice." I am proud to have been a part of the committee that produced this report, which has had the widest circulation of any General Assembly report, ever. Even non-Presbyterians bought copies in the thousands. Although the report was formally rejected, the church has never been the same, and this progressive "sex report" has become part of the history of the Protestant churches' struggle to address sexuality and spirituality issues in a humane and principled way. In spite of its official disapproval, or perhaps because of it, this resource remains in circulation, and people continue to form their own independent judgment of its merits. Even a decade after the 1991 report, the church still faces the same issues. Only now, it does so with diminished human and financial resources. Since the early 1990s, the church has restructured several times. Some national staff positions have been "restructured out." Local presbyteries continue to vote on questions of sexuality, especially on the ordination of lesbians and gay men. Meanwhile there are countless people of faith, not only Presbyterians but in all denominations, who are hurting and still crying out: "How long, O God, until we shall see justice in our churches?" Many marginalized Christians have also been "restructured out" or voted out. Who will hear their cries for justice?

Soon after the Special Committee on Human Sexuality completed its work, I joined the staff of the Center for the Prevention of Sexual and Domestic Violence, an international, multicultural, and inter-religious educational organization that mobilizes both religious and community leaders in response to sexual and domestic violence. I coordinate the Asian Pacific Islander program, as well as direct the overall training and educational program of the Center.

Very soon after the 1991 report was submitted to the General Assembly, word got out that I had voted for the controversial majority report. My professional life underwent close scrutiny, to say the least. Some Presbyterians looked at me as if I had the plague. Collegial relationships with other clergy were strained. The good news is that I survived this period of estrangement and, in fact, can claim that I am a survivor of the mean-spiritedness of people who had become terribly frightened by the passionate call we made to affirm justice-love as a way of right relationship with all people in every community.

Even as a member of the Presbyterian sexuality committee, I knew little about sexual and domestic violence. I had some textbook knowledge, but not much more. Since then, I have come to know more than I ever wanted to know about a range of violence against women and children. None of this makes me proud. I have had to come face to face, in an intimate way, with the pain and the wounds that women, children, and sexual minorities bear in their souls and bodies. I have stood side by side with victims and survivors as they shared their stories. I have mourned the death of those who did not survive the violence. I have also had to face my own everyday experiences of racism, sexism, and classism.

Survivors are the best mentors about these issues, along with experts in the field, some who are survivors themselves. From them I have gained deeper appreciation of how the church has been part of the problem because of its silence, denial, ignorance, and minimization of these problems. What do we make of the fact that, Sunday after Sunday, perpetrators of these many forms of violence sit in church pews and even stand behind pulpits? None of this makes me proud. In recent years, we have seen and heard in the news how religious leaders have been found guilty of abusing their power and authority. Again, I am not proud to admit this. Church members are hurting and continue to cry out, "How long, O God, will your justice be delayed?"

As I travel across and beyond this country to fulfill my calling at the Center, I continue to meet victims, survivors, and those who are engaged in healing the brokenness everywhere. This is both a sad and an inspiring experience. Sad, because the rhetoric of our confessional stance, that our chief end is to glorify God and enjoy God forever, remains only rhetorical insofar as half of humanity is prevented from reaching this end. What we say we believe must begin to match more clearly what we do. We need to embody—*incarnate*— our belief in true love and justice for all those for whom Christ lived and died. On the other hand, I have been inspired time and again by what I have seen. Out of the woundedness of body and soul, I have witnessed remarkable healing, albeit precious little of it. Marginalized voices and those of their advocates have cried out, spoken up, and called to action. This is good news.

Although one General Assembly failed to approve our progressive report with its resounding call for sexual justice, a subsequent Assembly mandated the creation of a denominational initiative on societal violence. I served on the team that focused on violence against women and produced a book, *Striking Terror No More,* that addresses violence against women, children, and the elderly.[2] Another initiative on domestic violence produced a resource called "Turn Mourning into Dancing!" Of this I am very proud and grateful. This policy statement is the result of a process that included wide consultation and participation throughout the church. It draws on biblical sources and insights from the Reformed tradition to address the root causes of domestic violence, and it examines the church's complicity in, as well as its constructive response to, the problem. The term "domestic violence" is used in this policy statement as an inclusive term, broadly encompassing the abuse found in child/child, parent or guardian/child, spouse/spouse, partner/ partner, and adult child/aging parent relationships, as well as the violence in sibling and dating relationships. I will be even more proud if and when the church implements the recommendations for social and ecclesiastical change that this latest report proposes. Every religious tradition must go beyond rhetoric and take vigorous *action* to dismantle systems that tolerate and support unattended patterns of abuse.

The moral wisdom of Asian American immigrant women

As an Asian American immigrant woman, I share the belief and analysis of feminist and womanist scholars that violence against women stems from a legacy of patriarchy and sexism that is widespread across cultures, including communities of color and, specifically, including Asian Americans. Rape and battering are not isolated acts of random violence, but tools of power and control within a culture shaped by sexism, racism, homophobia, and class elitism. As people of faith, we have much to learn about the history of violence against women of color in the United States and around the world.

Again, this is not a history in which to find much pride. It is in our best interest to learn from the abuses of the past and begin to redeem and transform these realities. Is it not the church's calling to participate in re-creating the world as God intends it, by making it possible for all God's creation to live in peace, harmony, justice, and love? The prophet Jeremiah said it loudly and clearly: "And do no wrong or violence to the alien, the orphan, and the widow" (Jer. 22:3). The Reformed theological tradition teaches that human beings are created in the image of God. Violence against human beings is violence against the image of God and, therefore, is violence against God's own self.

An Asian American feminist scholar, Dr. Nantawan Boonprasat Lewis, has written, "The history of violence against women of color, namely, Native Americans, African Americans, Asian Americans and Hispanic–Latin American groups, I submit, . . . is a history of an adversarial relationship between these women and the rest of the society — the dominant society and men and women of their own racial and ethnic backgrounds. It is a history of the intersection of colonialism, imperialism, racism, sexism, classism that at the present time is also intertwined with economic globalization."[3] To be more inclusive of the intersection of all the *isms,* we need to add heterosexism to this list. Queer women of color matter. Queer Asian American women matter. Their voices must be heard. The full multiplicity of women's experience has to be acknowledged if our work for justice is truly aimed at empowering all women.

Asian queer women's experiences

Filipina-lesbian and bisexual women in the Philippines and in the United States are part of a global, pan-Asian queer movement. These sisters have been both agents and beneficiaries of the international, grassroots liberation movement for gay, lesbian, and transgender rights over the course of the past twenty-five years.[4] Lesbian and bisexual women of color, both immigrant and U.S. born, are, like all women, subject to many forms of violence because they are women. The forms this violence takes are many: beatings, rape, sexual assaults, stoning, genital mutilation, forced prostitution, female circumcision, incest, emotional harassment, labor and economic exploitation, and homophobia. As Dr. Boonprasat Lewis maintains, "It is important to recognize that violence against women of color is not a contemporary issue but a historical reality that has significantly shaped the lived experience of not only the women and their racial groups but also the nation as a whole. Only the forms of expression vary based on the historical circumstance."[5]

Researchers and historians have only recently begun to examine the experiences of immigrant women in U.S. history and started the long process of uncovering the unique struggles of immigrant women in their various roles as wives, mothers, workers, and catalysts for change within their communities. As Chris Hogeland argues, it is important to examine the factors that have historically affected women's immigration in order to better understand their lives once here in the United States and work toward improving the conditions of their lives.[6] It is not within the scope of this essay to survey the historical oppression of all U.S. women of color and immigrant women, but suffice it to say that African American, Asian American, Latina/Hispanic, and Native American women have long memories of the oppression they have suffered and continue to suffer, within and outside their communities, because they are women and because they are women of color.

Asian American women, especially those in faith communities, have for the most part been silent about the violence done to their bodies, especially sexual and domestic violence. Again, as Boonprasat Lewis points out, the "marginalized history of Asian Americans in this country provides a good clue to their silence on this issue."[7]

Although I have spoken on this issue at several Asian American church gatherings, I have yet to be invited back after the initial conversation. Resistance to dealing with these realities is formidable, in large part because sexual and domestic violence is sustained by multiple structures of control, exploitation, and dehumanization, including racism, poverty, cultural imperialism, war, colonialism, religious fundamentalism, and heterosexism. Our work to end violence against women must, therefore, take account of all these factors. Further, as Margaretta Lin and Cheng Imm Tan suggest, "Because of the barriers of language, culture and economic disparities and the vagaries of racism and sexism, Asian and Pacific Islander victims of domestic violence suffer re-victimization at the hands of institutions designed to serve battered women."[8]

An Asian and Pacific Islander focus

The current ministry of which I am a part includes a commitment to identify and address the unique issues of traditionally underserved and seemingly hidden populations in North America, among them the Asian and Pacific Islander community. Asian and Pacific Islander Americans are one of the fastest growing ethnic groups in North America today. However, their increasing numbers are not directly proportional to the numbers seated in church pews every Sunday. Korean Americans, predominantly Presbyterian and one of the largest Asian groups, continue to grow and have been forming their own governing structures that raise new opportunities for education and advocacy.

Unfortunately, Asian and Pacific Islander (API) American Christians have not embraced the issue of violence against women as openly as API Americans who are not affiliated with the church. In fact, API American organizations *outside* the church have been engaged in this issue for many years. It is time, therefore, that API American churches break their silence around violence against women. If statistics are accurate—that one out of three girls has been sexually abused by the time she reaches the age of eighteen—then we have many church members, among them API Americans, who have personally experienced abuse. In other words, survivors as well as perpetrators sit in our pews, API Americans included.

Mail-order brides: Susana's story

Susana Remerata Blackwell was an API immigrant who did not survive her husband's violence. Her life as an abused immigrant woman embodies the intersection of some of the "isms" mentioned above. Susana came to the United States by means of marrying a military man whom she met through an advertisement in a magazine published in the United States. Mail-order brides, whether from Asia, Eastern Europe, or Central America, are vulnerable to abuse because of the inequality of relationships with their male partners. This inequality is compounded by the bride's immigrant status, race, and inadequate knowledge about her husband's society, language, and culture. In addition, these women encounter other barriers when they become victims of domestic violence: lack of access to medical, legal, and social resources; limited economic resources; and a general lack of support structures, including family.

Susana, who was seven months pregnant, and her two friends, Veronica Laureta and Phoebe Dizon, were murdered inside the King County courthouse in Seattle by Susana's estranged husband. The two women were assisting her in gaining her freedom from an abusive husband. On the day they were murdered, she was at the courthouse seeking legal protection from her abuser.

Susana was a "mail-order bride" from the Philippines.[9] Gabriela Network, Inc., a Philippines-U.S. women's solidarity organization based in San Francisco and Manila, views the mail-order bride industry, though legal, as trafficking in women. To name it as such is not to degrade the women, but rather to expose the exploitative nature of the industry. At the very least, efforts should be made to regulate these networks so that the women involved are less vulnerable to abuse. It is also important to ask who benefits from this industry. Surely, if justice is the test, no one should profit from the sale of human flesh. As Ninotscha Rosca of Gabriela says, "A paid-for wife is a slave for life."[10]

Trafficking, according to Aurora Javate De Dios, comes in a variety of forms through different channels:

> Women (and children) are deceived, lured, enticed and often forced into prostitution, bonded labor, sex tourism, military sexual slavery, pornography or sexual servitude in the guise

of marriage through matchmaking services, via mail, video, and magazine advertisements or other personalized forms of introduction. Somewhere in the complex web of modern-day trafficking are the women who dream only of creating a better life for themselves and their families, some of whom find death or abuse at the end of the rainbow.[11]

Although a longstanding practice, this too has been affected by the technological revolution. Matchmaking businesses have turned to electronic media and cyberspace. Moreover, at a recent international conference on the trafficking of women and children, it was noted that trafficking is a $7 billion industry that commodifies impoverished women and children and moves them from under-resourced countries to more wealthy consumers. Many of these women and children are from Asia.

Where, we must ask, is the outrage from polite members of our society? Who is willing to challenge the injustices that permeate extensive profiteering through abuse of the most vulnerable in our planetary community? The word is out: women and children's bodies continue to be commodified even as nations talk about trade agreements, tariffs, and sharing the profits of globalization. More needs to be done as the silences are broken.

The call for a culturally competent church

Effective ministry with abused women and children requires both an understanding of the dynamics of violence against women and children and an analysis of the social conditions that give rise to and exacerbate the experiences of victims. Any analysis must also include bicultural, if not multicultural, perspectives. Increasing numbers of immigrant women, men, and children are arriving, while large second and third generations are already in place.

Of course, not all Asian and Pacific Islander Americans are Christians. However, API congregations in North America are significant community institutions, serving as gateways for new immigrants and, at the same time, as a link to the old country. There is an urgent need for informed, sensitive, and competent leadership in local congregations where women and children often turn first for resources in time of crisis. In general, a congregation is better positioned to assist people when it is equipped with a good understanding of the cultural background of those it is trying to serve. It almost goes without saying that there are cultural considerations that effective advocates and resource providers must acknowledge in their work with API victims and survivors of sexual and domestic violence.

There are over eighty subgroups in Asia, the Pacific Islands, and Southeast Asia, each with its own language or languages, traditions, custom, culture, and ritual. The cultural background of clients includes country of origin, immigrant or refugee experience, degree of assimilation or acculturation, rural or urban attitudes, religious beliefs, and generational differences. It is important to keep an open mind about such cultural variations when trying not to make judgments based on behaviors. As in all cultural evaluations, each consideration is best assessed individually, according to each personal profile. Culturally competent advocates will want to take the following influential values into account.

Sex as taboo

Issues related to rape, incest, and sexual assault involve great sensitivity and typically are not talked about openly. A victim may feel further isolated due to lack of support and information. Because of the shame that a woman may experience after a sexual assault, she will most likely feel more comfortable with a female service provider, but the choice should be hers.

Reputation and family honor

Shame and denial are key factors in disclosing information. A victim may make decisions based on how it will affect her family versus how it will impact herself. In many Asian cultures, a good family reputation may be valued over other positive values, including wealth. A female may be considered "damaged goods" and no longer marriageable, due to her supposed loss of virginity.

Cultural barriers

Stigmatization often operates to prevent people from getting help from resources beyond the extended family. Some persons may be ashamed of seeking help outside the family or community, and there is often fear and mistrust of law enforcement and other authorities, who may not have been helpful in past experiences. For many immigrants, fear of deportation may prevent victims from disclosing accounts of abuse. Lack of knowledge about immigrants' rights and the law is a further barrier, which congregations can correct by providing access to knowledgeable community resources. Because API women have to deal with the constraints of their own cultures, as well as an indifferent and sometimes hostile mainstream culture, most API victims obtain little assistance from service providers that are authorized to help them.

Communication barriers

Differences in communication styles may not be understood and these differences, including nonverbal cues, may be misinterpreted. For example, in API cultures, direct eye contact is considered disrespectful and aggressively challenging. Therefore, if an error needs to be identified, the correction is best done indirectly, in a manner that supports the person's self-respect.

Using interpreters

The preference of a victim should be the deciding factor in determining use of an interpreter. Typically, it is best to use female interpreters whom a victim does not know personally. While one victim might prefer someone from outside her community, another victim may feel safer working with an interpreter who is from her own culture group. The interpreter should be not only fluent in the language, but also trained regarding sexual and domestic violence.

Confidentiality

Although it is very important to insure confidentiality (unless the victim is a minor), some women may prefer disclosure to a person who is not a member of the community.

Overall, these issues are not significantly different for API and non-API victims of sexual and domestic violence. However, it is important to educate service providers about cultural differences in order to meet people where they are and enhance the possibility that survivors will have access to community services.

Shame as positive and negative

API Americans, especially immigrants, are strongly influenced by the cultural value of keeping family problems within the family. When faced with violence in intimate relationships or between family members, the decision to reveal it beyond the family enclave runs directly into this cultural taboo. Disclosure of abuse can be the cause of great shame to an API family; it is frequently seen as airing one's dirty linen in public.

Many ethnic groups resonate with the culture of shame or of "saving face." Although not unique to the Asian culture, shame remains a major barrier for individual victims, as well as the community, in addressing domestic violence. However, shame has a positive and a negative side. Positively, shame may aid in calling a perpetrator to account or stir the community when it is shamed for not helping a victim. Negatively, shame becomes a barrier to victims when it prevents them from seeking help from the community or beyond. Within API communities, educators, leaders, and organizers have begun to access shame as a resource, not as a roadblock, shifting away from "victimization is a shameful experience" to the alternative message that "assaulting another person is shameful behavior." All of this helps victims to break community silence.

During one of my training trips to the Philippines, a church worker and an activist shared an example of how their barrio had begun to address domestic violence within its midst. The women had organized and devised a plan to support each other if anyone was subjected to abuse. While I was there, one of them was in an abusive situation, and the women agreed to beat their pots and pans, no matter what time of day or night, whenever the woman's husband started to beat her. The victim also would beat her pans, if she was able, until every woman in the group heard the signal, surrounded the house of the victim, and beat their pots and pans until the husband left the house. By that time, the whole barrio knew who the abuser was. He was publicly shamed until he stopped beating his wife, ran away, and came back to face a barrio council, or *barangay*, which called him to account and meted out the consequences of his abusive behavior.

In Seattle, the API community's response to the 1995 murders of Susana and her friends was a community effort to shift the shame from the victims to the abuser. Moreover, the community argued that it was shameful that the King County courthouse had refused to install security measures on their premises until someone was murdered. The community also insisted that it would be shameful if, as a Filipino community, we did not educate ourselves so that we could prevent other women from being abused and murdered. Calling the community into account has resulted in establishing the Asian Pacific Islander Women and Family Safety Center.

Facing expanded challenges

Additional challenges provoke us to reflect on the church's role in responding to our community's cry for life and self-determination. We long for the day when women will be able to sing our songs when and where we want to sing them, not as demanded by taunting requests to sing as foreigners in a strange land. In order for this day of hope to come, there are many dimensions of Asian Pacific Islander life that justice-loving people need to attend to:

- the status and role of women and children in Asia and the Pacific Islands;
- the relationship of the API community to the larger surrounding community in terms of racial tolerance, tension, and violence;
- the influence of Eastern religious traditions;
- the gender injustice between women and men;
- the cultural and religious beliefs and practices regarding family roles, sexuality, and violence;
- the sexual exploitation, sex industries, and trafficking in women and children as primary economic activities in Asia and the Pacific Islands;
- the role of North American countries in promoting the sexual exploitation of women and children through militarism, sex tourism, "mail-order bride" businesses, and multinational corporations;
- the experiences of immigration to North America, including sexual assault;

- the varying degrees of assimilation (or desire to assimilate) within the Asian Pacific Island communities;
- the intergenerational life experiences; and
- the relationships within the diverse cultures of API communities.[12]

Although many organizations in North America, as well as in the countries of origin, are organizing to end violence against API women, not enough of us focus on the role of religious communities in addressing these problems. I am hopeful that Asian American congregations will break their silence so that women can fully enjoy the blessings of God and have life in all its abundance. This is a challenge not only for our community; churches must make it safe for women to confront their woundedness. This may mean putting in place a ministry that makes disclosure by victims possible and provides resources to help them gain strength when they do. This may also challenge churches to provide ministries for calling perpetrators of abuse to account. Perhaps most importantly of all, this may inspire churches to model a genuine "spirituality of life" by affirming sexuality in all its goodness and mourning whenever sexuality is distorted or violated.

The work we are called to is, quite literally, a matter of saving lives. The church actually embodies the spirituality that it proclaims, about God in Jesus Christ who lived and died so that all might live fully. I was taught by missionaries that God makes life possible for all, regardless of race, gender, sexual orientation, culture, or abilities. The ministry of preventing sexual and domestic violence embodies a spirituality of healing: healing the bodies and spirits of women and others who become empowered to articulate a faith that strengthens them for much more than endurance alone. We seek a theology and ministry of mutual empowerment, not of passive acquiescence in suffering, our own or that of others.

What will make a difference? Faith, hope, and love, for sure. But in contemporary language we might say: to embody a culture of life, not death; to resist violence in all its forms; and to see to it that no one will ever be given carte blanche to do violence, abuse power, or try to make maleness and other markers of social privilege seem naturally superior, entitled to authority, and "right."

When we all engage in ministries of resistance and renewed hope, we might well burst into song. In singing loudly, proudly of self-determination and freedom, we give ourselves and others good cause to rejoice and thank God.

Notes

1. Author unknown; found in Sujata Warrier and Vicki Coffey, "Achieving Effective Domestic Violence Public Education in a Diverse Society: A Solution-Oriented Approach," a Working Discussion Paper of the National Domestic Awareness Month Project.

2. *Striking Terror No More: The Church Responds to Domestic Violence,* ed. Beth Basham and Sara Lisherness (Louisville: Bridge Resources, 1997).

3. Nantawan Boonprasat Lewis, "Facing Our Wounds: A History of Violence against Women of Color," paper delivered at the APPARI Conference, University of California at Berkeley, August 2002.

4. *Filipino Americans: Transformation and Identity,* ed. Maria P. P. Root (Thousand Oaks, Calif.: Sage, 1997), 244–45.

5. Boonprasat Lewis, "Facing Our Wounds."

6. Chris Hogeland, "Immigrant Women in United States History," in *Domestic Violence in Immigrant and Refugee Communities: Asserting the Rights of Battered Women* (Family Violence Prevention Fund, Coalition of Immigrant and Refugee Rights and Services, Immigrant Women's Task Force, and the National Immigration Project of the National Lawyers' Guild, Inc., 1991).

7. Boonprasat Lewis, "Facing Our Wounds."

8. Margaretta Lin and Cheng Imm Tan, "Holding Up More Than Half the Heavens: Domestic Violence in Our Communities, A Call for Justice," in *The State of Asian America,* ed. Karin Aguilar-San Juan (Boston: South End Press, 1994), 326.

9. In *Working with Battered Immigrant Women: A Handbook to Make Services Accessible,* produced by the Family Prevention Fund in 1992, Leti Volpp and Leni Marin suggest that "mail-order-bride" is a derogatory term that has evolved to characterize dating and marriage relationships between people from different countries.

10. Quoted in Thelma Burgonio-Watson, "Seeking Justice, Seeking Healing: An Asian Pacific Islander Perspective," *Journal of Religion and Abuse* 1, no. 4 (1999): 38.

11. Aurora Javate De Dios, "Trafficking in Women: A Human Rights Issue," *Women on the Move: Proceedings of the Workshops on Human Rights Abuses against Immigrant and Refugee Women,* Vienna, Austria, June 1993.

12. Burgonio-Watson, "Seeking Justice, Seeking Healing," 39–40.

17

Setting the Captives Free

Same-Sex Domestic Violence
and the Justice-Loving Church

Marvin M. Ellison

Two theological insights have guided me in writing this essay. First, ministry begins where the pain is. Ministry begins with suffering, but must not end there, which leads to the second insight. Setting captives free is an inescapable mandate for Christian faith communities. In Luke's Gospel, Jesus inaugurates his public ministry by proclaiming that God's Spirit "[has] sent [him] to proclaim release to the captives, and recovery of sight to the blind, to let the oppressed go free" (Luke 4:18). In taking up this ministry, we too seek to enlarge and strengthen community while promoting the well-being of each member. Given the entrenched character of evil and injustice, such work is not for the fainthearted.

Among the evils we may encounter is violence between intimates. Although sometimes approached as a problem of miscommunication, poor anger management, or conflict run amuck, battering is best seen as analogous to hostage taking.[1] One party within an intimate relationship uses a variety of coercive tactics to hold another person hostage. The abuser may even resort to killing violence in order to ensure the other person's final submission and then, in one last defiant act of control, commit suicide in order to evade accountability.

Because of widespread societal denial about domestic abuse, these issues are always difficult to address in ministry. For those wishing to respond to such injustice within *same-sex* relationships, I venture to say that additional courage and insight will be needed because of two complicating factors, namely, the disrespect for gay, lesbian, bisexual, and transgender people and the devaluing of same-sex relationships that is so common in this culture. As one survivor put the matter, "Before you can acknowledge [same-sex] battering, you must first acknowledge [gay and] lesbian relationships."[2]

In thinking about setting captives free in relation to same-sex domestic violence, I want to consider the freedom agenda of two distinct, yet overlapping, groups. First, as a gay man I wish to address the gay, lesbian, bisexual, and transgender communities and especially those harmed by battering and other forms of intimate violence. While at least some public attention has been given to bias and hate crimes, that is, to violence *against* sexual minorities, far less attention has been given to violence *within* same-sex relationships, that is, to violence perpetrated by some gay people against other gay people. Specific efforts are, therefore, required to "make the invisible visible."

Second, as a Christian ethicist, I struggle alongside many others to transform those elements within Christianity that are racist, classist, sexist, and homophobic, so that this faith tradition may be genuinely safe, hospitable, and respectful of all people. I am well aware how Christianity, at least in its culturally dominant configurations, has legitimated the oppression of gay people, including the sanctioning of overt persecution. Therefore, the second group I want to address is the *non-gay* majority, especially those who long to make a difference as advocates for a just peace throughout the social order. However, pastors, counselors, and other leaders will, at best, be ineffectual and, at worst, harmful as long as they remain entrenched in cultural myths about intimate violence or bound by ideological claims about homosexuality.[3] Because of such cultural captivity, well-meaning people of faith often lack insight about how to name same-sex domestic violence as an ethical problem and, therefore, fail to frame an adequate pastoral, congregational, and community response. They, too, need setting free.

In my judgment, faithful, liberating action depends on acquiring moral vision in two senses: first, on our gaining proper perspective about the matter at hand, and second, on our being grasped by a compelling moral vision of nonviolent, mutual relations that can truly enhance our common humanity. As William Sloan Coffin suggests, "The primary religious task these days is to try to think straight. Seeing clearly is more important even than good behavior, for redemptive action is born of vision."[4]

I offer this as a case study in the renewal of a Christian social ethic of sexuality and family life. My wager is this: churches will not be helpful to gay men and lesbians affected by domestic violence—and, in fact, may compound their suffering—unless and until faith communities recognize and publicly affirm same-sex relationships as morally desirable, legitimate ways of expressing intimate love. Peacemaking in relation to same-sex domestic violence requires justice advocates who are positive about *gay* sexuality, respectful of *same-sex* relationships, and at the same time *in*tolerant of abuse, whether it occurs among gay or non-gay intimates. If people of faith want peace for those among them who are gay and lesbian, they must seek justice *for* as well as justice *in* same-sex relationships. Therefore, when all is said and done, I have a quite traditional, even conventional theological message to convey: if you want peace, seek justice.

To give a roadmap for the discussion to follow, I first briefly examine battering in heterosexual relationships and then turn to analyze some similarities and differences in abusive same-sex relationships. I conclude with reflections about the difference it might make if faith communities shifted from what I call a "theology of disrespect" to an "ethic of solidarity and resistance."

Male battering of female partners: a matter of sexist power and control

During the last twenty-five years, feminist activists and social theorists, including feminist theologians and church leaders, have raised consciousness about domestic violence as a pervasive social problem for heterosexual couples. What is known about male violence against women, including battering, is known because of the courage of women who have come forward and told their stories, engaged in self-reflection and theory-building, and developed a grassroots social change movement to champion nonviolence within family and other social relations. The domestic violence movement offers literally lifesaving resources to countless numbers of women and their dependent children. Each year, as many as 4 million women in the United States are battered by their male partners. Statistics document that, in fact, "a woman is more likely to be assaulted, injured, raped, or killed by her male partner than by any other assailant." In addition, "forty percent of all homeless women and children in this country are fleeing domestic violence."[5]

Contrary to popular misunderstandings, battering is not about one person's "losing control" in a relationship. Rather, abuse is a pattern of coercive behaviors by which one partner seeks to establish and maintain control over the conduct, thoughts, and beliefs of another. As such, battering is purposeful behavior, chosen by the batterer for a reason, namely, in order to gain something that he desires: power and control over his partner. No psychological or sociological profile is predictive of which men are likely to batter, but batterers share a common belief system: that intimate relations require someone to be in charge, that the man is entitled to control "his" woman, that violence (or threatening violence) is permissible as well as effective in establishing such control, and, finally, that his abusive behavior will result in few if any negative consequences for himself.[6]

Because a man makes a choice to batter his partner, he alone is responsible for the abuse. At the same time, battering is a larger, more complex problem than the actions of any single batterer or even the sum total of abuse by all batterers combined. Battering is violent behavior, Susan Schechter observes, that is "individually willed yet socially constructed."[7] The problem lies not only within individual batterers, but also in the social order. On this score, the wider community bears a responsibility to critique sexist cultural norms that condone male violence against women and children. That deconstruction includes debunking theological notions of male superiority and of a man's right to discipline family members, a right that some men act out violently.

Although sexism does not, strictly speaking, cause any man to be violent, it does provide cultural legitimation for such choices. When institutions, including the church, fail to challenge sexist beliefs, they collude with batterers by tacitly supporting male entitlement to control female partners. As survivors tell us, silence and denial allow men's justifications to stand without challenge. When no one interrupts the victim blaming, women themselves are held responsible for supposedly "provoking" the violence against them. Therefore, community silence about domestic abuse increases men's power to batter and evade accountability. Minimization and trivialization of the problem give batterers a license, as it were, to coerce their partners without having to fear that they will encounter negative consequences.

Insofar as sexist oppression lies at the root of male battering, peacemaking requires a countercultural, oppositional stance. The ongoing cultural work of transformation requires developing "habits of the heart" and mind that convey deep respect for women, support their empowerment, and reinforce women's right to safety and well-being. Justice advocates must see the life-and-death urgency of debunking sexist norms that devalue women and of altering institutionalized power arrangements that grant men unequal social status and privilege.

Not all violence in intimate relations is gender violence, however. Ending male violence against women, a deeply desirable goal, will not by itself eliminate partner abuse. Another story must be told, listened to, and acted upon.

Making visible the invisible: domestic violence among same-sex partners

As with heterosexual domestic violence, what is known about same-sex battering is known because of the courage of gay men and lesbians to come forward, tell their stories, and share their moral wisdom. In *Men Who Beat the Men Who Love Them,* David Island describes in the third person the experience of his co-author Patrick Letellier:

> The last two years of [Patrick's] four-year relationship with his lover, Stephen, had been typified by bruises, humiliation, and psychological abuse. Stephen had kicked, struck, punched, and slapped him. He had shoved and thrown Patrick up against walls and down onto closet floors. From ridicule and harassment, Patrick knew guilt, shame, confusion, and loneliness. Stephen had threatened to kill him more than once.[8]

Such testimony speaks of abuse both similar to and different from heterosexual battering. Research documents that "domestic violence occurs at approximately the same rate in gay and lesbian relationships as it does in heterosexual unions."[9] Furthermore, same-sex victims suffer the same types of abuse as heterosexual women endure at the hands of their batterers, including physical, emotional, psychological, and sexual abuse. So, too, over time the abuse typically escalates in duration and severity. In addition, victims of same-sex violence often stay for the same reasons that battered heterosexual women stay: not because they like or accept the abuse, but because they love their partner and are invested in making their relationships work, they believe in their ability to change the batterer, they blame themselves for the abuse, and they fear reprisals should they leave. Moreover, many victims are further trapped because they lack economic resources and other supports that would make it possible for them to live independently, especially if they have dependent children. Others stay because it may be safer to remain with a batterer than leave and risk the danger of escalating violence.

Although same-sex abuse reflects many of the characteristics of heterosexual domestic violence, a primary difference is how a heterosexist social environment complicates matters. Free-floating homophobia provides a control mechanism not available to heterosexual batterers. For example, a lesbian batterer may exercise her power to "out" (or threaten to out) her partner and thereby extend her control by relying on homophobic prejudice to isolate her partner further from her family, her employer, and even their landlord. A gay-negative cultural environment not only isolates victims, it masks abusive behavior as a serious problem and gives it no challenge. In such a social context, without access to reliable family support, social services, or a friendly criminal justice system, battered gays and lesbians are not likely to seek assistance from the outside. If they do, they are not likely to be helped.

One ongoing task in justice-making ministries is making the connections between people's personal pain and larger social ills. In this case, the change agenda must include not only assisting victims and holding batterers accountable, but also changing the wider cultural context that sustains anti-gay oppression. Another task, equally important, is to provide a clear naming of same-sex battering as wrongful, unethical conduct. However, certain obstacles make such naming difficult. Donna Cecere, a survivor of domestic abuse, offers testimony that illuminates the problem:

> We were together for two years. The abuse began early on, though I didn't know enough then to make such a connection. Though a lesbian feminist activist for years at that point, I still thought of battering as, first, a male-against-female act, and second, as being a physically violent act. *I had no concept* of what emotional, psychological, and spiritual abuse was about.[10]

Lacking an interpretive framework that names the violence as unacceptable and assigns responsibility to the batterer, people often end up telling a story, usually a story about the persons being abused and what *they* did wrong to cause their own grief. However, as we know also from anti-racism and other justice struggles, justice-making depends, first and foremost, upon truth-telling. As long as victims are blamed or their reality is discounted, as frequently happens when the abuse is between same-sex partners, no liberating action is possible. Many people hold on to a settled belief that abuse can happen only when the recipient of violence ("the victim") has less social power and status than the abuser. Survivors of same-sex abuse tell a different story: that abuse can and does occur even when the parties have roughly equal social power and status. It happens when one person is willing to abuse their power and role, has the opportunity to abuse, and chooses to abuse—and when the community fails to stop the violence.

For victims of same-sex battering, naming the abuse, being heard, and being taken seriously is made more difficult by the tendency to interpret domestic violence exclusively through a heterosexual lens. If battering is defined exclusively as male battering of female partners, and if all intimate violence is presumed to be sexist in origin, then these presumptions mitigate against recognizing women who are abusive or men who are victimized. Again, as Donna Cecere acknowledged, she "had no concept" of heterosexual women's violence or of lesbian battering. Without the power to name the abuse *as abuse,* she "didn't know enough," as she put it, "to make a connection." An analytical framework that relies exclusively on gender/sexism to assign the roles of perpetrator and victim will not readily clarify for gay men or lesbians (or for that matter, hetero-sexual men) their own experience as victims or as victimizers. Nor will it help keep the focus where it rightly belongs, on the abusive behavior as the moral problem, along with a sociocultural context that promotes power as unilateral control. Similarly, in both church and society, because homosexuality itself has long been identified as sinful or alternatively pathological, many people mistakenly identify the problem as homosexual identity rather than as partner abuse. Held captive by such cultural obfuscations, people may look and look, but they will not see.

Making sense of battering, including same-sex battering, requires developing a theoretical framework that appreciates how violence as a social control mechanism is generally tolerated in this society, how it can be used by and against anyone, and how grasping what is going on requires keeping the focus on the behavior of the abusing partner rather than on the victim's gender or social identity. At the same time, the interpretive framework must take into account the larger social environment, in this case the "holding context" of heterosexist values and power dynamics, which greatly expands the opportunity for the abuse to go unchecked. Heterosexism provides a convenient cultural pretext for not seeing same-sex abuse as wrongful or significant enough to warrant the majority community's time and attention.

Another obstacle to naming same-sex battering is the LGBT community's own inclination toward self-protection in a hostile cultural context. The truth about same-sex battering remains hidden, in part, because of the shame experienced by those directly affected by the abuse and, in part, because of the reluctance of an oppressed community to go public with its problems and thereby give ammunition for further vilification of gay culture. Drawing attention to intimate violence *within* the community seems unnecessarily provocative and self-incriminating. (On this point, I find Traci West's *Wounds of the Spirit* helpful in documenting a similar reluctance in communities of color.) However, a lack of responsiveness to battering in same-sex or mixed-gender relationships only perpetuates the problem by not holding abusers accountable and neglecting the needs of victims for safety and support.

As a social problem, same-sex battering requires a social response. Not only the gay and lesbian communities, but also the heterosexual community at large must intervene in order to insure the safety of victims and hold batterers accountable. Together, we bear responsibility to convey the message that coercive control, whether in same-sex or other relations, is unacceptable and will not be tolerated. Our moral credibility on this matter depends on matching our rhetoric with policies and programs that offer effective strategies aimed at prevention, as well as crisis response.

From a theology of disrespect to an ethic of solidarity and resistance

The subtitle of Lutheran theologian Joy Bussert's book on battering, "From a Theology of Suffering to an Ethic of Empowerment,"[11] suggests how a justice-loving church might respond to domestic violence in heterosexual relations and, by implication, to same-sex battering. Becoming educated about these matters means letting go of our innocence about domestic injustice, recognizing that intimate violence is a pervasive social problem, and owning up to how patriarchal Christianity has long encouraged women and other nondominant groups to endure rather than protest their victimization, especially at the hands of controlling husbands, masters, parents, bosses, and so forth.

The work of liberation, of setting captives free, begins with listening to and believing victims' stories, taking their anger seriously, critiquing the social and religious traditions that legitimate social subordination, welcoming the rising power of oppressed peoples, and reconstructing a Christian theological ethic that truly honors each person's humanity while denouncing violence within any and all social relations.

In terms of our specific topic, setting free those held captive in abusive same-sex relations requires a willingness to listen to and learn from gay, lesbian, bisexual, and transgender survivors of domestic abuse, welcoming their anger, supporting their empowerment, engaging in a critique of socially and religiously sanctioned homophobia, and reconstructing a Christian theological ethic that truly honors gay people and identifies same-sex abuse as a violation of a commonly shared humanity. Theologian Carter Heyward expresses a theological foundation for this justice ministry this way: "The God whom Jesus knew and loved never calls us to leave ourselves behind or forget our own worth and, at the same time, calls us never to forget that others matter as much as we do. In God, we are called to hold together our own lives and those of others as equally worthy."[12]

Marie Fortune, founding director of the Center for the Prevention of Sexual and Domestic Violence in Seattle, asserts that the religious community has typically responded to family violence with denial. At the same time, the church has a theological mandate to advocate justice and peace, which obligates people of faith to break the silences and respond proactively to these concerns. "Violence is destroying families," Fortune writes. "If religious institutions and agencies are concerned with saving families, they must place a high priority on the needs of people suffering from such abuse and on the programs that seek to prevent it."[13] To this I would add that it is also imperative that the church publicly name violence as both personal and structural, and further, recognize that some of the families being destroyed by such violence are gay, lesbian, bisexual, and transgender families.

Here's the rub: Little evidence exists to show that hierarchical, controlling religious institutions or their leadership have been, or are now, truly invested in easing the suffering of even *heterosexual* victims of domestic hierarchy. Denial and minimization of male violence against women and children remain quite formidable obstacles to justice-making in and for families. Add to that the historically anti-gay posture of the church, and is it any wonder that the absence of strong moral leadership in our churches is even more pronounced whenever those suffering from abuse happen to be gay? The sad fact of the matter is that very few Christians hold themselves morally accountable for reducing violence *against* gay people, and yet, without that kind of public moral commitment, who will ever believe that our call for ending violence *within* same-sex relations is credible?

Fortune rightly insists: "The sum of all efforts to address violence in the family in religious communities must be justice-making."[14] Her own work on sexual and domestic violence and that of other Christian feminists incorporate a principled call for justice for gays and lesbians and an end to anti-gay violence.[15] However, even within

their explicitly justice-focused theological discourse, same-sex domestic abuse remains, by and large, invisible. The difficulty this poses
is that whenever a problem is not adequately named or made sufficiently visible, a proper response cannot be given. As Fortune herself
concludes, "By refusing to acknowledge the problem—by refusing to
accept any responsibility for the conditions that condone the battering of spouses and elderly adults and the physical and sexual abuse
of children—society allows such abuse to continue."[16] My point is:
should we not also be naming, more explicitly and without apology,
the wrongness of same-sex battering? Otherwise, church and society (which means we ourselves) will—by default—be allowing this
abuse to continue.

James Poling follows Fortune's lead in outlining three principles
for guiding a justice ministry in relation to domestic abuse. The first
priority is to promote the safety of those harmed, the second is to
call the abuser to accountability (and transformation), and the third
is to restore the integrity of the relationship, if possible. However,
if "the harm is too great, the damage too deep, [or] the resistance
of the abuser to change [is] too formidable," then it may be necessary to "mourn the loss of that relationship and work to restore the
individual."[17]

These are useful principles for dealing with the *relational* dynamics
of battering, but as Poling and Fortune themselves recognize, justice-
making requires more than addressing the needs of the individual
victim and abuser. The social context that legitimates *same-sex* abuse
must itself be transformed, including cultural norms that support
controlling institutional patterns and personal behaviors, as well as
the devaluing of gay people. Both crisis intervention and abuse prevention must be grounded in an explicitly *public* affirmation of the
dignity of gay men, bisexuals, and lesbian women and of the moral
goodness—the inviolability—of same-sex relationships.

Respect for gay people and their intimate partnerships is essential
for framing a credible Christian ethic of nonviolence. Philosopher
Richard Mohr points out that the phrase "adding insult to injury"
identifies two types of evil that a comprehensive nonviolent ethic
must address. On the one hand, evildoing refers to the physical
harms and injuries that reduce a person's happiness. These typically
elicit sympathy from others. On the other hand, evil refers to those

indignities, including name-calling and invectives, that a person suffers not because of something he or she has done, but because of who that person is perceived to be. The appropriate response to such insult is not sympathy, but rather outrage and our redoubled efforts to communicate respect for that person's dignity. Disrespecting a person does grave harm because insults attack a person *as a person* in his or her humanity. "If our regard for others does not include respect," Mohr writes, "we fail to treat them as persons, and treat them instead as lesser beings."[18] A Christian theology of nonviolence must, therefore, do more than object to violence in intimate relations. It must call for the honoring of gay people and their full lives, including their loves. It is only by demonstrating such clear, consistent respect that *non-gay* people will ever gain sufficient credibility to call gay and lesbian people to account whenever they, too, misuse power.

Religious leaders, including pastors and counselors, in responding to same-sex domestic violence, would do well to follow the guidelines outlined earlier: first, safety; second, accountability; and then, restoration, if possible. Moreover, listen with respect and care when someone discloses a history of abuse; make referrals to community resources, including the criminal justice system, if the abused person agrees; and collaborate with other community leaders and agencies to put response services in place if they are lacking. However, the primary work of ministry, I dare say, is not crisis intervention or even "putting out fires," as important as that work truly is. Rather, the primary calling is to preach, teach, and embody the gospel as liberating, life-giving good news—and, God willing, to exemplify mutual respect in all our social interactions. Justice ministries must cogently identify and promote culturally diverse models of intimacy and community based on radical respect, power-sharing, and nonpossessive partnership. Above all, domestic violence must be named as a social injustice that most certainly has personal ramifications, but cannot be resolved only as an "interpersonal problem."

At this juncture, a difficulty arises because so many religious people, including pastors, operate with a privatized model of ministry. Ministry becomes viewed narrowly as a "helping profession" that provides support and care for individuals and families in crisis. From this vantage point, doing good means offering services to victims or so-called "needy people," but does not necessarily imply empowering people to seek their own liberation and freedom. With respect to professional ethics in ministry, the norm of beneficence, especially a paternalistic notion of doing good *for* others, has unfortunately become the overriding obligation for many clergy. Well-meaning people thereby neglect the centrality of the norm of justice for the Christian moral life and fail to take seriously how freedom requires standing *with* the oppressed and, in this instance, with the LGBT community.[19] In contrast, liberating ministries of care are intimately linked to, and invested in, ministries of justice-making, on the alert for making the connections between caring for the well-being of persons and re-forming community through shared empowerment.

Standing in solidarity with gay men and lesbians and working to correct power imbalances within families and other social relations will take courage on the part of any faith community. In particular, working to end same-sex domestic violence will require people to work through their fears that in becoming advocates of justice and nonviolence for gay people, they risk becoming gay-and-lesbian-identified (i.e., known publicly as gay friendly or even as a "gay church") and thereby, face losing status and funding. This fear is not peculiar to those of us connected to the church. This fear has, at times, nearly paralyzed community organizing among feminists, for example, who have committed themselves to social change but nonetheless, often "put on the brakes" when confronted with lesbian-baiting. "For my politics," Suzanne Pharr counters, "if a woman's social change organization has not been labeled lesbian or communist, it is probably not doing significant work; it is only 'making nice.'"[20] Similarly, we might ask, what if—what if—churches regularly took moral inventory about how often *they* manage to "catch hell" for *their* justice advocacy? If they're not experiencing some measure of grief, may we not conjecture that "making nice" has taken precedence over making justice? If so, the power of the gospel has been domesticated.

Advocating justice as mutual respect, care, and power-sharing requires matching rhetoric with action. When a church says "all are welcome" but has no track record of anti-racism, anti-sexism, or anti-homophobia action and no history of explicitly gay-affirmative outreach, the message conveyed is a resounding lack of interest in the lives and struggles of gay people. Perhaps there's a begrudging willingness to include them, but only as long as they remain invisible as gay. However, a ministry of "don't ask, don't tell" is hardly liberating or healing of the violence within and surrounding people's lives.

In contrast, a justice ministry will seek, without distinction, to "bind up the wounds" of all who have been harmed. It will work ceaselessly to restore power and dignity to those who have been wronged by oppressive social structures. Its watchwords will be solidarity, the joy of shared struggle, and a certain "moxy," or moral fearlessness.

In conclusion, a pivotal lesson to be gained from addressing same-sex domestic violence may be stated this way: in a cultural context of diverse human sexualities, a theology of nonviolence must critique not only the violence *in* relationships, but also the violence, including the disrespect, directed *against* relationships. In my judgment, the church's credibility for offering a liberating, healing word, as well its efficacy in "setting captives free," depends on whether its commitment to ending violence is broadly inclusive and universal in scope. No one—not you, not I, not anyone else—should be left out, and no one should be made to suffer alone. As an ethics colleague frames the matter, "If there is a single Christian duty, task, or project, it is not to give to others, but to create and be in community, [the kind of community] in which [all] people can give, contribute, and feel valuable [and valued]."[21] As I see it, that's the kind of ministry truly worthy of our time, our commitment, and our very lives.

Notes

1. Ginny NiCarthy, *Getting Free: A Handbook for Women in Abusive Relationships* (Seattle: Seal Press, 1982, 1986), especially 285–304. NiCarthy cites Amnesty International's research about prisoners of war and reproduces a "chart of coercion," which depicts the brainwashing tactics used to control people psychologically as well as physically. As NiCarthy points out, "Most people who brainwash their intimate partners use methods similar to those of prison guards, who recognize their physical control is never easily accomplished without the cooperation of the prisoner" (286). Emotional and psychological abuse always accompanies and intensifies physical and sexual abuse.

2. Claire M. Renzetti, "The Poverty of Services for Battered Lesbians," in *Violence in Gay and Lesbian Domestic Partnerships,* ed. Claire M. Renzetti and Charles Harvey Miley (New York: Harrington Park Press, 1996), 66.

3. Studies indicate that while battered women may often turn to their pastors for help, they rank the helpfulness of the assistance they received at the very bottom in comparison to other sources of support and counsel. As Carol J. Adams reports, "Women who turned to their clergy for marital guidance stayed longer with their abusers, and the abuse did not subside." Her reading is that clergy by and large are overly confident about their knowledge and skills in assisting people in abusive, dangerous relationships. Clergy too often do not realize the life-threatening nature of battering, the importance of protecting the victim's safety by maintaining strict confidentiality, or how to interpret what is going on when an abuser's and a victim's stories differ dramatically. Without specialized knowledge and skills, pastors and counselors may fail to help and, in fact, cause more harm. Carol J. Adams, *Woman-Battering* (Minneapolis: Fortress, 1994), 5–6.

4. William Sloan Coffin, *A Passion for the Possible: A Message to U.S. Churches* (Louisville: Westminster John Knox, 1993), 2.

5. Adams, *Woman-Battering,* 12.

6. On the underlying belief system that reinforces the batterer's sense of entitlement, see Barbara Hart, "Lesbian Battering: An Examination," in *Naming the Violence: Speaking Out about Lesbian Battering,* ed. Kerry Lobel (Seattle: Seal Press, 1986), 182–83.

7. Susan Schechter, *Women and Male Violence: The Visions and Struggles of the Battered Women's Movement* (Boston: South End Press, 1982), 238.

8. David Island and Patrick Letellier, *Men Who Beat the Men Who Love Them: Battered Gay Men and Domestic Violence* (New York: Harrington Park Press, 1991), xxi.

9. Pam Elliott, "Shattering Illusions: Same-Sex Domestic Violence," in *Violence in Gay and Lesbian Domestic Partnerships,* ed. Claire M. Renzetti and Charles Harvey Miley (New York: Harrington Park Press, 1996), 1.

10. Donna J. Cecere, "The Second Closet: Battered Lesbians," *Open Hands* 3, no. 2 (fall 1987): 12; emphasis added.

11. Joy Bussert, *Battered Women: From a Theology of Suffering to an Ethic of Empowerment* (New York: Lutheran Church in America, Division of Mission in North America, 1986).

12. Carter Heyward, *Saving Jesus from Those Who Are Right: Rethinking What It Means to Be Christian* (Minneapolis: Fortress, 1999), 122–23.

13. Marie M. Fortune, *Violence in the Family: A Workshop Curriculum for Clergy and Other Helpers* (Cleveland: Pilgrim, 1991), 5.

14. Ibid., 19.

15. Marie Marshall Fortune, *Sexual Violence: The Unmentionable Sin* (New York: Pilgrim, 1983), especially chapter 3, "Reframing the Ethical Questions," 42–98; and also *Love Does No Harm: Sexual Ethics for the Rest of Us* (New York: Continuum, 1995). See also "Homophobia and Violence: An Unholy Alliance," *Working Together* 6, no. 3 (spring/summer 1986): 5–6. Carol Adams includes a section entitled "A Lesbian Partner as Abuser" in her first chapter on naming in *Woman-Battering,* 35.

16. Fortune, *Violence in the Family*, 3.

17. James Newton Poling, "Preaching to Perpetrators of Violence," in *Telling the Truth: Preaching about Sexual and Domestic Violence,* ed. John S. McClure and Nancy J. Ramsay (Cleveland: United Church Press, 1998), 72. See also Marie M. Fortune and James Poling, "Calling to Accountability: The Church's Response to Abusers," in *Violence against Women and Children: A Christian Theological Sourcebook,* ed. Carol J. Adams and Marie M. Fortune (New York: Continuum, 1995), 451–63.

18. Richard D. Mohr, *A More Perfect Union: Why Straight America Must Stand Up for Gay Rights* (Boston: Beacon, 1994), 59.

19. Karen Lebacqz, *Professional Ethics: Power and Paradox* (Nashville: Abingdon, 1985), especially 126–31.

20. Suzanne Pharr, *Homophobia: A Weapon of Sexism* (Inverness, Calif.: Chardon, 1988), 25.

21. Gary David Comstock, *Gay Theology without Apology* (Cleveland: Pilgrim, 1993), 20.

18

Clergy Sexual Misconduct

A Justice Issue

Anne Underwood

This essay is informed by research and writing of the past decade, particularly by feminists within the faith and legal communities on issues of power imbalance. These materials are filtered through the experiences of the author — an attorney who is Catholic and works professionally with Jewish, Christian, and Unitarian faith groups.[1] The essay suggests that, with regard to clergy abuse of power sexually, some of the vocabulary and approaches of secular culture need to be incorporated into the teachings and practices of faith communities. It lauds those who have lifted sexual activity out of the shroud of morality and onto the stage of justice-making. The focus here is on ordained clergy because, in their own minds and, appropriately or not, in the hearts of many laity, clergy possess the unique power of numinosity or holiness.[2] However, every minister, lay or ordained, who has a position of authority within a faith community is accountable to the principles of conduct articulated below. "Sexual misconduct" is used to encompass all forms of misuse of power sexually: abuse of minors, sexual malfeasance with adults, and sexual harassment.

Publicizing power

The past decade moved far toward recognizing clergy sexual misconduct as a public issue of justice rather than simply as a private concern about morality. Like other forms of ministerial misconduct, sexual misconduct is a matter of justice because it arises from abuse of power, involves the improper use of status, and violates trust.[3]

Clergy misconduct may be financial, emotional, physical, or sexual. None is simply a personal harm done privately between the minister and another. Each violates the trust of an individual, the congregation, and the commissioning body. Each private act has a public face. The public face is occasionally shown when clergy embezzle congregational funds. Loss of church funds incites discussion and public action. It is far rarer to hear congregations talk about sexual misconduct by their pastor. In religious culture, the interaction of power and money are public issues, the interaction of power and sex remain largely closeted as private concerns.

At least since Augustine, Christian traditions have compartmentalized sex as a "morality" issue. When ministers engage in inappropriate sexual conduct, it has been typically viewed as a moral failure. Because the church sees morality as its special purview, if sexual misconduct has been addressed at all, it has been as an internal church matter. This mentality, coupled with traditional concerns about government interference in religious affairs, has meant that the lessons, laws, and adjudicatory forums of secular society are often ignored if not outright rejected by local congregations, denominational officials, and their attorneys.[4]

This essay extends sexual conduct beyond the realm of morality into the sphere of justice-making — by no means a new endeavor.[5] How a person uses sexuality in the context of relationship is the subject of moral inquiry. Moral assessment here is not derivative from absolutes about sex. Sexualizing a ministerial relationship is not excused as a problem of sex; rather, it is critiqued as a problem of inappropriate use of power. This problem is compounded by a society in which having power is considered "sexy." For some, the exercise of power incites an erotic charge. For others, being the individualized object of power may elicit an erotic response. The gender, social, and economic constructs implicit in the "power as sexy" phenomenon are recognized, but lie beyond the scope of this essay.

This essay also challenges the assumption that only the synagogue or church has the authority and language to speak to the issue of sexual misconduct in its midst. To the contrary, key concepts that shape secular discussion about sexual misconduct must also inform ecclesiastical discourse. Justice, public accountability, ability to give consent, and standards of ethical conduct need to modify denominational discourse that up to now has favored mercy, private acts, relational dynamics, and holiness codes as guiding principles.

Excluding the norms and concerns of secular society from theological and ecclesiastical discussions about power, morality, and sexuality displays both ignorance and arrogance. Considerations broader than those entertained by most denominational leaders must inform and also frame the discussions at both congregational and judicatory levels. The experience of laity must be heard, as well as the desires of clergy. If this does not happen, our faith communities will be less safe than local health clubs and shopping malls, especially for children and other vulnerable people.

Power as intrinsic to ministerial relationships

Within the Jewish, Christian, and Unitarian Universalist traditions, no contemporary individual is born with the power or status of "religious leader." Such power and status are acquired. At one end of the spectrum, power and status are conferred on clergy through ordination according to the teachings and traditions of most denominations. On the other end, power and status, along with respect and trust, are earned by ministers—both lay and ordained—as they fulfill honorably the expectations placed on them as community leaders. Moreover, power does not exist in a vacuum. Power is relational, and in itself it is neither good nor evil, but morally neutral. How it is used in relationship to others becomes the justice issue.

Almost every person possesses some degree of personal power in most situations. Social and economic status, gender, age, race, and professional role can augment or diminish that power. Ideally, there is mutuality of power in most adult relationships. The power of each person, although different, balances that of the other. In a friendship, one person may be highly educated while the other is the town's best carpenter. One spouse may have higher earning capacity, but the other has stronger interpersonal skills. While people defer to the knowledge, expertise, or skills of friends or family in some aspects of life, those same relatives or friends defer to them in other aspects. There is mutuality of need and reciprocity of response. Power differentials shift within varying situations but remain overall in balance.

Perhaps the clearest example of power imbalance is that between adult authority figures and children. Society's ethical and legislative laws recognize this and require that adults be held responsible for the well-being of children in their parental or professional care. The most horrendous abuse of power is the sexual, physical, psychological, and emotional abuse of a child. When professionals, among them doctors, teachers, and clergy, do this, it betrays community trust as well as the child's. There are, however, other forms of abuse of power by clergy and other professionals that are recognized as highly damaging to individuals and as perpetrating great injustice within communities. In particular, the sexualization of a professional relationship with vulnerable people is viewed as a violation of trust, as a breach of the special duty owed by professionals to those served, and as manipulation of an inherent power differential. Recently, religious communities have also begun to identify this form of power abuse as clergy sexual misconduct.

Whether to define the role of clergy as a profession or as a calling is debated in many seminaries. While important to the ordained, it is a distinction without a difference to most laity. Indeed, designating a category of the faithful as *kleros* and setting them apart from the *laos* based on calling can be offensive. Jewish traditions have never elevated the ordained, although the good rabbi is typically exalted as teacher and, by extension, as community leader. Christian theologies teach that through baptism all are called. Some of those called in baptism also accept positions of ordained leadership as *kleros*.

Parishioners and others who are "in relationship" with clergy, based on the clergy's leadership position, can be as susceptible to power abuse as patients and clients of doctors, therapists, and lawyers. In each relationship, the professional is given access to aspects of the person's life not readily visible or available to others. Unlike the intimacy of family or friendship, there is little mutuality or reciprocity of access. The doctor does not bare a chest for the patient to examine; the attorney does not produce personal records for the client to review; and the therapist does not discuss her or his own emotional frailties. While clergy may share their own faith struggles in a general way and discuss aspects of their personal lives with congregants, it is they, not the congregants, who deliver the sermon at the Friday shabbat service, the Saturday mass, or Sunday morning worship and who are authorized to interpret the Scripture and teachings of the faith. (The question of whether all persons at all times are equally vulnerable in relation to their rabbi or pastor will receive reflection later in this essay.)

Addressing sexual abuse as a justice issue is different from addressing it as a morality concern. While it may be less threatening to define sexual misconduct as a personal failure and essentially one of sexual morality, it is more honest to examine how religious institutions abet people who use power in unjust ways, including sexually.[6] This requires holding all members within a community of faith accountable for monitoring safety and good conduct of its leaders.

Numinosity as power

Many clergy have difficulty admitting they hold power in relation to congregants. On the one hand, they may acknowledge having ecclesiastical power as functionaries in a hierarchy or as presiders within a liturgical context. On the other hand, they claim that clerical status does not significantly influence how others respond to them outside of those specific ecclesiastical and liturgical roles. Quite properly, they may wish an end to the *kleros-laos* distinction in daily interactions. Regrettably, most laity are unable to separate the power of the leadership role from the personhood of the clergy. Laity of all traditions frequently profess a sense of numinosity about their clergy even when the clergy person does not cultivate it.[7] Women cite as the most frequent reason they "went along with" sexual conduct in clergy counseling sessions their belief that clergy are "more holy" and possess "special access to God's will." Child victims of sexual abuse by parish clergy report similar feelings.

Whether cultivated or merely tolerated, numinous power is difficult to manage. It may be humbling for clergy to acknowledge that a "phenomenon" rather than their own personal kindness or brilliance is the primary source of another's trust and respect for them. However, when clergy are able to own this unique power as theirs, they can use it more readily and appropriately for the common good. Numinosity is a power that comes with the professional role or office. It gives clergy an authoritative voice in controversial public forums, as well as access to the most intimate moments in people's lives. In both places, clergy are thereby privileged to speak truth to the powerful and offer comfort and hope to the afflicted.

Legislative and judicial lessons for managing power imbalance

In the past twenty years the secular world has developed language to identify previously unnamed wrongs and to rename old wrongs in new ways. With that naming has come awareness that the abuse of power fuels those wrongs. Abusers rather than victims are being held accountable. Two examples are especially relevant to an examination of clergy sexual misconduct.

Example one:

Until the late 1970s, rape was prosecuted as a "sex crime." The leading cause of rape was considered to be women themselves: dressing in provocative clothing, drinking too much, or being out after dark. Their behaviors were used to justify the rapist's action. Today, every state prosecutes rape as a crime of violence. The penis is identified as a weapon, not as a wayward sex organ. The behavior and demeanor of the victim is rarely allowed into evidence. Rape is no longer excused as a crime of sexual passion; it is rather a crime of sexual violence.

Example two:

Until the mid-1980s, civil courts had no language to describe, much less censure, sexual harassment. In 1986, when the U.S. Supreme Court heard the first case addressing sexual harassment as a form of sex discrimination, few attorneys could articulate the standards for a sexual harassment claim.[8] Today, thanks to Clarence Thomas and Bill Clinton and to the development of policies and educational programs in many work places, most people can describe at least some elements of sexual harassment.[9] It is now understood that certain relationships create an inherent imbalance of power. The Supreme

Court noted in the 1986 case that there is an inherent imbalance of power between a supervisor and employee. The Court implied that there cannot be an assumption that an employee would feel free to withhold consent for a sexual relationship with her supervisor. The Court observed that while a sexual relationship in the presence of a power differential might be voluntary (no gun held to the head, no economic retaliation), it might not be welcome.

The federal government and the states regulate certain behaviors in many work places and most educational institutions.[10] To comply with these statutes, as well as the holdings from six Supreme Court cases addressing sexual harassment,[11] all government agencies, public and private educational institutions, and major employers have policies on sexualized behavior in the educational or work place. These policies define and prohibit sexual harassment.[12] Most also prohibit or advise against so-called consensual relationships where there is an inherent power imbalance (professor-student, supervisor-supervisee, counselor-counselee).

To determine if conduct constitutes harassment or if a relationship is consensual, most courts apply the "reasonable person" (in the victim's status) standard and look to the impact on the alleged victim, not the intent of the alleged harasser. This is a reversal of traditional tort and criminal law inquiry where the *mens rea* of the accused is the lens through which judgment is reached. In matters of harassment, the courts are applying the experience of the victim to determine whether the alleged conduct is problematic. In theological language, this might be called taking "the view from below," and faith communities might be both wise and compassionate to adopt it.

In addition to the above regulatory measures, state licensing boards and professional certifying associations have or are creating ethics codes that explicitly prohibit sexual relationships between those licensed and those served.[13] In some states criminal and civil law prohibit sexualized relationships between counselors and counselees and between doctors and patients, among others. Some laws cover licensed pastoral counselors and include parish clergy in counseling situations. These secular forums recognize that minding the power differential is the responsibility of the professional. This is true even when the other person tries to sexualize the professional relationship or has equal or greater personal power outside the work connection. If the professional cannot harness the sexual energy appropriately, it is her or his duty to terminate the work with the person. The pastoral response to another's refusal to accept limits on inappropriate conduct in a pastoral relationship is recognition of one's own limitations with that person. The ethical action called for is termination of the relationship with an appropriate referral to another professional.

Currently, clergy conduct within congregational settings is subject to review only by the standards and practices of the particular denomination or local church. These vary greatly across and even within denominations. Moreover, enforcement often depends on the particular official in charge. Laity and other clergy experiencing harassment (or worse) by clergy within a synagogue or church have very limited recourse. Until the late 1980s, relatively few cases involving clergy sexual misconduct were filed in state courts. Denominational lawyers argued successfully for dismissal of many of those on First Amendment grounds. The use of similar arguments to deflect prosecution of credible allegations of child abuse and molestation of adult counselees raises issues of justice that have been so eloquently articulated by Catholics during the 2002 revelations of abuse by some priests and cover-ups by bishops.

The court cases and the 2002 crisis have exposed the scandal of leaders committed to protecting an institutional structure (and those privileged in it) at the expense of the message of care for the most vulnerable. While retaining faith in God, some laity express loss of trust in institutional religion by whatever name it franchises itself. The First Amendment guarantees of noninterference with religious beliefs and practices were not intended to shield religious bodies from the consequences of criminal conduct or of the abuse and misuse of their own power. Denominations may wisely look to secular laws and professional codes for setting at least minimal standards of conduct for their members and leaders. Out of a faith tradition's special call to do justice should come its own policies and processes. However, secular practices should provide at least a floor. The ceiling of the edifice constructed to address sexual misconduct can, and should, soar much higher.

Clergy abuse of power sexually

Sexualized power abuse by ministers takes many forms. While the severity of the immediate and long-term impact may vary, all abuse violates trust. Some instances are crimes, such as pedophilia (sexualized relating with a prepubescent child of either gender), ephebophilia (sexualized relating with a pubescent minor of either gender), and rape. Every denomination should mandate immediate reporting to local authorities about such offenses. The state is empowered and equipped to investigate these acts as crimes. Faith communities may also investigate and confront these crimes as sin, but not to the exclusion of engaging state criminal processes.

In faith communities, most allegations of unwelcome sex come from women who are either in the conversion process or receiving counseling for bereavement or for marital, economic, or health problems.[14] These women are typically vulnerable and susceptible. Many have low self-esteem and are traumatized. In order to heal, they need safety to shed their psychological, emotional, and spiritual clothing, as it were. As physicians are expected not to misuse touch when examining a disrobed patient, so clergy are expected not to touch inappropriately the vulnerabilities of congregants or counselees. Emerging wisdom says that no emotionally exposed, vulnerable person can give meaningful consent to a sexual relationship *ever* with the person to whom she or he has turned to facilitate healing or conversion. There may be physical touching and spiritual/emotional intimacy, but there ought not be eroticized touching or sexualized intimacy. These require mutuality of power for consent to be authentic. Persons seeking pastoral care are unable to give consent freely and knowingly at that particular time of their lives, in that particular setting, or afterwards to the particular counselor.

Unfortunately, the fact that a person bringing forth allegations may also show manifestations of vulnerability can cause inexperienced church investigators, adjudicators, and advocates for clergy accused of sexual misconduct to name the complaint falsely as an overreaction on the part of a "needy" person, especially if the accuser has any history of prior abuse or instability. While the accuser appears to lack credibility, the clergy person holds a respected position, is typically confident if not charismatic, and has a history of success. Often the accuser is pictured as a "sick flake" or a "scheming, lying, destructive manipulator." The social as well as personal vulnerability of these women personifies the problems of the power differential inherent in many clergy-parishioner relationships. Mandating safeguards to protect those without power (or with relatively less power) is at the heart of doing justice.

Sexualizing relationships with vulnerable people is immoral, but the nature of the immorality is not sexual. Like power, sex acquires its moral value only in relationship. Sexual abuse of adults or minors is not predicated on sexual orientation or marital status (the majority of pedophiles are married heterosexual men), nor is the immorality in the relationship a function of orientation or marital status. The essence of the immorality is the abuse of trust and power. The relationship is immoral because it is inherently imbalanced and nonconsensual.

Sexuality as gift: how can clergy use it?

At their best, prohibitions against sexual contact between clergy and parishioners do not reinforce a sex-negative theological stance, but rather affirm the power and positive aspect of eros in all human relationships. Adopting a "pro-sex, anti-abuse" stance requires acknowledging that in many circumstances eros's power also necessitates its restraint. The desert mothers and fathers understood this well. Their monastic rules against certain forms of intimacy between individuals within community respected how the power of eros can alter the focus of personal and community relations. The eros alive between two people becomes transformed (and is meant to be transformed) into energy for sustaining the life of the entire community. The rules that eliminated particular sexualized relationships were kept in place so that the community would be a safe place for the exploration and realization of spiritual intimacy among (and between) women and men.

Ministers do not check their sexuality at the door of any relationship. Indeed, eros as "energy for life and connection" promotes growth through developing prudent intimacy with others. Ministers can offer the gift of spiritual and emotional intimacy for its own wondrous, awesome sake. Theirs can be an intimacy of dialogue, prayer, and touch, given without fantasies or expectations of the sexualized "more."

Prohibitions against sexual contact between clergy and parishioner are based on the ethical principle of respect for persons. Rabbi Yoel Kahn speaks to all faith traditions when he says,

> Our religious interpretation of sexuality is measured not according to whether acts are permitted or forbidden, nor ritually pure or impure, but whether the relationship as a whole and its specific expression is just or unjust, contributing to or diminishing from holiness....Accordingly, we must consider the long-term impact and possible consequences of our actions.

He notes that a just sexual relationship must occur "between equals—people who are peers in maturity, independence, and personal and physical power."[15]

Can clergy ever have a just relationship with a parishioner? Since the pioneering work of Marie Fortune,[16] the words "clergy," "sex," and "parishioner" when strung together have spelled some form of abuse by clergy.[17] In *The Cry of Tamar: Violence against Women and the Church's Response,* Pamela Cooper-White confirms this view. She writes, "I have found that a majority of ministers who enter into romantic or sexual relationships with parishioners do so primarily because there is an imbalance of power between them at the onset, and because they need to reinforce and heighten the intensity of that power dynamic."[18] A review of the literature suggests that it is clergy, rather than laity, who are asking when, if, and how sexual intimacy between clergy and parishioner can occur. And, every clergy person seems to know someone who has married a congregant and is living happily ever after.

Karen Lebacqz and Ronald Barton tackle the question of an exception to the presumption against clergy-congregant intimacies and offer structural guidelines for protecting both parties.[19] If there has been a counseling relationship, the presumption becomes a rule: no sexual intimacy, ever. In other circumstances, the burden of overriding the presumption lies always with the rabbi or pastor. He or she must demonstrate absence of coercion, mutuality of desire, and equality to give consent. There can be no secrecy about the relationship; congregational leadership must know. In addition, dual relationships must be avoided by the "other" finding a different clergy person for pastoral support. This approach comports with the sexual harassment analysis set forth by the Supreme Court. Both view the situation through the lens of the person with lesser power. Both hold the person with greater professional power accountable if the relationship ends in ways experienced as harmful by the other. That is what justice requires.

Individual and corporate accountability

To eliminate clergy sexual misconduct, faith communities need to ask of each and every minister: is this a person of integrity capable of integrating personal power with the mantle of authority a leadership position confers? Or is this a person so lacking in self-awareness and healthy self-esteem that the mantle is sought as compensation? The relevant questions are not about sexual orientation or sexual experiences, but rather about the person's understanding of power and his or her awareness and acceptance of personal limitations. In Jewish communities, are rabbis able to be true servants and teachers of Torah and at the same time refrain from exploiting their leadership? In Christian churches, what is the person's readiness to be a member of the Body of Christ in ministry when ministry invites access to an often-sacramental intimacy? These questions ought to be the primary points for discernment.

Clergy who comprehend, acknowledge, and honor their power will not violate trust through sexual misconduct. Selecting and supporting these people will go far toward eliminating abusive situations that now require accountability among all people of faith for violations that have occurred in the past. Accountability, as understood here, is not a private affair any more than is an act of sexual misconduct. Both are communal issues. While appropriate personal confidentiality for all must be honored, there can be no secret deals and no agreements to cover up and "just move on." Justice is a public act done with and by the authority of the entire community. It is not the prerogative of an anointed few.

Catholic ethicist Richard M. Gula writes, "Accountability is a way of doing justice toward the community.... The covenantal obligations we undertake as ministers warrant holding us accountable in order to protect others from being harmed." He quotes Protestant ethicist William May: "In professional ethics today, the test of moral seriousness may depend not simply upon personal compliance with moral principles but upon the courage to hold others accountable."[20] Compliance with moral principles is a private decision with public ramifications. Holding others accountable for their injustices is a public act with private and communal consequences. Both are necessary in faith communities.

Treating others with respect lies at the heart of the Jewish, Christian, and Unitarian Universalist traditions. Within its own governance, each must build consistent and enforceable standards accompanied by structures of uniform communal accountability for clergy sexual misconduct. Doing justice, loving mercy, and walking humbly requires nothing less of both clergy and laity who seek to respond faithfully to God's call to be in community.

Notes

1. This essay contains the author's opinion and overview of certain legal situations. It does not purport to contain specific answers to or recommendations for legal issues. The author, editors, and publisher are not engaging in legal advice. Legal advice should be sought from an attorney in the jurisdiction where the cause for questions arises.

2. For a definition of numinosity, see note 7.

3. "Power" means the ability to influence or control one's environment and people in it. "Status" refers to the position one occupies in relation to others within particular social, economic, cultural, and religious institutional systems.

4. The First Amendment to the U.S. Constitution instructs: "Congress shall make no law respecting an establishment of religion, or prohibiting the free exercise thereof." The framers of U.S. democracy wanted to insure the right for citizens to hold religious beliefs and practice their faith without government interference. Religious beliefs are absolutely protected. Religious practices, or conduct flowing from sincerely held religious belief, are generally protected, absent compelling reasons otherwise. The First Amendment does not cover conduct that is not incidental to religious belief. For example, religious bodies are not exempt from criminal statutes and from most municipal ordinances involving public order and safety although those statutes and ordinances cannot single out or unduly burden religious practice. Denominational attorneys frequently are successful in arguing that cases alleging sexual misconduct during spiritual counseling, confession, or other encounters between clergy and congregants must be dismissed. They argue that for a court to explore conduct in those settings would implicate government examination of the fundamental beliefs and practices of the faith community. On the other hand, in cases that reach trial, denominational attorneys use these same

considerations to refute liability claims against the religious body for clergy sexual misconduct. They argue that such conduct is not part of the tenets or practice of the faith and that the church as employer cannot be responsible for the clergy's conduct because it was neither foreseeable nor condoned nor part of the clergy's employment. There is legitimate concern about courts stepping into the realm of clergy training, hiring, supervision, and retention. However, the tenor of argument and litigation tactics employed by denominational attorneys have eroded trust by many laity. It appears that religious bodies care less for the safety and well-being of their members than for the reputations of their clergy and maintenance of church endowments.

5. The editors of this volume and the rest of the committee that prepared "Keeping Body and Soul Together: Sexuality, Spirituality, and Social Justice" were among the first to recognize sexual misconduct as a justice issue in the early 1990s. They wrote, "The framework of this report places the discussion of sexuality squarely in the context of justice. No issue tests our capacity to seek justice for all concerned parties like that of clergy sexual misconduct" (*Presbyterians and Human Sexuality 1991* [Louisville: Presbyterian Church (U.S.A.), 1991], 69). This understanding is reflected more recently in *Living the Sacred Trust: Clergy Sexual Ethics, A Resource on Clergy Misconduct of a Sexual Nature for Cabinets and Boards of Ordained Ministry of the United Methodist Church,* published by the General Board of Higher Education and Ministry (no publication date given). Its editors write, "When boundaries and relationships sacred to the office [clergy] are violated, the focus must be on the misuse of power" (vi). The United Church of Christ has in its codes for authorized ministers the vow, "I will not use my position, power or authority to exploit any person." This is applied to pastoral sexual misconduct in the denomination's *Guidelines for Resourcing Committees on the Ministry* (Local Church Ministries Parish Life and Leadership Ministry Team, May 2001), 34.

6. Two of many examples are Campus Crusade for Christ and the deacons of Detroit's Rosedale Park Baptist Church. Neither removed or censured Haman Cross Jr. after his 1998 court testimony acknowledging sexual contact with three women parishioners with whom he had counseled. Intercourse with one was established. The deacons kept Cross as senior pastor, but put a window in his office door. Campus Crusade for Christ continues to send him as a speaker to high school and college gatherings throughout the United States. Lynn Flynn, "Breaking Faith," *World on the Web* 17, no. 12 (March 30, 2002).

7. Karen Lebacqz and Ronald Barton in *Sex in the Parish* (Louisville: Westminster John Knox, 1991) offer an excellent discussion of how Protestant clergy and laity view the numinous aspect of the clerical role. The authors clarify that "numinous refers to the divine, the holy, the spiritual, the 'supernatural,' the mysterious." Reporting on their research, they cite the words of a pastor who says, "I believe that, always, we who are clergy carry a certain invisible mantle of authority or spirituality or human embodiment of the spirit." This means that clergy "are more to most parishioners than we desire or usually recognize" (110ff.).

8. *Meritor Savings Bank v. Vinson,* 477 U.S. 57 (1986). A bank teller terminated a lengthy sexual relationship with her supervisor. After being fired, she sued the

bank claiming the relationship had never been consensual and that she had felt harassed by the supervisor's attentions. The Court ruled that harassment constitutes discrimination and that an employer could be found liable for the conduct of its supervisory employees.

9. At the time of the Thomas hearings, some members of the white Establishment muttered that this must be a racial situation: two African Americans feuding and testing the boundaries. A few years later, the Establishment's own president engaged in behavior remarkably similar to that alleged against Thomas. The muttering stopped. Those who would label the 2002 revelations of cover-up and sexual abuse within the Roman Catholic Church as only a "Catholic problem" should take heed.

10. The federal government prohibits discrimination based on sex (as well as race, color, religion, or national origin) in most work places through Title VII of the Civil Rights Act of 1964 *as amended* and in educational institutions through Title IX of the Education Amendments Act of 1972. In religious bodies, Title VII covers only nonministerial employees. The same is true for most state antidiscrimination laws. Clergy and laity, in their relation to clergy in a faith community, are neither accountable to nor protected by these laws.

11. *Ellerth,* 524 U.S. 742 (1998), *Oncale v. Sundowner Offshore Servs., Inc.,* 118 S.Ct.998, 76 (1998), *Faragher v. City of Boca Raton,* 524 U.S. 775 (1998), *Gebser v. Largo Vista Independent School District,* 118 S. Ct. 1989 (1998), *Meritor Savings Bank v. Vinson,* 477 U.S. 57 (1986), *Harris v. Forklift Systems, Inc.,* 510 U.S. 17 (1993).

12. The EEOC definition of sexual harassment is most frequently used by employers and government agencies: "Unwelcome sexual advances, requests for sexual favors, and other verbal or physical conduct of a sexual nature constitutes sexual harassment when (1) submission to such conduct is made either explicitly or implicitly a term or condition of an individual's employment, (2) submission to or rejection of such conduct by an individual is used as the basis for employment decisions affecting such an individual, or (3) such conduct has the purpose or effect of unreasonably interfering with an individual's work performance or creating an intimidating, hostile, or offensive working environment." 29CFR 1604.11. Educational institutions add "educational" to employment situations.

13. Examples of associations of clergy with ethics codes addressing expectations for sexual conduct include the Association for Clinical Pastoral Education, Inc., the Association of Professional Chaplains, the American Association of Pastoral Counselors, and the Central Conference of American Rabbis.

14. Gary Schoener, a psychotherapist who has worked on more than twenty-five hundred cases of clergy sex abuse, says, "Priests who victimize women are far more common than those who victimize boys." Former priest and psychologist Richard Sipe believes that at any given time, approximately 20 percent of Catholic priests are involved with women, as opposed to 4 to 6 percent who abuse minors. Jeff Anderson, one of the leading plaintiff's counsel for clergy sexual abuse cases, says, "Church officials historically have been much quicker to blame girls than boys. When women come forward the response has been, 'Well, what did you do to seduce them?'" Jane Lampman, "A Wider Circle of Clergy Abuse," *Christian Science Monitor,* June 14, 2002.

15. Yoel H. Kahn, "Making Love as Making Justice: Towards a New Jewish Ethic of Sexuality," in *Sexuality: A Reader,* ed. Karen Lebacqz and David Sinacore-Guinn (Cleveland: Pilgrim, 1999), 587.

16. Marie Fortune in *Is Nothing Sacred? When Sex Invades the Pastoral Relationship* (San Francisco: HarperSanFrancisco, 1989) was the first to call sexualization of the pastoral relationship a violation of professional ethics and sexual abuse. In the same year, psychiatrist Peter Rutter published *Sex in the Forbidden Zone: When Men in Power—Therapists, Doctors, Clergy, Teachers, and Others—Betray Women's Trust* (New York: Ballantine Books, 1989). These books provided the theoretical frame to remove such relationships from the realm of "private, consensual affairs," subject only to moral scrutiny, into the public arena of social justice.

17. Fortune and others classify clergy who engage in sexual relationships with parishioners or counselees by placing them along a continuum from "wanderers" to "predators." No loophole is granted for authentic, romantic engagement in these contexts.

18. Reprinted in Rev. Jean Torrence, "Clerical Misbehavior Occurs in Many Faiths," *Omaha World-Herald,* on-line edition, May 20, 2002.

19. Lebacqz and Barton, *Sex in the Parish.*

20. Richard M. Gula, *Ethics in Pastoral Ministry* (Mahwah, N.J.: Paulist, 1996), 61, 62, and 63.

Part Five

Struggle and Hope

Keeping Body, Soul, *and Earth* Together

Revisioning Justice-Love as an Ecological Ethic of Right Relation

Daniel T. Spencer

> To be in relation to everything around us, above us, below us, earth, sky, bones, blood, flesh, is to see the world whole, even holy.
> —Terry Tempest Williams[1]

> We love well when we seek right-relatedness with all others and when we seek relations of genuine equality and mutuality, where there is shared power and deep respect....To do justice-love means seeking right-relatedness with others and working to set right all wrong relations, especially distorted power dynamics of domination and subordination.
> —"Keeping Body and Soul Together"[2]

To be in relation with everything around us is an inescapable characteristic of who we are as earth creatures, members of integrated ecosystems that constitute the whole earth community. We breathe, we eat, we excrete, and we commune. Each of our actions within and on our habitats, our earth homes, is affected by and in turn affects countless others, human and otherkind, who count earth as home. It is inescapable: we are fundamentally relational beings at every level of our makeup, biological, psychological, emotional, spiritual. By our very nature, we cannot *not* relate to others.

To be in right relation with everything around us is our moral and spiritual calling. The qualities of each of our actions within and on our habitats, to each other, human and otherkind, determine the moral nature of the habitats and communities we inhabit and construct, the quality of our "home life." To intuit, understand, and commit to this at a deep level—a deeply felt and lived level—is indeed "to see the world whole, even holy." For those of us steeped in the biblical tradition, it is to live within the prayer of the 1991 World Council of Churches conference: "Come Holy Spirit, Redeem Your Whole Creation."

In naming the ethical norm that grounds this moral calling "justice-love," the authors of the Presbyterian report "Keeping Body and Soul Together: Sexuality, Spirituality, and Social Justice" weave together the best moral insights of the biblical tradition with our contemporary experience of the Spirit's liberating and redemptive movement in our midst. Justice-love integrates two biblical mandates as inseparable dimensions of God's activity and our calling in the world to ground an ethic of sexuality and right relation "for the flourishing of all creation."[3] In doing so, "Keeping Body and Soul Together" articulates a profound ethic of right relation grounded in "erotic justice" that allows us to see and live out our sexuality, the most intimate parts of our relational selves, in the broader context of human community and social relations.

Despite occasional references to all of creation, however, the framework for this ethic of justice-love remains largely human-centered. While the connections of right relation in sexuality to social justice are named and explored, left largely unattended are the connections of erotic justice to ecological justice — the moral claims that living within diverse, dynamic, and increasingly damaged ecosystems and habitats shared by other humans *and* by otherkind make on us. How might a critique of anthropocentrism, humanity's too-often self-absorbed isolation from and oppression of the earth and otherkind, reveal to us the eros of earth as a necessary grounding for a sexual ethic of right relation?

In my book *Gay and Gaia: Ethics, Ecology, and the Erotic*, I argued "that the erotic energy that most deeply connects us with others also can point to a deeper ecological connection with all of creation."[4] What might an ethic of justice-love look like when worked out in an ecocentric rather than anthropocentric context, where right relation is understood as taking place at each level of our lives, from the erotic to the ecological, from our most intimate to our most planetary ways of connecting? Finally, what does ecology have to do with sexuality, with living out an ethic of justice-love?

In this essay I revisit the arguments of "Keeping Body and Soul Together" with these questions in mind. My thesis is that the erotic and the ecological are deeply intertwined, that the more we connect deeply with the erotic in right relation to each other and to earth, the more able we are to live ecologically in mindful, sustainable, and joyful ways. The more we re-member and re-create our connections to earth and our fellow earth creatures who share our earthly habitats, the richer, more sustainable, and more just our erotic and sexual connections to each other will be. Hence, in this essay I follow the structure and arguments of "Keeping Body and Soul Together," examining each through an "ecological hermeneutic," in hopes of deepening and expanding this already rich ethic of justice-love as right relation.

The time: a call to rethink sexuality

The authors of "Keeping Body and Soul Together" rightly begin their analysis by examining how the contemporary social-cultural context frames the perceived current crisis in sexuality. They observe at least six "upheavals in the sexual landscape" of contemporary culture that give shape to the crisis. While they focus on the social dimensions of these changes, it is worth noting in passing that several also have important ecological dimensions:

- Medical developments that have expanded sexual and reproductive choice while extending human lifespans have altered fundamentally not only intrahuman relations but how humans impact our natural environments whether through increased and increasingly toxic medical byproducts, widespread experimentation on animals for medical research, or through increased use of resources across longer and more affluent lifespans.

- The pandemic of HIV/AIDS and the broad array of other sexually transmitted diseases are as much ecologically shaped phenomena as they are socially constructed; our social-sexual patterns of behavior are embedded in ecological relations that largely shape how and why sexual diseases play out in human and nonhuman communities.

• The commercialization and exploitation of sexuality in the economic market takes place within a broader context of the commodification of virtually every aspect of the natural world. Everything from wilderness to water to wildlife increasingly is seen as a "resource" whose monetary value and contribution (or impediment) to the economy can and should be calculated to determine its "best use" for human profit.

• Deeply entrenched patterns of sexual abuse and violence, particularly against women and children, increasingly are understood as linked to abusive patterns toward nonhuman life. As ecofeminists have long argued and several studies have confirmed, for example, abuse of pets and animals is a leading indicator of abuse of women and children.[5]

While this is not the place to develop these observations in depth, they serve to remind us that human social behavior in general and sexuality in particular always take place within, and in turn deeply affect and are affected by, the broader ecological context in which we are embedded. This is illustrated especially in what the report describes as a "massive, deep-seated crisis of sexuality in this culture," a result of "a massive cultural earthquake, a loosening of the hold of an unjust patriarchal structure built on dehumanizing assumptions, roles, and relationships."[6] Symptomatic of this crisis is the burgeoning growth in the pornography industry, which typically portrays sexuality in terms of unequal relations of dominance and subordination, such that "good sex" requires inequalities of power and status between women and men that reflect and reinforce unjust patriarchal relations. The result? "Human intimacy is distorted into human estrangement, exploitation, and pain."[7]

Yet I would argue that this distortion in human relations is symptomatic not only of tears in our social fabric, but within the ecological weft and woof, as well. With the destruction of particular "nature-cultures"[8] across the globe by the march of economic globalization of the market has come the increased commodification and alienation of our relationships at all levels, to each other, to otherkind, to earth itself.[9] The authors note correctly that "how we name reality determines what we see and understand."[10] Seeing the crisis of sexuality only as part of a broader social crisis while missing the even broader grounding of the ecological crisis—or, perhaps, ecosocial crisis—is to limit and ultimately distort our understanding both of where we are and where we need to be.

What is needed today is to reframe all ethics within an ecological context and framework—*not* to lose the so-needed specificity of focus on sexuality, but to locate it accurately and comprehensively. As the authors note, the crisis in sexuality occurs within the historical movement toward gender justice and the backlash it has created, but this in turn is taking place within a broader historical movement of reorienting human relations to each other and to otherkind at all personal, social, and ecological levels. This movement is centered not only in social justice efforts to build human relations of right relation across lines of gender, race, and class, but also in ecological justice. The ethical mandate in these times of increased economic commodification and exploitation of all life is to rethink ethics as right relation at all levels, human and other. Sexual ethics and justice is a critical part of this mandate, perhaps the most intimate part for many, but it cannot and must not be separated or divorced from other dimensions of what it means to live in right relation with others. We are integrated beings, not dualistic or dichotomized constructs, who live simultaneously in webs of relationship with others—human and otherkind—that incorporate the many dimensions of who we are: physical, sexual, spiritual, emotional, mental.

This first section of the report ends by noting the church's special calling to respond to those who suffer. If "God's intention is for the full flourishing of all creation,"[11] then the church's ministry must be at the margins, where "pain sets the agenda," "from there to speak with compassion and gratitude for God's own gracious, extravagant love for this world."[12] An important challenge is not to divorce our sexual selves from our ecological selves as we move to the margins, to see how an ethic of justice-love as right relation understood ecologically as well as socially can help to reintegrate sexuality into a broader ethic of right relation at all levels of lives.

The challenge: reclaiming a passionate spirituality of justice

What would it look like to envision justice-love as right relation at all levels? The authors intuit this in arguing that our call to holiness is one of inclusive wholeness: "God's transforming and redemptive power is working not to merely preserve the holiness of the elect, but also to secure the wholeness of all persons and the integrity of creation."[13] Moreover, "to do justice-love means seeking right-relatedness with others and working to set right all wrong relations, especially distorted power dynamics of domination and subordination."[14] Key to this, the authors note, is embracing the erotic as a moral good, and the need to develop an erotic spirituality. I will return to this theme and develop it further in later sections, but I note here that the key to this is connecting the eros of humans to the eros of the earth: affirming that the erotic experienced in calling each other to intimate connection is both earthy and earthly. False dualisms separating heaven from earth, male from female, spirit from nature, and biblical from "pagan" have taught us to fear the erotic and distrust its connection to right relation. Yet eros as the "passionate desire for intimate connection," far from contradicting the justice and compassion to which we are called, is the necessary prerequisite for it. The authors note that the root of compassion is humility; the root of humility is *humus* — the earth, earthiness, soil. The eros of earth and our intimate connection to earth and hence to God is what grounds our erotic connection to each other and makes possible a passionate spirituality of justice.

The resources: authority, sources, and norms

"Keeping Body and Soul Together" gives a thoughtful overview of how the traditional Christian sources of Scripture, tradition, experience, and reason inform theological and ethical reflection about sexuality. My only reminder is that, whatever the ultimate source of these — and as Christians, we affirm that it is the Spirit that works through these to reveal God's word to us — they are always mediated by the earth. Whatever else humans are, we are embodied earth creatures. We are *of* the earth, and in a real sense we *are* earth in our make-up and identity. As feminists have re-minded us, all that we know comes through embodied, earthly experience.[15] Even that which feels disembodied is a reminder that we are grounded in earth. Sexuality in particular is an embodied, earthly, and earthy reality. As we draw on Scripture, tradition, and experience as sources, we need to remember, too, that each has also been mediated by the earth, by our bodies, in particular nature-cultures, in particular places and times. This is especially important in examining the diverse strands within Scripture on sexuality — each produced within and at least partially reflecting a particu-lar ecosocial location, a distinctive nature-culture that may or may not shed light on our own time. The same is true of tradition and experience. Locating each ecologically and socially as products of particular nature-cultures is vital for understanding the ways they may speak to us today.

Similarly, with respect to theological norms, we must include ecological sustainability and respect for earth within the norms of justice-love. The authors argue that "the theological vision of in-clusive wholeness provides us with a powerful normative vision for sexual and social relations."[16] And *ecological* relations. As ethicist Daniel Maguire reminds us about contemporary levels of ecological destruction: "If current trends continue, we will not."[17] A healthy, sustainable earth with diverse, healthy habitats is vital both for human flourishing and for God's vision of all creation flourishing together.

The problem: a patriarchal model of gender inequality and its ethic of social control

The authors of "Keeping Body and Soul Together" correctly name the primary problem of sexuality today as the patriarchal model of gender inequality and ethic of social control that forms the ground-ing of sexuality. Central to this model are dualistic understandings of reality combined with the hierarchical valuing and disvaluing of the paired opposites of each dualism. The report identifies three dualisms: body-spirit, where the superior spirit must control the in-ferior body (a source of temptation and sin, and hence to be viewed with suspicion); male-female, where historically men are active and in control while women are passive and to be controlled; and a dualism between freedom and structure, where the desire to control sex and sexuality has limited rather than enhanced our moral agency to be in responsible and freeing relation with each other. These three dualisms in turn interact, identifying men with the superior spirit and women with the inferior body (and sexuality), leading to a male-oriented ethic where women's sexuality must be controlled. Same-sex relationships have no place in such a dualistically structured and rigid world. Social relations based on sexism and heterosexism are the result.

Yet missing from this analysis is another critical dualism that has long shaped Western society and perhaps is reflected in the report itself: the dualism of nature-culture. Here nature serves as resource and passive stage for the activity of human culture, where God's central concern is human redemption. Combined with the dualisms listed above, nature has been feminized and imaged either as the nurturing "Mother Nature" who provides for (and cleans up after) male-created culture, or nature is the "wild woman" who threatens "man's" survival and hence must be domesticated and controlled.[18] Similar dualistic constructs have operated within heterosexism to identify lesbians and gay men as either "unnatural" or outside of nature (where natural sexuality is identified with procreative heterosexuality), or as too close to nature in the sense of homosexual behavior being "like animals," "lower" than what should correspond to human culture.[19]

When sexual ethics as right-relatedness refers explicitly only to the human social and cultural realm, simply assuming nature as passive backdrop, it risks reproducing the nature-culture split that has been so damaging historically both to the natural realm and those segments of human culture associated with it. Yet, as Carolyn Merchant argues, "Nature-culture dualism is a key factor in Western civilization's advance at the expense of nature....If nature and women, Indians and blacks are to be liberated from the strictures of this ideology, a radical critique of the very categories of nature and culture, as organizing concepts in all disciplines, must be undertaken."[20] The otherwise excellent structural analysis of sexuality and its social construction the authors offer is incomplete at best, and distorted at

worst, without recognizing how the nature-culture dualism has operated to help perpetuate "the unjust cultural arrangements which
stigmatize and devalue human sexual diversity."[21] Sexuality must be
understood within the realm of both nature and culture, or better,
as an integrated ecosocial reality within particular nature-cultures,
if we are to envision how best to integrate it within an ethic of right-
relatedness. This is particularly critical for responding to the report's
call to dismantle sexism and heterosexism.[22]

The possibility: gender and sexual justice and a Christian ethic of empowerment for wholeness and responsibility

The next section of "Keeping Body and Soul Together" outlines a bold
call for Christian sexual ethics to be grounded in gender and sexual
justice that fosters moral agency in each of us to bring wholeness and
responsibility to all of our relations, sexual and otherwise. Critical to
this is moving away from focusing on questions of form rather than
substance in sexual relationships—such as whether the relationships
are heterosexual in form, or whether the formal context is state- and
church-recognized heterosexual marriage, rather than whether such
ethically vital criteria such as mutual consent, respect, fidelity, and
commitment structure all of our relationships, regardless of their
form. They note "an ethic centered upon formal criteria...can unwittingly allow persons to fixate, for example, on whether persons
are properly conforming to patriarchal norms. Substantive questions
about justice and love are simply skirted."[23]

I affirm that this is the necessary shift in focus and grounding
required for sexual ethics in our time. But again, the grounding
must be expanded to include attention to other dimensions of justice
that shape profoundly the possibilities for realizing such qualities
as authentic mutuality, consent, and agency in our relationships.
Elsewhere in this collection other authors have drawn attention to
several of these dimensions: Mary Hobgood, for example, examines
the place of economic justice in an ethic of sexuality while Kelly
Brown Douglas poses a similar question on issues of race and sexuality. The authors of "Keeping Body and Soul Together" also recognize
this, in arguing in this section that

personal meanings of human sexuality and institutional dynamics and policy issues must be reshaped to assure greater
well-being and dignity for all persons. We are social beings,
and the quality of our interpersonal relations is, to a great
extent, dependent upon the quality of our social-institutional
dynamics . . . love flourishes only where justice is secured.

To this I would integrate attention to ecological justice as a critical grounding for at least two intertwined reasons. First, for the
flourishing of human relations in general, and sexuality in particular, ecological sustainability is a vital prerequisite. Matters of human
justice and flourishing simply cannot take place without healthy
and whole habitats within which our relations take place. This is
particularly critical for the most marginalized within human communities. It is precisely the economically oppressed, and especially
communities of color, who most suffer the effects of ecological degra-
dation. The resultant poverty and adverse effects on human health
sharply undercut the possibilities for right relation and result in
social conditions of violence and abuse that typically manifest themselves at the most intimate levels of relationship and against the most
vulnerable sectors of society, namely, women and children. Second,
integrating ecological justice with other dimensions of justice as the
grounding of an ethic of sexuality will continue to remind us that our
relations take place within a broader ecosocial context, and that the
goal of an ethic of sexuality is to integrate it within a broader ethic
of right relation at all levels of life.

Attention to two further aspects of this ethic can facilitate this
more comprehensive integration. First, there is the issue of epis-
temology: how we see and know reality. Liberation and feminist
theologians have sensitized us to the fact that where we stand, where
we are located in the social fabric, shapes how we see and understand reality. This needs to be expanded to examine where we each
stand within our respective ecological-social fabrics, our particular
"nature-cultures," as ethicist Nancie Erhard terms it. An anthropocentric lens, whether consciously or unconsciously, too often simply
filters out nonhuman nature as part of the reality "that counts" in
moral reflection. Right relation then corresponds only to the human

realm, leaving unexamined the quality of our relations to other dimensions of nonhuman nature and how they impact and are impacted by our sexuality. Hence the "epistemological privilege of the oppressed"[24] that liberationist theologies and ethics employ must include an ecological dimension in acknowledging that nonhuman otherkind, as well as marginalized sectors of the human community, make up the oppressed whose perspectives on reality are now centered in moral reflection. An ethic of responsibility and wholeness viewed from an ecoliberationist standpoint sees this responsibility extending to, and wholeness experienced within, the whole of the particular nature-cultures where each of us is located.

Second, the authors rightly lift up two elements critical to a revisioned sexual ethic of empowerment for wholeness and responsibility: valuing the goodness of our created sexuality and commitment to reclaiming eros and passion. Our sexual ethics needs to remember constantly that we share these embodied realities in continuity with the nonhuman members of our world, and that an ethic of right relation celebrates that our connectedness with nonhuman nature — particularly our sexuality — is an integral part of our created goodness and moral calling. For too long the nature-culture and body-spirit dualisms that have shaped the Western, European Christian heritage have consigned sexuality to the inferior nature/body realm. In reclaiming the goodness of our embodied sexual selves, we must not inadvertently divorce ourselves from the rest of nature where our embodied, sexual selves are located. Hence, the report's stated commitment to guaranteeing "the bodily integrity and self-direction of every person"[25] is an ethical vision that should inform not only our intrahuman relations, but our relations with all of God's created body-selves.

Eros itself is perhaps the most embodied energy we have that connects us simultaneously to each other, to God, and to nonhuman nature. The authors argue the need to convey "the divine eros as intrinsic to God's own energy and God's passion for connection and communion,"[26] to which I would add "to all of creation." The joyful pleasure of the erotic experienced in right relation is central to our moral calling and is one of the deepest sources of knowing our interconnectedness with others. The converse is also true: when we repress or cut ourselves off from eros, that energy does not disappear, but rather typically reappears in distorted forms of abuse: physical, mental, emotional, spiritual. When our sexuality and spirituality are integrated within the eros of right relation at all levels of our lives, it results in what Marvin Ellison aptly has termed a "spirituality of earthly delight."[27] Moral agency for right relation lies in reintegrating the erotic and the ecological, connection and communion at each level of living.[28] As Terry Tempest Williams has noted, "D. H. Lawrence writes: 'There exist two great modes of life—the religious and the sexual. Eroticism is the bridge.'"[29]

The patterns: enhancing and protecting intimacy and right-relatedness

"Keeping Body and Soul Together" closes the first section with the charge to seek "an eroticism that is both pleasurable and ethically principled,"[30] where we celebrate the gifts of community and intimacy, honor the diversity of families, and respect both partnered and single persons as sexual-spiritual persons. What might this charge look like understood within an explicitly ecological context? What might it mean to celebrate community and intimacy, to honor diversity within our total nature-cultures, ecologically and socially?

I believe the key to beginning to respond to these questions lies in rediscovering and reclaiming eros as that passion for connection and communion at all levels of our lives.[31] Terry Tempest Williams captures this intuition brilliantly in her book *Red: Passion and Patience in the Desert*. In her essay "The Erotic Landscape," she writes, "Eroticism, being in relation, calls the inner life into play. No longer numb, we feel the magnetic pull in our bodies toward something stronger, more vital than simply ourselves. Arousal becomes a dance with longing. We form a secret partnership with possibility."[32] She goes on to ask, "I wonder what walls we have constructed to keep our true erotic nature tamed. And I am curious why we continue to distance ourselves from natural sources."[33] Throughout *Red*, Williams describes her erotic encounters in connecting to different elements of the natural world in the red rock country of her native Utah: a morning wrapped in the limbs of a gnarled juniper, joining with friends to rub mud from the Little Colorado River all over their bodies, strad-dling her body on slick rock as water drips slowly onto her from a slot in a canyon wall. Beyond the pure pleasure of these moments comes a deep sense of connectedness that leads to a deeper sense of know-ing: knowing oneself in relation to that which one has experienced intimately.

It is the fear of this intimate knowledge through erotic connection that emerges in distorted eros, particularly the objectification of the other that characterizes pornography. Drawing on the work of Audre Lorde, Williams wonders:

> Could it be that what we fear most is our capacity to feel, and so we annihilate symbolically and physically that which is beauti-ful and tender, anything that dares us to consider our creative selves? The erotic world is silenced, reduced to a collection of objects we can curate and control, be it a vase, a woman, or wilderness. Our lives become a piece in the puzzle of pornogra-phy as we go through the motions of daily intercourse without any engagement of the soul.[34]

I believe it is this engagement of the soul in all our motions that makes the erotic the needed grounding for an ethic of right rela-tion. And, as Williams writes, the fullest engagement of the soul takes place when we reintegrate the erotic in our body-selves with all of nature around and within us: "Here lies our dilemma as human be-ings: Nothing exists in isolation. We need a context for eros, not a pedestal, not a video screen. The lightning we witness crack and charge the night sky in the desert is the same electricity we feel in our-selves whenever we dare to touch flesh, rock, body, Earth. We must take our love outdoors where reciprocity replaces voyeurism, respect replaces indulgence."[35]

To be in relation with everything around us is an inescapable char-acteristic of who we are as earth creatures. To be in right relation with everything around us and within us is our moral and spiritual calling. Keeping body, soul, *and earth* together is the necessary place to start for visioning a sexual ethic of right relation at all levels of our lives.

Notes

1. Terry Tempest Williams, *Red: Passion and Patience in the Desert* (New York: Pantheon Books, 2001), 104.
2. *Presbyterians and Human Sexuality 1991* (Louisville: Presbyterian Church [U.S.A.], 1991), 9.
3. Ibid., 7.
4. Daniel T. Spencer, *Gay and Gaia: Ethics, Ecology, and the Erotic* (Cleveland: Pilgrim, 1996), 4.
5. See, for example, Carol J. Adams, "Woman Battering and Harm to Animals," in *Animals and Women: Feminist Theoretical Explorations*, ed. Carol J. Adams and Josephine Donovan (Durham, N.C.: Duke University Press, 1995), 55–84; Carol J. Adams, *The Sexual Politics of Meat: A Feminist-Vegetarian Critical Theory* (New York: Continuum, 1990); and Carol J. Adams, *Neither Man nor Beast: Feminism and the Defense of Animals* (New York: Continuum, 1994).
6. *Presbyterians and Human Sexuality 1991*, 3.
7. Ibid.
8. Ethicist Nancie Erhard has coined the term "nature-culture" to remind us that the moral habitats we inhabit are inextricably linked to the biophysical habitats we know as home, that historically nature and culture have developed together in particular places into interwoven "nature-culture" communities of people, animals, plants, and place. See Nancie Erhard, "Moral Habitat: Ethos and Agency for the Sake of Earth," Ph.D. dissertation, Union Theological Seminary, New York, 2002.
9. For an excellent analysis of how the increasing globalization of capitalist economies has led to a thorough commodification of sex and sexuality, distorting or blocking the capacity of the erotic to serve as a vehicle of justice and mutuality, see Marvin M. Ellison, *Erotic Justice: A Liberating Ethic of Sexuality* (Louisville: Westminster John Knox, 1996).
10. *Presbyterians and Human Sexuality 1991*, 3.
11. Ibid., 7.
12. Ibid., 6.
13. Ibid., 7.
14. Ibid., 9.
15. See, for example, Joan L. Griscom, "On Healing the Nature/History Split in Feminist Thought," *Heresies: A Feminist Publication on Art and Politics* 4, no. 1 (1981); Isabel Carter Heyward, *The Redemption of God: A Theology of Mutual Relation* (Washington, D.C.: University Press of America, 1982); Carter Heyward, *Touching Our Strength: The Erotic as Power and the Love of God* (San Francisco: Harper & Row, 1989); Rosemary Radford Ruether, "Toward an Ecological-Feminist Theology of Nature," in *Readings in Ecology and Feminist Theology*, ed. Mary Heather MacKinnon and Moni McIntyre (Kansas City, Mo.: Sheed and Ward, 1995), 89–93; and Susan Griffin, "Split Culture," in *Readings in Ecology and Feminist Theology*, 94–104.
16. *Presbyterians and Human Sexuality 1991*, 13.
17. Daniel Maguire, *The Moral Core of Judaism and Christianity: Reclaiming the Revolution* (Minneapolis: Fortress, 1993), 13.

18. For a historical analysis of how these images have emerged and operated in Western culture, see Carolyn Merchant, *The Death of Nature: Women, Ecology, and the Scientific Revolution* (San Francisco: HarperCollins, 1980).

19. See Spencer, *Gay and Gaia,* 80–81, for discussion of these constructs and how they operate within sexism and heterosexism.

20. Merchant, *The Death of Nature,* 143–44.

21. *Presbyterians and Human Sexuality 1991,* 16.

22. For a detailed analysis of this, see Spencer, *Gay and Gaia,* especially chapters 3 and 4.

23. *Presbyterians and Human Sexuality 1991,* 19.

24. For a helpful discussion of the epistemological privilege of the poor and oppressed in Latin American liberation theologies, see José Míguez Bonino, *Toward a Christian Political Ethics* (Philadelphia: Fortress, 1983), 42–44. Alice Walker in *The Color Purple* (New York: Harcourt Brace Jovanovich, 1982) makes a similar point when her character, Celie, quotes her lover Shug in remarking, "You have to git man off your eyeball, before you can see anything a'tall" (168).

25. *Presbyterians and Human Sexuality 1991,* 22.

26. Ibid., 21.

27. Ellison, *Erotic Justice,* 121. Note that I am *not* here calling for a romanticizing of our relations to nonhuman nature. There is much in the natural world that is destructive to human well-being as there is in our human communities. Romanticizing eros, whether directed toward other humans or nonhuman nature, distorts the resulting relationships by not allowing us to see and experience the other within the other's authenticity. Rather romantic love projects a false image onto the other and in relating to that image does damage to the integrity of the other in relation. Though it is hard work, I believe that an ethic of right relation at all levels calls us to guard against romanticizing our relations and thus avoiding the hard work of relating authentically to others, both human and otherkind, who are both deeply connected to and different from us.

28. For further development of this claim, see Spencer, *Gay and Gaia,* chapter 11: "Erotic Ecology: Interconnection and Right Relation at All Levels."

29. Williams, *Red,* 109.

30. *Presbyterians and Human Sexuality 1991,* 23.

31. Perhaps prophetically, just as I was trying to type this line, Ellie, my cat, chose that moment to leap onto my lap, rubbing herself against my chest and purring loudly, insisting on a moment of interspecies communion, connection, and eros!

32. Williams, *Red,* 106.

33. Ibid.

34. Ibid., 108.

35. Ibid., 111.

20

Coming to Our Senses

Erotic and Economic Discipleship and
the Transformation of Gender

Mary E. Hobgood

"For the church to minister adequately to the realities of people's lives," insists the 1991 Presbyterian report on human sexuality, "there must be a critical assessment of our cultural context and of the social forces which shape and misshape human sexuality personally and corporately." Additionally, the report maintains that it is important to do a structural analysis of sexuality in order to "pay attention" to the "social meanings" that are given to our sexuality.[1] Such convictions indicate a clear realization: human sexuality is not simply a matter of personal experience and ethical decision-making, but also something structurally located within the entire fabric of complex social institutions.

In the material and ideological world of twenty-first-century capitalism, it is impossible to understand homophobia and the oppressive, exploitative dimensions of the Western sexual system without exploring how gender and heterosexuality have been thoroughly harnessed to the needs of capitalism. The social meanings given to sexuality (like the social meanings given to race, religion, culture, and all facets of capitalist life) are always in dialogue with economic arrangements.

While the Presbyterian report alludes to such connections, much work remains for their full articulation. This essay seeks to contribute to that work. I use a materialist feminist approach, which claims that relations of production under capitalism (not culture, consciousness, or discourse) have primacy in grounding all social relations and, therefore, should be the starting point for liberation theory and transforming praxis. All differences, including sexual difference and identity, have been shaped to support capitalism's dual drive to accumulate surplus profit and achieve elite managerial control over human bodies and their environments.[2] In this essay I argue that capitalist goals of limitless profit making and managerial control require (and reproduce) a system of gender polarization in order to function adequately.

Gender polarization, or what I am calling *heterogender,* includes the notion that men and women, instead of sharing a common humanity, are "opposites" in attributes and talents. When social benefits and burdens are unfairly distributed between men and women, heterogender provides the rationale. Heterogender also reinforces a powerful set of beliefs that teach people to fear and devalue embodiment and the sensuous world. Moreover, the abstract, anti-body, and hierarchical values and behaviors deemed appropriate to persons gendered as male are considered superior to the concerns about embodiment, care giving, and communal well-being associated with persons gendered as female.

As we will see, both family and economic systems serve "masculine" goals of hierarchy and profit making. Scholars have identified the alternative values of loyalty and community building as "social capital."[3] However, human connection and the nurturing work that enables social capital are "feminized," disparaged, and largely unrealized in capitalist political economy, precisely because such feminized values interfere with the power-over relations sought by domestic and foreign policy. In demeaning what has been associated with women's communities and the "feminine," both the economic and erotic systems erode human potential to live in just relationships with ourselves, others, the nonhuman world, and God. By not respecting human limitation and vulnerability, both power-over eroticism and cutthroat capitalism are dangerous to all life because they ignore our radical interdependence with each other and the larger world. This essay explores ways in which the economic and erotic systems work in tandem to create hierarchy and desensitize people to our mutual vulnerability and consequent need for connection and just relations with others. Capitalist eroticism precludes consciousness of a shared vulnerability that is the absolute precondition for an ethical sexuality.[4]

As I focus on the interconnection of the sex-gender and economic systems, I assume a dialectical relationship between the major systems within our political economy. That is, I assume that capitalist eroticism is both shaped by and reinforces the economic system and, furthermore, that the economic system is both shaped by and reinforces the sex-gender system. To interfere with one is to threaten or destabilize the other. Otherwise said, the sex-gender system under capitalism is also an economic system, and the economic system is a thoroughly gendered system. Each depends on the other to function. Both sexual *and* economic justice and, indeed, the survival of our own humanity and of the sensuous world itself depend on transforming the gender system. My contention is that the structures and ideology of heterogender, which disparage interdependence while sacralizing power-over relations, comprise the "social forces" and "cultural context" for both erotic and economic injustices that the Presbyterian report urges us to examine.

In an earlier essay on the dialectical relationship of the sex-gender and economic systems, I focused primarily on the marriage relationship within capitalism.[5] Here I extend consideration of the capitalist gender system beyond the sexual regulation of traditional marriage. In particular, I focus on work and culture: the importance of heterogender for the primacy of low-wage work in the global economy and the increasing amounts of unpaid labor in the marriage economy; the proliferation of "masculinized" technologies that sell limitless virtual realities to desensitized people; and the erosion of social capital insofar as masculinized values, behaviors, and products monopolize family and civic life. In expanding the capitalist erotic beyond the marriage relationship, I have moved from a focus on enabling pluralism in sexual relationships to an equally important focus on being faithful to relation or connection. The critique of erotic connection based on ownership, the subject of my previous work, is amplified here by a critical assessment of how the political economy interferes with authentic erotic connection. We need better assessments of the various obstacles to sensuous connection that are now proliferating in capitalist culture. While the following discussion hardly exhausts how erotic life is distorted by economic imperatives, I believe it extends the analysis needed about the social forces that are misshaping human sexuality.

As I hope the ensuing discussion will illuminate, nonconformity to the behaviors and values of the prevailing sex-gender system poses certain dangers to capitalism, including the erosion of work hierarchies, the destabilization of heterosexist consumer-oriented marriage, and the transformation of cultural values that disparage care giving. In addition, the fear that gender fluidity will unsettle the status quo necessitates that so-called queers, that is nonconformists to the sex/gender system, suffer multiple forms of social hatred. Gay, lesbian, bisexual, and transgender people are under enormous pressure to assimilate and be co-opted by becoming *de*sexualized, *dis*passionate, and "good" (read safe). Queers may receive some measure of acceptance if they become as sexually and politically predictable ("normal") as everyone else. However, whenever they defy heteronormativity by their appearance, social scripts, sexual practice, and social values, and whenever they refuse to assimilate into suburbia, become lucrative markets for corporations, or mimic marriage in their partnerships, they threaten not only the sexual system but also the political economy itself.

The extent of this challenge is enormous. As a consequence, the pressure toward co-optation is real and powerful. Gaining a deeper understanding of how gender polarization and heterosexist marriage are essential to maintaining capitalist culture and political economy will help us see that homophobia is not just a matter of mistaken attitudes. It is rather a pillar of the complex political economy that surrounds us. No one challenges it without paying a price. Furthermore, liberation from homophobia, I contend, is not possible without economic justice and cultural transformation.

Heterogender and the marriage economy

Philosopher Linda Singer connects the erotic and economic sectors of political economy by observing that "in capitalism workers are constantly in the position of having to exchange their bodily capacities for wages or marriage."[6] No matter the goods of marriage some individuals enjoy, and no matter the advantages U.S. women within the top 20 percent of income earners have gained, most women, especially those with children, require a partner for economic support. Since wages have always been insufficient for most women to

sustain themselves and their families comfortably, marriage has offered the best economic arrangement for most (not to mention men
who benefit from women's unpaid sexual, household, and nurturing
labor).

At the beginning of this millennium, the Washington-based Center
for Policy Alternatives reported that in twenty-four states the me-
dian income of full-time employed women was below the federal
poverty line.[7] This situation well serves capitalist political economy
by making the majority of women economically dependent on marriage and the system of heterogender. Their economic dependence
justifies both their unpaid labor in marriage and their low wages in
the labor market. In addition, heterogendered marriage guarantees
free domestic labor for a majority of male workers who remain stag-
nant or downwardly mobile in the lower sectors of the working class.[8]
The fact that men as a group receive sexual and domestic services
from women helps elite investors by assuaging men's exploitation
in the work place. Marriage also guarantees the free reproduction of
the next generation of taxpayers and workers. As a consequence, the
marriage system helps keep social reproduction as cost effective as
possible.

Today's low-wage economy is particularly dependent on the marriage structure, as evidenced by the Bush administration's proposal
to use $300 million of scarce welfare funds for marriage promo-
tion programs for poor women.[9] Pushing poor women into marriage
will supposedly serve to cut down on welfare spending and free up
even more of the public treasury for corporate raiding. Perhaps even
more importantly, having increasing numbers of women married
normalizes sexual services, reproduction, cleaning, and care giving
as unpaid (slave) labor. This, as previously noted, is essential for
justifying the underpaid, super-exploited labor of most workers in
an economy that increasingly generates low-wage service sector jobs
that resemble housework.

In summary, while marriage and family structures are in enormous transition, the ideology of their traditional forms serves as a
powerful regulating ideal in the service of capitalism. The marriage
system naturalizes reproductive (including nurturing and household) labor as unpaid. It regulates sex in the service of work discipline and produces surplus erotic needs that can become another

site for selling products and making profits. Under such conditions, Singer contends, the traditional family no longer produces sufficient reproduction or erotic satisfaction for free, but instead has turned itself into a site of consumption where fertility clinics, adoption and surrogacy agencies, fast-food franchises, and providers of maid, nanny, and sexual services can expand profits. As she concludes, the point of capitalist marriage is to "expand the ways and forms in which sexuality, both reproductive and erotic, can become [a source for profits] and [can] preserve sexual [and female-gendered] labor which is ideally unpaid."[10] The marriage system, therefore, teaches the very youngest members of society the necessity of social hierarchy and socializes people to be compliant within a status quo organized around consumerism and dominant/subordinate relations.

Heterogender and the global economy: women's labor as the glue of globalization

Gender polarization is crucial to the functioning of capitalist society because it also creates a sexual division of labor that benefits capitalists globally. This hierarchalizes the value of human labor and justifies the super-exploitation of female workers and racially subordinated men who are "feminized" insofar as their market work becomes associated with women's free (slave) household labor. Twenty-first-century structures of class and race are overlaid with the gender system to create a super-exploited global working class comprised primarily of poor women of color. As Rose M. Brewer observes, these arrangements make the class system invisible, as if sexism, racism, and the culture of meritocracy alone could explain why current structures of capitalism produce increasing amounts of low-wage work and the "economic lock-out" of the global majority.[11]

Gender in capitalist society is really heterogender in the service of a marriage system that allows men to benefit from women's unpaid domestic labor. Heterogender also allows investors in a service economy to benefit from the underpaid market labor of all workers, male and female, who are engaged in the public extension of housework. It has become increasingly important to characterize work done by women and "feminized" men as less valuable because almost 80 percent of new jobs in the U.S. economy are low-wage service sector jobs.[12] Who will do this work if not properly heterogendered women or men who fail to meet the requirements of masculinized white affluent status? How will the economy continue unobstructed if the gender and race systems cease to hide the fact that low wages for the many are essential to profits for the few? It becomes clear, as well, that homophobia serves as a crucial tool of the economic system, because it enforces gender polarization and normalizes the exploitation of "less valuable" laborers.

Neocolonialist "structural adjustment policies" rely on heterogender to meet what has become an escalating crisis in capitalism. This crisis is intensifying because the structural need for limitless profits creates growing contradictions in the economic system. The crisis includes the destruction of resources and ecosystems, as well as making all aspects of life into products, from family needs and civic life to all of sensuous reality. Indeed, the disparagement of the sensuous feminized world is essential to the newest arena of masculinized profit making, the production of technologized (virtual) realities sold for profits. Such dynamics of the capitalist engine generate a number of problems: impoverished worker-consumers; saturated markets (since increasingly fewer people can buy); the decimation of health, education, and welfare for the many (since services are privatized to yield profits for the few); gross pollution of air, water, and land; depleted natural resources; cutthroat competition; and intensifying income polarization everywhere. In turn these conditions necessitate "quick fix" policies.

In response to cutthroat competition, national and global policies encourage unlimited access to even cheaper workers and resources, a tendency that places more and more workers at the bottom of the economic hierarchy. To address impoverished worker-consumers and saturated markets, quick-fix policies endorse a relentless search through "free trade" for untapped markets throughout the world. This gives advantage to the economically powerful, but at the horrific cost of destroying struggling local economies. Because competition in this atmosphere also makes corporate survival more tenuous, taxpayers' money is less likely appropriated for the collective good and

instead is diverted to bail out "corporate citizens." Globalization policies favor this raiding of public treasuries through tax breaks for
the rich and subsidies to corporations. Corporate interests, under increasing stress from the internal contradictions of the system, force
national governments to come to their rescue by passing neoliberal
economic reforms. These so-called reform policies massively reduce
labor costs and environmental protection even further, again for the
immediate benefit of capitalist lending institutions and corporate
profit-making endeavors.[13] Because of the long-term effects of these
policies, this neoliberal cure is worse than the capitalist disease.

When economies are hit with decreased public spending on such
necessities as health, education, welfare, low-income housing, and
transportation, one of the consequences is an increase in women's
unpaid labor. Under policies of globalization, Two-Thirds World
women are not only increasing their unpaid family labor, they are
also increasingly exporting their underpaid wage work abroad. To
benefit investors and serve the luxury needs of the world's affluent
minority, poor countries have always been export platforms for agricultural and other products. Now they are diversifying their exports
as the process of relentless exploitation penetrates every last possible
resource for profit generation. Poor countries are exporting not only
their children for adoption into affluent families in the First World,
but also their children's mothers. As women and families find themselves unable to absorb the costs of globalization policies, women's
nurture and care are becoming major exports from poor countries
and fueling new industries. In her study of immigrant workers in the
global economy, Grace Chang shows how women's exported sexual,
household, and nurturing work is increasingly the glue that makes
capitalism work in both Two-Thirds and First World countries.[14]

Women's labor provides the economic glue that keeps poor countries afloat while also meeting the needs of the affluent minority in
First World countries whose own public sector is eroding through
policies of economic "reform." Through the remittances they send
home, migrant women sex-workers, domestic laborers, nannies, and
health-care workers hold up Two-Thirds world economies, decimated
by centuries of capitalist colonialism, neocolonialism, and now globalization. They also offer the more affluent in First World countries

an opportunity to acquire cheap "women's work" as their own welfare state is being dismantled. Their labor, often illegal, creates a super-exploitable low-wage labor force, often in competition with welfare workers in the host country.[15]

By this means, the government-corporate-military alliance in affluent countries creates an expanding sector of indentured and sub-minimum-wage workers. As a consequence, low-paid women immigrants of color, including those with nursing degrees, are becoming the backbone of certain service industries, including the U.S. for-profit hospital and the home health care industries.[16] In addition, even educated Two-Thirds World women, among them Filipinas with college degrees, are providing affluent families in the First World with housecleaning, nanny services, and after-school care. This enables a minority of First World women professionals to pursue both careers and the paychecks necessary for upper-income lifestyles, even as their own public sector is diminishing. In the globalizing economy, class and race structures deeply condition the experience of gender.[17]

In Linda Singer's words, "Traditional liberal concerns for civil rights, individual freedom, right to privacy, and the principles of equality and equity" are no match for the "social logic that advocates increased surveillance and regulation of bodies in ways that support and reproduce hegemonic relationships of dominance."[18] A structural analysis of the sex-gender system begins to probe the extent to which human sexuality and the gender system have been thoroughly harnessed to the needs of capitalist profit-making and managerial control. Furthermore, such analysis demonstrates why challenging homophobia is so threatening in capitalist society. Homophobia, a chief enforcer of heterogender, is not just a matter of mistaken attitudes. It is a main pillar of the global economy.

Heterogender and the proliferation of an anti-body technological culture

An economic system based on individualism and profits for the few requires a culture to support it. To aid the processes of profit making for investors, capitalist culture diminishes healthy sensory experiences and tries to reproduce all of life, including social relations and the material world, into saleable products (commodities). Disparaging values and modes of interconnection that have emanated from women's communities, including underpaying caregiving work and disrespecting requirements for healthy interdependence, keeps people from coming to their senses. Capitalist values and practices force people to comply with structures and behaviors that promote "masculine" unshared power arrangements, including honoring social hierarchies and domination over the nonhuman world. Without values and behaviors that honor reciprocity, interdependence, mutually pleasurable touch, delight in the sensuous world, and nurturing care, people suffer impoverishment in their ability to be emotionally, spiritually, and physically connected to themselves and others. It is, therefore, important to deepen understanding of how gender-polarized values and practices endanger our bodily, familial, and civic lives.

The highly regulated sexual system of compulsory heterosexual monogamy is not the only element in capitalist material and ideological environments that disconnects people from their bodies, emotions, and experience of the world. Ethicist Linda Holler discusses how the ubiquitous presence of both sensory deprivation and sensory overload are key factors in promoting the "flight from the body." A culture saturated by technological advertising and the consumption of endless virtual worlds creates material environments that disconnect us emotionally and morally from ourselves, others, and the nonhuman world.[19] These disembodied environments have enormous consequences for knowledge and relationships. Not only our ability to relate to others but cognitive knowledge itself is rooted in the quality of our sensory experiences. Quite simply, Holler says, human touch alters brain chemistry.[20] Touch, or lack of it, alters our intellectual capacity, either increasing or diminishing it. Our bodies, brains, and social/material environments are connected in an unending dialectic.[21]

A healthy person is one who has found the right balance in sensory experience, including a preponderance of nurturing touch. People with too little sensory experience, such as children who are neglected or people who spend most of their waking hours in computer-created worlds, are disconnected from their bodies and potentially diminished in their capacity to form satisfying social relations. People lacking rich sensory experience and loving interaction with others are alienated from feelings and from their potential to relate to themselves and others. *Being emotionally numb and under-related to the material and social world, they become unaware of the true consequences of their actions and have a high tolerance to inflict pain.* They also are susceptible to feeling disorders such as autism (being overwhelmed by sensory experience) and schizophrenia (being overcome by thought processes).[22] It is not difficult to imagine using such terms to characterize the antiseptic culture of government bureaucracies, military tribunals, corporate boardrooms, church hierarchies, and academic offices.

Since health is found in sensory balance, an overload of sensory experience functions similarly to sensory deprivation by alienating people from themselves. Such sensory overload, so ubiquitous in capitalist society, is engendered by violence and trauma, by constant bombardment of advertisements and excessive amounts of information, and by the stress of capitalist work schedules.[23] As previously noted, lack of balanced sensory experience is thought to be at the root of most addictions whenever people "substitute anesthetizing behavior for encounter and intimacy."[24] Whether through sensory deprivation, sensory overload, or both, it is clear that opportunities for bodily alienation proliferate in capitalist societies. Whenever people do not feel at home in their bodies, their ability to realize their vulnerability and interdependence is impeded, as is their ability to perceive the true impact of their actions. The morality of social relations is thereby placed in jeopardy.

Heterogender and the erosion of social capital in family and civic life

Lack of balanced sensory connection is due not only to technologized culture, but also to increasing stresses on the family, given the labor market of twenty-first-century capitalism. In keeping with Linda Singer's observation of the family as a site of increasing consumption, economists David Cecil and Julia Heath claim that the family, traditionally a primary source of nurturing touch, is being universally transformed by overwork and commodification.[25] Nurturing, reciprocal activities in constant interaction with the sensuous world, such as baking, cooking, gardening, cleaning, bathing, and reading together, are being eroded in family life. Not only are adult women and men working outside the home for longer hours than previous generations, the nurturing, reciprocal activities of family life are being sold for profit in the service economy. In the stressed two-earner family, household activities are increasingly being "contracted out." As Cecil and Heath point out, "The rich tapestry of human relations [in families] is reduced to transient [impersonal] exchanges."[26] Sensuous activities are withering that engender non-market values of loyalty, trust, reciprocity, interdependence, continuity, and sharing—activities regarded as social capital and defined by Cecil and Heath as "encompassing the binding relationships of caring labor [and] also civic engagement."[27] The low-wage service economy is hardly an ethical substitute for the social capital that values caring labor and is oriented toward mutual delight and the common good. (Cecil and Heath also argue that eventually the erosion of social capital will contribute to the demise of the market system itself because markets require some modicum of social cohesion to function.[28])

Increasingly, interactions that express human feeling are being replaced with impersonal, profit-oriented activity in an electronically mediated "virtual" world. We are in peril when the social capital necessary for friendship, intimacy, fulfilling social relations, and planetary survival is so rapidly diminishing. What Linda Holler calls "culturally induced feeling disorders" are on the rise. Their fallout is found in myriad forms of addiction and violence.[29] In this context, coming to our senses is truly subversive activity and the *sine qua non* of ethical practice, family and community well-being, and survival itself.

Finally, there is a direct relationship between increased self-alienation and rising authoritarianism, but how does constricted sexuality, lack of nurturing touch, sensory deprivation and overload, and the disparagement of service in low-wage commodification promote the intensification of hierarchy, authoritarianism, addiction, and abuse? As a beginning point, I find Mark D. Jordan's assessment of authoritarianism in the Roman Catholic hierarchy instructive. In *The Silence of Sodom: Homosexuality in Modern Catholicism,* Jordan provides an interpretation of the connection between self-contempt and the power-over dynamics of ecclesiastical hierarchy.[30] He suggests that the power-over dynamics of hierarchy and infallibility are connected to the deep self-alienation of the men who run the church, especially homophobic men who are alienated from their masculinity and often from their own sexual orientation as gay men. As Jordan explains, the machinery of the hierarchy provides the means by which homophobic gay men oppress other gay men and, I would add, white women and people of color who are over-associated with their bodies and sexuality.

Feminist theologian Carol Christ makes a similar observation: theologians who show contempt for their own limitations often seek relief and distraction by creating an anti-sensual theology that aids them in denying both their self-hate and their connections to vulnerable others.[31] Authoritarianism and abuse of others is intimately linked to alienation from one's body, emotions, sensuality, and need for interdependence. The poet W. H. Auden recognized this phenomenon when he acknowledged that "as a rule it was the pleasure-haters that became unjust."[32]

Conclusion

This analysis begins to explore the depth of "the [economic] forces which shape and misshape human sexuality" and our ability for friendship, intimacy, and democratic community life.[33] It is increasingly clear that the systems of gender polarization and heterosexist marriage are absolutely essential to the sexual division of labor that makes the unpaid and underpaid labor of providing care seem "natural." This gender division is also increasingly essential to the profit-making needs of capitalism. Feminized labor undergirds the global capitalist economy as profits become ever more dependent on all types of devalued service work.

However, the unjust organization of work in family and society is not the only goal of heterogender. As noted, the sex-gender system also has a powerful set of cultural beliefs that teach people to fear embodiment and sensuality and to disrespect the fundamental human need for connection with others. Philosopher Ann Ferguson agrees with economist Deborah Stone that revitalized family and civic life (and, I would add, the very transformation of gender) depend on developing an oppositional cultural politic that seeks to increase the market value of caring labor.[34] This politic must also seek to transform a culture that numbs people with sensory deprivation and overload and fuels an addictive, authoritarian society. Our society is fast becoming out of sync with spiritual and ecological realties and at home only in isolated virtual worlds.

The practice and meaning of gender and sexuality, as orchestrated in the family and global economies, tolerate only what supports the powerful. Given the extent to which the sex-gender system has been made to serve capitalism, many scholars argue that we do not yet have a theory and practice of sexuality (or economics for that matter) adequate to the human libido.[35] How could we, when sexuality and intimacy require honest sharing of our reality? Capitalist society encourages flight from reality and from the vulnerability, finitude, and interdependence that define who we are. As Karen Lebacqz contends, there is no ethical sexuality — and, as this essay argues, no ethical economy — without acknowledgment that we are vulnerable persons who require right relations with one another and with the nonhuman world for our happiness and survival. It is, of course, more difficult to imagine what good and just erotic-economic arrangements would look like than it is to critique unjust erotic-economic systems. Sadly, outrageously, we are a people grossly underexposed to a full spectrum of erotic and economic possibility. Consequently, as Mark Jordan suggests, serious moral assessments of homosexuality (and, indeed, of all sexual and economic practice) must await a time when women and men of diverse sexualities, races, and classes can truly enjoy a context of freedom.[36]

While inaugurating a meaningful erotic and economic discipleship requires many things, understanding the connections between sexuality and political economy makes clear that economic transformation and fundamental change in class relations are necessary for an ethical sexuality. Granted, making connections between the sexual and political economies is a novel thing to do, especially because

Christian reflection on sex has historically focused largely on the behavior of individuals. However, sexual relations are not the product of discrete individual relations alone, nor is sexuality what happens only between individuals. Rather, at any given moment our sexuality is what is allowed or promoted by massive social systems, especially the economic one. As this exploration has made clear, our sexuality is thoroughly infused with values and power arrangements rooted in a capitalist economic system. It is, therefore, past time for churches to deprivatize their understanding of human sexuality and sexual morality.

The problem for gay, lesbian, bisexual, and transgender people, as Nicola Field suggests, is not heterosexism. Rather, the problem is a political economy that requires (male-dominant) heterosexuality to be the normative pattern for social and sexual relating.[37] Given this key insight, the struggle necessary to undo heterosexism and homophobia will be formidable. In conjunction with the market's requirement to make profits from family life, civic relations, and the material world, heterogendered values and practices further erode social capital. When humans, gay and non-gay alike, have little opportunity to engage in nonmarket relations, we are impoverished in our ability to create reciprocal, trusting, and interdependent relations. As a consequence, our emotional, spiritual, communal, and sexual lives—our very humanity—are at stake.

Activities that are deeply rooted in human touch and sensuous connection increase social capital and our capacity to advance our humanity in family and civic life. They include running households (and other forms of economies) that democratically provide provision for all, political work that strengthens community, and various experiences of being over doing, including artistic work, revised sports games, and other forms of play, such as sexual exploration and contemplative prayer. *Economic and erotic relations shaped by a humanizing justice emanate from sensuous connections, not from market relations or moral and theological dogmas.* Communities all over the world, from the Revolutionary Association of the Women of Afghanistan (RAWA) to the Honduran feminist organization of Christian Community Development (CCD), are creating and nurturing social capital as they build new forms of democracy.

These are the concerns and the hopes that churches should be addressing in relation to erotic and economic discipleship. As the Presbyterian report advocates, churches need more sophisticated understanding of the complex social forces that shape all our lives. The better we understand the links between the sexual and political economies, the more we will be able to comprehend how the sex/gender system and the capitalist political economy are one system. The odds may also be enhanced for us to be able to push this destructive system into crisis and redesign the rules of the game to benefit everyone.

When such structural analysis is lacking, our sexual and economic ethics, including gay liberation theologies, suffer from being simplistic. Therefore, struggling for sexual and economic justice will also require us to struggle intellectually, especially to make sense of the growing political alliances among queers, straight allies, people who suffer from racism and sexism, and the world's impoverished majority. After all, these justice-lovers are the best teachers to show us how neither their interests nor ours — both sexually and economically — are well served by capitalism and how hope lies in struggling together for a very different day.

Notes

1. *Presbyterians and Human Sexuality 1991* (Louisville: Presbyterian Church [U.S.A.], 1991), 14, 15.

2. Rosemary Hennessy and Chrys Ingraham, "Introduction: Reclaiming Anticapitalist Feminism" in *Materialist Feminism: A Reader in Class, Difference and Women's Lives,* ed. Rosemary Hennessy and Chrys Ingraham (New York: Routledge, 1997), 1–14.

3. Julie Matthaei, "Healing Ourselves, Healing Our Economy: Paid Work, Unpaid Work, and the Next Stage of Feminist Economic Transformation," *Review of Radical Political Economics* 33, no. 4 (fall 2001): 464–65.

4. Karen Lebacqz, "Appropriate Vulnerability: A Sexual Ethic for Singles," in *Sexuality: A Reader,* ed. Karen Lebacqz with David Sinacore-Guinn (Cleveland: Pilgrim, 1999), 129–35.

5. Mary E. Hobgood, "Marriage, Market Values, and Social Justice: Toward An Examination of Compulsory Monogamy," in *Redefining Sexual Ethics*, ed. Eleanor H. Haney and Susan E. Davies (Cleveland: Pilgrim, 1991), 115–26.

6. Linda Singer, *Erotic Welfare: Sexual Theory and Politics in the Age of Epidemic* (New York: Routledge, 1993), 56.

7. Linda Carney-Goodrich, "The Party That Gave Us Welfare Reform Claims It Will Fight for All the People,"*Sojourner* 26 (October 2000): 24.

8. Michael Zweig, *The Working Class Majority: America's Best Kept Secret* (Ithaca, N.Y.: Cornell University Press, 2000), 28–34.

9. Robert Kuttner, "Kids Left Out of Bush's 'Wedding Welfare,'" *Boston Globe,* March 27, 2002, A 23.

10. Singer, *Erotic Welfare,* 37.

11. Rose M. Brewer, "Theorizing Race, Class and Gender," in *Materialist Feminism,* 241.

12. Lawrence Mishel, Jared Bernstein, and John Schmitt, *The State of Working America, 1998–99* (Ithaca, N.Y.: Cornell University Press, 1999), 173.

13. For a more lengthy exploration of these dynamics, see my *Dismantling Privilege: An Ethics of Accountability* (Cleveland: Pilgrim, 2000), 63–106.

14. Grace Chang, *Disposable Domestics: Immigrant Women Workers in the Global Economy* (Cambridge, Mass.: South End Press, 2000).

15. Chang shows how the government and media criminalize and pathologize both immigrant and welfare workers and how divide-and-conquer tactics are used against them. For example, welfare workers receive no wages and few public benefits, and immigrant workers receive sub-minimum wages and often have no access to the public sector and public benefits. See her *Disposable Domestics,* 155–84.

16. Ibid., 131–34.

17. Ibid., 123–54.

18. Singer, *Erotic Welfare,* 120.

19. Linda Holler, *Erotic Morality: The Role of Touch in Moral Agency* (New Brunswick, N.J.: Rutgers University Press, 2002).

20. Ibid., 29.

21. Ibid., 77.

22. Ibid., 39–82.

23. Ibid., 31–32, 127–39.

24. Ibid., 139.

25. David H. Cecil and Julia A. Heath, "To Market, to Market: Imperial Capitalism's Destruction of Social Capital in the Family," *Review of Radical Political Economics* 33, no. 4 (fall 2001): 401–14.

26. Ibid., 410.

27. Ibid., 409.

28. Ibid., 412.

29. Holler, *Erotic Morality,* 127.

30. Mark D. Jordan, *The Silence of Sodom: Homosexuality in Modern Catholicism* (Chicago: University of Chicago Press, 2000).

31. Carol Christ, "Reverence for Life: The Need for a Sense of Finitude," in *Embodied Love: Sensuality and Relationship as Feminist Values,* ed. Paula M. Cooey, Sharon A. Farmer, and Mary Ellen Ross (San Francisco: Harper & Row, 1987), 51–64.

32. Quoted in Virginia Ramey Mollenkott, *Sensuous Spirituality: Out from Fundamentalism* (New York: Crossroad, 1993), 158.

33. *Presbyterians and Human Sexuality 1991,* 14.

34. Ann Ferguson, "Back to the Grassroots," review of Johanna Brenner's *Women and the Politics of Class*, in the *Women's Review of Books* 19, no. 2 (September 2002): 18.

35. See, for example, Singer, *Erotic Welfare,* 146; Jordan, *The Silence of Sodom,* 3; and Eleanor H. Haney, *Vision and Struggle* (Portland, Maine: Astarte Shell Press, 1989), 98.

36. Jordan, *The Silence of Sodom,* 3.

37. Nicola Field, "Identity and the Lifestyle Market," in *Materialist Feminism,* 259–71.

21

Marriage Troubles

Rita Nakashima Brock

During the 1996 U.S. elections, the news media mocked Dick Morris. The inventor of "traditional family values" was accused of having dropped them around his ankles when he was caught with a prostitute. He was political advisor to President Bill Clinton, who later faced his own sexual scandal with Monica Lewinsky. If we assume, however, that the behavior of Morris and Clinton violates traditional Christian family values, we would be wrong for most of the church's history. Many theologians assumed that sex outside of marriage was necessary to preserve the family, and they advocated social policies on that basis.

Prostitutes were a necessary evil, according to Thomas Aquinas, as they were permitted by God to prevent chaotic eruptions of sinful male lust. "Sewers," he notes, "are necessary to guarantee the wholesomeness of palaces."[1] In other words, prostitutes protected "good" wives from their husbands' immoral, lustful demands. Prostitutes supposedly exhibited the sexual licentiousness inherent in all women, which good women repressed. The most "holy" women, like the most "holy" men, were supposed to follow a celibate vocation. Aquinas's view was typical, that being married and sexually active was less spiritual than celibacy. In this same period, virulent homophobia also developed.[2]

During the Protestant Reformation, which abolished vows of celibacy, marriage became the sole vocation for women. This change was not necessarily a social or legal advance. Marriage had long been the instrument of women's subordination, a subordination found in the Bible and used by theologians to describe human relationships in obedience to God: the wife was to the husband as humanity was to God. By the end of the twentieth century, most

Christian churches, Catholic and Protestant, had acknowledged that sexism was a sin. They have not, however, scrutinized one major social institution perpetuating sexism—marriage.

Many feminist Christians, myself among them, have struggled with how to put two contrary impulses together in our lives. We have sought to do work to which we feel called and which feeds our souls. The more educated and professionally successful we become, however, the less suited we are for the traditional roles of married women. Women are supposed to want relationships with men who are dominant — who earn more money, are professionally more powerful, are older, better educated, and taller than we are. When marriage is based on gendered roles of dominance and subordination, the creation of egalitarian, intimate relationships becomes a countercultural choice, at odds with the social, economic, and cultural pressures that influence our everyday lives. This choice challenges the core gender structure of traditional marriage.

The movement to legitimate same-sex marriage presents a similar challenge. This essay explores the intersection of these challenges to heterosexual marriage as an institution structured by sexism. The church avoided consecrating marriage for a millennium, a history related to its understandings of sexuality and celibacy. This history of ambiguity around marriage and sex relativizes the supposed sanctity of marriage and raises questions about what makes intimate relationships ethical. In examining this Christian legacy historically, ethically, and theologically, I will offer ways to think anew about ethical marriage, loving sex, and nondominating images of God, all of which open ways for Christians to accept the legitimacy of same-sex marriage.

Troubles with marriage

Marriage defines women as property, as does the tenth commandment: "You shall not covet your neighbor's house; you shall not covet your neighbor's wife, or male or female slave, or ox or donkey, or anything that belongs to your neighbor" (Exod. 20:17). Throughout the history of Europe and its colonies, marriage laws have been patchwork and fluid but consistently premised on the subordination of women to the patriarchal family ownership system. The Western system of marriage is rooted in Roman traditions in which heterosexual coupling was premised on male dominance. A man could use, without obligation, any woman for sex—slave, captive, servant, prostitute, or client—under his authority and economic control. A man could also have one or more concubines, whom he did not control but who were usually dependent on his financial largess. When women married, laws required that they turn their bodies and economic assets over to their husbands, who had unlimited sexual access to their wives.[3] A common element of ancient marriage was the expected rape of the bride.[4] Though mutual consent was an element of some Roman marriages, women consented to the legal status of property if they married. Unmarried women continued to be categorized as the children of their fathers, no matter their age. Elizabeth Cady Stanton, who chose to marry because she loved her husband, observed that marriage made women "legally dead."[5]

Marriage has been a tool of male dominance, economic exploitation, and violence. Its laws historically granted the husband conjugal rights that obligated the wife to domestic responsibilities without compensation and without the right to refuse sex. In return, as "head of household," the husband was supposed to provide financially for the entire family.

Contemporary marriage laws reflect some of this history. When my father died in 1976, a married woman could not have her own credit history. My mother had to use my father's credit rating even though she had worked for pay outside the home for much of her adult life. Such economic inequalities tend to remain in the background of day-to-day gender relationships and often become more of a problem when marriages end. A more acute and constant problem is women's loss of bodily integrity. This loss can extend even to unmarried women. For example, in 1997, a woman in Peru who was sexually assaulted was required by law to marry her rapist if he so requested, allowing him freedom from criminal prosecution,[6] a policy resembling the rape codes in Deuteronomy:

> If a man meets a virgin who is not engaged, and seizes her and lies with her, and they are caught in the act, the man who lay with her shall give fifty shekels of silver to the young woman's father, and she shall become his wife. Because he violated her he

shall not be permitted to divorce her as long as she lives. (Deut. 22:28–29)

Violence against women is a pernicious and enduring aspect of marriage relationships, behavior found in images of God. As biblical scholar Renita Weems has noted, domestic violence is sanctified as a right of God to discipline Israel in prophetic books such as Ezekiel and Hosea.[7]

Until recently in the United States, a man could rape his wife with impunity because legal definitions of rape exempted a husband from prosecution, and rape in marriage was not uncommon.[8] Over the centuries, the church tolerated domestic violence and sought to regulate the conditions under which women could be beaten by their husbands.[9] Still today, twelve times more women are murdered by husbands and family members than by strangers.[10] While violence in intimate relationships is not limited to heterosexual marriage, the loss of married women's bodily integrity has impeded legal action against such violence.

Few responsible adults would consider signing a binding contract without reading it, especially a contract stipulating that one partner would cease to be a full legal person and both parties intended to adhere to that agreement for life. However, people do so when they marry. Marriage contracts are not only legally binding, but also difficult and expensive to circumvent by private agreements between individual parties. Women and men committed to equal, respectful relationships, if they enter a legal marriage, will face the imposition of the state into their private lives. Legal marriage was not designed to be an egalitarian institution and carries this legacy of gender inequality. Feminists have worked to change some of the sexist laws and policies governing marriage in the United States, but the amount of change varies state by state.

Through the participation of their clergy, churches endorse this state system. The U.S. constitutional division between church and state disappears in the marriage ceremony; clergy act on behalf of the state and are granted authority as agents of the state.[11] The involvement of clergy gives sanction to this unequal marriage system and confers holiness upon it. However, as long as legal marriage subordinates women, it will remain unethical, even when sanctioned by the church.

Troubled by marriage

For half of the history of the church, Christian theologians were troubled by marriage and did not regard it as sacred. Priests did not officiate at ceremonies, and the church had no policies governing marriage. The church understood marriage as a civil ceremony, for both political and religious reasons.[12] When Christianity began, the Roman empire had already instituted policies that required its citizens to marry. The empire enforced this obligation through taxation and other legal pressures, beginning with Caesar Augustus's Julian Laws in 19 and 18 B.C.E., which created a more systematic form of marriage. Roman marriage carried the obligation of procreation as a duty to the state. Under the empire, life expectancy was twenty-five years, infant mortality was high, and common diseases, such as malaria and dysentery, and constant warfare required a five-child birthrate per woman to forestall a decline in population among Roman citizens (and with it a corresponding decline in tax revenues to support the empire).[13] Among the privileged classes who benefited most from imperial largess, marriage was a social and economic contract arranged by heads of households to establish family linkages, create heirs, and maintain dynasties. Procreation was possible elsewhere; marriage protected legal heirs, including the children of servants who had been used to provide offspring for the master.

To understand the impact of such policies on women, we might consider what it would mean for a girl to be married in early adolescence to a man two or three times her age. She was often raped on her wedding night. She would spend most of her time confined to the home and be expected to bear children as early and as often as possible without access to adequate medical care. The majority of her children would die before they reached adulthood, and she would not survive to see her youngest children become adults.[14]

Slaves, poor peasants, and other marginalized people had the legal status of property and were forbidden legal marriage. Many of the earliest Christians came from these marginalized groups. They believed baptism, not birth, conferred their kinship status with each other. Hence, Christians regarded legal marriage as an ambiguous institution because of its strong connections of loyalty to the Roman state. Resistance to state marriage evolved early in Christianity, especially through practices of asceticism. Ascetic men saw sexual abstinence, even within marriage, as an act of defiance against Roman oppression. In their abstinence they were living, they believed, freer lives, more closely embodying a divinely transformed human order. Sexual orientation was not at issue; heterosexual sex within marriage was the problem.

This desire to live a spiritual ideal was, of course, not easy. Many of the desert "fathers" struggled with sexual fantasies and bodily urges (Origen reportedly cut off his own testicles). While such things may sound pathological to modern ears, the struggle was important to Christian life for religious and political reasons (the two were not separated). The celibate body symbolized a new life to come so that even Adam and Eve, in their pre-fallen state, were envisioned as not engaging in sex. Abstinence showed they were free of the corruptible flesh. Even nonabstinent Christian households were influenced by abstinence as a sign of life under divine governance.[15]

The first documented ceremonies for life-long, committed, loving relationships were created for same-sex couples, which the church later used as a model for marriage rituals.[16] These early ceremonies affirmed before witnesses a couple's love that was personal, committed, and had a spiritual dimension. These same-sex relationships developed in monasteries and may or may not have included sexual activity. Nonetheless, they present an alternative to the marriage system of Rome.

This history should caution us against valorizing heterosexual marriage as the ideal Christian commitment. The tradition, beginning with Paul, held a negative view of marriage because it was wedded to heterosexual sex and to duties that distracted Christians from the work of God. Love was independent of this structure, essential neither to marriage nor to sex. While inscriptions on early Christian sarcophagi give touching evidence of love between husbands and wives and between parents and their children, such love was not required in the definition of marriage, and it was not expected.

The contemporary movement to ban same-sex marriage seeks to protect heterosexual marriage. However, Christians in this movement do not understand their own tradition's well-grounded wariness of this institution. Moreover, prohibiting same-sex marriage will not address the unethical structures of traditional marriage, and it is these structures that should be transformed, not defended or "protected" from change.

In theological terms, traditional heterosexual marriage is sinful because it is unjust. The sanctification of marriage has inscribed as sacred unethical structures between men and women, subordinating women to men, denying women bodily and sexual integrity, and sanctioning domestic violence. This unjust system is further entrenched theologically by the use of marriage as a model of divine-human relationships, in which God is presented as husband, i.e., as representing the masculine side of the power equation. This hierarchical gender structure as divinely ordained upholds the virtue of women's obedience to male power:

> Wives, be subject to your husbands as you are to the Lord. For the husband is the head of the wife just as Christ is the head of the church, the body of which he is the Savior. Just as the church is subject to Christ, so also wives ought to be, in everything, to their husbands. (Eph. 5:22–24)

Paul makes a similar point, in a more convoluted way, in 1 Corinthians 11:3–10, but only after he has said,

> To the unmarried and the widows I say that it is well for them to remain unmarried as I am. But if they are not practicing self-control, they should marry. For it is better to marry than to be aflame with passion.... He who marries his fiancee does well; and he who refrains from marriage will do better.... [A widow] is more blessed if she remains as she is. And I think that I too have the Spirit of God (1 Cor. 7:8–9, 40 NSRV).

Marriage, it seems, is a lesser state of life than being single.

Proposing marriage as a model of divine-human relationships bases faith on a problematic relationship in which love is inessential. Paul's primary language about marriage is power, submission, and control: submission of the wife to her husband, and control of lust to avoid sinning. When he speaks of love in marriage, it is in the framework of this power system. He does not mention procreation or the care of children. Meanwhile, Paul extols love as the highest good, even above faith, in 1 Corinthians 13:13. However, he delivers his message of love not for married couples, but for the diverse members of the church and to encourage the use of everyone's gifts within a caring community. If marriage is less than the best life for Christians, why should Christians seek its parallel in relation to God?

Same-sex relationships disrupt the power inequalities of gender embedded in heterosexual marriage, though of course not all same-sex relationships avoid structures of domination and submission. They do not begin, however, with the inequality of heterosexuality as a structural assumption of the relationship. This disruption of gender and power may be one reason why homosexuality has become such a flashpoint of theological controversy. Those who object to same-sex marriage use a number of reasons, including that heterosexual marriage is biologically, morally, and culturally "normal" or "natural" because of its procreative purpose. While sex has a biological basis in human beings, marriage does not. In fact, marriage is neither "natural" nor "sacred," and sex has uses other than procreation, including the expression of love. In other words, an unethical institution has been naturalized as a model for all sexual relationships.

The roles and behaviors associated with gender and what we do with our feelings, where we direct them, and even how they are prompted are a complex mixture of biology and cultural constructions passed on to us from birth. Because we are taught sexual values and attitudes from an early age, we may feel as if they are inherent. However, sexual attitudes, attractions, behaviors, and relationships vary extensively both within and across cultures. All could be deemed "natural" in the same way marriage is. Some people and cultures appreciate and allow same-sex relationships; others condemn and reject them, giving evidence that societies are a major shaping factor in sexual behavior and attitudes.

Over the long history of contested marriage laws in the United States, the same arguments are repeated. Interracial marriage is "unnatural." Giving women economic independence and the right to work will undermine the structures preserving marriage. Using birth control is "unnatural" and takes away the primary procreative reason for marriage. Allowing divorce violates the life-long arrangements cemented by marriage.[17]

The use of these recurring, persistent defenses of marriage is slippery and rests on the fabricated idea that marriage is "natural." However, the fact that marriage is legal does not make it "natural," just, or ethical. If we rely on a state-defined, sexist institution to determine the morality of intimate relationships, we abrogate our responsibility for ethical discernment. Focusing on protecting heterosexual marriage prevents us from examining what various life choices exist for ethical love, responsible sexual behavior, and long-term commitments. We need a more complex understanding of what makes adult intimate relationships moral.

Troubles with sex

Christian ambivalence about heterosexual marriage is part of our struggle with human sexuality. Heterosexual sexuality has been politically charged, given its early connection to Roman marriage.[18] It is not inconceivable that Thomas Aquinas's argument allowing prostitution emerged from a strategy to minimize rape and battering in marriage and thereby reduce the anguish and trauma of family violence. Whether or not such a strategy was successful, the fact remains that the church often profited from the taxation of prostitution.[19]

Until the Protestant Reformation, most major Western Christian theologians were troubled by sexuality and wrote about the body and sex from a perspective that believed celibacy to be a higher spiritual state.[20] Augustine's theology of sex was one of the most influential from late antiquity. According to his *Confessions,* his non-Christian father was sexually profligate outside his marriage to a Christian woman. Augustine himself had a difficult adolescence, followed by a fifteen-year relationship with a concubine who bore him a son. Even though Augustine's achievement of faithfulness defied the model of his father, he later dismissed it as "the mere bargain of lustful love."[21] Elsewhere, he concedes, in the abstract, that a faithful concubine can be considered a wife.[22] However, when his mother betrothed him to an adolescent woman of the appropriate social class (a typical marriage arrangement of the time) he abandoned his unnamed concubine. Augustine refused to marry and eventually became a monk.

From Augustine we inherit a notion of human nature that connects sin with sexual passion. He found evidence for original sin in his "unruly member," which convinced him that his moral will could not control his sexual urges and feelings. Without such control, the soul was helpless to submit to God. Hence, the very fact that humans are conceived in a rebellious will, grounded in sexual passion or lust, transmits this sin from generation to generation. Powerless to help ourselves, we must submit our wills to divine grace.

Sex was a duty of marriage for the purpose of procreation. Married sex was not required to include love or to be enjoyable — in Augustine's case the very capacity of sex to provide pleasure was troubling. Men often found social and emotional intimacy, whether sexual or not, with other men and not their wives. Augustine had such friendships with men, which were more emotionally and intellectually satisfying to him than the one he had with his concubine. Of these friendships, he says, they "[proceeded] from our hearts as we gave affection and received it back, and shown by face, by voice, by the eyes, and by a thousand other pleasing ways, kindled a flame which fused our very souls together, and, of many, made us one."[23] John Boswell's research on early holy union ceremonies in Christianity found a similar early Christian preference for same-sex intimacy.[24] As Augustine's example demonstrates, same-sex friendship was voluntary and mutual, an intimacy in marked contrast to the gender dominance structured into heterosexual marriage.

The Protestant reformers of the sixteenth century are widely regarded as having a more positive view of sex and marriage because they abolished monasticism and repudiated celibacy. Protestants rejected the idea that abstinence resulted in a more spiritual state and opened the door to considering a positive relationship of sexuality to faith. However, most Protestant reformers did not peer far through that door. Their rejection of celibacy rested on their negative assessment of it as a means of acquiring grace.[25] Calvin disapproved of celibacy only when those who had chosen this path could not stay on it. Although Calvin was willing to grant that sex within marriage had a positive function in relation to procreation as a divinely ordained act, he warned that the marriage bed should not become a nest of licentiousness.[26] The Reformers continued to view sexuality quite negatively outside the confines of married, procreative sex. Protestant marriage thus narrowed the focus of sexual life to marriage and confined women to this subordinated role and vocation.[27]

Reformers such as Luther took the harshest possible reading of Paul to mean that the original equality of Adam and Eve had been shattered by Eve's disobedience. Because of her sinful nature, Eve was to be subordinate to Adam, as all wives were to be subject to their husbands.[28] This theology implies that traditional marriage is a punishment, not a blessing. During this same historical period, social policies defined the conditions under which a man could beat his wife. When the Protestant reformers closed convents, they denied women one of the few legitimate avenues of escape from domestic violence, sexual abuse, forced pregnancy, and illiteracy. In addition, women were more isolated from adult relationships, once provided by convents, of emotional and intellectual intimacy with other women.

This sex-only-within-marriage legacy has produced Christian theological and ethical language about sex that focuses primarily on control, sin, rules, and guilt. The control of sexuality and the marital rules by which it is governed have determined whether we should feel guilty about or enjoy sexual activity. This theology of human sexuality constricts and denies the fullness and complexity of human sexuality and reinforces men's dominance and women's obedience to male power and authority, paralleling submission to God. Augustine's influential conceptual mistake was making his masculine experience of sex into an all-encompassing theory of human nature, with sexual passion as a problem — an indication that "man" was fallen.

Still troubled

Life for Christians in the West has changed dramatically since Paul, Augustine, Luther, and Calvin, but our cultural attitudes, theologies, and ideas have been slow to follow. Perhaps this is because until very recently, the most privileged men who benefited most from male dominance and racial inequality created our policies and laws.

Feminist legal scholars and activists have worked for over a century to change sexist laws and policies.

An increasing number of men, such as Michael Eric Dyson, James Nelson, James Poling, and John Stoltenberg, as well as authors in this collection, have joined feminists in examining the harm caused by systems of male dominance. For men to do so requires the deconstruction of dominance structured into masculine socialization.[29] Dyson writes in a letter to his wife Marcia,

> The truth is, Marcia, that for the most part black men have been unwilling to confront inequalities between ourselves and the women in our lives, inequities that we deeply invest in and justify by all sorts of philosophical and rhetorical gyrations...as black men we have a hard time seeing ourselves as oppressors, as doing to black women what has wrongfully been done to us. So many of the black women in our lives...overlook [our difficulties] at times,...make their peace with them, thereby inviting their own downfall.[30]

Christian marriage must be remade into an ethical institution, regardless of how law and policy define it. A reassertion of traditional values, based in women's inequality, reinscribes injustice. Women's lives today challenge the social practices, economic structures, and stereotyped roles on which traditional marriage was based.[31] In addition, young adults spend, on average, a decade or more before marriage being hormonally, physically, and emotionally ready for sexual activity, and they act on that capacity before committing to long-term relationships. This long period of adolescent sexual maturity has created a stage of human life in which sexuality is seen as an aspect of self, not as a function of marriage and procreation. However, most Christians receive little guidance for this period of sexual life beyond "just say no."

This guidance is crucial because the modern emphasis on personal sexual fulfillment has not eliminated sexism. The old dynamics of gender and power still haunt heterosexual relationships. The negative Christian view of sex has, in turn, produced a reaction based in a view of sexual freedom that dissociates it from values or relationships. As John Stoltenberg argues,

> Sexual-freedom advocates have cast the issue only in terms of having sex that is free from suppression and restraint...sexual freedom on a more personal level has meant sex that is free from fear, guilt, and shame — which in practical terms has meant advocacy of sex that is free from consequences, sex that is free from ethical distinctions, sex that is essentially free from any obligation to take into account one's consciousness that the other person is a *person.*[32]

This libertarian reaction to puritanical sex parallels Augustine's callous dismissal of his concubine as a "mere bargain of lustful love." In the modern version, the sexual partner is also the object of lust in a performance of desirability and sexual mastery. As in patriarchal marriage, masculinity is constructed on the basis of dominating attitudes toward sex and women. Because of their own greater freedom and personal income, women can also play such roles of power.

Traditionally, even within monasticism, the church tolerated prostitutes as an outlet for lust, which allowed for exploitative sex that did not touch the soul or strain church coffers with legitimate offspring of church officials. Actually loving someone intimately was understood to interfere far more with spiritual life than uninvolved sex. Lust was tolerated; sex with love was suspect. In addition to monks, married men supposedly needed outlets to protect their wives from lust, as noted above. Lust could be impersonally expressed; love might lead to attachment and relationship. In today's version of such sex, masculine mastery is demonstrated not by celibacy, but by sexual prowess without attachments, a practice akin to monastic asceticism. The sexual behavior Stoltenberg describes shares with asceticism and traditional heterosexual marriage an assumption that masculine lust is expressed through power, an ethic now possible for even women to enact.[33]

This sex-love split resembles the fragmentation of the soul in the aftermath of violence. Violence was long accepted within marriage as an aspect of male dominance. Survivors of sexual abuse, rape, and family violence often lose awareness of their bodies—the site of painful memories. They separate body from feelings and intellect. Connecting them would require reliving pain that can be a descent into hell. Rather than make such a descent, survivors of violence sometimes live dissociated lives, with body, heart, mind, and soul unintegrated — with each part of the self not speaking to or being heard by the others.[34] Without the integrity of the self, responsible, self-respecting ethical decisions in intimate relationships are difficult. The Department of Justice Office of Crime Statistics reports high levels of intimate violence.[35] Many regard these statistics as underestimates.[36] A theology of intimacy that divides sex from love only reinforces the traumatic aftermath of such violence.

The Christian tradition confined sex to traditional marriage, thereby trapping women and men in a sinful system in which the only approved sex was within a system of dominance. However, sex free of sin was seen as virtually impossible, even in marriage, because of lust. Since love and sex together create the yearning for intimacy and sexual passion that was equated with lust, the union of sex and love could be dangerous to the soul. This Catch-22 has created veils of shame and guilt even around healthy sexual feelings. Latin American liberation theologians have suggested that sin, organized in its social dimensions within human systems of power, magnifies the abuse of power, especially in economic and political forms. Sin is a social phenomenon with a structured social and historical character.[37] Christian marriage is such a system of sin.

We must seek new criteria for understanding what makes sex ethical, not only because traditional marriage has enmeshed sex in an inescapable circular system of sin, but also because such an unjust ethic is less and less supported by contemporary social and economic conditions. Most adult women work and like having their own income. Women live longer, have fewer children in economically privileged societies, and outlive men in life expectancy. Child rearing now occupies perhaps one-third of an adult woman's life whereas a century ago it was her entire adult life, especially because she was likely to die before her youngest child became an adult. All marriages end by death or divorce, so most adults spend some part, often a significant part, of their lives unmarried. Heterosexual adults sometimes commit to long-term relationships without any intention of marrying or having children. Most adult sexual behavior deliberately avoids procreating. Protected sex has become a moral imperative not only because we live in an era of HIV/AIDS, but also because, to be ecologically responsible, we must limit the numbers of children we bring into the world. Hence, the decision to procreate must be carefully considered to be ethical.[38]

To make sex ethical, we find clues in Augustine's dilemma: he had sex with his concubine, but found intimacy with his male friends. He yearned for, but did not find, adequate intimacy and mutuality in his sexual relationship. Augustine's dilemma offers us important theological insight. His struggle between his will and his urges suggests that the human heart or psyche is a dimension of sexual feelings. Augustine believed that the ideal, spiritually uplifting moment of sexual relations occurs when body and soul are one, when the human will coalesces in love with the desire of the body. Unlike many of his contemporaries, he believed that Adam and Eve had sex before they knew sin and that there would be sex in heaven.

Augustine's relationship with his concubine led him to believe he could not control his sexual urges. At the same time, his relationship with her did not equal the emotional and intellectual friendships he had with men. He longed for the two to become one relationship, so that he could make love in loving friendship. However, the culture and structures of gender in his time may have stood in his way, despite evidence from his time that some men and women found such romantic unions.[39] Certainly, an attitude toward women revealed in his characterization of his concubine as a "bargain" led him to believe that such grace-filled sex in this life was impossible.

Augustine wished he could integrate the many dimensions of his life: values, feelings, spirituality, intellect, and will. The power structures of gender that prevented this integration haunt heterosexual relationships, structures to which men and women are still socialized. His dilemma is an invitation to re-imagine sexual relationships on the basis of love.

Augustine's friendships offer us an important insight into the quality of love among relative equals. Adult relationships are spiritually grounded and ethical when their values are egalitarian, when one member is not expected to sacrifice her or his life or talents for another's, when each contributes to the relationship, when each is free to be honest, and when each is able to thrive. In psychological terms, such relationships respect boundaries; they are based in respect for the separateness and differences among persons. The normal tensions and conflicts that emerge between human beings in

close relationship with each other can become oppressive or violent when one has considerable power over the other. Conflicts are
less likely to become chronically harmful within the freedom provided by a friendship among equals. Each person has a sense of
her or his own worth and power. This love is what Paul describes in
1 Corinthians 13.

Augustine paints, perhaps, too idealized a picture of what he
longed for, but could not experience. Such idealized expectations,
usually promoted as a reason to wait for sex until marriage, encourage the naive to think that one all-consuming relationship can
meet such needs rather than understanding that human needs are
met in a variety of ways.[40] If we idealize sexuality and lack space for
the complex truths of our lives, we will imprison a major part of intimacy that is truth. Without the freedom to be present as ourselves, in
our limitations and complex needs as well as our passions and joys,
we will not be much better off than when sex was seen as sin. Idealized sex is not an answer to sex as sin, any more than sex without
feeling for the other is an answer to repressed sex.[41]

If ethical intimacy is the joining of love and sex, then we must accept that such relationships sometimes do not endure for life. Love
cannot be ordered or legislated. Love is a voluntary act, based on
complex, often mysterious factors. Education, employment, family
commitments, trauma, and time change people's lives and how they
feel about them. When love changes, fades, or fails, it cannot be
commanded to reappear. Violence and emotional abuse are major
reasons that intimate relationships fail. These forms of coercion must
never be confused with ethical love. They are a betrayal of love.

"Belief in love, belief in the integrity of individual conscience,
is profoundly unsettling. . . . Each of us matters, . . . each of us must
choose for ourselves how to live."[42] Trusting the human heart will
not give us certainty or permanence, but it is the only avenue for
joining sexual life to the soul. Love can be reinforced and supported
by family and community systems, which should also provide accountability for responsible behavior when love ends. Moreover, such
systems provide support for those who grieve the loss of love.

Joining sex and love should not lead us to think of the two as the
same. There are many kinds of love, and sexual love is one dimension
of loving. Similarly, sexuality is not just what we do in a committed

relationship with another. Sex can bring pleasure without love of another, for example, through self-pleasure and the tactile wonders of the body.

The Christian tradition has relied upon fixed, act-centered rules to judge whether any sexual relationship is ethical, rather than on discerning how relationships are guided by principles of love, mutuality, responsibility, and pleasure. In addition, until very recently, few theologies have discussed the intrinsic goodness of sexual pleasure. To acknowledge sexual pleasure as a human good would be to place it into the framework of creation as blessing from God. Sex would then be valued for itself, as something creative of love and pleasure, not as an instrument used to obtain something else it serves, such as procreation or financial support.[43]

Same-sex marriage challenges us to make marriage ethical. Because too much joy and pleasure in sex have been suspect, heterosexual sexual activity has often been laden with tension and guilt. Same-sex marriage calls into question the hierarchical marriage system of gender that has separated sex from love. This challenge is not because all same-sex relationships are free of violence or domination, but because same-sex relationships are not constructed by gender hierarchy. They make evident the capacity of human beings to join sex with love in diverse ways.

Loving, egalitarian intimate relationships increase human and spiritual value. To increase the possibilities for loving is to increase the incarnation of love in the world. A diversity of intimate relationships can be ethical and are not determined by sexual orientation. Such relationships provide the larger society with adults in stable economic units, supporting each other financially, raising children, joining and supporting churches, and contributing in other ways to religious and civic life.

Unmarried God

We need new images of God to replace those of marriage with God as Lord, Husband, and Master. Fresh theological language and imagery offer us faith not as obedience, submission, and duty, but as a relationship of intimacy, mutuality, and responsibility.[44] Imagining God as beloved, friend, and wisdom is not new, but such images have been largely ignored, disparaged, or neglected by a tradition that defined faith in God as marriage.

The Song of Songs describes the love of those beloved to each other. Its joys and sexual love are not those of marriage, and yet this text was canonized as a model of the divine-human relationship. Feminist biblical scholar Phyllis Trible suggests it represents an image of return to the Garden of Eden when Adam and Eve were not punished for their sin with marriage.[45] Or perhaps it gives us an image of Augustine's hope for sex in heaven. Literary scholar Marcia Falk has translated it as a series of beautiful lyric love poems.[46]

While the Song of Songs never appears in the preaching lectionary, it has been a favorite of mystics who see its passionate love poetry as describing their God-infused lives. The intimate, whole-being sensibility of the text depicts a knowing closer to the Hebrew understanding of "to know" than the English sense of "knowledge." The Hebrew "to know" is used for sexual relationships, as well as for divine-human relationships. Hence, to know God as our Beloved is to be intoxicated by divine love and to know oneself as God's beloved.[47]

Love, of course, is not limited to sexual intimacy, and the image of God as Beloved is only one possible image for faith. Friend is another image of love, offered in John 15:15–17:

> I do not call you [slaves] any longer, because the [slave] does not know what the master is doing; but I have called you friends, because I have made known to you everything that I have heard from my Father. You did not choose me but I chose you. And I appointed you to go and bear fruit, fruit that will last, so that the Father will give you whatever you ask him in my name. I am giving you these commands, so that you may love one another.[48]

To be a true Friend is to commit to a relationship of love, respect, mutuality, and equality. In friendships, relationships of domination and subordination can be transcended because they are voluntary. As noted above, friendship is also sometimes related to sexual relationships, but many kinds of friendships exist. To befriend God is to stand with the world where the Spirit of God dwells and to know the presence of comfort and love is with us always.[49]

Throughout the biblical text, the divine spirit guides people, challenges them, comforts them, inspires them, disturbs them, and binds them to each other. This spirit is called many names: Ruah (breath), Shekinah (presence), Pneuma (spirit), Sophia (wisdom), Logos (word), and Paraclete (advocate). She appears when she is needed, but she does not always provide what we think we want. Rather, she disrupts narrow certainties by challenging our biases. She asks us to pay heed to what makes us uncomfortable, frightened, anxious. She heals wounds by coaxing us to face pain we cannot face alone. She inspires courage by grounding us in care and protection for ourselves and each other. She is not inwardly turning, but outwardly moving.[50] She cannot guarantee us certainty in life, but she gives us confidence in God. Ethical discernment and the ability to increase in judgment and responsibility come from our ability to respond to this spirit. This wisdom-spirit, Sophia, dwells in the world, in the flesh, and invites us to connect heart, mind, soul, and strength in our struggle to increase just love in the world.[51]

Christianity has lacked a tradition of just love in heterosexual marriage. The church's use of marriage has shaped a tradition that has separated sex from love, enforced the subordination of women, and ignored the spiritual dimensions of human sexuality and love. The movement for same-sex marriage provides us an opportunity to transform and redeem marriage as a place where love is bound with ethics, pleasure, and commitment. If we make marriage ethical, we will also need fresh ways to think of our relationship to God. This will all be to the good, strengthening Christian faith and community life. In moving Christian life toward greater mutuality, wholeness, and joy, we may see our diverse ways of loving as a gift of God, blessedness beyond measure.

Notes

1. Thomas Aquinas, *Summa Theologica,* II-II, q. x, art. ii; II-II q. lx, 2 and 5; II-II, lxxxvii, 2, ad 2; II-II, cxviii, 8, ad 4, in the edition translated by the English Dominicans, 22 vols. (London: Burns, Oates & Washburne, 1922).

2. John Boswell, in *Same-Sex Unions in Premodern Europe* (New York: Villard Books, 1994), notes that "from the fourteenth century on, Western Europe was gripped by a rabid and obsessive negative preoccupation with homosexuality as the most horrible of sins" (262).

3. John Boswell, *Same-Sex Unions,* provides an extensive discussion of the history of marriage in premodern Europe, including the minor presence in very late antiquity of romantic, voluntary relationships that sometimes involved marriages of more or less equals. "The notion of voluntary 'partnership' that lends itself to legal debate about contemporary marital arrangements would hardly have applied to matrimony before the late empire: it was...more like the adoption of the woman into the man's family. Moreover, *all* of these relationships have in common that the rigidly hierarchical nature of ancient social structures — everyone was bound through dependence or subordination to persons above and below her/him — were imported overtly into the relationships, even into marriage, so that emotional aspects were limited and shaped to a large extent by the social roles of the partners....Spouses who were actually 'in love' with each other were thought extraordinary and odd before the later empire" (38).

4. E. J. Graff, *What Is Marriage For?* (Boston: Beacon, 1999), 55.

5. For a discussion of marriage laws, see Virginia Sapiro, *Women in American Society: An Introduction to Women's Studies* (Mountain View, Calif.: Mayfield, 1998) and "The Gender Biases of American Social Policy," *Political Science Quarterly* 101 (1986): 221–38.

6. Calvin Sims, "Justice in Peru: Victim Gets Rapist for Husband," *New York Times,* March 12, 1997, section A.

7. Renita Weems, *Battered Love: Marriage, Sex, and Violence in the Hebrew Prophets* (Minneapolis: Fortress, 1995).

8. The Centers for Disease Control reports that 84 percent of rape victims do not report assaults. See their website at *www.cdc.gov/ncipc/factsheets/rape.htm* for an extensive bibliography on research. In 1979, Bob Wilson, a California state senator, said, "If you can't rape your wife, who can you rape?" At the time of the famous Greta Rideout case in 1979 in Oregon, in which a woman accused her husband of rape, only four states made rape in marriage illegal. Since that time, most state legislatures have made rape in marriage illegal. See Diana Russell's *Rape in Marriage* (Bloomington: Indiana University Press, 1990), and the CDC website for an extensive discussion of victim impact and statistics.

9. See Rita Nakashima Brock and Rebecca Ann Parker, *Proverbs of Ashes: Violence, Redemptive Suffering, and the Search for What Saves Us* (Boston: Beacon, 2001), for a discussion of advice and theology used by Christians that entrap women in situations of abuse and violence.

10. *When Men Murder Women: An Analysis of Homicide Data,* a report published by the Violence Policy Center (VPC Communications, 1140 19th St. NW, Washington DC 20036, 202-822-8200 ext. 105), analyzes 1997 FBI one-on-one homicide statistics, providing a state-by-state listing. A VPC report on 1996 statistics shows the same twelvefold difference between stranger and acquaintance homicide.

11. For a discussion of this collapse between church and state, see Rebecca T. Alpert's essay, "Religious Liberty, Same-Sex Marriage, and the Case of Reconstructionist Judaism" in *God Forbid: Religion and Sex in American Public Life,* ed. Kathleen M. Sands (New York: Oxford University Press, 2000).

12. Boswell, *Same-Sex Unions:* "Sporadic blessings and local offices of marriage no doubt existed in the early Middle Ages...but did not coalesce for centuries

into a coherent or obligatory liturgical tradition in eastern or western Europe" (164–65).

13. Arthur E. R. Boak and William G. Sinnigen, *A History of Rome to A.D. 565,* 5th ed. (New York: Macmillan, 1965), 281ff.; and Peter Brown, *The Body in Society: Men, Women, and Sexual Renunciation in Early Christianity* (New York: Columbia University Press, 1988).

14. In the Roman catacombs, the majority of graves are those of infants and children.

15. Brown, *The Body in Society.*

16. John Boswell, in *Same-Sex Unions,* notes that historically marriage had many economic and social functions that most modern people would no longer accept as necessary components of marriage. However, today personal affection and commitment are accepted. Hence, he concludes that the early holy union ceremonies in the church were marriages. "In almost every age and place the ceremony fulfilled what most people today regard as the essence of marriage: a permanent romantic commitment between two people, witnessed and recognized by the community" (281).

17. E. J. Graff, *What Is Marriage For?* Discusses these many contestations in defense of marriage, 251–53.

18. Brown, *The Body and Society.*

19. Rita Nakashima Brock and Susan Thistlethwaite, *Casting Stones: Prostitution and Liberation in Asia and the United States* (Minneapolis: Fortress, 1996), 129–30.

20. See John Boswell, *The Kindness of Strangers: The Abandonment of Children in Western Europe from Late Antiquity to the Renaissance* (New York: Pantheon Books, 1988) for a discussion of the fate of oblates promised to the church at a young age. The monastic code was severe with regard to children and what we now understand as needs for nurturance.

21. *Confessions* IV, ii, 2.

22. Boswell, *Same-Sex Unions,* 31.

23. *Confessions* IV, x, 13.

24. Boswell, *Same-Sex Unions.*

25. Martin Luther, *Works,* ed. Jaroslav Pelikan et al. (Philadelphia and St. Louis: Muhlenberg and Concordia, 1955ff), 68:278.

26. John Calvin, *Institutes of the Christian Religion,* IV.xii.18, trans. F. L. Battles, *Library of Christian Classics,* 20 and 21, ed. John T. McNeill (Philadelphia: Westminster, 1960).

27. This history is drawn from the introduction and chapter 8 in *Casting Stones.*

28. Luther, *Works,* 44:1–8.

29. James Poling, *The Abuse of Power: A Theological Problem* (Nashville: Abingdon, 1991), includes a perceptive portrait of sexual offenders and their relationship to masculine socialization.

30. Michael Eric Dyson, *Between God and Gangsta Rap: Bearing Witness to Black Culture* (New York: Oxford University Press, 1996), 189.

31. E. J. Graff, *What is Marriage For?,* discusses the evolution of the purpose of marriage into the contemporary model of personal fulfillment and happiness and presents a case for same-sex marriage.

32. John Stoltenberg, "Pornography and Freedom," in *Making Violence Sexy: Feminist Views on Pornography,* ed. Diana E. H. Russell (New York: Teachers College Press, 1993), 67.

33. Evolutionary theories of the last century attempted to "naturalize" this ethic through "evidence" in animals of similar behaviors that emphasized the value of male promiscuity and female faithfulness. Evolutionary biologist Sara Blaffer Hrdy in *Mother Nature: Maternal Instincts and How They Shape the Human Species* (New York: Ballantine Books, 1999) exposes the gender biases and inadequate research of these theories.

34. Judith Herman, *Trauma and Recovery* (New York: Basic Books, 1992) is a definitive work on the impact of violence on survivors, used internationally. *Proverbs of Ashes,* chapter 5, gives a personal account of the lingering consequences of sexual abuse.

35. See *www.ojp.usdoj.gov/bjs.*

36. For an example of why Department of Justice numbers are suspect, see Mark Fazlollah, "City, National Rape Statistics Highly Suspect," *Philadelphia Inquirer,* January 8, 2001. As of March 2003, this article was available at *www.womensnews.org/article.cfm/dyn/aid/398.*

37. See Gustavo Gutiérrez, *A Theology of Liberation* (Maryknoll, N.Y.: Orbis, 1973).

38. Christine E. Gudorf, *Body, Sex, and Pleasure: Reconstructing Christian Sexual Ethics* (Cleveland: Pilgrim, 1994).

39. John Boswell, *Same-Sex Unions:* "One does encounter in antiquity, especially under the empire, heterosexual relationships based less on property and status considerations and more closely corresponding to what later ages would call 'lovers': i.e., two people involved in a romantic relationship without a predominant coercive element, either legal (as in slavery) or economic (as in concubinage)," 39.

40. See, for example, the essay by Mary Hobgood in *Redefining Sexual Ethics: A Sourcebook of Essays, Stories, and Poems,* ed. Susan E. Davies and Eleanor H. Haney (Cleveland: Pilgrim, 1991).

41. Susan Griffin's *Pornography and Silence* (New York: Harper & Row, 1981) is an analysis of the denial of the erotic in exploitive sex, i.e., the repression of feeling for the use of sex as mastery and control.

42. Graff, *What Is Sex For?,* 253.

43. Christine E. Gudorf proposes such a framework in *Body, Sex, and Pleasure.*

44. A sample of recent works with fresh images and ideas includes Sallie McFague, *Models of God: Theology for an Ecological, Nuclear Age* (Minneapolis: Fortress, 1987); Carter Heyward, *Touching Our Strength: The Erotic as Power and the Power of God* (San Francisco: Harper & Row, 1987); *Weaving the Visions: New Patterns in Feminist Spirituality,* ed. Judith Plaskow and Carol Christ (San Francisco: Harper & Row, 1989); Dorothee Soelle, *Thinking about God: An Introduction to Theology* (New York: Trinity Press International, 1990); *Lift Every Voice: Constructing Christian Theologies from the Underside,* ed. Susan Thistlethwaite and Mary Potter Engel (San Francisco: Harper & Row, 1990); and Delores Williams, *Sisters in the Wilderness: The Challenge of Womanist God-Talk* (Maryknoll, N.Y.: Orbis, 1993).

45. Phyllis Trible, *God and the Rhetoric of Sexuality* (Philadelphia: Fortress, 1978).

46. Marcia Falk, *Love Lyrics from the Bible: A Translation and Literary Study of the Song of Songs* (Sheffield: Almond Press, 1982).

47. John Boswell, *Same-Sex Unions,* notes the use of brother-sister language in antiquity referring to sexual lovers or husbands and wives who were equal (41–42).

48. The NRSV uses the word "servant" instead of the literal Greek, "slave." "Slave" is also translated as "disciple" in some English versions. The interrelationship of the words "slave," "servant," and "disciple" shows the structure of domination and subordination inherent in such images of relationship.

49. Elizabeth Johnson, *Friends of God and Prophets: A Feminist Theological Reading of the Communion of Saints* (New York: Continuum, 1998).

50. Michael Welker's *God the Spirit,* trans. John Hoffmeyer (Minneapolis: Fortress, 1994) is a comprehensive study of the biblical and theological meaning of the spirit of God.

51. Elisabeth Schüssler Fiorenza discusses the relationship of Sophia to Jesus in *Jesus: Miriam's Child, Sophia's Prophet: Critical Issues in Feminist Christology* (New York: Continuum, 1994).

22

No More Second-Class Members

Rethinking the Church's Continuing Debate over the Ordination of Lesbian, Gay, Bisexual, and Transgender Persons

Virginia West Davidson, Michael D. Smith, and Jane Adams Spahr

Despite decades of debate, conflict over human sexuality continues to persist unabated in the church. Many congregations and denominations still find it difficult even to talk about sex, let alone achieve consensus or compromise on tough issues. The situation is all the more problematic when the issues are sexual orientation and gender identity. Deep divisions exist and show no signs of going away any time soon.

This conflict over sexuality issues in the church is focused primarily on ordination. In most cases, lesbian, gay, bisexual, and transgender persons are told they are welcome to be members of congregations, but are prohibited from holding offices or positions of ordained leadership. It is argued that electing and ordaining LGBT persons to office amounts to approving of their sexuality in a way that granting church membership does not. Many LGBT persons who believe themselves called to ordained ministries continue working to change the noninclusive policies and practices of their denominations. Others leave, refusing second-class membership.

Both sides of the ordination debate are engaged in various activities of education, witness, demonstration, legislative initiative, and judicial action in efforts to affect the policies and practices of their denominations. We turn our attention specifically to LGBT ordination in the Presbyterian Church (U.S.A.), beginning with the 1991 report,

"Keeping Body and Soul Together." Although other denominations and religious traditions have different institutional dynamics, we believe a close examination of this struggle in the PCUSA provides a useful case study to consider not only the immediate goal of LGBT ordination, but also to rethink the model of ordained leadership.

We continue to be participants in these denominational struggles, one as an openly lesbian pastor and the other two as heterosexual allies. Our thesis is that justice requires more than granting LGBT people access to ordination, important as that goal is. Justice also requires a serious rethinking of ordination itself and of the prevailing model of professionalized ministry. We continue to ask ourselves, is ordination *really* "holy ground," or is it not a mechanism that insures patriarchal control and blocks the free sharing of gifts by and for all God's beloved people?

In offering our analysis, we gladly meld our voices together because joint authorship is so much in keeping with our commitments to promote collaborative models of ministry and to share power and leadership between women and men of all sexual orientations, as well as Christians and other people of faith (or of no faith). Although we take collective ownership of this essay, a discerning reader may detect a particular individual's voice at certain points, not as a soloist but more as a lead singer with very good back-up vocalists! Because of Mike's gifts as a savvy navigator of Presbyterian polity and a consummate strategist for progressive groups within the church, his voice guides the opening discussion of the intricate contours of denominational fights over ordination. As a pastor and "lesbian evangelist" within the church, Janie takes the lead in speaking about why (at least some) LGBT folks continue to find ordination an important issue. Rightly she connects this struggle with the commitment to live faithfully in partnership with God and with other justice-loving people. Finally, Ginny, snowy-haired "het" ally and courageous activist for gender, race, and sexual justice, continues the conversation by pushing the critique of clericalism and calling for a partnership model of ministry.

The struggle for LGBT ordination in the PCUSA

For Presbyterians, the ordination issue is made particularly difficult by their longstanding tradition of ordaining elders and deacons as well as ministers of the word and sacrament. Presbyteries (regional governing bodies) have the power and responsibility for ordaining ministers while sessions (governing bodies of congregations) ordain elders and deacons to positions of leadership in congregations. Persons are ordained to all three offices by the same "laying on of hands" and answering constitutional questions about faith, theology, the authority of Scripture, historical church Confessions, and polity (church law). Thus, the prohibition on ordaining LGBT persons to office prevents not only the ordination of clergy, but also each congregation from choosing and ordaining LGBT members as lay leaders.

In 1978, the Presbyterian Church established a policy declaring that homosexual behavior is sinful and precludes ordination to church office.[1] (The language of church policy is almost exclusively confined to the term "homosexual" in restricting same-gender sexual relations. Church policy is virtually silent on bisexuality and transgenderism, but would affect bisexual and transgender persons in same-gender relationships.) In 1991, the General Assembly (the annual meeting of denominational delegates, or commissioners) rejected the report of the Special Committee on Human Sexuality, "Keeping Body and Soul Together," and its recommendation that gay men and lesbians could be ordained. Since 1991, continuous activity has taken place to overturn the 1978 policy, and four groups have been in the forefront working for change. The efforts of these growing organizations, especially in the last decade, are an important part of the PCUSA struggle regarding LGBT ordination.

More Light Presbyterians

More Light Presbyterians is the successor organization to Presbyterians for Lesbian and Gay Concerns (PLGC) and the More Light Church Network (MLCN). PLGC brought lesbians, gays, and their allies together for legislative and advocacy work at the denomination's General Assemblies and organized chapters in several cities. MLCN's work was within congregations, providing education, pastoral care, resources, and encouragement for churches to become More Light congregations, willing to declare and act upon their opposition to the denomination's restrictive ordination policy. On

January 1, 1999, PLGC and MLCN joined to become More Light Presbyterians (MLP).

The "More Light" name is taken from the 1620 sermon of an English Puritan pastor, the Rev. John Robinson, as he sent those seeking religious tolerance off to the New World: "We limit not the truth of God to our poor reach of mind—by notions of our day and sect—crude, partial and confined. No, let a new and better hope within our hearts be stirred, for God hath yet *more light* and truth to break forth from the Word."[2]

The mission of MLP is to "work for the full participation of lesbian, gay, bisexual and transgender people of faith in the life, ministry and witness of the PCUSA."[3] To help accomplish its mission, the MLP board employed Michael Adee, an "out" gay elder, as a full-time national field organizer in May 1999. A second organizer, the Rev. Katie Morrison, an "out" lesbian minister, was added two years later. There are now 110 More Light Churches in the PCUSA (most of whom have "irregularly" ordained LGBT elders and deacons), over 450 congregations identified as welcoming churches that have offered some kind of a statement of welcome to LGBT people, and twenty-five MLP chapters in cities and at college and seminary campuses.

National MLP conferences have been held annually for several years. MLP is an active, visible presence each year at General Assembly as it works not only to pass legislation to overturn church policy, but to achieve justice, acceptance, and affirmation of persons of all sexual orientations. The organization also provides legal counsel and financial support to those who have had charges filed against them for violating the denomination's ordination policy.

That All May Freely Serve

In November of 1991, the Downtown United Presbyterian Church in Rochester, New York, called the Rev. Dr. Jane Adams Spahr, an open, self-affirming lesbian ordained to the ministry in 1974, to be one of its co-pastors. The 1978 policy prohibiting ordination of LGBT persons contains a "grandparent clause," stating that the ordinations of persons ordained prior to 1978 will not be affected by this action. Following the congregation's action, the Presbytery of Genesee Valley approved the call and voted again in January of 1992, upon motion to reconsider, to uphold its decision. The action was appealed to the Permanent Judicial Commission of the Synod of the Northeast, which voted nine to one to uphold the presbytery's action. However, the Synod decision was appealed to the General Assembly Permanent Judicial Commission, which voted twelve to one to set aside the call, finding it to be contrary to the standards of the PCUSA.

The Downtown Church took action to form an organization they named "That All May Freely Serve" and invited Janie to hold the position of Evangelist (lesbian evangelist, to be specific). In affiliation with the Westminster Presbyterian Church in Tiburon, California, Janie has remained a minister member in good standing of Redwoods Presbytery in Northern California. Her new calling was to share the good news of God's all-embracing love as she traveled throughout the United States speaking about the injustice of the current policy and the need for a fully inclusive church.

In 1996, TAMFS began creating "regional partnerships" in order to enlarge opportunities for others to "person" the issue and provide education and organization to change church policy. By 2000, TAMFS had eight regional partners and a national office located at the Downtown Church. By 2002, all of the regions had full or part-time staff, and Lisa Larges was employed as regional partnership coordinator. Since 1999, TAMFS has held national conferences annually and has been a growing presence at General Assemblies, working to realize the goal of their mission: "an inclusive church that honors diversity and welcomes lesbian, gay, bisexual, and transgender persons as full members. Full membership includes eligibility for ordination to the offices of elder, deacon, and pastor."

The Shower of Stoles Project[4]

On September 16, 1995, Martha Juillerat, an openly lesbian Presbyterian pastor, set aside her ordination. That day, eighty Presbyterian ministers sent Martha their clergy stoles as a public witness to those barred from serving their church because of their sexual orientation and to give voice to those forced to choose between serving in silence and losing their livelihood. As word circulated about this outpouring of support, Martha began receiving stole after stole in the mail, and the Shower of Stoles Project (SOSP) was born. By spring of 1996, over two hundred stoles had been received (not all of them from clergy, but additionally from musicians and others using the stole as symbol). At the General Assembly in June of 1996, 350 stoles made their appearance, not at a display location, but on individuals who wore them all day, every day. This colorful, artistic collection of stoles has become a powerfully embodied symbol of loss to the church of gifted leadership.

The SOSP was incorporated in May of 1997 and quickly became ecumenical. At the close of 2002, the stoles numbered just over one thousand, with eighteen denominations and several countries represented. They have been displayed in varying numbers in congregations, denominational meetings and conferences, colleges, and seminaries across the United States and Canada and at each General Assembly since 1996. Martha works full time as project director.

Though employing different operating styles and organizational structures, MLP, TAMFS, and the SOSP have formed a close working partnership because of their common commitment and are now referred to as the "Three Sisters" in Presbyterian circles.

The Covenant Network of Presbyterians[5]

The Covenant Network of Presbyterians (CNP) is a broad-based national group of clergy and lay leaders committed to upholding a progressive, Reformed vision of the church and to removing the constitutional impediments to the ordination of gay and lesbian Presbyterians. CNP was formed in 1997 to work specifically for the passage of Amendment 97-A to the PCUSA *Book of Order.* This amendment would have allowed sessions and presbyteries to ordain gay and lesbian persons whom they believed to be called to ordained office. The proposed amendment was approved by the General Assembly but failed to get the required affirmative vote by a majority of the 173 presbyteries. Five years and three "amendment campaigns" later, CNP continues its work to remove constitutional restrictions to ordination.

Among Presbyterian advocacy groups, CNP's special focus is attempting to reach, inform, persuade, and mobilize the broad middle of the church in order to build a majority for change. Consequently, its leadership includes well-known pastors, seminary presidents, and former General Assembly moderators such as CNP founding co-moderators Robert Bohl and John Buchanan. Pamela Byers serves as executive director, and a second staff person, Tricia Dykers Koenig, was added in 2001 to be national organizer. In 1998, CNP set out its vision in "A Call to Covenant Community" and asked individuals and governing bodies in the church to sign their names in support of the declaration. The statement did not mention LGBT persons specifically, but rather called for the denomination to trust sessions and presbyteries to ordain people who are qualified and called by God. The statement has since been affirmed by more than eighteen former moderators of the General Assembly, twenty-five hundred ministers, three hundred sessions, five presbyteries, and thousands of Presbyterian elders, deacons, and members.

The Covenant Network is organized to affect votes related to ordination in presbyteries and General Assemblies and offers advice and support for sessions and officers confronting challenges posed by current ordination standards. CNP holds an annual conference, issues publications, and seeks local and regional opportunities for study and dialogue on ordination issues.

Efforts to change ordination policy

We will now look briefly at major actions during the last decade that sought to change church policy on ordination of LGBT persons. The original policy decision of the General Assembly in 1978 was just that, a policy established by the GA. The question was soon asked about the status of the policy. Was it binding, or was it to be considered merely guidance for the church, leaving those who disagreed free to follow their conscience? The Stated Clerk of the General Assembly, William P. Thompson, ruled that the policy constituted "definitive guidance" and had the status of a constitutional mandate. (Years later, when no longer in office, Thompson changed his mind and publicly expressed regret over his earlier decision.[6]) The language in the constitution upon which the definitive guidance was based, section G-6.0106a in the *Book of Order*, stated that a requirement for ordination to church office is that the church officer's "manner of life should be a demonstration of the Christian gospel in the church and in the world."[7]

The status of the policy remained unresolved, however, as many refused to grant "definitive guidance" the authority of the constitution. The matter came before the General Assembly in 1993, which invoked a provision whereby a General Assembly can establish an "authoritative interpretation" of the constitution and voted to declare the "definitive guidance" policy to be an authoritative interpretation. Many believed that this would settle the issue, but it didn't. The issue then became the status of an authoritative interpretation. Did *it* carry the same weight as the constitution itself?

Those opposing LGBT ordination then took the next step by proposing an amendment to the Book of Order at the 1996 meeting of the General Assembly that would make the policy part of the constitution. The amendment would add a section "b" to G-6.0106a:

> Those who are called to office in the church are to lead a life in obedience to Scripture and in conformity to the historic confessional standards of the church. Among these standards is the requirement to live either in fidelity within the covenant of marriage between a man and a woman (Directory for Worship-4.9001), or chastity in singleness. Persons refusing to repent of any self-acknowledged practice which the confessions call sin shall not be ordained and/or installed as deacons, elders, or ministers of the Word and Sacrament.[8]

The proposed amendment was passed by the General Assembly and then ratified, as church polity requires, over the next few months by a majority of presbyteries by a vote of ninety-seven to seventy-four. The very next General Assembly, meeting in Syracuse in 1997, sought to nullify the new prohibitive constitutional provision by passing an amendment to replace the new section G-6.0106b with:

> Those who are called to office in the church are to lead a life in obedience to Jesus Christ, under the authority of Scripture and instructed by the historic confessional standards of the church. Among these standards is the requirement to demonstrate fidelity and integrity in marriage and singleness, and in all relationships of life. Candidates for ordained office shall acknowledge their own sinfulness, their need for repentance, and

their reliance on the grace and mercy of God to fulfill the duties of their office.[9]

Although it was passed by the General Assembly, the proposed amendment failed by a significant margin (59–114) to win an affirmative vote by the presbyteries. Once again, the hopes of those seeking to open the way for LGBT ordination were dashed.

With the defeat of the amendment, the church called for a three-year process of study and dialogue on the issue of LGBT ordination (once again, as it had in 1993), urging a respite from more attempts to change the constitution. Thus, the next action by General Assembly was in 2001 when, by a vote of 317–208 (60 percent), an amendment was sent to the presbyteries that, if approved, would remove all barriers to LGBT ordination. The amendment would strike G-6.0106b from the constitution and amend the preceding section, G-6.0106a, by adding a new sentence: "Their suitability to hold office is determined by the governing body where the examination for ordination or installation takes place, guided by scriptural and constitutional standards, under the authority and Lordship of Jesus Christ."[10] The General Assembly action also stated that all related interpretive statements concerning the ordination of homosexual persons since 1978 would be given no further force or effect if the amendment received a positive vote in the presbyteries.

Immediately following the General Assembly, individuals and groups on both sides of the issue began intensive work to secure votes in the presbyteries for their position. Those supporting LGBT ordination were encouraged in their efforts by the strong (60 percent) vote of the General Assembly. However, hopes were dashed once more as the presbyteries voted to defeat the amendment by a margin even greater than the last time, 46–127.

Committed to "the long haul," the "Three Sister" organizations (MLP, TAMFS, and SOSP) and the Covenant Network have all continued their efforts to remove the ban against LGBT ordination. However, the focus of the struggle has shifted in large measure since the 2002 General Assembly, where no amendment affecting ordination standards was passed. Instead, several judicial cases began to be filed against open LGBT ministers and elders.

The issue goes to court

As in the United States governmental system in which, as legislative issues bog down, courts often become the arena for resolving conflict, so too within the Presbyterian Church, the conflict about LGBT leadership has moved into the court system. Prior to the meeting of the General Assembly in June 2002, fifteen important cases involving ordination of LGBT persons were filed in the ecclesiastical courts of the PCUSA. They were all remedial cases, that is, cases alleging that a governing body (session, presbytery, synod, or General Assembly) has committed (a) an irregularity, an erroneous decision or action, or (b) a delinquency, an omission or failure to act. Such cases seek a remedy for the alleged irregularity or delinquency. Some of the cases challenged actions of presbyteries involving ministers (including Jane Adams Spahr) and candidates for ministry, but most were filed against sessions, alleging that they violated G-6.0106b in ordaining LGBT elders.

Permanent Judicial Commissions (PJC) exist in each of the 173 presbyteries, fifteen synods, and the General Assembly, and cases can be appealed from presbytery PJCs to synod PJCs and finally to the General Assembly PJC. The judicial decisions upheld the restrictive ordination policy, though in several instances the cases were determined by technicalities or dismissed. For example, an irregularity might be found, but no remedy or relief was possible except an admonishment to refrain from repeating the action.

Some cases call for interpretation of the language of G-6.0106b, and advocates of LGBT ordination view some of these interpretations favorably. A case in point is *Ronald L. Wier v. Session,* Second Presbyterian Church of Ft. Lauderdale, Florida, decided by the General Assembly PJC on April 14, 2002. Wier alleged an irregularity/delinquency relative to the session's ordaining an elder whom Wier claimed was a practicing homosexual. In its decision the PJC said,

> The complaint did not allege that the accused is a self-acknowledged, practicing homosexual. Instead, the complaint simply alleged that the accused was a "practicing homosexual." When, as here, a complaint alleges a violation of constitutional standard that may have consequences to a person's reputation, career, or friendships, a greater degree of pleading specificity

is required. A complaint making such an allegation must assert factual allegations of how, when, where, and under what circumstances the individual was self-acknowledging a practice which the confessions call a sin.

In the instant case, even if one assumes the allegation of "practicing homosexual" were true, the complaint fails to meet the specificity that G-6.0106b compels in that it did not allege any specific details. The plain language of the *Constitution* clearly states that disqualified persons must have self-acknowledged the proscribed sin. Self-acknowledgement may come in many forms. In whatever form it may take, self-acknowledgement must be plain, palpable, and obvious and details of this must be alleged in the complaint.[11]

Since Wier's complaint failed to comply with the PJC's interpretation of the specificity required of G-6.0106b, the PJC ruled that the complaint lacked a claim upon which relief could be granted and dismissed the case.

The outcome of this case established a precedent, making it more difficult for opponents of LGBT ordination to be successful in such remedial cases. The Wier decision clearly makes it harder for governing bodies to discriminate. In the end however, anyone who specifically self-acknowledges a practice that the Confessions call a sin is ineligible to be ordained. This presents a dilemma for LGBT persons. Some may choose not to reveal the details of their intimate relationships so that they can continue to serve. Others will be unable, in good conscience, to deny the sanctity of their relationships by refusing to answer questions when asked; instead they will choose to tell the truth.

The cases filed during the four months following the June 2002 General Assembly took a new turn. These twenty-four new cases are disciplinary actions. In contrast with remedial cases, which are filed against a governing body, disciplinary cases are those in which a church member or officer may be censured for an offense contrary to Scriptures or the Constitution of the PCUSA. Censure can include removal from office or membership.

Many of the cases are against "out" LGBT persons, who are already serving as elders or ministers and whose governing bodies of jurisdiction have not sought to raise an issue with their ordinations ("don't ask, don't tell"). Allegations made in most of these cases claim the accused are in violation of their ordination vows, which include affirmation of the authority of Scripture, church confessions, and polity. In some cases, specific reference is made to G-6.0106b.

Some sessions and presbyteries have shown reluctance to pursue such disciplinary cases and have dismissed them, usually on grounds that the charges lack specificity. Yet some of the accused have made clear their desire to see the case through to the end, intending to be honest about their sexuality and relationships. It is too early to predict the outcome of what has been termed a "season of litigation." The "Three Sisters" have declared their preference for a "season of illumination," a time to shine the light on issues of LGBT ordination and, more specifically, on the values and actions of both those who welcome and those who oppose an inclusive church.

With this picture of what has happened regarding LGBT ordination since the 1991 report, we explore now the stakes of ordination for those still treated today as second-class members in the church.

Ordination continues to be important: LGBT persons partnering with God

Ordination is the key issue on which problems of access are most focused. Those who would withhold ordination contend that LGBT individuals are an abomination in the eyes of God. LGBT persons are accorded second-class status and regarded as unworthy. They are not affirmed in the light of their faith or their actions of service, freely given as they endeavor to live with integrity and trust in God's grace.

Many have left the PCUSA and other faith traditions because these traditions are seen as harmful, damaging, and just plain wrong in defining LGBT individuals as "less than" and evil. Others stay and work for change within and among communities that once welcomed them, yet now treat them as strangers in their midst. For them, staying means not settling in, but inviting and moving the church to be the place of hospitality they believe it can be.

LGBT individuals understand the call to ordained ministry to be so intertwined with their full identity that to separate sexuality from spirituality is to deny the very creations that God has made, whole persons responding to God's call with their full being. Dualism, inherited from Greco-Roman times, is perpetuated when LGBT individuals are seen only as sexual rather than whole persons. The words used to exclude women from the priesthood in the third century—licentious, promiscuous, mysterious, dirty, bad, immoral, temptress—are the same words used even now to define LGBT persons, thus denying their callings and positions of leadership in the church.

Because they understand the connections among oppressive systems, many LGBT individuals are conscious of the church as a patriarchal system. They are painfully aware, as well, of scapegoating that blames victims of oppression and gives others license to inflict spiritual and physical violence in order to "save souls," outrageously doing so "in the name of God"! The work of justice to end this violence is seen by LGBT people as a crucial part of the movement of liberation and of their faith journeys. Many commit their very lives to achieve justice and freedom for themselves and all others who are marginalized and despised.

Pursuing LGBT ordination today involves much more than arguing with those who question whether LGBT persons believe in God, take the Bible seriously (but not literally), affirm that tradition matters, and seek to live faithful lives. In our judgment, it requires a fundamental rethinking of ordination, a project that follows from what we believe about God, how we experience God, and our relationship with God. Our view of God affects our re-visioning of leadership, faithfulness, and power.

God is our beloved—the one who is all-loving, loving each of us unconditionally. The one who is both within and transcendent. The one who loves all of creation. The one who calls us into partnership with her to work together for justice and love in a world longing for such justice and love. God does not seek or claim power over creation; rather God empowers creation to live in the fullness of what, in wholeness, it (and we) are called to be.

By calling us into partnership with her and to be her beloved community, God invites us to be healthy people, that is, to live in relationship with each other and the earth as friends, or, as Irene Monroe names us, "partner passengers" on a journey together.[12] This view of God moves us away from hierarchical models for structuring the church to ones of mutuality and reciprocity. We envision our friendships, communities, and all socially constructed institutions shaped at their core by trust and love, functioning as partners toward the human freedom God wills for everyone.

Breaking with clericalism: renewing leadership among equal partners

Commitment to a God of partnership, who calls each of us to be equal partners with God and one another, has profound implications for leadership and ordination in the church. We believe that sexism and heterosexism engender discrimination against LGBT ordination and that patriarchy undergirds both. Therefore, revisiting ordination requires careful analysis of issues of power, control, and injustice. In doing so, we dare to question whether it is even possible for ordination, *as we know it*, to exist without its accompanying hierarchical status and power. Our interest is not in promoting ordained, professionalized ministry, but rather ministry as mutuality in partnership. In critiquing ministry and church order, we speak as Anglo-American feminists and heirs to a particular church tradition. We do not seek to speak for sisters or brothers with different racial, ethnic, or religious perspectives. Their experiences in and understanding of the liberation struggle are theirs to tell. We value and benefit from their unique insights, while recognizing the limitations of our study.

In the early 1970s, the United Presbyterian Church in the U.S.A. responded to growing pressures from women and people of color for fair representation on its boards and agencies, both as staff and as elected members. Equal employment opportunities and affirmative-action programs became encouraging signs of greater openness and acceptance of those who had never before been included in church structures. Simultaneously, there were other voices raising concerns about a growing clericalism in the church. Clergy frequently wrote and spoke about what they believed the ministry of the laity should be, while in response, the laity often silently resisted being told what they should do.

Language perpetuates the problem. The terms "clergy" and "laity" define a permanent unequal relationship between two classes of people. Laity refers to the body of church members differentiated from those ordained to the Ministry of Word and Sacrament, who are the "professionals." The laity, comprising the vast majority of the church, is defined not in terms of its own identity, but in relation to this relatively small group of clergy. Clergy are seen as active agents in ministry, the laity as those receiving ministerial care. In Presbyterian governance, some lay people who are elected by their congregations and ordained ideally help to equalize power with clergy. However, even with this move toward parity, clergy (and especially male clergy) hold disproportionate power, even as some lay people hold power and privilege over other lay people. Not surprisingly, such relationships of permanent inequality create either passive and uninvolved or discontented and critical people in the pews.

What are the alternatives to this disempowering model of leadership? If the focus were on *function* or *purpose,* rather than *position* or *office,* would the model differ? What if the focus were on enabling genuine partnership? By valuing relationships and mutuality in the practice of ministry, rather than separation and authority, would the model need to change? Is ordination—the setting apart of some for rule and governance—a barrier to truly egalitarian communities of faith?

Feminism is the struggle of women (and their male allies) to free themselves from all sexist and hierarchical structures, including religious institutions. The structures of the church continue to marginalize and subordinate women, whether ordained or not, as well as men who are not ordained. The paradoxical nature of oppression is that both the oppressor and the oppressed are losers in systems structured according to power and privilege, although this is seldom perceived since the realities of patriarchal systems are so familiar as to be almost invisible.[13] Furthermore, hierarchical organizations provide "patriarchal dividends" to those who hold special status, honor, and authority.[14] For many reasons, structures of inequality within the church are virtually unrecognized or intentionally unacknowledged, yet all who participate in hierarchical systems contribute to structures of injustice.

Although feminism is a particular perspective shaped by the experiences of women, its insights and teachings are applicable to everyone in the church — women and men, children and youth, ordained ministers, and church members. Feminism begins when women define themselves and their own relationship to faith traditions. Self-definition as subjects is key. Thus, a Christian feminist assessment of the present clergy/laity model anticipates a more egalitarian community in which laity are no longer defined only in relation to clergy, but define themselves as co-equal partners in ministry. Such a body would truly be the *laos*—the whole people of God with diverse gifts for ministry. Indeed, *all* ministries begin with baptism, with God's radically inclusive welcome of us as equally beloved children!

Partners in ministry emphasize connections and relationships rather than differences. When individuals are intentional in discerning gifts for the work at hand, the result is what Letty Russell calls a "circle of interdependence." As she explains, "Ordering is explored through inclusion of diversity in a rainbow spectrum that does not require that persons submit to the 'top,' but rather that they participate in the common task of creating an interdependent community of humanity and nature."[15] Similarly, Diarmuid O'Murchu writes in *Quantum Theology* that "humanity today hungers for genuine love, the ability to interrelate and interconnect...out-growing our man-made competitive and destructive isolation."[16] By choosing to pursue integration instead of fragmentation, partnerships avoid either/or distinctions wherever possible and favor affiliation and mutuality in relationships.

For most of us, learning to be partners in ministry will mean entering new and strange landscapes where the old, familiar practices give way—too slowly and often with great reluctance—to the new and unfamiliar. Walter Brueggemann reminds us, however, "A royal (or dominating) consciousness leads people who are shut out to despair about the power for new life."[17] Alternatives to dominant, exclusive models of leadership will enliven and energize communities and call forth faithfulness in response. New ways of being church could generate surprising gifts from its members.

The issue is not insisting on an exact equivalence of gifts, but seeking to discern which gifts are needed for the tasks to be accomplished. Though all parts of the body are different, all parts are necessary to constitute the whole. Individually, members will contribute differently at various times, depending on the need. Thus, working as partners, we develop gifts that were formerly hidden or unrecognized; in addition, we might each acquire new skills!

Implicit in the "body" image is awareness that partners, or parts of the body, will do well when they are most able to trust and accept one another. This involves a willingness to risk mistakes or failures along the way. Furthermore, partners, when they learn and communicate with each other, seek to balance being both "listener" and "speaker." As Letty Russell suggests, "we learn to be partners by being partners."[18]

To be called to ministry is never merely an individual endeavor; rather, it is always a call to join with other believers, to participate corporately, and at times to discover new partners because of what needs to be done together. This image of partnership or co-ministry suggests communities of co-equal disciples. Unlike patriarchal structures with "top down" authority, partnerships encourage multiple authorities, depending on occasion and circumstance.[19] Leadership and power, defined as "the capacity to implement," are not static and fixed, but move from one individual to another, as the necessary gifts are used for the work to be done.[20] An *authority of purpose* replaces an *authority of position*.

In true partnerships, power is as much the ability to *be* moved or changed as it is to move or change others. Partnerships model ministry *with* rather than *to* others. This means that any working group must include the individuals for whom the program is intended and in more than token numbers. This egalitarian model offers a vision of new possibilities for the whole people of God as partners and friends of Christ.[21] By living and working with others in relationships and making new connections, we gain new knowledge and deeper insight. In her 1990 study of mainline Protestantism, Barbara Wheeler observes: "By modeling leadership as potentially an opportunity open to many members at one time or another, rather than only those whom the seminary prepares for leadership—that is, the clergy—will we begin* to break the power of clericalism."[22]   *fix

A growing acceptance and lasting comfort as partners in ministry will no doubt develop slowly at first. The practice of *being* partners demands periods of energy and intense concentration, followed by times of reflection and consolidation. Perseverance, commitment, and making new friends who will join us are all necessary for this journey. We grow into its practice by living as co-equals, attentive to one another and to the voices in the world around us, in the grand enterprise of reshaping and receiving ever-new life. Rethinking sexuality and LGBT ordination might well involve replacing sexist and heterosexist structures—including even ordination itself—with new, more faithful models of partnership in which all gifts and calls to ministry are realized.

In conclusion, we recognize that the struggle for LGBT ordination, within the PCUSA and elsewhere, is far from over. We see it continuing as the primary "hot button" issue for years to come, and surely as long as LGBT persons and their heterosexual allies find second-class membership unacceptable and unfaithful to God's inclusive love in Jesus Christ. God's calling of LGBT individuals to ordained leadership should be recognized and honored, but that is only part of the struggle. The alternative, and already emerging, partnership model of leadership will perhaps take even longer to become a reality. With hope and a measure of feistiness, we persist in both struggles, confident in the power and promise of justice-love.

Notes

1. *The Church and Homosexuality* (New York: United Presbyterian Church in the U.S.A., 1978), 61.

2. "Building a Church for All God's People," brochure of More Light Presbyterians, 2002.

3. Ibid.

4. Information on the Shower of Stoles Project is extracted from material provided by Martha Juillerat, project director.

5. Information on the Covenant Network of Presbyterians is extracted from material provided by Pamela Byers, executive director.

6. William P. Thompson, "How My Mind Was Changed," *Called Out With: Stories of Solidarity,* ed. Sylvia Thorson-Smith, Johanna W. H. van Wijk-Bos, Norm Pott, and William P. Thompson (Louisville: Westminster/John Knox, 1997), 18–22.

7. *The Constitution of the Presbyterian Church (U.S.A.), Part II, Book of Order* (Louisville: Presbyterian Church [U.S.A.], 2001–2), G-6.0106a.

8. Ibid., G-60106b.

9. *Minutes of the General Assembly, Part I, Journal* (Louisville: Presbyterian Church [U.S.A.], 1997), 89–90.

10. *Minutes of the General Assembly, Part I, Journal* (Louisville: Presbyterian Church [U.S.A.], 2001), 401.

11. *Minutes of the General Assembly, Part I, Journal* (Louisville: Presbyterian Church [U.S.A.], 2002), 340–41.

12. The phrase is Irene Monroe's and introduced at a CLOUT (Christian Lesbians OUT) conference.

13. Nora Johnson, "Housewives and Prom Queens, Twenty-five Years Later," *New York Times Book Review,* March 20, 1988, 33.

14. R. W. Connell, *The Men and the Boys* (Berkeley: University of California Press, 2000), 25.

15. Letty M. Russell, *Household of Freedom: Authority in Feminist Theology* (Philadelphia: Westminster, 1987), 34.

16. Diarmuid O'Murchu, M.S.C., *Quantum Theology* (New York: Crossroad, 1998), 89.

17. Walter Brueggemann, *The Prophetic Imagination* (Philadelphia: Fortress, 1978), 62.

18. Letty M. Russell, *Growth in Partnership* (Philadelphia: Westminster, 1981), 39.

19. Ibid., 33.

20. Jean Baker Miller, M.D., *Toward a New Psychology of Women,* 2d ed. (Boston: Beacon, 1986), 116.

21. Elisabeth Schüssler Fiorenza, *Discipleship of Equals* (New York: Crossroad, 1993); also, *In Memory of Her: A Feminist Theological Reconstruction of Christian Origins* (New York: Crossroad, 1983).

22. Barbara G. Wheeler, "Uncharted Territory: Congregational Identity and Main Line Protestantism," in *The Presbyterian Predicament,* ed. Milton J. Coalter, John M. Mulder, and Louis B. Weeks (Louisville: Westminster/John Knox, 1990), 62–89, especially 85–86.

Related Titles from The Pilgrim Press

Between Two Gardens:
Reflections on Sexuality and Religious Experience
James B. Nelson

Theologian and ethicist Nelson seeks to stimulate a further re-examination of human sexuality and the Christian experience. Rather than asking the typical question of: What does faith say about human sexuality?, he more pertinently asks: What does sexuality say about faith — theology, Scripture, tradition, and the meaning of the gospel? With this more existential perspective in mind, Nelson explores a wide range of sexual and medical issues.

ISBN 0-8298-0681-4
Paper, 196 pages, $13.00

Body, Sex, and Pleasure: Reconstructing Christian Sexual Ethics
Christine E. Gudorf

Drawing on Scripture, natural law, historical and contemporary Catholic and Protestant theology, the social sciences, and the lived experiences of today's women and men, Gudorf presents a carefully crafted and systematic reconstruction of Christian sexual ethics. Her aim is to engender appreciation, not rejection and shame, of our bodies and our sexuality. It is a provocative and compelling call to all women and men to reject the damaging influence of body/soul dualism—and ultimately, to do justice to the Incarnation, the central revelations of Scripture, and human dignity.

ISBN 0-8298-1062-5
Paper, 276 pages, $16.00

Constructing the Erotic: Sexual Ethics and Adolescent Girls
Barbara J. Blodgett

In this thought-provoking work, Barbara J. Blodgett challenges "feminist theologies of the erotic" through a critique of feminist theologians, an exploration of developmental theories, and an examination of adolescent girls' narratives. In response, she constructs an alternate sexual ethic for adolescent girls based on establishing appropriate trust.

ISBN 0-8298-1478-7
Paper, 200 pages, $20.00

Introducing Body Theology
Introductions in Feminist Theology series
Lisa Isherwood and Elizabeth Stuart

Because Christianity asserts that God was incarnated in human form, one might expect that its theologies would be body affirming. Yet for women (and indeed also for gay men) the body has been the site for oppression. *Introducing Body Theology* offers a body-centered theology that discusses cosmology, ecology, ethics, immortality, and sexuality in a concise introduction that proposes and encourages a positive theology of the body.

ISBN 0-8298-1375-6
Paper, 168 pages, $17.00

Science, Scripture, and Homosexuality
Alice Ogden Bellis and Terry L. Hufford

The collaborative work of a biblical scholar and a biology professor, this book is written in a highly accessible manner, addressing Scripture passages relating to homosexuality and explaining the foundation of genetics and the growing evidence suggesting an organic basis for sexual orientation. The prevailing message its progressive authors wish to convey is that "the role of the homosexual, as well as the heterosexual, within the Church should be based upon common criteria for all." Ideal for church school discussion.

ISBN 0-8298-1485-X
Paper, 128 pages, $12.00

To order (M–F, 8:30am–4:30pm, ET),
call 800-537-3394, fax 216-736-220ʳ
or visit our Web site at www.pilgrimpres

Prices do not include shipping and han
Prices subject to change without noti